Social Science and Philosophical Analysis:

Essays in Philosophy of the Social Sciences

Michael Martin

Copyright © 1978 by

University Press of America™
division of
R.F. Publishing, Inc.
4710 Auth Place, S.E., Washington, D.C. 20023

All rights reserved
Printed in the United States of America

Library of Congress Catalog Number: 78-51142
ISBN: 0-8191-0478-7

To My Wife

PREFACE

Printed in this volume are a number of my papers, many of which have appeared in philosophical journals, on various aspects of philosophy of the social sciences. The purpose of this collection is not only to gather these papers together in a convenient form but also to provide a text that can be used in the classroom, if not as an introduction to philosophy of the social sciences, at least as a supplementary volume covering most of the major arguments in the field.

In order to facilitate the book's use in the classroom, I have provided an introductory essay and a brief introduction to each section of the book. Since many of my papers are critiques of contemporary work in philosophy of the social sciences, students are urged to read the papers and books which I discuss. Frequently my papers have themselves occasioned further discussion in the journals. In so far as I am aware of such discussions I have cited them in my introductions. Students are urged to read these papers as well.

Although the responsibility for the mistakes in these essays is my own, many people are responsible for my writing them and bringing them together in one volume. It will become evident to a reader of these essays that I have often been stimulated to write by what others have said well or badly or by what they have failed to say. I am grateful to them for their stimulation. Jane Martin, the person to whom this book is dedicated, has helped me in many ways; without her none of these essays would have been written, let alone published in one volume. My former teacher, Israel Scheffler, has always been supportive and has provided a model of clear critical thinking for me. I would also like to thank Judith Bleiwas Wilkis for her careful typing of the introduction and of those essays which are not reprinted from previous articles. Finally, I would like to thank the editors and publishers who have granted me permission to reprint the following essays:

"The Explication of a Theory," Philosophia, 3, 1973, 179-199; "Theoretical Pluralism," Philosophia, 2, 1972, 341-349; reprinted by permission of Philosophia.

"An Examination of the Operationists' Critique of Psychoanalysis," Social Science Information, 8, 1969, 65-86; reprinted by permission of Social Science Information.

"On the Conceivability of Mechanism," Philosophy of Science, 38, 1971, 79-86; "The Objectivity of a Methodology," Philosophy of Science, 40, 1973, 447-450; "The Explanatory Value of the Unconscious," Philosophy of Science, 31, 1964, 122-132; reprinted by permission of Philosophy of Science.

"The Scientific Status of Psychoanalytic Clinical Evidence," Inquiry, 7, 1964, 13-36; "Mr. Farrell and the Refutability of Psychoanalysis," Inquiry, 7, 1964, 80-98; "Situational Logic and Covering Law Explanations in History," Inquiry, 11, 1968, 388-399; reprinted by permission of Inquiry and Universitets Forlaget, Oslo, Norway.

"Neurological Reduction and Psychological Explanation," Philosophy of Social Science, 1, 1971, 161-170; "Causal Importance and Objectivity," Philosophy of Social Science, 4, 1974, 157-168; "Explanation in Social Science: Some Recent Work," Philosophy of Social Science, 2, 1972, 61-81, reprinted by permission of Philosophy of Social Science.

"Value Judgements and the Acceptance of Hypotheses in Science and Science Education," Philosophic Exchange, 1, 1973, 83-100; reprinted by permission of Philosophic Exchange.

"The Philosophical Importance of the Rosenthal Effect," Journal for the Theory of Social Behaviour, 7, 1977, 81-96; reprinted by permission of Journal for the Theory of Social Behaviour and Basil Blackwell, Oxford, England.

"Description and Objectivity," Philosophy Research Archives, 2, 1977; reprinted by permission of Philosophy Research Archives.

"Are Cognitive Processes and Structure a Myth?" Analysis, 33, 1973, 83-88; reprinted by permission of Analysis.

"Review of Berger and Cioffi (eds.): Explanation in the Behavioral Sciences, Synthese 26, 1973, 324-336; reprinted by permission of Synthese and D. Reidel Publishing Co.

"The Body-Mind Problem and Neurophysiological Reduction," Theoria, 37, 1972, 1-14; reprinted by permission of Theoria.

"Methodological Individualism and the Reduction of Cultural Anthropology to Psychology," Scientia, 9-10, 1969, 489-502; reprinted by permission of Scientia.

"Understanding and Participant Observation in Cultural and Social Anthropology," Boston Studies in the Philosophy of Science, Vol. 4 1966-1968, eds. M. Wartofsky and R.S. Cohen, (D. Reidel Publishing Co., 1969) 303-330; reprinted by permission of D. Reidel Publishing Co.

"Winch on Philosophy, Social Science and Explanation," The Philosophical Forum, 23, 1966, 29-41; reprinted by permission of the Philosophical Forum.

"Popperian Anthropology," Methodology and Science, 4, 1971, 41-79; reprinted by permission of Methodology and Science.

"An Explicative Model of Theory Testing," Zeitschrift Für Allgemeine Wissenschaftstheorie, 1, 1970, 228-242; reprinted by permission of Zeitschrift Für Allgemeine Wissenschaftstheorie.

CONTENTS

PREFACE		iv
INTRODUCTION		1
PART I	THEORY CONSTRUCTION IN PSYCHOANALYSIS AND PSYCHOLOGY	
	INTRODUCTION	7
1.	THE EXPLICATION OF A THEORY.	8
	POSTSCRIPT (1977) ON EXPLICATION	29
2.	AN EXPLICATIVE MODEL OF THEORY TESTING.	30
3.	AN EXAMINATION OF THE OPERATIONISTS' CRITIQUE OF PSYCHO-ANALYSIS.	45
4.	THE EXPLANATORY VALUE OF THE UNCONSCIOUS.	65
5.	MR. FARRELL AND THE REFUTABILITY OF PSYCHOANALYSIS.	76
6.	ARE COGNITIVE PROCESSES AND STRUCTURES A MYTH?	95
7.	THEORETICAL PLURALISM.	101
PART II	OBJECTIVITY AND VALUE JUDGEMENTS	
	INTRODUCTION	111
8.	DESCRIPTION AND OBJECTIVITY.	114
9.	VALUE JUDGEMENTS AND THE ACCEPTANCE OF HYPOTHESES IN SCIENCE AND SCIENCE EDUCATION.	141
10.	CAUSAL IMPORTANCE AND OBJECTIVITY.	159
11.	THE PHILOSOPHICAL IMPORTANCE OF THE ROSENTHAL EFFECT.	171
12.	THE OBJECTIVITY OF A METHODOLOGY.	188
PART III	EXPLANATION AND PREDICTION	
	INTRODUCTION	193

13. EXPLANATION IN SOCIAL SCIENCE: SOME RECENT WORK. 195
14. SITUATIONAL LOGIC AND COVERING LAW EXPLANATIONS IN HISTORY. 216
15. SOCIAL SCIENTIFIC PREDICTION AND OPEN CONCEPTS. 228
16. A NEW INTERPRETATION OF VERSTEHEN. 233
17. REVIEW OF BORGER AND CIOFFI (EDS.): EXPLANATION IN THE BEHAVIORAL SCIENCES. 237

PART IV REDUCTION

    INTRODUCTION 251

18. THE BODY-MIND PROBLEM AND NEUROPHYSIOLOGICAL REDUCTION. 253
    POSTSCRIPT (1977) ON NEUROPHYSIOLOGICAL REDUCTION. 267
19. NEUROLOGICAL REDUCTION AND PSYCHOLOGICAL EXPLANATION. 268
20. ON THE CONCEIVABILITY OF MECHANISM. 278
21. METHODOLOGICAL INDIVIDUALISM AND THE REDUCTION OF CULTURAL ANTHROPOLOGY TO PSYCHOLOGY. 286

PART V TECHNIQUES OF VALIDATION

    INTRODUCTION 301

22. THE SCIENTIFIC STATUS OF PSYCHOANALYTIC CLINICAL EVIDENCE. 303
23. UNDERSTANDING AND PARTICIPANT OBSERVATION IN CULTURAL AND SOCIAL ANTHROPOLOGY. 327
24. JUSTIFICATION BY VERSTEHEN. 355

PART VI CRITIQUE OF ALTERNATIVE PHILOSOPHIES

    INTRODUCTION 369

25. WINCH ON PHILOSOPHY, SOCIAL SCIENCE AND EXPLANATION. 370
26. POPPERIAN ANTHROPOLOGY. 383
27. THE PHILOSOPHER OF SOCIAL SCIENCE AS PARTICIPANT OBSERVER. 422

INTRODUCTION

The Values of Philosophy of the Social Sciences

Why is philosophy of the social sciences worth studying? Two reasons can be given. First, such a study will help improve our understanding of the social sciences. The social sciences are among the most fascinating studies in which people can engage. Yet many of us, while knowledgeable about many of the details of the social sciences, have a confused or at least limited view of their purpose, methodology and implications. Philosophical study of the social sciences can often eliminate this confusion; it can present a more balanced picture of the social sciences, and can provide illumination of them. For example, many people who have studied psychology assume without question that it some day will be reduced to physiology. Other people with a psychological background are equally confident that such a reduction is impossible. As we shall see, both parties have too simple and a <u>priori</u> a view of the issue. Getting clear on what reduction involves cannot but help people improve their thinking about psychology since in psychological theorizing reduction plays a crucial role. One task of philosophy of the social sciences is to analyze concepts such as reduction.

Second, oddly enough the study of philosophy of the social sciences may indirectly help one to improve one's understanding of the natural sciences. This is because one often learns to understand things in terms of contrasts: for example what life is by contrasting it with death and what love is by contrasting it with hate. In a similar way one learns what the natural sciences are by contrasting them with the social sciences. It is sometimes claimed that the natural sciences are experimental sciences, ones concerned with establishing general laws and theories, while the social sciences are not experimental and are interested in studying the particular, not the general. Yet not all the natural sciences are experimental (astronomy is not) whereas some of the social sciences are experimental (parts of social psychology are). Moreover, some social sciences are interested in establishing general laws (cross cultural studies in cultural anthropology are) and some natural sciences are not (natural history oriented biology is more interested in studying particular species in their natural habitats than in developing theories or general laws). In its attempt to provide a general picture of the social sciences philosophy of the social sciences may then indirectly produce a better understanding of the natural sciences by giving a more balanced and accurate picture of the social sciences.

Different Conceptions of Philosophy of the Social Sciences

Since this book consists of essays in philosophy of the social sciences, it may be a good idea to say something about what that field of inquiry is. But this is not as easy as it sounds, for there have been different conceptions of it.

(1) One traditional conception is that philosophers should attempt to bring the various social sciences under some general perspective. This may be accomplished in at least two different ways. One way would be for the philosopher to provide some classification scheme in which all the major methods of the social sciences could be understood and related.[1] A second way would be to construct some grand explanatory theory in which a wide variety of social phenomena could be explained and understood. The theories of Karl

Marx and Sigmund Freud can be viewed as an example of this approach.

There is no doubt that these two conceptions of philosophy of the social sciences have merit. It is very important to have a classification that illuminates the methods used in the social sciences. Far too often it is wrongly assumed that the social sciences use only one means of investigation and a classification scheme may point up this error very well. Furthermore, the attempt to unify a wide variety of social data under one theoretical framework, a la Marx or Freud, is also very important. Such an attempt, if successful, would give us deeper understanding of social reality and would provide us with powerful theories analogous to those found in the physical sciences.

These views have certain limitations, however. In some classification schemes the social sciences are accepted in too uncritical a spirit. The philosopher of the social sciences should not just bring the social sciences under some unifying scheme but should critically evaluate them. Furthermore, this view of philosophy of the social sciences neglects the value of philosophical analysis. Philosophers not only need to cast their nets wide but (to mix metaphors) to probe deeply. There is much that needs clarifying in the social sciences and this may take detailed analysis rather than a classification scheme. For example, social scientists sometimes claim that the method of participant observation enables them to understand a primitive culture. But the term "understand" is used ambiguously in the literature. Part of the job of the philosopher of social sciences is to unravel this ambiguity and provide the needed clarification.

The Marx-Freud conception of the philosophy of the social sciences as a super theory builder and synthesizer is not without its problems either. First, it is not clear that philosophers have any special training or talent for this sort of system-building. Certainly in contemporary times the major attempts at this have been made by theoretically inclined social scientists rather than by philosophers. In any case, such a task will not be undertaken here. Secondly, it is not obvious that such a unifying theory is possible in the social sciences at this time. At present the development of theories of lesser scope may be more fruitful. Certainly the failure of the Marx-Freud type of unification gives one little confidence in this approach to philosophy of the social sciences.

In short, I do not rule out a philosopher of the social sciences performing a synthetic function. Indeed, a classification scheme of scientific methods is very useful and is something to which a philosopher, trained in methodological issues, can be expected to make a contribution. However, other synthetic functions, e.g. that of providing a general explanatory theory, may be better left to theoretical social scientists.

(2) One newer conception of the philosophy of the social sciences has the philosopher analyzing the concepts and methods of the social sciences. The philosopher dissects the social sciences revealing unclarities and ambiguities and exposing gaps in arguments. There is no doubt that this approach is valuable. The special training of philosophers in logic and analysis makes them especially suited to this job. Analysis of social scientific concepts such as operational definitions, function and <u>verstehen</u> will be found in this book.

However, as it is often practiced this approach has problems. First, exclusive concern with analysis can blind the philosopher to a more comprehensive picture of the social sciences. It is easy for philosophical analysis to become an end in itself instead of a tool that can be useful for understanding and critically evaluating the social sciences. Second, some philosophers have supposed that the analysis of concepts and methods of the social sciences can proceed in an a priori armchair fashion. However, this is not so. The analysis of social scientific concepts and methods requires rather intimate knowledge of social science literature, both substantive and methodological.

Third, philosophical analysis may be wrongly used as a justification for the status quo since an analysis of a concept or method is often taken as a justification of that concept or method, which it is not. But rightly used, philosophical analysis is a critical tool for exposing weaknesses and limitations.

(3) Another conception of philosophy of the social sciences views the philosopher as a social critic, evaluating the social uses and abuses of social science, specifying the responsibilities of social scientists and suggesting moral guidelines for social scientific research. Too often the social scientist shows gross irresponsibility. For example, some anthropologists were lured by the C.I.A. to work for their nefarious schemes in Southeast Asia. Concerned as they are with ethical problems and trained in ethical theory, philosophers can make useful contributions to this sort of social criticism.

However, such a view of philosophy of the social sciences is surely not complete. It neglects both the synthetic and the analytic job of philosophy. These two tasks are not only compatible with social criticism but they complement it. It may well be the case that in order to have a good grasp of the social scientist's social responsibility a unified picture of the social sciences is needed. Furthermore, philosophical analysis of certain key social scientific conceptions can be useful in any critique of the uses of social scientific findings. Thus, for example, a philosophical analysis of the concept of intelligence may be quite helpful in evaluating the results of the intelligence tests used in education. How can one tell whether people should be separated educationally on the basis of intelligence tests unless one has a clear understanding of what intelligence is?

(4) Still another conception of philosophy of the social sciences has the philosopher constructing theories of social scientific growth in order to answer such questions as how social scientific knowledge best grows. Although this conception is a new one in contemporary philosophy of science, its proponents argue that it was advocated by classical philosophers of science such as Mill and Bacon. Historical origins aside, this view of philosophy of the social sciences is important and has been too long neglected.

Philosophers can and should surely make contributions to theories of scientific growth. Once again this view taken by itself has limitations. It is not, however, incompatible with the other views of philosophy of the social sciences considered above, but rather it is complemented by them and in turn complements them. In order to construct theories of social scientific growth it may be very useful to have a comprehensive view of the methodology of the social sciences. In order to determine whether the testing of a plurality of theories of, for example, the functions of magic is more conducive to the growth of social scientific knowledge than the testing and revision of one theory, it may be helpful if certain key terms are analyzed: function, magic, growth of social scientific knowledge.

Is Philosophy of the Social Sciences Necessary?

So far I have argued that four conceptions of philosophy of the social sciences are important but limited. This does not necessarily mean that every philosopher of the social sciences needs to practice in accordance with all four. Some philosopher may specialize in the construction of theories of scientific growth, others may specialize in the philosophical analysis of social scientific concepts and methods, still others may concentrate on the social criticism of scientific theories and the use of social scientific information. Nevertheless, the work of one philosopher of the social sciences engaged in one type of enterprise may be useful for another philosopher engaged in another type: the various conceptions complement one another.

But the question arises as to whether philosophy of the social sciences is really necessary. Could not all the things that philosophers of the social sciences do be done by social scientists? Theoretically minded social scientists have attempted to provide a synthetic picture of social scientific methodology; they have clarified and analyzed their concepts and methods; they have raised questions about the responsibility of social scientists and have criticized the use of social scientific information. Social scientific information and research are essential to evaluating theories of social scientific growth and social scientists seem capable of making such evaluations. Given these facts, what special contribution can philosophers make? Is philosophy of the social sciences really necessary?

The above query certainly indicates that there is no sharp difference between a social scientist and a philosopher of the social sciences. This, however, does not show that there is no difference, or that philosophy of the social sciences has no right to exist. The difference is a matter of degree and emphasis. The philosopher's concern is primarily one or more of the four functions outlined above, indeed he or she is usually a specialist in one or more of them. However, the typical social scientist approaches these four tasks, if at all, not as his or her primary function, but as part—perhaps a small part—of it. As a consequence, the social scientist's work on these tasks may not be as painstaking and thorough as the philosopher's. Furthermore, it is a rare social scientist who can transcend his or her occupation and look at its methodology and the use of its theories objectively. Loyalty to one's discipline and blindness caused by being too much involved in the situation under consideration make the job of critic very difficult. Philosophers of the social sciences are more frequently free of this loyalty and blindness and, as a result, their critiques and analyses tend to be more hard hitting. Finally, because of their special training, philosophers of the social sciences should be more able to take on the four tasks mentioned above. For example, philosophers are specially trained in analysis and ethical theory. Social scientists do not usually have much of this type of training.

This is not to suggest that philosophers of the social sciences do not have hangups of their own. They may be insensitive to social scientific problems because they are too distant from the scene of battle, too ready to press into service philosophical apparatus which has dubious application and relevance, too quick to criticize before they understand and appreciate. Philosophers of the social sciences consequently constantly need to check their work against social science literature and the critical opinion of actual working scientists.

Philosophical Orientation

Although a fully articulated and comprehensive philosophy of the social sciences will not be presented in the essays printed here, it will not be difficult to tell where my philosophical sympathies lie. In general I will maintain that the social sciences and the natural sciences have basically the same methodology.

With respect to theory construction I will argue that a narrow operationist methodology is inappropriate. However, I will also argue that social scientific theories should be testable. I will resist any attempt to rule out a priori explanatory hypotheses that appeal to unobservable entities and processes and will maintain that whether such hypotheses are acceptable depends on the role they play in a testable explanatory theory.

I will maintain also that the social sciences, like the natural sciences, can be objective despite the Rosenthal Effect, despite judgements of causal importance and despite claims that social scientists are committed to value judgements via their descriptions. I will attempt to refute the view that the social sciences and history have a fundamentally different logic of prediction, explanation and understanding than do the natural sciences and I will defend the covering law model of explanation against some important criticisms. I will moreover argue against interpretations of Verstehen that attempt to put a priori limits on the type of explanation allowed in the social sciences.

I will argue that the reduction of holistic sciences to individual sciences and of psychology to neurology cannot be ruled out on a priori grounds. Although I will argue that the social sciences have basically the same methodology as the natural sciences, I will not maintain that the social sciences are free from methodological criticism. I will show that there are grave problems involved in validating clinical interpretations and that the traditional stress on participant observation does not seem to be justified.

In short, the methodology that will be defended in these essays might be called a neo-positivist position. However, certain differences in emphasis from the typical positivist position will be seen. First, modern positivists have not been interested in theories of scientific growth. I believe this to be a mistake. Although I do not put forth a theory of scientific growth in these essays, I do consider the evidence which would be relevant to an examination of such theories. I argue that theories of scientific growth should be evaluated by empirical evidence of a certain kind. Elsewhere I have called this a plea for empiricism in matters methodological.[2]

Although positivists have been concerned about the explication of scientific concepts, little or no work has been done on the explication of scientific theories. Such explications are taken seriously in these essays.

Positivists have had a particularly wrong headed view of Verstehen, one which seems to bear no relation to the way in which Verstehen was traditionally understood; consequently their arguments against Verstehen have been irrelevant. I believe that I understand Verstehen and reject it on proper

5

grounds. Thus Scriven's and Krimerman's interpretations of Verstehen are not put in some a priori mold but are critically examined in their own right.

Footnotes

1. Paul Diesing attempts to do this in his book _Patterns of Discovery in the Social Sciences_ (Chicago: Aldine-Atherton, 1971). Some of Diesing's views are evaluated in my essay, "The Philosopher of Social Science as Participant Observer," printed in Part VI of this volume.

2. See my paper, "How to Be a Good Philosopher of Science: A Plea for Empiricism in Matters Methodological," in a forthcoming volume of the _Boston Studies in the Philosophy of Science_.

PART I: THEORY CONSTRUCTION IN PSYCHOANALYSIS AND PSYCHOLOGY

Social scientists develop and test theories. In this section problems connected with scientific theorizing, especially theorizing in the fields of psychoanalysis and psychology, are examined.

One problem is the relation between theory and observation. On one widely accepted view theories are reducible either to actual or to possible observations. A variant of this view, discussed in "An Examination of the Operationists' Critique of Psychoanalysis," is operationism, the doctrine that in order to be scientifically meaningful theoretical concepts must be reduced to concepts referring to the physical operations of measurement and their results.

A problem closely related to the first is that many theories in the social sciences are unclear and ambiguous. One consequence of this unclarity is that the relation between the theories and their observational base or support is unclear. It is therefore difficult to tell what the theories assert and what empirical observations are relevant to evaluating them. One way of curing this problem is to "operationalize" the unclear concepts in theories.

The problem posed by unclear theories is taken up in several of the papers in this section. In "The Explication of a Theory" the general problem of explicating unclear theories is discussed, while a particular application of this problem is considered in "An Explicative Model of Theory Testing." The question of whether psychoanalysis is an empirically testable theory is explored in "Mr. Farrell and the Refutability of Psychoanalysis"[1] and the attempt to operationalize psychoanalysis is discussed in "An Examination of the Operationalists' Critique of Psychoanalysis."

Another problem raised by theorizing in psychoanalysis and psychology is the use of concepts, for example, the unconscious, which philosophers find problematic not just because of their unclarity but because they are connected with controversial issues in the philosophy of mind. I discuss the problematic character of psychological concepts in two papers: Arthur Pap's and A.C. MacIntyre's views on the unconscious are criticized in "The Explanatory Value of the Unconscious" and in "Are Cognitive Processes and Structure a Myth?" Norman Malcolm's Wittgensteinian criticism of cognitive psychology is evaluated. In both instances I argue that concepts such as the unconscious and cognitive structure should be treated no differently from concepts in natural scientific theorizing and that arguments purporting to show that such concepts are methodologically unsound are invalid.

A final problem to be discussed in this section is that of the number and variety of theories social scientists should use in different research areas. Should they work with many rival theories? Are there methodological advantages to a pluralistic approach to theorizing? The view called theoretical pluralism which was popularized by I. Lakatos and Paul Feyerabend is discussed in the paper entitled "Theoretical Pluralism."

Footnotes

1. Farrell replied to my critique in his paper, "A Note on Dr. Martin's Senses of 'Refutable,'" *Inquiry*, 1964, 99-103.

THE EXPLICATION OF A THEORY*

MICHAEL MARTIN

Recent discussions of the concept of explication in science have concentrated on the explication of a scientific term or concept.[1] Typically one term or concept is said to explicate another term or concept. However, it is also possible to think of explication as taking place on a larger scale. One can think of an explication of a theory and hence of one theory explicating another theory. Now, although the concepts of inexactness and imprecision which are indirectly relevant to the explication of a theory have been discussed in recent philosophy of science literature,[2] little work indeed has been done directly on the concept of the explication of a theory. Popper has spoken of the explication of a theory.[3] But, as we shall see, Popper's analysis does not seem to capture the intuitive notion of the explication of a theory. Kuhn has spoken of the articulation of a paradigm.[4] But, as we shall see, Kuhn's notion is quite unclear and what it has to do with the explication of a theory is uncertain. Elsewhere I have suggested an explicative model of theory testing in which the explication of a theory was discussed.[5] To my knowledge, Popper's discussion, my earlier discussion and perhaps Kuhn's discussion are the only works directly bearing on this important notion.

---

* I would like to express my thanks to Israel Scheffler, John Mullen, and Richard Von Dohlen for reading an earlier draft of this paper and making helpful criticisms.

MICHAEL MARTIN

In this paper I will first critically consider Popper's notion of the explication of a theory. The problem with Popper's analysis will lead us to a discussion of the vagueness of certain theories. After distinguishing two types of vagueness in theories and their relevance to theory testing I will present a formal analysis of the explication of a theory. With this analysis before us we can consider Kuhn's notion of the articulation of a paradigm and the relevance of our analysis to the history of science. In the last section of the paper I will consider the various decisions involved in the explication of a theory considered in terms of our analysis.

POPPER'S NOTION OF THE EXPLICATION OF A THEORY

Popper's view of the explication of a theory seems to be this: Let T* be the explicatum and T be the explicandum. Now T* can be said to explicate T iff T* has deductive consequences C_1' & C_2' & ... C_n' under special conditions which are close approximations of the deductive consequences[6] of C_1 & C_2 & ... C_n of T and C_1' & C_2' ... C_n' are more accurate than C_1 & C_2 ... C_n.[7] Thus, Popper seems to suggest that Newton's theory is the explicatum of Galileo's theory and Kepler's theory which in turn are the explicanda. Popper says, "Newton's theory unifies Galileo's and Kepler's. But far from being a mere conjunction of these two theories — which play the part of explicanda for Newton — it corrects them while explaining them. The original explanatory task was the deduction of the earlier results. It is solved, not by deducing them, but by deducing something better in their place: new results which, under special conditons of the older results, come numerically very close to these older results, and at the same time corrects them. ...What is brought out strongly by (this) ... situation... is the fact that the new theory cannot possibly be *ad hoc*. ...Far from repeating its explicandum, the new theory contradicts it and corrects it. In this way, even the evidence of the explicandum itself becomes evidence for the new theory".[8]

EXPLICATION OF A THEORY

We have no quarrel with Popper's account except the label. Why call T* the explicatum? It is important to realize that there is an important disanalogy between Popper's notion of the explication of a theory and the notion of explication as it is usually understood in philosophical literature. The notion of explication is usually associated in the literature with Carnap.[9] According to Carnap an explication occurs when a more exact concept replaces a less exact concept. It is clear from the context of Carnap's writing that by 'more exact' Carnap meant 'less vague' and not 'more accurate'. Explication for Carnap was a cure for the vagueness of certain concepts. Recent writing on the notion of explication has also interpreted explication in this way.[10] Clearly the correct analogical extension of the term 'explication' to cover theories should be in terms of decreased vagueness and not in terms of increased accuracy. An explicatum of a vague theory — the explicandum — would be a less vague theory. But in Popper's account the explicatum is more accurate — not necessarily less vague. Thus for Popper, Newton's theory is a more accurate theory than Kepler's but not necessarily a less vague theory.

What is needed is some account of the explication of a theory in terms of decreased vagueness. Popper's discussion — however valuable it might be — does not meet this need. First of all, we need to ask ourselves the question: What is a vague theory? Secondly we need to ask: What is wrong with a vague theory?

TWO TYPES OF VAGUENESS IN THEORIES

To say that a theory is vague may mean at least two different things. First a vague theory may be a theory which has vague empirical consequences. The empirical consequences of the theory would be couched in language that is vague. Secondly, a theory may be vague in the sense that it is unclear what empirical statements the theory entails.

Presumably these two senses are independent of one another. There could be a theory which had vague consequences yet it was perfectly clear what these vague consequences were. On the other hand, there could be a theory such that it was uncertain which non-vague consequences it had. Usually, however, both types of vagueness go together. Vague theories are often vague in both senses at once. For a wide class of sentences it is impossible to determine whether these sentences are consequences of the theory or not; moreover, the members of this class of sentences are vague. Psychoanalysis is surely a theory of this kind. In certain cases it is not clear what sentences psychoanalytic theory entails and also the sentences one is unclear about are vague. Let us call the first type of vagueness *consequence vagueness* and the second type of vagueness *deductive indeterminacy*. We will consider each type of vagueness in turn.

CONSEQUENCE VAGUENESS

The observable consequences of a theory can be vague in at least two ways. First of all, the consequences of the theory may contain predicates which are vague in that it is sometimes impossible to determine in principle whether the predicates apply or not. The phrase "impossible to determine in principle" is meant to indicate that the problem is not a pragmatic one. The problem is not lack of evidence or information such that if one obtained such information one would be able to apply the predicate. Vague predicates, by definition, are predicates such that for a certain range of entities they neither do apply nor do not apply. This entails that within this range of cases the law of excluded middle fails.

If such predicates appeared in the deductive consequences of a theory, then under certain circumstances, it would be impossible in principle to tell whether the consequences were true or false. Let us call such consequences *inexact*. For example, suppose that a theory entails 'Ba' where 'B' is a vague predicate and 'a' is the name of an entity which is in the range of 'B's vagueness. Then it would be impossible in principle to say whether the predicate 'B' applies to a or whether the predi-

EXPLICATION OF A THEORY

cate '~B' applies to a. Thus it would be impossible in principle to tell whether 'Ba' is true or false.

Such indeterminancy in the application of a predicate may occur for several reasons. One major reason is that there might be criteria for the application of 'B' which were in conflict. Suppose 'B' is 'is a tributary' and suppose a is some river. Now there might be two independent criteria for the application of 'B', viz.: (1) length of the river, (2) volume of the water flow. It might be the case that these two criteria were in conflict in regard to a; hence it would be impossible to say whether a was B or not. Now if a theory has inexact consequences of this kind, the situation can be cured by making some decision between the conflicting criteria or perhaps by using new criteria. Of course it may not be possible in one sense to eliminate all inexactness in the deduced consequences of a theory. Nevertheless, it may be possible to reduce to zero the range of *actual* cases where it is impossible in principle to tell whether or not the predicate applies. For example, if two new criteria are chosen for 'is a tributary' there might be cases in which the criteria would be in conflict. However, there might not be any actual cases where the decision was in doubt. In this sense, at least, inexactness can be *completely* eliminated.

Secondly, a theory may have consequences which are stated in some quantitative concept. Nevertheless there may for practical reasons be great uncertainty in applying the concept. For example, the measuring procedure may be unreliable and subject to wide experimental error. There may also be a theoretical reason for the uncertainty, namely the existence of independent criteria for the application of the measurable concept. Consider a consequence of some theory in medicine; namely that some patient has a disease with an incubation period of time t. Now on one criterion of incubation of D, $t = 5$ days, and on another criterion $t = 10$ days. The length of the incubation period t would be within the interval of 5 to 10 days. The longer the interval the vaguer the prediction would be. Let us call a consequence of this type *theoretically imprecise*. The cure for this sort of vagueness is not to develop more reliable measuring procedures. Rather one must find some new measurement in which the interval is shorter or else choose one of the measurements, and not use the other. In either case the theoretical imprecision would be decreased. As in the case of inexactness it might be impossible to eliminate theoretical imprecision in all possible cases where the concept's application was in question. Nevertheless it does seem possible in all actual cases to eliminate theoretical imprecision relative to some unit of measurement. For example, relative to the unit of a day it does seem possible to develop criteria of incubation which are in agreement for all actual cases. Thus there might be no theoretical imprecision, i.e., the period of incubation for actual cases would have no spread measured in terms of days.

DEDUCTIVE INDETERMINACY

To say that a theory is deductively indeterminate with respect to a set of sentences S is to say that it is impossible in principle to decide whether the sentences in S do or do not follow from the theory because of the informal nature of the theory. Just as in the case of a very vague predicate 'B' it is impossible to tell in principle in a wide range of cases whether 'B' applies or not, so with a very deductively indeterminate theory it is impossible to tell in principle in a wide range of sentences whether these sentences follow or do not follow from the theory. The deductive indeterminacy of a theory is a function not of the vagueness of the consequences of the theory but of the lack of logical rigor of the theory, its degree of formalization.[11] Theories are more or less deductively indeterminate depending on their degree of formalization.

Suppose we find the following statements in a sociological treatise:

> "Lack of specificity is closely associated with lack of tribal harmony; furthermore, group cohesiveness involves tribal harmony. We know from field work that the Bunyoro lack specificity."

EXPLICATION OF A THEORY

What is supposed to follow from these statements? In particular, can one infer that the Bunyoro lack group cohesiveness? It is unclear whether this does or does not follow because of the unclarity of such connecting terms as "closely associated with" and "involves". For example, it is unclear whether lack of specificity is a sufficient condition or a necessary condition of tribal harmony; and it is unclear whether tribal harmony is a necessary or a sufficient condition for group cohesiveness.

Of course, given certain interpretations of the terms "closely associated with" and "involves" the conclusion "The Bunyoro lack group cohesiveness" follows. Thus letting $Sx = x$ has specificity and $Tx = x$ has tribal harmony and $Gx = x$ has group cohesiveness and $b =$ Bunyoro and letting "is closely associated" and "involves" mean "is a sufficient condition for" one can construe the above passage as follows:

(1) $(x)(\sim Sx \supset \sim Tx)$
(2) $(x)(Gx \supset Tx)$
(3) $\sim Sb$

So construed

(4) $\sim Gb$

follows deductively. But on another interpretation it does not. For example, if we interpret "is closely associated with" to mean "is a necessary condition of" then (1) becomes

(1') $(x)(\sim Tx \supset \sim Sx)$

Clearly (1') (2) and (3) do not entail either (4) or its negation.

Let us suppose further that in light of the entire sociological treatise neither interpretation is preferable; that it remains unclear after reading the entire treatise how these connecting phrases should be interpreted. Thus it is impossible in principle to determine whether '$\sim Gb$.' is entailed or not by the theory as expounded in the sociological treatise; it is impossible in the sense that given the unclear syntax of the theory as it is expounded in the treatise one does not know whether "$\sim Gb$" follows or whether it does not. Thus, we will say that the theory is deductively indeterminate with respect to "~Gb."

It is important to notice that the theory is not deductively indeterminate with respect to all sentences. Presumably from the passage cited one can unequivocally deduce:

(5) Either specificity is closely associated with tribal harmony or Bunyoro lacks group cohesiveness.

(5), unlike (4), clearly follows from the passage cited since the deduction of (5) does not turn on the unclear syntax of the language of the theory as it does in (4). Moreover, it seems quite clear that the following sentence does not follow from the theory.

(6) Nixon is President of the United States.

This example illustrates how consequence vagueness and deductive indeterminacy may sometimes occur together. It is not clear if '~Gb' follows from the theory. But even if. ~Gb does follow, it might be unclear if '~Gb' is true or false. For "lacks group cohesiveness" may well be an inexact predicate and the Bunyoro may well be in the range of its vagueness. However, it should be clear that "lacks group cohesiveness" need not be an inexact predicate for '~Gb', to be deductively indeterminate with respect to the theory.

It is important not to confuse the notion of deductive indeterminacy with certain properties of formal deductive systems, or with certain results in proof theory. For the property of deductive indeterminacy is a property of non-formal systems — systems that are poorly articulated formally. Such systems lack a clear syntax, clear rules of formation or transformation, and so on. The results of proof theory, e.g. that certain formal systems are incomplete or that there is or is not a decision procedure for a certain branch of logic or mathematics, presuppose a clear and rigorous formulation.

EXPLICATION OF A THEORY

To be sure, the most rigorously formulated theory retains the property that if no proof or disproof of some sentence has been found we cannot tell whether or not the sentence follows from the theory. However, if the theory is complete we can be assured that such a proof or disproof exists; it is possible in principle to find a proof or disproof. But in the case of a deductively indeterminate theory it is impossible in principle to find a proof or disproof of a certain sentence – not because the theory is incomplete in the technical logical sense but because of the theory's lack of logical rigor. Incomplete theories in the technical logical sense clearly do not lack logical rigor. Indeed, a necessary condition for a completeness or incompleteness proof is that the theory be rigorously formulated.

The cure for deductive indeterminacy is to reshape the theory in a more rigorous and clear way. The job of the explicator of a deductively indeterminate theory can perhaps be specified in terms used by Scheffler in another context. His task consists "in a formal specification of the branch (or science) in question, in such a way as to exhibit its logical skeleton, the systematic articulation of the basic ideas, definitions, assertions, and rules of inference. His goal is here not (in an important sense) to go outside of the branch of science under consideration, but rather to formulate its manifest content in an explicitly systematic way."[12]

TESTABILITY AND VAGUENESS

The vagueness of a theory – both in the sense of consequence vagueness and deductive indeterminacy – adversely affects the testability of the theory.[13] It is well known that if a theory has inexact consequences, it is more difficult to refute than if it has exact consequences. For if a theory has inexact consequences then it is sometimes impossible to determine whether the consequences are true or false. Hence it is impossible to test the theory *via* these consequences. For example if 'Ba' is an inexact consequence of a theory T, then since it is impossible to tell whether 'Ba' is true or false it is impossible to test T *via* testing 'Ba'. If a theory has theoretically imprecise consequences then under certain conditions[14] it will be more difficult to refute the theory than if it has precise consequences. For normally the more theoretically imprecise the consequences the more evidence is compatible with the theory. For example there is more evidence compatible with the deduction that disease D has an incubation period of 5-10 days than with the deduction that disease D has an incubation period of 5 days. However, the latter deduction is less precise than the former. Hence, theory T_1 with the consequence that disease D has incubation period of 5-10 days is harder to refute than theory T_2 with the consequence that disease D has incubation period of 5 days.

A theory with deductive indeterminacy is also difficult to test but for a different reason. It may be unclear whether some alleged test of the theory is really a test since it is impossible to decide whether some sentence describing the test situation logically follows from the theory. Thus it may be impossible given a theory with deductive indeterminacy to know whether the sentence is a test implication of the theory.

Small wonder then that scientists have been interested in replacing vague theories by less vague ones. Small wonder, that is, that they have been interested in explicating theories. The question is: Can we make this notion of explication more precise? Can we, as it were, explicate the notion of explication of a theory?

TESTABILITY AND AUXILIARY HYPOTHESES

Before we explicate the notion of explication of a theory the role of auxiliary hypotheses in explication and theory testing should be considered. It has often been pointed out that theories are not tested in isolation but against a background of other assumptions. Test implications follow from a whole complex of hypotheses and a negative test does not uniquely determine which hypotheses in the complex are false. Furthermore, various alternative adjustments exist for bringing the experimental evidence into accord with the complex.

In a similar manner consequence vagueness and deductive indeterminacy may be the result of a complex of hypotheses and not of any isolated hypothesis; in order to eliminate vagueness many hypotheses in the complex may need to be clarified and alternative ways of clarifications are possible.

For purposes of simplicity in our formal definition of explication, we will consider the theory T to be explicated as a complex of hypotheses — what might normally be called a theory and its auxiliary hypotheses; the explicated theory T* will also be considered a complex of hypotheses, a complex which results from clarification of T, in order to eliminate consequence vagueness or deductive indeterminacy. In order to bring this clarification about certain aspects of the original complex must be reconstructed.

For example, in the case considered above, a reconstruction in order to eliminate some deductive indeterminacy might consist in construing "is closely associated with" as "is a sufficient conditon of". The question normally arises whether this construal itself can be considered as an auxiliary hypothesis. Thus one might wonder whether the following is an auxiliary hypothesis which when added to the rest of the social theory of our example and other auxiliary hypotheses enables us to deduce '$\sim Gb$'.

(6) Lack of specificity is a sufficient condition of lack of tribal harmony = Lack of specificity is closely associated with lack of tribal harmony.

In most cases to treat (6) in this way would be misleading. For (6) may not be a factual assumption for which evidence is relevant at all; (6) may be more like a recommendation or proposal to use terms in a way thought to be fruitful for scientific purposes. We will consider this point in more detail toward the end of the paper, when we consider decisions involved in explications of theories.

MICHAEL MARTIN

FORMALIZATION OF THE EXPLICATION OF A THEORY

Since there are two ways in which a theory can be vague — consequence vagueness and deductive indeterminacy — we shall define two different notions of the explication of a theory: (1) Explication of a theory in terms of improving deductive indeterminacy, which we call explication$_1$ and (2) explication of a theory in terms of improving consequence vagueness, which we will call explication$_2$.

EXPLICATION$_1$ OF A THEORY

Let T* be the explicatum and T be the explicandum. Let S_1 be the set of all sentences entailed by T and S_2 be the set of all sentences not entailed by T and S_3 be the non-empty set of all sentences for which it is impossible in principle to determine whether they are entailed or not entailed by T, because of the lack of rigor of T.[15] Let K_1 be a subset of S_3 that is entailed by T* and K_2 be a subset of S_3 not entailed by T*. Then, we may define "completely explicates", in terms of deductive indeterminacy as follows:

T* completely explicates$_1$ T iff T* entails S_1 and T* does not entail S_2 or any subset of S_2, and $K_1 \cup K_2 = S_3$.

And we may define "explicates$_1$" in terms of deductive indeterminacy as follows:

T* explicates$_1$ T iff T* entails S_1 and T* does not entail S_2 or any subset of S_2 and $K_1 \cup K_2 \neq \Lambda$.

Thus T* completely explicates$_1$ T in the sense that it entails everything that T entails and does not entail anything that T does not entail and T* entails or does not entail everything that it is impossible to decide whether T entails or does not entail. Thus T* preserves what is clear about T but clarifies what was unclear. An explication$_1$ that is not complete only clarifies part of what is unclear. That is in an explication that is

EXPLICATION OF A THEORY

less than complete T^* either entails or does not entail some of the sentences of S_3 but not all. Thus the union of K_1 and K_2 is not empty.[16]

With the help of the above apparatus we can define a notion we introduced elsewhere:[17] the notion of an explicative consequence of a vague theory T.

C is an explicative$_1$ consequence of T relative to explicatum T^* iff $C \in K_1$.

EXPLICATION$_2$ OF A THEORY

Let T^* be the explicatum and T be the explicandum. Let S_4 be the set of all sentences entailed by T which are neither inexact nor imprecise. Let S_5 be the set of all sentences not entailed by T and let S_6 be the non-empty set of all sentences entailed by T which are either inexact or imprecise. Let S_7 be a set of sentences constituted as follows: For each sentence in S_6, exactly one sentence which is a clarified version is a member of S_7. Furthermore, S_7 contains only clarified versions of the sentences in S_6. Let K_3 be some non-empty subset of S_7. Then, we can define "completely explicates$_2$" in terms of consequence vagueness as follows:

T^* completely explicates$_2$ T iff T^* entails S_4 and S_7 and does not entail S_5 or any subset of S_5.

and we may define "explicates$_2$" in terms of consequence vagueness as follows:

T^* explicates$_2$ T iff T^* entails S_4 and K_3 and does not entail S_5 or any subset of S_5

Thus, in a complete explication$_2$ of T, T^* preserves what is clear and clarifies everything that is not. In an explication$_2$ that is less than complete T^* preserves what is clear and clarifies some things that are not; that is K_3 is a proper subset of S_7.[18]

Again, with the above apparatus the notion of an explicative consequence can be defined,

C is an explicative$_2$ consequence of T relative to T*
iff C ϵ K$_3$.

EXPLICATION IN THE HISTORY OF SCIENCE AND KUHN'S NOTION OF THE ARTICULATION OF PARADIGM

How well the two notions of explication analyzed above apply in the history of science is unclear. It is plausible, however, to suppose that theories are explicated in ways approximating to explication$_1$ and explication$_2$ only in certain stages of scientific development. Often when a theory is first proposed in a certain domain it is vague. The theory subsequently is clarified and cleaned up by investigators working with the theory in the domain. In other words, the investigators draw explicative consequences from the theory. The clarified and cleaned-up version of the original theory is however usually called by the same name as the original. This sameness of name, however, should not blind us to the change that has occurred. Thus although T* and T may be called by the same name, this usage should not hide an ambiguity. T* is not the same as T but a clarified version of T.

Thus the drawing of explicative consequences from a theory, as we have conceived it, would occur at least in what Kuhn has called periods of normal science – periods of science in which the details of theories are worked out – rather than in periods where major conceptual revolutions are taking place. Indeed, the view of explication presented above may appear to bear a close analogy to Kuhn's notion of the articulation of a paradigm which is on his view an essential aspect of periods of normal science.

However, the unclarity of the notion of paradigm pointed out by reviewers of Kuhn's book carries over to his notion of the articulation of a paradigm[19]. Hence it is uncertain whether my view is similar to Kuhn's view in important and relevant respects. If one simply identifies paradigms with theories – something Kuhn does not do – Kuhn's thesis would be that much of normal science consists in the articulation of the accepted theory of the period. The problem now is to know what articulation means. In particular, does articulation and specification of a theory amount to what I have called explicating a theory in either of the two senses analyzed?

Again this is not clear. But there is some reason to think that Kuhn in some places at least has something quite different in mind. Kuhn speaks of the "empirical work undertaken to articulate the paradigm resolving some of its residual ambiguities and permitting the solution of problems to which it had previously only drawn attention".[20] It seems that in this passage, at least, Kuhn considers the articulation of a paradigm as an experimental or empirical enterprise.

However, the drawing of explicative consequences as we have conceived it, is a conceptual endeavor. To be sure, such a task may be influenced or justified by experimental results. Moreover, empirical research may be preceded by the drawing of explicative consequences. But the empirical research is not "undertaken to" explicate a theory.

In other places Kuhn seems to have in mind something much closer to what we have called an explication of a theory. In speaking about the theoretical work — in contrast to the experimental work — undertaken in the articulation of a paradigm he says:

Some of the problems... aim simply at clarification by reformulation. The *Principia*, for example, did not always prove an easy work to apply, partly because it entailed some of the clumsiness inevitable in a first venture and partly because so much of its meaning was only implicit in the application... Many of Europe's brilliant mathematical physicists repeatedly endeavored to reformulate Newton's theory in an equivalent but logically and aesthetically more satisfying form. They wished, that is, to extract the explicit and implicit lessons of the *Principia* in a logically more coherent version, one that would be less equivocal in the application to the newly elaborated problems of mechanics.[21]

In this passage at least the brilliant mathematical physicists Kuhn refers to may be either explicating$_1$ or explicating$_2$ Newton's *Principia*. They may be reformulating the theory in such a way that either explicative$_1$ or explicative$_2$ consequences can be drawn. Thus if we restrict paradigm to theories and restrict articulation to the theoretical reformulation Kuhn speaks about in the above passage, our notion of explication$_1$ or explication$_2$ may provide an analysis of Kuhn's notion of the articulation of a paradigm. Thus:

> The *Principia* as reformulated by Hertz is an articulation of Newton's original *Principia* = the *Principia* as reformulated by Hertz either explicates$_1$ or explicates$_2$ Newton's original *Principia*.

Whether this analysis does capture Kuhn's intention is difficult to say since Kuhn is unclear; whether this analysis captures the import of Hertz's endeavor is a question in the history of science that we will not pursue.[22] In any case, however well this analysis captures Kuhn's meaning or however well it captures the import of Hertz's endeavor, there are differences between Kuhn's view and ours which need to be emphasized. The articulation of a paradigm (whatever exactly this might mean) occurs only in periods of normal science. But periods of normal science are, according to Kuhn, periods in the history of established sciences; Kuhn's examples are all taken from physics and chemistry. Although we do not question the fact that theories are explicated in periods of normal science and in traditions of established science we do not want to restrict explication to these periods or to these sciences. For example, the explication of theories goes on in behavioral and social sciences. Kuhn, however, would consider these sciences without any dominant paradigm – i.e., sciences in a pre-paradigm stage. Furthermore, Kuhn emphasizes the unquestioning attitude of experimenters to the paradigm; their great faith that the paradigm can be articulated to solve all puzzles. Such an attitude is not an essential part of explicating a theory as we conceive of it. Indeed, many of the experimenters who explicate a theory in the social sciences, e.g. psychoanalytic theory, are very skeptical of the theory.

DECISIONS IN THE EXPLICATION OF THEORIES

Whatever the relevance of the notion of the explication of a theory to understanding Kuhn's notion of the articulation of a paradigm and whatever the relevance of the notion of the explication of a theory to understanding certain periods or stages in the history of science, when a scientist is confronted with a vague theory he has various decisions to make. His first decision is whether to explicate the theory or not. If he decides to explicate, he must decide whether the explication should be complete or partial. If he decides on a partial explication, the further question arises, how partial? [23] But even if he answers these questions, further decisions are necessary. In an explication$_1$ he must decide, for example, which members of S_3 should be entailed by T^* and which should not be. In an explication$_2$ he must decide which clarified versions of the sentences in S_6 should be included in S_7. Since there may be several plausible clarified versions of each sentence in S_6, one of these plausible versions must be picked.

The basis for such decisions will vary from context to context and will be relative to the type of decisions one is making. Thus if the decision is whether to explicate completely or partially or not at all, the decision should undoubtedly be decided on economic grounds broadly conceived. One must "trade off" the time and energy involved in explication with the results one expects to achieve and the purposes of the inquiry. Some theories may not be worth explicating very much; other theories may be worth the time and energy involved in a complete explication; still others may show so little promise they are not worth explicating at all.

However, the situation may differ when it comes to decisions concerning which sentences of S_3 should be entailed by T^* or which sentences should be included in S_7. Here it might be necessary, given certain purposes, to do biographical scholarship. After all, what a scientist means in propounding a theory may be quite different from the theory that is propounded. Furthermore, what a scientist meant to say may be revealed in his books, letters, old lecture notes, oral communications, and so on. Exegetical analysis of such material might well reveal that what a scientist meant to say was much clearer than the well publicized and standard statements[24] of the theory. Thus given certain purposes, one should prefer explicatum T_1^* over T_2^* or T if T_1^* is closer to the author's intention than T_2^* is. Exegetical analysis may not be able to establish that T_1^* is closer to the author's intention. that T_2^*. It may only be able to eliminate several explications which are not in keeping with the author's intentions at all.

For example, even if it is not possible to pinpoint exactly what sentences are to be included in K_1 or K_2, it might be possible to rule some possibilities out; again, even if it might not be possible to say which sentence is the most plausible interpretation of some sentence in S_6 it might be possible to rule out those which are the least plausible.

However, given other purposes such exegetical analysis may be irrelevant. One might not care what the creator of the theory meant or intended. The task might be to find an explication that is methodologically fruitful rather than exegetically plausible. If so, the considerations that would be relevant would be of many types. For example, simplicity might be an important consideration since, other things being equal, one should prefer explicatum T_1^* over T_2^* of T if T_1^* is a simpler theory than T_2^*. But usually more is involved. An explicatum might be preferred over another if it is in keeping with a historical trend. Past explicators of the theory — or at least of theories of a certain type — have done so and so; hence, to preserve historical continuity, it might be argued, it is a good idea to continue explication along certain lines. Whether this is a good argument will depend on how fruitful the whole historical trend has been.

EXPLICATION OF A THEORY

However, whatever the basis for such decisions in explicating theories it is usually a good policy to bring them out in the open. Too often explications of theories are not recognized as such and the basis of the decisions involved in such explications is unclear and arbitrary. Although it is perhaps not possible to eliminate all arbitrariness in such decisions there is no *apriori* way of knowing this in advance and decisions in explications could well be subjected to more rational scrutiny and criticism than they usually are.

BOSTON UNIVERSITY
BOSTON, MASSACHUSETTS 02215
USA

NOTES

[1] Joseph F. Hanna, "An Explication of 'Explication'" *Philosophy of Science*, 1968, pp. 23-42.

[2] See for example, D.H. Mellor, "Inexactness and Explanation" *Philosophy of Science*, 1966, pp. 345-359; D.H. Mellor, "Imprecision and Explanation", *Philosophy of Science*, 1967, pp. 1-9; D.H. Mellor, "Experimental Error and Deducibility" *Philosophy of Science*, 1965, pp. 105-122; R.G. Swinburne, "Vagueness, Inexactness and Imprecision" *British Journal for the Philosophy of Science*, 1969, pp. 281-297; Pharmendra Kumar, "Logic and Inexact Predicates" *British Journal for the Philosophy of Science*, 1967, pp. 211-222; S. Korner, *Experience and Theory* (London, 1966).

[3] Karl Popper, "The Aim of Science" *Ratio*, 1967, pp. 24-35.

[4] Thomas Kuhn, *The Structure of Scientific Revolutions* (Chicago, 1962).

[5] Michael Martin, "An Explicative Model of Theory Testing" *Journal for General Philosophy of Science*, 1970.

[6] The phrase "the deductive consequences" is left ambiguous deliberately; it could mean "all deductive consequences" or "some deductive consequences". The best way to reconstruct Popper's view here is uncertain since it is unclear if Popper would consider one theory as explicating another theory if the one entailed some of the same consequences as the other.

[7] In order to avoid unacceptable consequences one must regard T* as devoid of redundant elements. Otherwise a Theory T_*' which consists of T* plus some arbitrary theory $T_•'$ would fulfill the above conditions and the explicate T. Such a result would surely be unacceptable. How exactly one should specify the lack of redundancy is an open question.

[8] Popper, *op. cit.*, p. 33.

[9] Rudolf Carnap, *Logical Foundations of Probability* (Chicago, 1962).

[10] Hanna, *op. cit.*

MICHAEL MARTIN

Cf. Richard Rudner, *Philosophy of Social Science* (Englewood Cliffs, New Jersey, 1966). p. 50.

[2] Israel Scheffler, *The Anatomy of Inquiry* (New York: 1963), p. 4.

[3] We are discussing here factual theories and not normative theories, e.g., a theory of subjective expected utility. In normative theories there is no problem of testability; however, with vague normative theories there is an analogous problem of not being clear on what the theories prescribe. Thus vague normative theories have what might be called the problem of "followability." I owe this point to John Mullen.

[14] It should be noted that just because theoretical imprecision is reduced it does not mean that practical imprecision is. Indeed, just the opposite is true. Reducing the interval of theoretical imprecision may put the prediction beyond the range of available reliable measuring procedures.

[15] This impossibility in principle can be clarified as follows: Suppose to each sentence p of T corresponds a set of sentences $\{q_1...q_n\}$ which contains all of the most plausible interpretations of p. Thus in the example above if p = Lack of specificity is closely associated with lack of tribal harmony and group cohesiveness involves tribal harmony and Bunyoro lack specificity, then the set $\{q_1...q_n\}$ would include the sentences q_1 and q_2 where q_1 = (x) ($\sim$Sx $\supset \sim$Tx) & (x)(Gx $\supset$ Tx) & $\sim$Sb and q_2 = (x) ($\sim$Tx $\supset \sim$Sx) & (x) (Gx $\supset$ Tx) & $\sim$Sb. Now assuming p = T it is not possible in principle either to derive or not derive a sentence r from T if there is no *uniform* deductive relation holding between the q's and r. Thus if r_1 = $\sim$Gb then r_1 can neither be derived nor not derived from T since on one plausible interpretation q_1, r_1 is entailed and on another plausible interpretation q_2, r_1 is not entailed. Thus there is no uniform deductive relation holding between the q's and r. Consequently r_1 is a member of S_3. On the other hand if r_2 = Either specificity is closely associated with tribal harmony or Bunyoro lack group cohesiveness, r_2 is derivable from the set of q's under all plausible interpretations. Consequently r_2 is in set S_1. On the other hand if r_3 = Nixon is President of the United States, then on none of the plausible interpretations is r_3 entailed from $\{q_1...q_n\}$, so r_3 is in set S_2.

[16] It is also possible to define a weaker notion of explication. Sometimes one is particularly interested only in someproper subset of sentences of S_3, e.g. S_3' and not interested in any of the rest of S_3. A complete explication$_1$ relative to *this* interest would be achieved when T* either entailed or did not entail all of the sentences in S_3' and entails S_1 and did not entail S_2 or any subset of S_2; a partial explication$_1$, then, would be achieved when some but not all of the sentences in S_3' were either entailed or not entailed by T* and T* entailed S_1 and did not entail S_2 or any subset of S_2.

[17] Martin, *op.cit.*

[18] A weaker notion of explication$_2$ could be developed along the lines suggested in note 16.

[19] See Dudley Shapere. "The Structure of Scientific Revolutions", *Philosophical Review*, 1964, pp. 383-394.

[20] Kuhn, *op. cit.*, p. 27.

[21] *Ibid.*, pp. 32-33.

[22] There is some historical reason to think that Hertz's reformulation was based at least in part on a consideration of the vagueness of Newton's theory in its original form. First Hertz complained that some crucial terms in the theory, e.g. 'force' were not defined with sufficient clarity. Secondly, he complained that some alleged deductions from the theory did not meet acceptable standards of logical rigor. The first complaint seems closely connected with what we have called consequence vagueness: unless 'force' was clearly defined those consequences of Newton's theory which contained the term 'force' would be inexact or imprecise. The second complaint is similar to what we have called deductive indeterminacy: the logical status of the theory is such that it lends itself to putative deductions from the theory which in fact do not meet acceptable standards of logical rigor; strictly speaking, therefore, it is impossible to tell whether some inferences "made from the theory" are really logical consequences of the theory after all. See Heinrich

Hertz, "Two Systems of Mechanics," *Philosophy of Science*, eds., Danto and Morgenbesser (New York: 1960), pp. 349-365.

[23] For a discussion of decisions involved in formalizing a theory see Rudner, *op. cit.*, pp. 49-53.

[24] I owe the idea of exegesis in the explication of a theory to Mr. Richard von Dohlen.

POSTSCRIPT (1977) ON EXPLICATION

I now see a serious problem in my analysis of the explication of a theory. What is usually meant by the explication of a theory is that a clearer version of the theory replaces the original one. The explicatum and explicandum are the same theory. Unfortunately, my two definitions of the explication of a theory allow for the possibility that the explicatum and explicandum are completely different theories. For example, T* might be Skinnerian conditioning theory and T might be psychoanalysis. The conditions specified in my definitions might be fulfilled, but we would not want to speak of T* explicating T.

In order to eliminate this problem, identity criteria for theories might be built into the definition. Unfortunately, philosophers of science have done little work on the topic of theory identity.[1] The problems involved in providing such criteria seem very difficult. For example, one might suppose that T* is the same theory as T IFF T* has all the same basic principles and themes as T, and conversely. However, this suggestion seems to suffer from at least two basic problems: (1) When is a basic principle in T* the same as a basic principle in T? The present analysis seems to have pushed the problem back to the problem of specifying the identity criteria for principles and themes. (2) Is the "all" stipulation too strong? Could not a theory T* lack some of the basic principles and themes of T and still be considered the same theory?

At the present time I know of no clear way out of these problems. I will, therefore, simply add the clause, "...and T* is the same theory as T," to both definitions and will leave the criteria of sameness unspecified.

Footnotes

1. I was made aware of the problem with my analysis and the need for criteria of theory identity by reading an unpublished paper by Richard Burian. Burian is one of the few philosophers I know who has taken the problem of theory identity seriously.

An Explicative Model of Theory Testing

MICHAEL MARTIN

Summary

The official view of theory testing in the philosophy of science, the deductive model, does not reflect the way ambiguous, vague and ill formulated theories are tested. A new model of theory testing, the explicative model, is outlined which reflects how such theories are tested. This model is illustrated in the actual testing of psychoanalysis, a typical case of an ambiguous, vague and ill formulated theory and is contrasted with Kuhn's notion of the articulation of a paradigm.

One of the dogmas of contemporary philosophy of science is that a theory is tested by testing its deductive consequences. This account may be called the deductive model of theory testing. Now whether the deductive model of theory testing is an illuminating account of some theory testing we will not decide here. One suspects that this model applies mainly to theories in highly developed sciences and even then only at certain times and at certain points.

Be that as it may, I will argue that this model is at least not illuminating in certain areas of theory testing. In particular, I will argue that such a model of theory testing is not appropriate to testing theories that are unclear, ambiguous and ill formulated. Put in a different way I will argue that this model does not give an adequate account of the scientific testing of some "unscientific" theories. Typically, however, unscientific theories are considered to be those theories which do not have clear and unambiguous deductive consequences — those theories that cannot be tested according to the deductive model of theory testing. I will use as an illustration the scientific testing of psychoanalytic theory — a contemporary example of a theory of this "untestable" kind. I will suggest a different model of theory testing — a model based on the notion of explication — which will illuminate at least the scientific testing of psychoanalysis. In conclusion I will relate the explicative model of theory testing to Kuhn's notion of the articulation of a paradigm.

THE DEDUCTIVE MODEL OF THEORY TESTING AND ITS PROBLEMS

One might say that the official view of theory testing in contemporary philosophy of science is this: From a hypothesis and initial conditions plus perhaps auxiliary hypotheses, consequences are logically deduced; these consequences are tested; testing these consequences indirectly tests the theory.[1]

This deductive model of theory testing runs immediately into the following problem. Some theories are so ill formulated, ambiguous and vague that they seem to have no logically derivable empirical consequences. Nevertheless scientific testing of such theories goes on. It has been argued, for example, that psychoanalytic theory does not have clear empirical deductive consequences.[2] The inference that psychoanalysis cannot be tested seems to be unwarranted, however, since many aspects of psychoanalytic theory have been tested.[3] Thus the curious problem arises of a supposedly untestable – hence unscientific theory – apparently being tested.

Deductive theorists may take either of two stands in the light of this argument. On the one hand they may say that the testing of psychoanalysis shows that psychoanalysis does have testable deductive consequences, appearances notwithstanding; on the other hand they may argue that psychoanalysis was not actually tested by the studies referred to, but rather some other theory – equivocally called "psychoanalysis" – was tested.

The first retort seems to me to be the easiest to meet. It is not true that psychoanalysis as it was originally stated by Freud and his followers has testable consequences that can be deduced from the theory.[4] Indeed, many experimental psychologists, sociologists and anthropologists who

---

[1] See for example Karl Popper, *The Logic of Scientific Discovery*, New York: Basic Books, 1959, pp. 32—33. — Carl G. Hempel, *Philosophy of Natural Science*, Englewood Cliffs, N. J.: Prentice-Hall, 1966, chap. 2. — Arthur Pap, *An Introduction to the Philosophy of Science*, New York: The Free Press, 1962, pp. 142—143. — Edward H. Madden. *The Structure of Scientific Thought*, Boston: Houghton Mifflin, 1960, pp. 3—13. — John Patrick Day, *Inductive Probability*, New York: Humanities Press, 1961, pp. 52—79.

[2] See for example Ernest Nagel, "Methodological Issues in Psychoanalytic Theory," *Psychoanalysis, Scientific Method, and Philosophy*, (ed.) S. Hook, New York: New York University Press, 1959. — Karl Popper, *Conjectures and Refutations*, New York: Basic Books, 1962, pp. 34 ff.

[3] See for example R. R. Sears, *Survey of Objective Studies of Psycho-Analytic Concepts*, New York: Social Science Research Council, 1943. — E. R. Hilgard, "Experimental Approaches to Psychoanalysis," *Psychoanalysis As Science* (ed.) E. Pumpian-Mindlin, Stanford: Stanford University Press, 1952. — B. A. Farrell, "The Scientific Testing of Psycho-Analytic Findings and Theory," *The Study of Personality* (ed.) H. Brand, New York and London: Wiley and Chapman Hall, 1954. — H. Orlansky, "Infant Care and Personality," *Psychol. Bulletin 46* (1949) No. I, pp. 1—48. — I. L. Child, "Socialization," *Handbook of Social Psychology* (ed.) G. Lindzey, Cambridge: Addison-Wesley, 1954, Vol. II.

[4] See for example Peter Madison, *Freud's Concept of Repression and Defense: Its Theoretical and Observation Language*, Minneapolis: University of Minnesota Press, 1961. — Michael Martin, Review of Peter Madison, *Freud's Concept of Repression and Defense, Its Theoretical and Observation Language, Philosophy of Science*, 1964, pp. 186—188. — Michael Martin, "Mr. Farrell and the Refutability of Psychoanalysis," *Inquiry*, 1964, pp. 80—98. — B. A. Farrell, "A Note on Dr. Martin's Senses of 'Refutable,'" *Inquiry*, 1964, pp. 99—103. — B. A. Farrell, "The Status of Psychoanalytic Theory," *Inquiry*, 1964, pp. 104—123.

test psychoanalysis admit this.[5] They do not claim to deduce consequences from the theory in their testing of it. One naturally wonders then what they do in testing the theory.

Their procedure seems to be this: In testing psychoanalysis they attempt to mold or reformulate the theory — or rather parts of the theory — into testable propositions. Their procedure is in this way creative for in testing psychoanalysis they do not leave everything as it is; they shape it, clean it up, and sharpen it. The experimental investigator gives the theory an experimental meaning it did not originally have. This procedure may, of course, be called "deducing consequences from the theory" but now "deducing" means something quite different from what it means in logic books. In any case, the actual evidence from the history of experimental psychoanalysis puts the burden of proof on the deductive theorist who would maintain that the deducing of empirical consequences, in the technical logical sense of "deducing," is going on appearances notwithstanding.

The procedure of experimentalists in testing psychoanalysis is in certain important respects like the procedure of judges in interpreting some law passed by a legislature. In many judicial interpretations meanings of key terms in a law become crystallized, the range of the application of the law is defined, and in the process the law often takes on a significance it lacked in the books or the mind of the legislator. Moreover, each previous judicial interpretation is usually taken into account — added to or modified — by other judges in later interpretations. It has been argued that because of this the process is creative and the view that judges always deductively apply already made laws is an illusion.[6]

The analogy between judicial interpretation and experimental "interpretations" (or "explicative consequences" as I shall call them later) of psychoanalysis is striking. In the process of testing, the experimental meaning of key terms becomes crystalized, the scope of the theory becomes defined, and the theory takes on a significance it lacked in psychoanalytic writing or even in psychoanalytic thought. Moreover, each previous experimental reformulation is usually taken into account —

[5] See Michael Martin, "Mr. Farrell and the Refutability of Psychoanalysis," *Inquiry*, 1964, pp. 86—87.

[6] I am not here advocating the extreme position of some legal realists that statutes are never deductively applied and that judges have complete freedom in all cases to modify statutes in any way they see fit. See for example John Chipman Gray, "The Judge as Law-Giver," *The Nature of Law* (ed.) M. P. Golding, New York: Random House, 1966, pp. 187—199. Nevertheless, it does seem to be true in a wide range of cases that statutes may be so unclear and ambiguous that it is unclear whether they apply. In cases of this sort judges must clarify and sharpen the law in applying it — they must interpret it. This interpretation is not arbitrary, however; it may be governed by considerations of public policy and other critical standards. See Ronald Dworkin, "Judicial Discretion," *Journal of Philosophy*, 1963, pp. 624—638. This does not mean, however, that there is one correct interpretation. See Gerald C. MacCallum, "Dworkin on Judicial Discretion," *Journal of Philosophy*, 1963, pp. 638—641. Indeed, the notion of a correct interpretation in cases of this sort may be quite misleading.

added to or modified by other experimenters working in the same area. It may be argued that because of the creative process of experimental testing, in psychoanalysis the deductive model of testing is an illusion.

The second possible retort of the deductive theorist is harder to answer. It might be said that the theory that experimenters actually test is not psychoanalysis in its original sense but a cleaned up experimental version of it. Thus psychoanalysis$_1$ (the original version) is not tested or even testable since empirical consequences cannot be derived. Psychoanalysis$_2$ (the purified version) has been tested because testable consequences have been derived and compared with experimental evidence. In this way the deductive model could be preserved.

There is no doubt that one could talk in this way. Whether one does or not is surely a matter of convention. However, one may wonder whether such a manner of speaking is convenient and illuminating.

In the first place, on this construal one could never say that this or that experiment tested Freud's original theory. Rather one would have to say that the experiment tested some other theory — equivocally called "psychoanalysis." But it is not convenient to speak in this way. For sometimes, at least, some experiments do seem to have some relevance to Freud's original statements even if psychoanalysts tend to deny their relevance.[7] Indeed, it may be partly this obstinacy of psychoanalysts that makes it inconvenient to preserve the deductive model of testing. One wants to say that some experiments *ought* to test psychoanalysis; psychoanalysts ought not to deny the relevance of any *prima facie* negative evidence; psychoanalysis should not be permitted to be above empirical evaluation.[8] Yet the insistence that only theories with deductive empirical consequences can be empirically evaluated does indeed put psychoanalysis beyond the pale of empirical inquiry.

Moreover, another implication of the present defense of the deductive model of testing is that each new experimental translation of the original theory is a new theory: Thus we have psychoanalysis$_1$ (the original untestable theory), psychoanalysis$_2$ (the theory as reformulated by experimenter X), psychoanalysis$_3$ (the theory as reformulated by experimenter Y) and so on. The term "psychoanalysis," unless subscripts were used, would be astonishingly ambiguous. But again it is awkward to suppose this. When one speaks of "psychoanalysis" in these contexts one does not ordinarily suppose it has this great ambiguity and it would be inconvenient to suppose it did.

That this way of speaking is unnatural and inconvenient is surely obvious. The above analogy to legal interpretation brings out this awkwardness even more. It would be inconvenient to say that in certain judicial decisions a *new* law was created by the judge and subsequently

---

[7] Cf. B. A. Farrell, "A Note on Dr. Martin's Senses of 'Refutable,'" *Inquiry*, pp. 99—103.
[8] This sort of justified indignation is expressed well by Popper. See Popper, *Conjectures and Refutations*, pp. 34 ff.

deductively applied by him to the case before his bench although one could say this. But surely although a deductive theory of judicial interpretation could indeed be preserved in this way such a way of talking has an *ad hoc* ring.

AN EXPLICATIVE MODEL OF THEORY TESTING

What seems to be needed — at least for theories like psychoanalysis — is a new and more appropriate model of theory testing. A model is available in Carnap's notion of explication. Carnap used the term "explication" to refer to a particular kind of definition. Explication, according to Carnap, "consisted in transforming a given more or less inexact concept [explicandum] into an exact concept [explicatum] or rather, in replacing the first by the second." Carnap notes:

> In a problem of explication the datum, viz., the explicandum, is not given in exact terms; if it were, no explication would be necessary. Since the datum is inexact, the problem itself is not stated in exact terms; and yet we are asked to give an exact solution.
> ... It follows that, if a solution for a problem of explication is proposed, we cannot decide in an exact way whether it is right or wrong. Strictly speaking, the question whether the solution is right or wrong makes no sense because there is no clear cut answer. The question should rather be whether the proposed solution is satisfactory, whether it is more satisfactory than another one, and the like.[9]

Carnap goes on to suggest as requirements for an adequate explicatum for a given explicandum: (1) similarity to the explicandum, (2) exactness,[10] (3) fruitfulness, and (4) simplicity.

Now it seems to me that much of what Carnap says about the explication of concepts can be carried over to theories.[11] One might say for a first approximation that an explication of a more or less inexact and

---

[9] Rudolf Carnap, *Logical Foundations of Probability*, Chicago: The University of Chicago Press, 1962, pp. 3—4.

[10] Popper has pointed out that the notion of exactness is context bound; exactness is always exactness *for* a particular purpose. See Popper, *Conjectures and Refutations*, p. 283 n. I believe that Carnap would agree with Popper's contention.

[11] Popper has on at least one occasion spoken of explication in connection with theories. But he seems to have in mind something rather different from the present thesis. See Karl Popper, "The Aim of Science," *Ratio*, 1957, p. 33. Popper here suggests that Newton's theory is an explicanda of Galileo's and Kepler's theories (the explicandum) in the sense that Newton's theory has as deductive consequences certain propositions which Galileo's and Kepler's theories are approximations of; thus Newton's theory corrects and contradicts Galileo's and Kepler's theories. But the notion of explication considered here is introduced in connection with a more inexact, unclear theory (the explicandum) being transformed into a less inexact and unclear theory (the explicanda); I take it that although Galileo's and Kepler's theories are approximations to certain deductive consequences of Newton's theory, they need not be less exact, i.e. precise and clear; in particular their exactness and clarity does not stand in the way of testing them.

unclear theory T would consist in transforming T into more exact terms, where "exact" and "clear" would be defined in terms of testability and logical rigor.[12] As in the case of the explication of a concept, the explication of a theory is strictly speaking neither correct nor incorrect but more or less satisfactory for the purpose at hand. Moreover, the requirements for an explication of a concept would be more or less the same for the explication of a theory. The transformation should preserve certain relevant similarities; it should increase exactness, i.e. testability and logical rigor; it should be fruitful, e.g. lead to further transformation and relate to other research in the area; it should be simple, that is at least as simple as the other requirements permit.

There is one aspect of Carnap's notion of explication which may be misleading when carried over to the explication of theories. In Carnap's notion of explication, the explicatum "replaces" the explicandum, but this would not seem to have any obvious analogue in theory testing. There is no obvious "explicatum" that replaces psychoanalytic theory (the "explicandum").[13] Since Carnap defines "explication" in terms of replacement, it seems misleading to use this term to designate the proceedings involved in testing psychoanalysis.

Let us therefore use different terms. Instead of speaking of the explicatum of a more or less imprecise theory, let us speak of an explicative consequence of the theory; instead of speaking of giving an explication of a theory, let us speak of drawing an explicative consequence from the theory. An explicative consequence C of a more or less imprecise theory T would be a proposition resulting from some clarification, reformulation, and sharpening up of theory T (plus perhaps some auxiliary hypotheses). Typically, explicative consequences C_1, C_2, ..., C_n of some imprecise theory T would no more replace theory T than deductive consequences C_1', C_2', ..., C_n' of some rigorously stated theory T' would replace T'.

It should be noted that drawing explicative consequences from a theory and testing these consequences may involve explication of concepts in Carnap's sense. Thus, in order to test psychoanalysis experimenters may give an explication of certain specific terms, e.g. castration threat. However, drawing explicative consequences from a theory need not involve explication in Carnap's sense. Carnap seemed to construe explication as a replacement of individual terms. However, in drawing explicative consequences of a theory the clarification may be of much larger units than individual terms. An experimenter may reformulate whole sentences or even large sections of the theory as a unit; he need

---

[12] For an account of degrees of formalization of a theory see Richard Rudner, *Philosophy of the Social Science*, Englewood Cliffs, N. J.: Prentice Hall, 1966, pp. 47–53.

[13] The theory is in general explicated piece-meal; thus one aspect of the theory is replaced by a clearer formulation. For an attempt at wholesale explication, see Albert Ellis, "An Operational Reformulation of Some of the Basic Principles of Psychoanalysis," *Minnesota Studies in the Philosophy of Science* (ed.) H. Feigl and M. Scriven, Minneapolis: University of Minnesota Press, 1956, Vol. I.

not proceed by explicating individual concepts and then combining the results.

The modification of Carnap's notion of explication when applied to theories would scarcely change the criteria of adequacy. It would make no sense to say that some explicative consequence C was validly or invalidly drawn from a theory T; as in the case of the explication of a concept there is no question of correctness or incorrectness for the canons of deductive logic do not apply. Explicative consequences of a theory would be more or less adequate and their adequacy could be judged in terms roughly equivalent to the requirements that Carnap suggests for the explication of concepts. The propositions drawn as explicative consequences should be more exact than the part of the theory they are drawn from; they should preserve relevant similarities with that part of the theory they are drawn from;[14] they should lead to fruitful results; they should increase simplicity to the extent that it is compatible with fulfilling the other requirements, and so on.

In sum, I have suggested a model of theory testing different from the standard deductive model: imprecise, unclear and ambiguous theories are tested by drawing explicative consequences from these theories and testing these consequences. Let us see in detail how this works in an actual context of theory testing.

SOME EXAMPLES OF DRAWING EXPLICATIVE CONSEQUENCES

Experimental investigators who wish to test psychoanalysis usually follow one of two procedures:

(1) Some investigators simply assume that certain evidence would be relevant for evaluating some aspects of the theory. Their assumptions do not seem to be based on any specific statement or statements of Freud or other psychoanalysts, but rather their assumptions seem "reasonable" to them — they seem to be in accordance with what one might expect a clear empirical consequence of the theory to be if the theory had some clear empirical consequences. Their attitude is best characterized as "If this evidence is not relevant for evaluating psychoanalysis, then what is?" Certain psychoanalytic concepts may suggest to these investigators in a very rough way the sort of empirical evidence that would be relevant. They take these suggestions and give them some concrete empirical meaning. Because of the vagueness and ambiguity of the theory, there is a wide range of what seems "reasonable" to different investigators; the theory itself does not enable one to decide between opposing explicative consequences. Presumably, opposing explicative consequences would have to be judged on the basis of fruitfulness, simplicity etc.

(2) Other investigators work much more closely with the original text of the theory. Instead of making "reasonable" assumptions after con-

---

[14] As in the case of exactness what is relevant will be dependent on the problem at issue.

sidering the theory in some general way, these investigators take specific statements of Freud or his followers and reformulate them so they are testable; or they perform some experiment and then look for some statement of Freud or his followers which could be formulated in a way such that their experiment could be considered a test of it. Again because of the vagueness and ambiguity of the original statement of psychoanalytic theory, great latitude is possible in the reformulations. Thus conflicting explicative consequences would again have to be judged in terms of fruitfulness, simplicity etc.

Let us examine some examples of these two sorts of ways of drawing explicative consequences.

Explicative Consequences based on General Considerations

The difficulty connected with the verification of propositions about the Oedipal situation is well known. Hook, for example, has related some humorous stories about the reluctance of contemporary psychoanalysts to say what evidence would count against a boy having an Oedipus complex.[15] To some investigators, however, the vagueness of the theory is no problem. They simply specify certain evidence that seems to them in accordance with the theory; they *give* the theory clear empirical meaning. In short, they draw explicative consequences.

Robert R. Winch,[16] for example, although confessing that it is "difficult to subject [psychoanalysis] to nomothetic empirical tests,"[17] suggests that it is reasonable to assume that certain evidence would indicate the presence of an unresolved Oedipus complex. As far as one can tell, Winch does not get his suggestion for the "data bearing on the Oedipus hypothesis" from any specific statement of Freud or his followers. In any case, Winch suggests that (a) statements by a person that the person loves the opposite sex parent more than the same sex parent and (b) a person's lack of commitments leading toward marriage, e.g. lack of dates, no engagements, etc., would be relevant evidence. Winch suggests that if psychoanalysis is true, then we should expect to find that people who acknowledge that their greatest love is for their opposite sex parent tend not to be committed to marriage, i.e. not to date, not to be engaged, etc. Naturally, stated in this way, this aspect of the Oedipal hypothesis is easy to verify. Its verification is just a matter of having people fill out questionnaires containing such questions as, "Which parent do you love the most?" and "How often do you date?" and of analyzing the results statistically.

---

[15] S. Hook, "Science and Mythology in Psychoanalysis," *Psychoanalysis, Scientific Method and Philosophy* (ed.) S. Hook, pp. 212—224.
[16] Robert R. Winch, "Some Data Bearing on the Oedipus Hypothesis," *Journal of Abnormal and Social Psychology 45* (1950), pp. 481—489.
[17] *Ibid.*, p. 481.

But surely this sort of evidence seems no more "reasonable" than other potentially contradictory evidence. Why should we not expect, for example, to find that men who acknowledge that they love their mother more than their father tend to have *more* dates, etc., with girls who remind them (unconsciously) of their mothers? Why should we not find that men who actually love their mothers more (unconsciously) *say* just the opposite, as in reaction formation? It seems that these and other assumptions are just as plausible as Winch's assumptions. In short, the theory is simply not stated in a way that enables clear empirical consequences to be inferred. Winch *specifies* that the evidence he cites is in accordance with the Oedipus theory, but psychoanalytic writing does not. To Winch it may seem perfectly reasonable; to others, e.g. Child in a review of the experimental literature on the Oedipus complex,[18] it seems far removed from the original theory.

Perhaps the most common kind of criticism leveled at the sort of experimental design that Winch has produced is that it is not subtle enough; experiments of this kind do not get at the *unconscious* motivation of the people involved. S. M. Friedman,[19] in an elaborately designed experiment, has attempted to get over this problem. He argues that real Oedipus feelings would be manifested only in projective tests. One projective technique he used was to show a series of pictures to boys and girls. These boys and girls were asked to make up stories about the pictures. One picture shown to boys was of a boy standing in a room by an open door; in the room also, facing the boy and seated at a table, was a woman (the mother-figure). One picture shown to girls was exactly the same except that a girl was standing by the door instead of a boy. Now according to Friedman, one can "predict" from psychoanalytic theory (combined with certain principles of Lewin's field theory)[20] that, in general, in telling stories about the pictures boys, because of their "Oedipal needs," will produce more fantasies in which the child moves *toward* the mother-figure than will girls.

It is literally false, of course, that one can make a "prediction," in the sense of drawing any logical conclusion, from psychoanalytic theory (even when combined with Lewin's field theory) of the kind Friedman mentions. What Friedman means, surely, is that this sort of conclusion seems "reasonable" to him. It seems to him plausible that boys will express their desire for their mother in the symbolism of their fantasies and that, in the light of field psychology, this would be manifested in

---

[18] I. L. Child, "Socialization," *Handbook of Social Psychology*, ed. G. Lindzey, p. 669.

[19] Stanley M. Friedman, "An Empirical Study of the Castration and Oedipus Complexes," *Genetic Psychology Monograph 46*, pp. 61—130.

[20] *Ibid.*, pp. 106—107. According to Lewin, an object with "positive valence" in one's psychological field will draw the person toward the object. The opposite would be true with an object with "negative valence." See K. Lewin, "Behavior and Development as a Function of the Total Situation," *Manual of Child Psychology*, ed. L. Carmichael, New York: Wiley, 1946, pp. 805—806.

their stories about the picture by movement *toward* the desired object. But why is it not just as reasonable or plausible to suppose that boys, because of the "castration threat," produce fantasies in which the child moves *away* from the mother-figure? Again, why would we not suspect that girls would produce fantasies in which the child moves toward the mother-figure as much as or more than the boys, since girls would unconsciously wish to identify with their mothers to "obtain" their father's penis? Moreover, certain passages of Freud suggest that the normal children used in Friedman's experiment should not show *any* repressed "Oedipal needs."

In any case, we must not be led to believe that any "deduction" was made from the theory as Friedman seems to suggest. Rather, Friedman specified a clear interpretation that seemed to him reasonably in accordance with a vaguely stated theory. But that other interpretations are just as much in accordance with the theory should not be overlooked — interpretations that seem to account for practically all possible combinations of evidence, e.g. the child in boys' fantasies moving forward or backward, the child in girls' fantasies moving forward just as much as boys, moving not as much as boys, etc. If we accept Friedman's explicative consequence we are able to make a clear and unambiguous test of the theory that was impossible before. The rest of Friedman's "deductions" are of the same kind.

It is uncertain what Winch and Friedman could say to justify their drawing the explicative consequences they did draw over some conflicting explicative consequences they could have drawn. Presumably if they could justify their explicative consequences over alternatives they would have to do so on the grounds already mentioned: fruitfulness, simplicity, exactness, similarity. Although there is no *a priori* reason to suppose this could not be done Winch and Friedman make no attempt to do this in their studies. Thus the adequacy of Winch's and Friedman's explicative consequences remains in doubt.

Explicative Consequences based on Specific Passages

One of the most ingenious attempts to test the psychoanalytic theory of psychosexual development has been that of Gerald S. Blum.[21] Blum devises a projective test called the "Blacky test" to test the psychoanalytic theory of psychosexual development. The Blacky test consists of a series of cartoons portraying the adventures of a dog called Blacky (Blacky is a male dog when the test is given to boys and a female dog when it is given to girls). Various cartoon pictures of the series are supposed to portray in a symbolic and disguised form various stages of psychosexual development. In Cartoon II, for example, Blacky is pictured violently chewing a dog collar with the label "Mama" on it. This cartoon

---

[21] Gerald S. Blum, "A Study of the Psychoanalytic Theory of Psychosexual Development," *Genetic Psychology Monograph 39* (1949), pp. 3—103.

is supposed to represent "oral sadism," and various responses of the subjects to the cartoon are judged for their "oral sadistic" nature. In the first part of the test the subjects are asked to make up a story about the cartoon. The stories are rated in respect to their "oral sadism." The second part of the test asks the subjects the following question: "What will Blacky do next with Mama's collar?" Three multiple choice answers are allowed:

(1) Get tired of it and leave it on the ground.

(2) Return it to Mama.

(3) Angrily chew it to shreds.

Answer number (3) is supposed to indicate "oral sadism."

Cartoon III is supposed to test "anal sadism." Blacky is shown covering something with dirt between Mama's doghouse and Papa's doghouse. The examiner tells the subject: "Here Blacky is relieving himself (herself)." Again the subjects are asked to make up a story about the picture. The story is rated for anal sadism. In the second part of the test the examiner asks the following question: "How does Blacky feel about the training he's (she's) been getting?" Four multiple choice answers are possible:

(1) By relieving himself (herself) in the ways he's (she's) been taught, he (she) now has an opportunity to show his (her) family what a good dog he (she) can be.

(2) He (she) feels Mama and Papa are expecting too much of him (her) at this early stage.

(3) He (she) is very happy to have control of himself (herself).

(4) He (she) thinks he's (she's) got Mama and Papa right where he (she) wants them.

Answer (4) is supposed to indicate "anal sadism."

These and other similar cartoons were used in Blum's experiment with 119 males and 90 females in an elementary psychology class at Stanford. One of the main purposes of the test was to see if there were any significant differences between the responses to the tests of males and females. It turned out that in some cases there were no significant differences, but in many other cases there were. Blum then attempted to find *specific* statements in the writings of Freud and Fenichel that would indicate what one could "predict" about the differences between men and women, e.g. in respect to their anal and oral sadism. Let us examine in detail Blum's "predictions" on oral and anal sadism based on the writings of Freud and Fenichel.

In relation to the responses to Cartoon II (the oral sadism cartoon) Blum found significantly *more* women than men responding with answer number (3) (the oral sadism response). Blum then tried to find specific passages in Freud and Fenichel from which one could "predict" his results, thereby showing them to be in keeping with psychoanalytic theory. Blum found passages in Fenichel which he took to suggest that little girls have hostile feelings toward their mothers. Fenichel notes, for example:

> The most important experiences that precipitate, facilitate, impede, or form the change of object in girls are disappointments coming from the mother, which causes a turning away from her. Among these, weaning, training for cleanliness, and the birth of siblings have the most important repercussions . . . .[22]

Blum goes on to explain:

> The specifically feminine disappointment accounting for the greater antagonism in females is the lack of a penis, for which the mother is held responsible. Awareness of this lack remobilizes anal and especially oral elements, which are often characteristic of subsequent femininity.[23]

Blum cites another passage from Fenichel:

> It is understandable that this development is open to many disturbances and that conflicts about the preoedipal love for the mother play an important role in the neuroses of women. In normal development, too, the relationship of women to their mothers is more frequently ambivalent than in that of most men to their fathers. Some remnants of the pre-oedipal mother fixation are always found in women . . . .[24]

Blum also notes that Freud linked the little girls' hostility directly to oral frustration and he cites Freud who says:

> The [girl's] complaint against the mother that harks back furthest, is that she has given the child too little milk, which is taken as indicating a lack of love . . . .[25]

On the basis of these passages Blum maintains:

> Thus, psychoanalytic theory would predict oral sadism, which is an expression of pre-oedipal hostility toward the mother, to be more prevalent in females than in males.[26]

It is hard to see why any such conclusion can be "predicted" from the passages cited by Blum. Surely Freud's and Fenichel's statements are much too vague to permit any clear statement to be made about a difference of the kind that Blum mentions. In any case, Blum suggests on the next page, when he deals with "anal sadism," that women, according to psychoanalytic theory, tend to repress their aggression more strongly than men do, and he cites Freud to prove his contention.[27] Why, therefore, should we not expect women to show *less* oral sadism than men,

---

[22] Otto Fenichel, *The Psychoanalytic Theory of Neurosis*, New York: Norton, 1945, p. 89.
[23] Blum, *op. cit.*, p. 38.   [24] Fenichel, *op. cit.*, p. 90.
[25] Sigmund Freud, *New Introductory Lectures on Psycho-Analysis*, New York: Norton, 1933, p. 166.
[26] Blum, *op. cit.*, p. 38.   [27] Freud, *op. cit.*, p. 158.

or perhaps the same amount as men, since the strong oral sadistic drive might be equalized by the strong repression?

In relation to Cartoon III (the anal sadism cartoon), Blum found significantly *fewer* anal sadistic responses in women than in men. Blum tried to find specific passages in Freud from which one could "predict" his results, thereby showing them in keeping with psychoanalytic theory. Here Blum *does* cite passages (as he does not in relation to oral sadism) that suggest that women would repress their aggressions more than men. These passages, Blum believes, indicate that his results on anal sadism are compatible with psychoanalytic theory. But what Blum does not seem to realize is that these *same* passages indicate that his results on *oral* sadism are incompatible with psychoanalysis, i.e. women, because of stronger repression, should have less *oral* sadism on the Blacky test (which they did not). Moreover, Blum does not argue in relation to anal sadism (as he does in relation to oral sadism) that girls' hostility "remobilizes *anal* and especially oral elements, which are often characteristic of subsequent femininity."[28] (My italics). But if this argument can be used to prove that women should have more *oral* sadism, it can also be used to show that women should have more *anal* sadism. Viewed in this way, Blum's results on anal sadism are also incompatible with psychoanalysis. In short, Blum seems to use passages and arguments from Freud and Fenichel that make his results compatible with the theory without realizing that the same passages and arguments, used in a different way, would make his results conflict with the theory. Depending on what passages he cites and how he interprets the passages, many different and contradictory "predictions" can be made. And this is only to say that unambiguous and clear conclusions cannot be deductively drawn from psychoanalysis. Blum has *specified* a clear and unambiguous empirical meaning for psychoanalysis; he did not find it in the theory. In short, he drew explicative consequences from the theory.

As in the case of Winch and Friedman the adequacy of Blum's explicative consequences remains in doubt. Blum does not attempt to justify his explicative consequences in terms of the criteria already mentioned. Whether this justification is possible is uncertain.

KUHN'S NOTION OF THE ARTICULATION OF A PARADIGM

The view of theory testing presented above may appear to bear an analogy to Thomas Kuhn's notion of the articulation of a paradigm.[29] However, Kuhn's views on the articulation of a paradigm are not clear. The unclarity of the notion of a paradigm pointed out by reviewers[30] of

[28] Blum, *op. cit.*, p. 38.
[29] Thomas Kuhn, *The Structure of Scientific Revolution*, Chicago: University of Chicago Press, 1962.
[30] See Dudley Shapere, "The Structure of Scientific Revolution," *Philosophical Review*, 1964, pp. 383–394.

An Explicative Model of Theory Testing

Kuhn's book carries over to his notion of the articulation of a paradigm; hence it is uncertain whether my view is similar to Kuhn's view in important and relevant respects.

If one simply identifies paradigms with theories — something Kuhn does not do — Kuhn's thesis would be that much of normal science consists in the articulation and specification of the accepted theory of the period. The problem now is to know what articulation and specification means. In particular, does articulation and specification of a theory amount to what I have called drawing explicative consequences?

Again this is not clear. But there is some reason to think that Kuhn has something quite different in mind. Kuhn speaks of the "empirical work undertaken to articulate the paradigm resolving some of its residual ambiguities and permitting the solution of problems to which it had previously only drawn attention."[31] It seems that in this passage, at least, Kuhn considers the articulation of a paradigm as an experimental or empirical enterprise.

However, the drawing of an explicative consequence from a theory is a conceptual job. To be sure, such a task may be influenced or justified by experimental results. Moreover, empirical research may be preceded by the drawing of explicative consequences. But the empirical research is not "undertaken to" draw explicative consequences from a theory.

There are other differences between Kuhn's views and my own which need to be emphasized. The articulation of a paradigm (whatever exactly this might mean) occurs in periods of normal science. But periods of normal science are, according to Kuhn, periods in the history of established sciences; Kuhn's examples are all taken from physics and chemistry. I am insisting that at least in ill formulated theories, e.g. psychoanalysis,[32] the drawing of explicative consequences of the theory goes on; whether this is common practice in mature science I have not considered. Moreover, Kuhn emphasizes the unquestioning attitude of experimenters to the paradigm; their great faith that the paradigm can be articulated to solve all puzzles. Such an attitude is not an essential part of drawing explicative consequences. Indeed, many of the experimenters who draw explicative consequences from psychoanalysis are very skeptical of the theory.[33]

---

[31] Kuhn, *op. cit.*, p. 27.

[32] What the exact status of psychoanalysis is we need not decide here. But it is generally acknowledged by everyone except some psychoanalysts that psychoanalysis is not a science let alone a mature one. The judgment that psychoanalysis is not a science is usually based on a number of criteria: untestability in the deductive model sense, unreliability of psychoanalytic clinical evidence and the dogmatic attitude of many psychoanalysts. We may well accept this judgment and the criteria on which it is based and still maintain with perfect consistency that a particular kind of scientific testing, i.e. the drawing and testing of explicative consequences by experimental psychologists is wide spread. For an illuminating discussion of the status of psychoanalysis see B. A. Farrell, "The Status of Psychoanalysis," *Inquiry*, 1964, pp. 104—123.

[33] See for example W. Sewell, "Some Observations on Theory Testing," *Rural Sociology* 21 (1956), pp. 1—12.

CONCLUSION

I have suggested a new model of theory testing to illuminate those contexts of theory testing in which vague, ambiguous and ill formulated theories are tested — theories in which clear deductive consequences cannot be drawn. In these contexts explicative consequences can be drawn and these consequences can be tested. The actual testing of psychoanalysis illustrates this procedure.

How far one can apply this model is uncertain, but at least much of psychoanalytic theory testing is illuminated by its application. It may be that the testing of protoscientific theories in the history of science can be illuminated. But what limitations this model has cannot be determined *a priori*.

A final question about this model must be raised although it cannot be answered here. Since the explicative consequences of a theory are not deductive consequences, what relevance does a positive or negative test of an explicative consequence have for the truth or falsity of the theory? Thus suppose an explicative consequence C is drawn from theory T. Suppose further that C is judged false in the light of experimental evidence. Can we infer by modus tollens that the theory is false? Clearly not since, as I have already pointed out, explicative consequences are neither validly nor invalidly drawn. Presumably, then, we could not *logically* infer from a false explicative consequence to the falsehood of the theory from which it was drawn.

What could one say? There are a number of alternative approaches. Let me mention just two. One could say that testing the explicative consequences of a theory is not a test of the theory's truth; it is a test of rather the heuristic value of the theory — its ability to generate by drawing explicative consequences testable propositions. (Indeed one might argue that because theories like psychoanalysis are so vague, ambiguous and unclear they have no truth value to test; that psychoanalytic theory should be treated like a system of sentence schemata).

On the other hand, one might want to argue that some new type of logic should be developed to handle explicative consequences, a logic in which a negative explicative consequence could, by an inference somehow analogous to modus tollens, be used to falsify the theory from which the explicative consequence was drawn. Such a logic might permit us to say, for example, that since C is an explicative consequence of T and C is false and C is more simple and fruitful and preserving of relevant similarities than any contradictory explicative consequence of the theory, therefore T is false. Whether such a logic is possible or even meaningful is problematic.

MICHAEL MARTIN

An examination of the operationists' critique of psychoanalysis

> "Many of the objections against psychoanalysis have their origin in an overly narrow interpretation of the version of scientific empiricism commonly known as operationism with its stress on the rooting of all concepts in concrete manipulations and observations, and generally in a vaguely anti-theoretical attitude, rather than in a legitimate criticism of psychoanalytic theory." [1]
>
> Else Frenkel-Brunswik

When psychoanalysis first made its appearance on the intellectual scene at the turn of the century, it met with strong opposition. And although Freud gained almost universal recognition in the years that followed, psychoanalysis has continued to be severely criticized. In some cases, however, the criticisms brought against Freud's theory are obviously unjustified from a scientific point of view, for they turned upon certain *a priori* or religious theories of human nature which psychoanalysis seemed to undermine. We will not concern ourselves with those critics who clearly do not purport to base their criticism on scientific grounds. There is, however, one objection raised against psychoanalysis with which we must concern ourselves for it purports to be in the name of science. In America within the last thirty years psychoanalysis has come under attack from a methodological point of view known as "operationism". In this paper we shall examine the operationists' criticism.

Operationism considered

The rise of operationism in psychology

Operationism, first explicitly formulated by Bridgman in *Logic of modern physics* in 1927 [2], gained a secure foothold in American experimental psychology in the years that followed. Joining forces with some older behavioristic

---

1. E. Frenkel-Brunswik, "Psychoanalysis and the unity of science", *Proceedings of the American Academy of Arts and Sciences* 80, 1954, p. 274.
2. P.W. Bridgman, *Logic of modern physics*, New York, Macmillan, 1927.

trends [3], in a short time operationism became one of the most important methodological points of view in psychology. Allport, in a review of the changing trends in the leading psychological journals, reports that the first article mentioning operationism appeared in 1928 "close on the heels of Bridgman's book" [4]. Skinner reports that in 1931 he produced "the first explicitly operational analysis of a psychological concept" [5]. By 1939, with the trend rising rapidly five per cent of all the articles in the leading psychological journals mentioned operationism [6]. By 1945, presumably indicative of operationism's growing influence, *The psychological review* devoted its September issue to a discussion of operationism by psychologists and philosophers of science [7].

The complaint against psychoanalysis

Traditional psychology in general and psychoanalysis in particular came under the operationists' criticism. To the question "What is wrong with psychoanalysis as a science?" the operationists had a ready answer. While sometimes admitting that psychoanalysis had been heuristic, and had given new life to academic psychology, operationists insisted that psychoanalytic concepts were vague and imprecise. The way to make psychoanalysis scientific, the way to make its concepts clear and precise, was by means of operational definitions. Some operationists seemed to hope that the main body of psychoanalytic concepts could be so defined. Bridgman, the founder of operationism, commented: "In spite of the apparently unsatisfactory status of some of the constructs of the psychoanalyst it would appear that there is nothing fundamentally unsound at the foundations but that if one takes the necessary trouble and care everything can be put on a completely 'operational' basis" [8].

Pratt, one of the leading operationists in psychology, maintained: "Many generations of psychologists will spend their lives trying to translate the poetry of Freud into the prose of science" [9]. But as he argued elsewhere: "If the Freudian mechanisms [...] are thought of as picturesque words which do no more than summarize certain clinical observations, their meaning and defini-

---

3. S.S. Stevens, "Psychology and the science of science", in: P. Wiener (ed.), *Readings in the philosophy of science*, New York, Charles Scribner's Sons, 1953, p. 166.
4. G. Allport, "The psychologists' frame of reference", *Psychological review* 37, 1950, p. 10.
5. B.F. Skinner, "Rejoinders and second thoughts", *Psychological review* 52, 1945, p. 291.
6. Allport, *op. cit.*
7. E.G. Boring, P.W. Bridgman, H. Feigl, H. Israel, C.C. Pratt and B.F. Skinner, "Symposium on operationism", *Psychological review* 52, 1945, pp. 241-294.
8. P.W. Bridgman, "Comments", in: S. Hook (ed.), *Psychoanalysis, scientific method and philosophy*, New York, New York University Press, 1959, p. 282.
9. C.C. Pratt, *Logic of modern psychology*, New York, Macmillan, 1939, p. 164.

tion fall well within the range of operational procedure" [10]. But what does it mean to put psychoanalysis "on a completely operational basis"? What is "operational procedure"? In short, what is operationism?

The vagueness and ambiguity of the term

An examination of the operationists' literature and an empirical study of the actual use of the term by graduate students at Duke indicate that the term "operationism" has many different meanings [11]. Indeed, the term has even changed its meaning in Bridgman's own writings in at least two respects: 1) in what is to count as an operation, and 2) in the extent to which operations determine the meaning of a concept.

1) In *Logic of modern physics*, Bridgman, although mentioning briefly "mental operation", expounded a dominantly physical operationism. Concepts were to be defined in terms of the gross physical manipulations involved in observation and measurement. Length could be defined, *e.g.*, by the physical operations involved in laying off a foot rule [12]. But in later writings Bridgman explicitly expanded the meaning of "operation" to include many non-physical operations variously called "verbal", "mental", and "paper and pencil" operations [13]. In fact, in one formulation, an operation, according to Bridgman, is any act involved in the attempt "to reduce events to understandability" [14].

2) Bridgman maintained in his early writing that scientific concepts must be completely defined in terms of operations. He argued that a scientific concept "is synonymous with the corresponding set of operations" [15]. Later, however, he seemed to suggest something a little weaker in the statement that meaning "is to be sought [...] in operations" [16]. In 1938 this weaker thesis became explicit. He maintained then that operations were a "necessary" but not a "sufficient" condition for the determination of meaning [17], and in one of his last statements he argued that the "operational aspect is not by any means the only aspect of meaning" [18].

---

10. C.C. Pratt, "Operationism in psychology", *Psychological review* 52, 1945, p. 268.
11. H. Hart, "Towards an operational definition of the term 'operation' ", *American sociological review* 18, 1953, pp. 612-617.
12. Bridgman, *Logic of modern physics, op. cit.*, pp. 1-20.
13. P.W. Bridgman, "Operational analysis", *Philosophy of science* 5, 1938, p. 123.
14. *Ibid.*, p. 115.
15. Bridgman, *Logic of modern physics, op. cit.*, p. 5.
16. P.W. Bridgman, "A physicist's second reaction to Mengenlehre", *Scripta mathematica* 2, 1934, p. 103.
17. Bridgman, "Operational analysis", *op. cit.*, p. 116.
18. P.W. Bridgman, "The nature of some of our physical concepts", *British journal for the philosophy of science*, 1952, p. 257.

S.S. Stevens, a strong supporter of Bridgman in psychology, also expanded the meaning of "operation" from Bridgman's original emphasis on gross physical manipulation to include perceiving as an operation, *i.e.*, the operation of making a discrimination. Stevens argued: "When we attempt to reduce complex operations to simpler and simpler ones, we find in the end that discrimination, or differential response, is the fundamental operation" [19].

With this expansion of the meaning of terms by Stevens, combined with Bridgman's own extended use, the term "operation" came to cover almost everything. As Gustav Bergman has remarked about operationists: "They saw operations everywhere. At the one extreme, the scientist's perceptions were decked out to be a species of operations; and at the other, his verbal and computational activities were as so-called symbolic operations herded into the same corral" [20].

As the years passed, this tendency to expand and generalize the meaning of the term "operationism" seemed to spread. Operationism became identified with various general positions: Lundberg identified operationism with "empiricism" [21], Rapoport equated it with "the philosophy of science" [22] and Pratt maintained that operationism is nothing more than "the manner in which the present generation utters the familiar cry of science 'Be careful' " [23]. As Benjamin has noted : "As a consequence of this shift in the meaning of the term, operationism becomes readily identifiable with a wide range of positions extending from the narrow insistence that only quantitative methods may be used in science; through the vague demand that science be empirical as opposed to rationalistic, or metaphysical, or speculative, or any other notion with which the term 'empirical' is commonly contrasted; and ending with the extremely general position that any concept is operationally defined if it produces 'understanding' " [24].

Operationism narrowly conceived:
Two critiques of psychoanalysis

It may be wondered in the light of this broadening of the meaning of operationism, what the operationists' complaint against psychoanalysis really amounts to. As Margenau points out, an extremely generalized operationism of this kind "would not be saying much" [25]. But we must not forget our

19. Stevens, *op. cit.*, p. 164. See also S.S. Stevens, "The operational definition of psychological concepts", *Psychological review* 42, 1935, pp. 517-527.
20. G. Bergman, "Sense and nonsense in operationism", in : P. Frank (ed.), *The validation of scientific theories*, Boston, Beacon Press, 1956, p. 49.
21. G.A. Lundberg, *Social research*, London, Longmans Green, 1942, p. 89.
22. A. Rapoport, *Operational philosophy*, New York, Harper, 1953, p. viii.
23. Pratt, *Logic of modern psychology*, *op. cit.*, p. 81.
24. A.C. Benjamin, *Operationism*, Springfield, Ill., Charles C. Thomas, 1955, p. 42.
25. H. Margenau, *The nature of physical reality*, New York, McGraw-Hill, 1950, p. 232.

thing: not all operationists were so liberal and general in their view on what an operational analysis should be; hence they were not so liberal and general in their view on what was wrong with psychoanalysis. When they said that psychoanalysis should be "put on an operational basis", they were referring to something quite similar to the narrowly and strictly conceived operationism of Bridgman's early writings. In fact, two of the most extensive criticisms of psychoanalysis in the literature are formulated from the point of view of a narrowly conceived operationism; namely the criticisms of Albert Ellis and B.F. Skinner.

Ellis' critique. Albert Ellis, well-known for his critical writings on psychoanalysis [26] and clinical psychology [27], has attempted "to reformulate the main tenets of psychoanalysis" [28] from the point of view of a narrowly conceived operationism. The surprising thing about Ellis' attempt is that, although he believes that Bridgman's early "strict operationism [...] may be unduly restrictive" [29], he ends up in his reformulation with a position that is similar to Bridgman's early view. He proposes first of all "a liberal operationism". In this liberal formulation the only requirement seems to be that scientific theories should be in "the final analysis linked to operations". But "to be operationally meaningful, a statement must be confirmable at least in principle: that is to say, a scientific theory must be tied to observables at *some* point" [30]. It would seem then that Ellis' liberal view of operationism is identical with a liberal empiricism that requires only that scientific theories be confirmable. But although Ellis gives brief lip service to this account of liberal operationism or empiricism, when he actually comes to his "operational reformation of psychoanalysis" he does something quite different: "This, then, is modern operationism or empiricism. As applied to psychoanalysis, it means that psychoanalytic principles should be stated in terms so that they are, in some final analysis, in principle confirmable in terms of some ultimate observables. *In the following paragraphs, however, we shall attempt to be even more strictly operational than this in translating psychoanalytic principles into scientific language*" [31]. (My italics.)

Ellis' attempt to be "more strictly operational" amounts to the suggestion that the theoretical concepts of psychoanalysis be construed as "intervening

---

26. A. Ellis, "An introduction to the principles of scientific psychoanalysis", *Genetic psychology monographs* 41, 1950, pp. 147-222.
27. A. Ellis, "A critique of systematic theoretical foundations in clinical psychology", *Journal of clinical psychology* 8, 1952, pp. 11-15.
28. A. Ellis, "An operational reformulation of some of the basic principles of psychoanalysis", in: H. Feigl and M. Scriven (eds.), *The foundations of science and the concepts of psychology, and psychoanalysis*, Minneapolis, University of Minnesota Press, 1956, pp. 131-154 (Minnesota studies in the philosophy of science, vol. 1).
29. *Ibid.*, p. 132.
30. *Ibid.*
31. *Ibid.*, p. 135.

variables" [32]. Now the notion of intervening variables in psychology goes back to E.C. Tolman [33]. Tolman has suggested that human behavior (dependent variables) may be considered as a function of certain environmental stimuli (independent variables). Except in the case of simple reflexes this is a very complex function and we may find it necessary, according to Tolman, to break down this complex function into component functions. We do this by means of logically constructed intervening variables. Each intervening variable would be a certain function of given independent variables therefore the dependent variable would itself be a function of the intervening variables. The term "intervening variable", used by Tolman, was unfortunate for these constructs do not "intervene" between stimulus and response as the nervous system might be said to intervene [34]. Indeed, intervening variables for Tolman were merely manipulatory conveniences. They could not be identified with hidden mental or physiological processes of the organism for they involved no hypothesis concerning the existence of unobserved entities or processes.

MacCorquodale and Meehl, in a now well-known article, have distinguished two types of constructs used in psychology [35]. One type of construct they call "intervening variables". These constructs have the same meaning as Tolman's intervening variables for they are completely definable in terms of behavior; they refer to no unobservable entities, but have only a "summarizing character". But some constructs in psychology, e.g., in Hull's theory [36] are not completely definable in terms of behavior; they refer to unobserved events or processes, e.g., physiological processes. These unobserved events are usually inferred from certain observable manifestations of these events or processes. MacCorquodale and Meehl suggest that these constructs be called "hypothetical constructs", to differentiate them from intervening variables. Now Ellis accepts this distinction of MacCorquodale and Meehl and proposes that psychoanalytic concepts be construed as intervening variables, i.e., they should be completely defined in terms of behavior, despite the fact that intervening variables are of "limited usefulness in scientific theorizing" and that "hypothetical constructs take in the widest range of

---

32. *Ibid.*, p. 136.
33. E.C. Tolman, "The determiners of behavior at a choice point", *Psychological review* 45, 1938, pp. 1-41.
34. *Cf.* J.R. Maze, "Do intervening variables intervene?", *Psychological review* 61, 1954 pp. 226-234.
35. K. MacCorquodale and P.E. Meehl, "Hypothetical constructs and intervening variables", in: H. Feigl and M. Brodbeck (eds.), *Readings in the philosophy of science*, New York, Appleton-Century-Crofts, 1953, pp. 596-611.
36. See C.L. Hull, *Principles of behavior*, New York, Appleton-Century-Crofts, 1943 Some of Hull's concepts, *e.g.*, of "fractional anticipatory goal response", refer to hypothetical processes within the organism.

relevant phenomena, lead to maximum success in the prediction and explanation of behavior, and are heuristically necessary" [37].

But if hypothetical constructs have these advantages over intervening variables, why does Ellis recommend construing psychoanalytic theory in terms of intervening variables? Now Ellis does not deny that psychoanalysis could be legitimately construed in terms of hypothetical constructs, but he maintains that in the case of psychoanalysis it would be *best* to construe its theoretical terms as intervening variables. His reasons seem to boil down to this:

1) Psychoanalytic theory would be more easily confirmed or disconfirmed if it were formulated in terms of intervening variables;

2) Hypothetical constructs have never been shown to be necessary in psychoanalytic theory;

3) A formulation of psychoanalysis in terms of intervening variables would eliminate psychoanalytic "dogmaticism and fuzzy thinking" and possible erroneous and redundant aspects of psychoanalytic theory, and would encourage new hypotheses and experiments [38].

In summary, Albert Ellis has recommended for several reasons a narrowly conceived "operational" reformulation of psychoanalysis. He wants to construe psychoanalytic theory in terms of intervening variables, thus, in turn, defining psychoanalytic concepts completely in terms of behavior.

Skinner's critique. Like Ellis, B.F. Skinner is opposed to the use of hypothetical constructs in psychoanalysis [39]. But unlike Ellis, who seemed to acknowledge the superiority of hypothetical constructs in other areas, Skinner is opposed to their use in psychology generally and, perhaps, in any science [40]. According to Skinner: "Operationism may be defined as the practice of talking about 1) one's observations, 2) the manipulative and calculative procedure involved in making them, 3) the logical and mathematical steps which intervene between earlier and later statements, and 4) *nothing else*" [41]. Skinner maintains that all scientific definitions should be operational in this sense [42]. In relation to psychoanalysis he insists that Freud should have followed the "simple expedient of an operational definition of terms" [43].

---

37. Ellis, "An operational reformulation of some of the basic principles of psychoanalysis", *op. cit.*, pp. 132-133.
38. *Ibid.*, p. 136.
39. B.F. Skinner, "Critique of psychoanalytic concepts and theories", in : Feigl and Scriven (eds.), *op. cit.*, pp. 77-87.
40. B.F. Skinner, "Are theories of learning necessary?", *Psychological review* 57, 1950, pp. 193-216.
41. B.F. Skinner, "The operational analysis of psychological terms", *Psychological review* 52, 1945, p.270.
42. *Ibid.*
43. Skinner, "Critique of psychoanalytic concepts and theories", *op. cit.*, p. 87.

Theory and methods

Because of this narrowly conceived operationism, Skinner believes that all psychological theories "that appeal to events at some other level" are unnecessary [44]. To be sure, Skinner does not deny what theories that do contain hypothetical constructs have accomplished. He argues: "It would be foolhardy to deny the achievement of theories of this sort in the history of science". But, according to Skinner, theories of this kind are a luxury; they "are fun". "The question of whether they are necessary has other implications." [45] In relation to the hypothetical constructs of psychoanalysis, Skinner comments: "Whether we need similar constructs in the future prosecution of a science of behavior is a question worth considering" [46].

But why does Skinner think that such theories are unnecessary? First of all, although he has never explicitly said so, he seems to consider his own work as a demonstration of the fact that hypothetical constructs are unnecessary for the simple reason that he does not use them. He believes, for example, that he has restated the Freudian mechanism in terms of conditioning theory "without reference to Freudian theory" [47]. But Skinner also gives theoretical considerations to support his contention. Consider his attitude on the relevance of neurology for psychology. He argues that the study of neural events is not in the least useful in the study of human behavior, for whatever knowledge we gain of the nervous system, the causes leading up to the neural events and the effects of the neural events will eventually lead *outside* the organism: "Eventually a science of the nervous system based upon direct observation rather than inference will describe the neural state and events which immediately precede, say, the response, 'No, thank you'. These events in turn will be found to be preceded by other neurological events and these in turn by others. This series will lead us back to events outside of the nervous system and, eventually, outside the organism". [48] Our knowledge of the nervous system has not helped us determine the statistical relation *between* the environmental independent variable and the dependent behavioral variable. This relation could have been determined *without* any knowledge of neurology. But a knowledge of this relation is precisely what is needed to predict human behavior.

The same is true, according to Skinner, with the hypothetical constructs of psychoanalysis. We need not postulate some Freudian mechanisms to connect, *e.g.*, childhood toilet training and adult personality traits. If we know the childhood environmental stimuli and the adult behavior, a functional relation can be found directly between the stimuli and response. Hidden Freudian mechanisms can be dispensed with. Construed in this "opera-

---

44. Skinner, "Are theories of learning necessary?", *op. cit.*, p. 193.
45. *Ibid.*, p. 194.
46. Skinner, "Critique of psychoanalytic concepts and theories", *op. cit.*, p. 78.
47. *Ibid.*, p. 84.
48. B.F. Skinner, *Science and human behavior*, New York, Macmillan, 1953, p. 28.

Théorie et méthodes

tional" way, Freudian mechanisms need not be regarded as "what happens when a skillful wish evades a censor — but simply as ways of representing relationships among responses and controlling variables" [49].

In summary, Skinner, in this narrowly conceived "operational criticism" of psychoanalysis, has maintained that hypothetical constructs of psychoanalysis are unnecessary. From his point of view the observational relation between stimulus and response is all that is necessary.

Operationism criticized

We have reviewed operationism's rapid rise to methodological power in psychology and we have heard the operationists' complaint against psychoanalysis. We have seen that the term "operationism" has become so ambiguous that the complaint is unclear without further elaboration, while after elaboration it is evident in some cases that the term has been used so broadly that the complaint has become empty. Some operationists, however, maintained a narrowly conceived operationism; both Ellis and Skinner, despite differences in their reasons, share one view in their complaint against psychoanalysis : psychoanalytic theory should not be construed in terms of hypothetical constructs, but should be construed completely in terms of overt behavior. For Ellis this amounts to the insistence that psychoanalytic concepts be interpreted as "intervening variables", while for Skinner it comes to the contention that in psychoanalysis, as in any psychological theory, the relationship between stimulus and response is all that is necessary. Now we must determine whether this complaint against psychoanalysis is justified.

I will argue that these narrowly conceived operationist criticisms of psychoanalysis do not stand up under close scrutiny. My criticism will be divided into two parts: 1) general considerations from the logic of science to show that this type of operationism is untenable, 2) specific criticism of Ellis' and Skinner's argument against the use of hypothetical constructs in psychoanalysis.

General considerations from the logic of science

Dispositional terms: Explicit definitions. From the point of view of the logic of science psychoanalytic theory may be considered as a set of sentences formulated in a specific vocabulary. The extra-logical terms of the theory, for purposes of analysis, may be divided into two sub-sets — a set of non-observational terms, *e.g.*, "super ego", "Oedipus complex", and a set of observational terms, *e.g.*, "blushes", "remains silent". The set of observation sentences, *i.e.*, those sentences of the theory whose non-logical terms are all observational terms and are quickly decidable by some group of language

---

49. Skinner, "Critique of psychoanalytic concepts and theories", *op. cit.*, p. 84.

user, *e.g.*, English speakers. A sentence would be considered quickly decidable if a member of this group could decide whether to assert or deny the sentence in a few observations. Thus, for instance a sentence "Jones is blushing" presumably could be quickly decided by most users of the English language in a few observations if Jones was near and in plain view. On the other hand the sentence "Jones unconsciously hates his mother" could not be quickly decided by most English speakers in a few observations even if Jones was near and in plain view.

Moreover, the observational vocabulary is highly reliable, among the group specified. There would be a high probability that if one person of the group applied a term in a given situation so would another person and if one person applied a term on one occasion he would also in another occasion if there were no relevant differences. Thus, for example, it is highly probable that if one person applies the expression "is blushing" to Jones in a given situation so would another person, other things being equal.

Let us suppose further that the observation vocabulary is in terms of certain environmental stimuli and people's responses to these stimuli. Now the thesis of the narrowly conceived operationism considered above may be restated more precisely: All non-observable terms of psychoanalysis should be explicitly defined in terms of quickly decidable, highly reliable stimulus-response language specified above.

Consider a property term A from the non-observational vocabulary. The thesis of a narrowly conceived operationism would consist in the contention that A should be fully defined in terms of the observational vocabulary, *e.g.*, in terms of environmental stimulus S and behavioral response R. This definition might take the form

$$Ax. \equiv . Sx \supset Rx$$

i.e., a person x has (by definition) the property A if and only if he is such that under environmental stimulus S, he exhibits a behavioral response R. This thesis, then, would be tantamount to construing the terms of non-observational vocabulary as dispositional terms, *i.e.*, terms that designate dispositions on the part of people to display specific reactions under certain specific circumstances. For example, we could consider "anxiety" as a dispositional term, *e.g.*, by explicitly defining it in terms of obvious changes of a certain kind in a patient while he is free associating after he has been given an interpretation of a certain kind by a psychoanalyst. We might then define "anxiety" thus: "x is anxious if and only if, when x is told by his psychoanalyst that x hates his mother, then x blushes or stammers and the content of x's free association changes" [50].

---

50. Naturally, this definition and other definitions used in this paper are deliberately oversimplified. However, the definitions can be made as complex as one desires by additions to the antecedent or conclusion of the hypothetical statement. These additions will not affect the logical point that is being made.

But, as Carnap first noted [51], this kind of definition, on the standard extensional interpretation of logical connectives, is untenable. The conditional $Sx \supset Rx$ is false only in case the antecedent Sx is true and the consequent Rx is false; hence any person who does not satisfy condition S, *i.e.*, for whom the antecedent is false, would make the conditional as a whole true; consequently this person would be assigned the property A. In terms of our illustration any person *not* told by his psychoanalyst that he hates his mother would be anxious no matter what kind of behavior the person might exhibit.

A way out of this problem would be to interpret the "if [...], then [...]" not in the standard extensional manner, but as a subjunctive conditional, *i.e.*, "x is anxious if and only if, if x *were* told by his psychoanalyst that x hates his mother, then x *would* blush or stammer and the content of x's free association *would* change". But the problem with this interpretation is that it is not clear what the meaning of the subjunctive conditional amounts to. Despite several attempts at clarification [52], no fully satisfactory analysis is yet available. As Hempel has argued, the thesis that dispositional terms should be defined with the use of subjunctive conditionals "represents a program rather than a solution" [53].

Dispositional terms: Reduction sentences. Carnap has proposed another way of meeting this difficulty without recourse to subjunctive conditionals [54]. It consists in providing a partial, rather than a complete, specification of the meaning of a dispositional term. This is done by means of so-called reduction sentences. One form of reduction sentences is this:

$$Sx \supset (Ax \equiv Rx) \text{ [55]}.$$

It is important to notice that the use of extensional connectives no longer has the undersirable aspects of the first formulation, for if a person x is not under condition S, then the entire formula is true of him, but this implies nothing about whether the person does or does not have the property A. This approach construes operational definition as only a partial specification of the meaning of A in terms of the observational vocabulary and treats disposi-

---

51. R. Carnap, "Testability and meaning", in: Feigl and Brodbeck (eds.), *op. cit.*, pp. 52-53. See also C. Hempel, "A logical appraisal of operationism", in: P. Frank (ed.), *The validation of scientific theories*, Boston, Mass., Beacon Press, 1956, p. 65.
52. R. Chisholm, "The contrary-to-fact conditional", in: H. Feigl and W. Sellars (eds.), *Readings in philosophical analysis*, New York, Appleton-Century-Crofts, 1949, pp. 482-497; N. Goodman, "The problem of counterfactual conditionals", *Journal of philosophy* 44, 1947, pp. 113-128.
53. C. Hempel, "Fundamentals of concept formation in empirical science", *International encyclopedia of unified science* 2 (7), 1953, p. 25.
54. Carnap, *op. cit.* For an application of this method in psychology see S. Koch, "The logical character of the motivation concept", *Psychological review* 48, 1941, pp. 15-38.
55. Read: If Sx, then Ax if and only if Rx. For other forms of reduction sentences see Carnap, *op. cit.*

tional terms as "open", *i.e.*, provides for a set of different, and mutually supplementary, reduction sentences for a given term.

Thus we may partially define anxiety by the reduction sentence [56]:

"If x is told by his psychoanalyst that he hates his mother, then x is anxious if and only if x blushes or stammers and the content of x's free association changes".

And we may specify the meaning of anxiety further by other reduction sentences:

"If x is given an anxiety questionnaire, then x is anxious if and only if x's score falls in the upper 20 % of the distribution".

"If x is told that he will be given an electric shock, then x is anxious if and only if x's skin resistance drops 1 000 ohms or more".

And so forth.

But we never completely exhaust the meaning of "anxiety" in terms of observational vocabulary in this way [57]. It should be noticed, therefore, that the results of Carnap's analysis give little encouragement to the thesis of a narrowly conceived operationism, for the terms of non-observational vocabulary construed in this way are not completely definable in terms of the observational vocabulary.

However, this "openness of meaning" of the terms of non-observational vocabulary provided by reduction sentences should not be considered a disadvantage. Indeed, in all scientific theories we desire the possibility that our constructs may enter into further empirical connections. As Hempel has suggested: "In the case of theoretically fruitful concepts, we want to point to, and indeed count on, the possibility that they may enter into further general principles, which will connect them with additional variables and will thus provide new criteria of application for them. We would deprive ourselves of these potentialities if we insisted on introducing the technical concepts of science by full definition in terms of observables" [58].

However, even Carnapian reduction sentences do not do full justice to another dimension of non-observational language. Although they do provide for the "openness of meaning" of non-observational terms they do not provide an adequate account of the systematic character of such terms, *i.e.*, the systematic relation of one non-observational term to others in the

---

56. I am indebted to Mandler and Kessen for my psychological examples of the use of reduction sentences. *Cf.* G. Mandler and W. Kessen, *The language of psychology*, New York, John Wiley and Son, 1959, p. 117.

57. The only restriction on the use of reduction sentences is an empirical one, *i.e.*, the empirical compatibility of the defining conditions. Thus the following conditions should hold given the appropriate stimuli: x's skin resistance drops 1 000 ohms or more if and only if x's score falls in the upper 20% of the distribution; x's score falls in the upper 20% of the distribution if and only if x blushes or stammers, and x's free association changes. *Cf.* Mandler and Kessen, *ibid.*, p. 117.

58. Hempel, "Fundamentals of concept formation in empirical science", *op. cit.*, p. 29.

theory [59], *e.g.*, the relation between "anxiety" and "repression", "psychic energy", and so on.

It is this systematic relation which provides the explanatory scope, heuristic power and simplifying potential of a theory [60]. Once these interrelations are taken into account the proposal of the strict operationism seems even more untenable.

Specific criticism of Ellis and Skinner

Ellis. 1) It is difficult to know what Ellis means by his claim that psychoanalytic theory is "more difficult" to confirm or disconfirm when stated in terms of hypothetical constructs [61]. The only thing that is necessary to know in either the case of hypothetical constructs or intervening variables in order to confirm or disconfirm them is what empirical evidence counts for or against them. Now since intervening variables are supposed to be defined completely in terms of observables, we know this as soon as we know what the definition of the intervening variable is; with hypothetical constructs we know this when we know how these constructs are related to empirical observations. It may be true that psychoanalytic theory is difficult to confirm or disconfirm, but this is not *because* it has hypothetical constructs. If psychoanalytic theory is hard to confirm or disconfirm, it must be because it is not clear what the relation is between its hypothetical constructs and the empirical subject matter with which the hypothetical constructs are supposed to be indirectly connected. But the unclarity of this relation is not intrinsic to the use of hypothetical constructs. It seems to me, therefore, that Ellis has confused two different theses, one which may be true and another which is false; namely, the thesis that psychoanalytic theory as *it is now formulated* in terms of hypothetical constructs is more difficult to confirm or disconfirm than a reformulation of psychoanalytic theory in terms of intervening variables, and the thesis that the mere presence of hypothetical constructs in psychoanalytic theory makes it more difficult to confirm or disconfirm than a reformulation of psychoanalytic theory in terms of intervening variables.

As far as Ellis' own reformulation in terms of intervening variables is concerned, it may even be doubted that the former thesis is true. Ellis attempts to reformulate psychoanalysis in terms of a "basic operational vocabulary". This vocabulary is in terms of perception and response. Although he construes perception and response of a person in terms of the person's verbal and non-verbal behavior he seldom specifies precisely what

---

59. *Ibid.*, p. 36.
60. See C. Hempel, "The theoretician's dilemma", in: H. Feigl, M. Scriven and G. Maxwell (eds.), *Concepts, theories, and the mind-body problem*, Minneapolis, University of Minnesota Press, 1958 (Minnesota studies in the philosophy of science, vol. 2).
61. Ellis, "An operational reformulation of some of the basic principles of psychoanalysis", *op. cit.*, p. 136.

this behavior is. His reformulations of psychoanalysis in terms of this basic operational vocabulary are, therefore, sometimes as hard to confirm or disconfirm as the original.

Ellis' procedure is to quote from Freud and then to give an operational reformulation of Freud's idea in terms of perception and response. For example, in relation to oral eroticism, he quotes Freud [62]:

"The baby's obstinate persistence in sucking gives evidence at an early stage of a need for satisfaction which, although it originates from and is stimulated by the taking of nourishment, nevertheless seeks to obtain pleasure independently of nourishment and for that reason may and should be described as 'sexual' ". Then Ellis gives an "operational reformulation":

"Babies, through their oral perceptions, appear to obtain satisfaction independently of nourishment. We may describe this tendency of infants to seek oral stimulation as oral sensuality and may find confirmation of it through observing the behavior of infants in relation to their oral zones" [63]

It should be noticed that Ellis does not tell us what specific behavior is to be regarded as oral perception or satisfaction. It is difficult to see, therefore, why this "operational reformulation" is easier to confirm than Freud's original statement. Indeed, we seem to be in worse shape now with Ellis' vague references to the "behavior of infants in relation to their oral zones" as confirming evidence than we were with Freud's more specific suggestion that "persistent sucking" is to count as evidence.

2) To Ellis' argument that it has never been shown that hypothetical constructs are needed in psychoanalysis [64], one must ask what criteria Ellis is using for being "needed" or "not needed". But Ellis never explicitly tells us. Although it is doubtful that there is any conclusive argument to show that psychoanalysis can not be formulated completely in terms of observables, there are, as we have seen, grave logical problems involved in construing psychoanalysis in this way. So in several relevant senses of "needed" that have been specified in the literature, hypothetical constructs are indeed needed in psychoanalysis just as they are needed in other sciences.

But we might take another tack. We could take one of Ellis' own contentions, e.g., that hypothetical constructs in science "lead to maximum success in the [...] explanation of behavior" [65], and see if his operational reformulation preserves this quality. Consider his operational reformulation of the phallic stage [66]. To be sure, he tries to connect childhood and adult life by saying that childhood "sexual

---

62. S. Freud, *An outline of psychoanalysis*, New York, Norton, 1949, p. 28.
63. Ellis, "An operational reformulation of some of the basic principles of psychoanalysis", *op. cit.*, p. 143.
64. *Ibid.*, p. 136.
65. *Ibid.*, p. 133.
66. *Ibid.*, p. 143.

experiences may have important influences on adult sex and other behavior" and that this hypothesis may be confirmed by observation of childhood and adult sexual behavior, and by "calculating appropriate correlations between childhood and adult" behavior. And it tries to do this by hypothetical constructs such as the unconscious and repression [67]. But these possible correlations are precisely what Ellis leaves unexplained. To be sure, Ellis also gives an "operational reformulation" of "the unconscious" and "repression". But, first of all, these reformulations are in terms of behavior that itself needs explaining and, secondly, they are unrelated to the "phallic stage" reformulation, *i.e.*, Ellis' reformulation of repression and unconscious is not tied up in any obvious way with childhood sexual behavior and adult behavior. One can only conclude that Ellis' "operational reformulation" does not "lead to maximum success in the [...] explanation of behavior", and therefore that on Ellis' own ground hypothetical constructs *are* necessary in psychoanalysis.

3) It is not at all clear why Ellis believes that a formulation of psychoanalytic theory in terms of intervening variables would eliminate "dogmaticism and fuzzy thinking", whereas a formulation in terms of hypothetical constructs would not [68]. That there may be dogmaticism and fuzzy thinking among psychoanalysts no one can deny, but to believe that this can be cleared up by a reformulation of psychoanalytic concepts is surely to have too much faith in the powers of logical reconstruction. One suspects a better way to overcome possible "dogmaticism" and "fuzzy thinking" among psychoanalysts would be to make courses in logic and scientific method compulsory in the psychoanalytic training schools. Indeed, Ellis has elsewhere suggested something very similar to this [69].

Ellis' claim that possible erroneous and redundant aspects of psychoanalytic theory would be eliminated by a reformulation into intervening variables [70] is no more understandable than his claim concerning dogmaticism and fuzzy thinking. Now psychoanalytic theory may have erroneous and redundant parts but this surely cannot be traced to the use of hypothetical constructs. Definitions completely in terms of observables may also be erroneous and redundant. If we had clearly formulated rules linking hypothetical constructs to observables and a logically tight syntax linking hypothetical constructs to each other, what is erroneous and what is redundant could be found

---

67. We are not suggesting that this attempt is wholly satisfactory. But we are suggesting that the *attempt* to provide a conceptual bridge by means of hypothetical constructs is perfectly legitimate in scientific explanation.
68. *Ibid.*, p. 136. Again we may suspect that Ellis is confusing 1) psychoanalysis as it is now formulated, with 2) psychoanalysis formulated with hypothetical constructs.
69. Ellis, "An introduction to the principles of scientific psychoanalysis", *op. cit.*, p. 202.
70. Ellis, "An operational reformulation of some of the basic principles of psychoanalysis", *op. cit.*, p. 136.

just as easily in psychoanalysis as in a formulation in terms of intervening variables.

Finally, Ellis' reasons why a reformulation in terms of intervening variables would encourage new hypotheses and experiments are not stated. As has been shown elsewhere hypothetical constructs, and *not* intervening variables, seem to have heuristic value.

We must conclude that Ellis' arguments for construing psychoanalysis in terms of intervening variables are extremely unpersuasive, and lend no more plausibility to a narrowly conceived operationist criticism of psychoanalysis.

Skinner. 1) Now it would be absurd to deny the importance of Skinner's work in animal psychology; but it is one thing to admit his importance in this area, and another thing to believe that Skinner's own work is a demonstration that hypothetical constructs are unnecessary in theories of human behavior. The initial plausibility of the latter rests partly upon the apparent success of the application of Skinner's work in animal psychology in complex human situations. But, as Chomsky has shown in a devastating and detailed criticism of Skinner's book *Verbal behavior*, this success is *only* apparent, for Skinner "utilizes the experimental results [of the animal laboratory] as evidence for the scientific character of his system of behavior, and analogic guesses (formulated in terms of a metaphoric extension of the technical vocabulary of the laboratory) as evidence of its scope. This creates the illusion of a rigorous scientific theory with a very broad scope, although in fact the terms used in the description of real-life, and of laboratory behavior may be mere homonyms, with at most vague similarity of meaning" [71].

Consider just one of Chomsky's arguments that indicates that a "Skinnerian shift" from the laboratory using rats and pigeons to a real life situation involving people is completely untenable: Skinner's observational language is in terms of stimulus and response. In *Behavior of organisms*, part of the environment and part of the behavior of an organism are to be called "stimulus" and "response" only in the case that they are lawfully related [72]. Terms of causal description are not valid descriptions of causality until the defining properties of stimulus and response are specified and a functional relation is experimentally demonstrated to hold between them. But in *Verbal behavior*, an alleged application of this notion to human verbal behavior, the situation has changed. Skinner maintains the lawfulness of stimulus and verbal response at the cost of making these terms empty. Any verbal response is said to be under control of "subtle" properties of physical objects. But what these properties are cannot be determined until *after* the response is given. If we look at a red chair and say "red", the response is, according

71. N. Chomsky, "Review of *Verbal behavior* by B.F. Skinner", *Language* 35, 1959, p. 30.
72. B.F. Skinner, *The behavior of organisms*, New York, Appleton-Century-Crofts, 1938, p. 9.

to Skinner, "under the control" of the stimuli "redness"; if we say "chair", the response is, according to Skinner, "under control" of the total collection of properties "chairness", and so forth no matter what the response is [73]. It is evident that the word "stimulus" now has lost all its objectivity; stimuli are driven back into the organism for we can identify the stimuli only *after* we hear the response. Prediction of a response is therefore impossible [74].

It appears that at least part of Skinner's failure to apply his work in the animal laboratory successfully to human behavior is due to his belief that an appeal to hypothetical neural processes is unnecessary. Chomsky has argued that the phenomena of language learning cannot be completely accounted for by using only the Skinnerian categories of stimulus, re-enforcement and deprivation. Following K.S. Lashley, Chomsky has maintained that "the composition and production of an utterance is not simply a matter of stringing together a sequence of responses under the control of outside stimulation and intraverbal association, and that the syntactic organization of an utterance is not something directly represented in any simple way in the physical structure of the utterance itself"[75]. For according to Lashley, this syntactic structure is rather a "generalized pattern imposed on the specific acts as they occur", and "there are, behind the overtly expressed sequences, a multiplicity of integrative processes which can only be inferred from the final results of their activity" [76].

Chomsky argues that the fact that all normal children acquire grammar having great syntactical complexity with remarkable rapidity "suggests that human beings are somehow specially designed to do this", *i.e.*, they have complex neural tendencies to learn in specific ways. If this is true, then any attempt to account for the learning of language without prior understanding of these neural "integrative processes" will be unsuccessful [77]. But this is precisely what Skinner has attempted to do.

In short, it is far from obvious that Skinner's own work shows that hypo-

---

73. B.F. Skinner, *Verbal behavior*, New York, Appleton-Century-Crofts, 1957, p. 110.
74. Chomsky, *op. cit.*, p. 32. Chomsky points out many similar problems in Skinner's work.
75. *Ibid.*, p. 55.
76. K.S. Lashley, "The problem of serial order in behavior", in : L.A. Jeffress (ed.), *Hixon symposium on cerebral mechanisms in behavior*, New York, Wiley, 1951, quoted in Chomsky, *op. cit.*, p. 55.
77. *Ibid.*, p. 55. Chomsky has suggested that this "integrative process" of the nervous system is analogous to a logical deductive system, and that the theory of language can be considered as the study of the formal properties of this system. Thus Chomsky's suggestion amounts to the proposal that since little is known about the actual nervous system, a "model" of a deductive system may be used that can be more easily understood and manipulated, *i.e.*, we may find it useful to act "as if" the nervous system were a deductive system. Others have proposed that analogue and digital computers may serve as models of the nervous system. *Cf.* R.L. Gregory, "On physical model explanations in psychology", *British journal for the philosophy of science* 4, 1953-1954, p. 195.

thetical constructs are unnecessary in psychology. Indeed, if Chomsky is right, Skinner's work in language seems to suggest just the opposite.

2) We may agree with Skinner's theoretical contention that the cause and effect of hypothetical constructs, e.g., physiological or mental events, must eventually lead outside of the organism, but we deny what Skinner seems to conclude from this; namely that *therefore* hypothetical constructs are unnecessary, and that we should only concern ourselves with the functional relation between environmental and behavioral variables.

First of all, Skinner himself has admitted that beyond "the collection of uniform relationships lies the need for a formal representation of the data reduced to a minimal number of terms". Skinner, however, will not allow "theoretical constructs" that "refer to another dimensional system" [78], *i.e.*, what we have called hypothetical constructs, e.g., physiological processes and mental events. But as has been shown elsewhere [79] it is precisely systems with theoretical terms referring to hypothetical constructs that lend deductive and inductive systematization to a formalized body of data. Ginsberg, in his critique of Skinner, has noted the same thing; he has argued that we forfeit "systematic elegance", "economy of expression", and "scope" by giving up theories with hypothetical constructs [80]. According to Skinner's own criterion it would seem that hypothetical constructs are necessary in psychoanalysis.

Secondly, a Skinnerian formulation would also forfeit the suggestive powers that hypothetical constructs might offer in psychoanalysis. As Scriven has argued against Skinner: "Many of the great steps in the history of science have not only followed the sudden perception of familiar events in a new way, according to a new model [...] but [...] they could not have been made otherwise, for example, Lavoisier with the theory of combustion, Kepler with the planetary motions, Guericke and the spring of the air, and Freud and the unconscious wish" [81]. And, as Ginsberg has maintained: "Variables are not things like trees, 'out there' simply to be perceived like so many concrete existences. They are abstractions derived from or suggested by theories and often not otherwise obtainable" [82]. Feigl, therefore, seems quite justified in accusing Skinnerian type operationalists of having "thrown out the baby of fruitful hypothetical constructs with the bath water of transcendent speculation" [83].

78. Skinner, "Are theories of learning necessary?", *op. cit.*, pp. 215-216.
79. See Hempel, "The theoretician's dilemma", *op. cit.*
80. A. Ginsberg, "Operational definitions and theories", *Journal of general psychology* 52, 1955, p. 237.
81. M. Scriven, "Notes on the discussion between E. Frenkel-Brunswik and B.F. Skinner", in : P. Frank (ed.), *op. cit.*; *cf.* Hanson, *op. cit.*, pp. 1-50.
82. Ginsberg, *op. cit.*, p. 240.
83. H. Feigl, "Principles and problems of theory construction in psychology", in: W. Dennis (ed.), *Current trends in psychology theory*, Pittsburgh, University of Pittsburgh Press, 1951, p. 203.

Thirdly, Skinner has failed to provide an explanation of the relation between environmental and behavioral variables. Skinner has not provided any theory from which any lawful relations between environmental and behavioral variables can be deduced. Feigl [84], for example, has suggested that T is a theory of a certain domain if we can deduce (explain) all the empirical laws L of this domain from T. Scriven, using Feigl's analysis, has suggested that Skinner's position may be expressed by saying that there is no need to go beyond the L-level [85]. But, as Scriven has argued, it is a perfectly respectable, scientific question to ask why L's hold in a certain domain. In physics, for example, we answer the question why rarefied gases at normal temperature obey Boyle's Law by deducing Boyle's Law from the kinetic theory of gases. In a similar manner, it would be a legitimate scientific move to answer the question why there is a lawful relation L between childhood environmental variables and adult behavioral variables by deducing this L from a psychoanalytic theory, provided that the theory meets certain standards of a scientific theory, *e.g.*, confirmability, simplicity and so on.

One may, of course, by definition say that psychology should only concern itself with lawful relations among these variables. But as far as the question "Why do these particular L's hold in this domain?" is concerned, it is, as Scriven maintains, "quite obviously appropriate for *some* part of the scientific enterprise to be devoted to such questions". So any definition of psychology that ruled out an explanation of L would be a "persuasive definition" of psychology: "It is as though I were to say 'Chemistry is concerned to describe the composition and the interaction properties of all substances'. Then a man who tried to find out *why* an acid combines with a base to produce a salt would not be doing chemistry. Well, we could call him a physicist or a physical chemist instead, but there's nothing illegitimate about his activity; and we may reasonably expect his discoveries to be very useful to chemists" [86].

We can only conclude that Skinner has not shown that a psychoanalytic theory construed completely in terms of observables is desirable or that the relationship between environmental and empirical variables is all that is necessary.

Conclusion

An examination of general considerations of the logic of science as well as detailed consideration of Ellis' and Skinner's position give us good reason to question the narrowly conceived operationist critique of psychoanalysis.

---

84. H. Feigl, "Some remarks on the meaning of scientific explanation", in: Feigl and Sellars (eds.), *op. cit.*, pp. 510-515.
85. M. Scriven, "A study of radical behaviorism", in : Feigl and Scriven (eds.), *op. cit.*, pp. 94-96.
86. *Ibid.*, p. 95.

Psychoanalysts, therefore — insofar as they have opposed operationism in psychoanalysis — have been on the side of the angels. Unfortunately, some psychoanalysts have given the wrong reason and have drawn the wrong conclusions from their rejection of operationism. Consider a statement by Rudolf Ekstein: "The modern criterion for the validity consists in giving us the methods necessary in order to confirm or disconfirm theory. An example in physics where this task was undertaken is P.W. Bridgman's classic *The logic of modern physics* (1927). Bridgman sees in the concepts of physics not 'abstractions, but simply names for unique groups of experimental operations'. I believe that the philosophy of operationism has had its powerful influence on psycho-analysis as well, so that today we are confronted with the often voiced demand to review our concepts and to redefine them in operational form [...] I believe that Pumpian-Mindlin takes the middle way, and I am identified with this position. Pumpian-Mindlin suggests that the energy concepts in their present form cannot be reduced to operational propositions" [87].

This quotation seems to suggest that although the demand for operational definition in psychoanalysis is unreasonable at the present time it might not be at some other time; and the demand for the operational definition of all concepts is a reasonable demand in physics. But this would be a mistake. Such a demand would be unreasonable in the later stages of psychoanalysis as well as in physics.

Secondly, Ekstein fails to distinguish between the demand that all concepts in psychoanalysis be operationally defined (Ellis' strict operationism and Bridgman's 1927 position) with the demand that psychoanalytic assumption be indirectly testable (Ellis' liberal "operationism"). To demand the latter is merely to require some specifiable connection between the hypothetical constructs in psychoanalysis and empirical observation. This view has little to do with Bridgman's 1927 position.

Now whether psychoanalysis does have such specifiable connection is debatable [88]. But it is clear that the demand that it should have in order to be a testable scientific theory is hardly debatable.

---

87. R. Ekstein, "Discussion of E. Pumpian-Mindlin's Propositions concerning energetic-economic aspects of libido theory: Conceptual models of psychic energy and structure in psychoanalysis", in: L. Bellak (ed.), *Conceptual and methodological problems in psychoanalysis*, New York, New York Academy of Science, 1959, pp. 1061-1062 (Annals of the New York Academy of Science, 76).

88. See for example P. Madison, *Freud's concept of repression and defense, its theoretical and observation language*, Minneapolis, University of Minnesota Press, 1961; M. Martin, "Mr. Farrell and the refutability of psychoanalysis", *Inquiry* 7 (1), 1964, pp. 80-98.

THE EXPLANATORY VALUE OF THE UNCONSCIOUS

MICHAEL MARTIN

It is common knowledge that the notion of the unconscious is an essential part of psychoanalytic theory. In recent years, however, Arthur Pap and A. C. MacIntyre have argued that Freud's theory of the unconscious is not explanatory. But a close examination of Pap's and MacIntyre's arguments reveals that they are invalid. If one wishes to show that the theory of the unconscious is unexplanatory, different arguments will be necessary.

It is common knowledge that the notion of the unconscious is an essential part of psychoanalytic theory. In recent years, however, the explanatory value of the unconscious has been called into question. At least two philosophers—Arthur Pap[1] and A. C. MacIntyre[2] have argued that Freud's theory of the unconscious is not explanatory. Pap's and MacIntyre's criticisms, however, turn on entirely different analyses of the unconscious. On the one hand, Pap has argued that the unconscious should be construed as a "dispositional state" rather than as a hypothetical construct such as the electron in physics. On Pap's view, "dispositional states" are not explanatory. On the other hand, MacIntyre has argued that the unconscious, like the electron, can be construed as a hypothetical construct. But MacIntyre has maintained that the unconscious so construed, unlike the electron, is not explanatory.

Without wishing to defend psychoanalysis in general or the explanatory value of the unconscious in particular, I will argue that the arguments presented by Pap and MacIntyre are invalid and that if one wishes to show that the theory of the unconscious is not explanatory, different arguments will have to be presented.

I

1. *Pap's Account of the Unconscious.* Arthur Pap has suggested that "the unconscious" should be construed as a dispositional term. On Pap's view, dispositional terms are characteristic of the "pre-theoretical" stage of science. He believes that, usually, to ascribe a disposition is to issue a "promissory note" for the future discovery of a causal generalization which, together with relevant singular statements, i.e., statements of initial conditions, would explain an observed regularity.[3] In making dispositional statements in the pre-theoretical stage of science one *anticipates* the discovery of a causal law, but one does not assert the existence of such a law. Hence, one can *not* explain some given phenomenon by reference to dispositional states; one only promises that the phenomenon will be explained when some relevant causal law is found.

In relation to psychoanalysis, to ascribe an unconscious dislike to a person is,

---

[1] Arthur Pap, "On the Empirical Interpretation of Psychoanalytic Concepts," *Psychoanalysis, Scientific Method and Philosophy* (New York: New York University Press, 1959), ed. S. Hook, pp. 283-304.

[2] A. C. MacIntyre, *The Unconscious* (London: Routledge and Kegan Paul, 1958).

[3] Pap here presupposes Hempel and Oppenheim's "Studies in the Logic of Explanation," *Philosophy of Science*, XV, 1948.

according to Pap, to ascribe a dispositional state. Hence, it is a mistake to suppose that an item of a person's behavior is causally explained when one says that it expresses such and such unconscious dislike of another person; rather one is issuing a promissory note to the effect that the first person has some intrinsic property K, e.g., traumatic sexual experience in infancy, such that any person with the same intrinsic property K would probably react similarly in similar circumstances. The term "unconscious" cannot appear in any genuine causal explanation because its function is only to mark, not to solve, a problem of explanation. It marks the lack of some causal generalization. When such a generalization is found, this generalization will be used in explaining the behavior. At such a time the word "unconscious" will have no point; the promise will be fulfilled.

Pap is opposed to construing the unconscious as a hypothetical construct e.g., as subatomic particles in physics are usually construed, for two basic reasons:

(1) Pap maintains that phsychoanalysis cannot be legitimately compared with physics. He argues:

> A methodological justification of psychoanalysis by comparison with theoretical physics is out of place, because psychoanalysis is too young a science still to be in a position to lay a precise and solid theoretical foundation for its rough empirical generalizations.[4]

(2) Pap argues that uncritical acceptance of talk about unconscious mental events as hypothetical constructs arises from "a tacit objectification of psychological language." Pap seems to mean by this that it is logically impossible for a desire or a wish to occur without the subject of the wish or desire being aware of it when he introspects. This is because desires and wishes "are just the sort of 'private' states that are meant by the old-fashioned expression 'state of consciousness.'"[5]

There is then only an apparent similarity between an atom and an unconscious wish construed as a hypothetical construct. It is not part of the meaning of "atom," for example, that it cannot be seen; it is just a contingent fact i.e., the impossibility involved in not seeing an atom is just an empirical impossibility. But part of the meaning of the term "wish," for example, as it is ordinarily used, is the possibility of introspective awareness. So, to speak of unconscious wishes as "efficacious mental states" is not like speaking of an "invisible atom" but rather like speaking of a "shapeless cube."

2. *"Promissory Note" Analysis.* Whatever merits Pap's "dispositional" analysis of the unconscious may have, his analysis so warps the original and present day function of the concept of the unconscious that it is scarcely recognizable.

In the first place, when psychoanalysts talk about unconscious dislike, they are not "promising" the discovery of causal laws e.g., laws connecting childhood traumatic sexual experiences and adult personality; psychoanalysts are asserting that there *are* such laws. To be sure, psychoanalysts may be mistaken in their claims, and they would be surely hard-pressed to state these laws in any precise way, but this is not the point at issue. Thus Hartmann, in *Die Grundlagen der Psychoanalyse*, maintains that psycho-

[4] Pap, *op. cit.*, p. 290.
[5] *Ibid.*

analysis deals with causal laws, and argues: "We have *explained* a process when we have succeeded in discovering by what law it is governed."⁶

In the second place, psychoanalytic statements about the unconscious not only do *not* "promise" the discovery of causal laws, but on the contrary they purport to explain the causal laws that they assert, rightly or wrongly, to exist. Indeed, the whole purpose of the unconscious is to provide the explanatory connecting link between certain spatially and temporally separated, but supposedly lawfully related, phenomena e.g., certain childhood and adult behavior—relations that remains unintelligible otherwise. MacIntyre is surely correct when he says that in psychoanalysis:

> There is first the claim that it is a correlation between certain types of childhood experience and certain types of adult behaviour. Psychology owes an immeasurable debt to Freud for having suggested so clearly the existence of such correlations, but there is nothing peculiarly "Freudian" about them. Freud argues that a thrifty, somewhat ill-tempered attitude is the result in early life of the wrong sort of potting training or that adult attitudes to one's wife are in some cases correlated with childhood attitudes to one's mother.⁷

And he goes on to say:

> So far as theory is concerned, Freud pins everything upon a ... claim, that the reason why childhood events are correlated with adult experience ... is *because* memories have been repressed, have been operative in some form or other in the unconscious and have manifested themselves in overt behaviour.⁸

Pap is aware of the fact that psychoanalysts make causal assertions about the relation between childhood experiences and adult behavior, and that these laws can be used in explanations. Pap remarks:

> Thus psychoanalysts often succeed in tracing neurotic adult behavior to certain kinds traumatic experience in childhood. Also Freud's famous case of the bride's disappointment during her wedding night leading to a strange form of compulsive behavior falls into this category. Here we have genetic laws, of an imperfect probabilistic character. ...⁹

He goes on to say: "They [the genetic laws] can legitimately be used for probabilistic and in principle confirmable explanations of abnormal behavior patterns."¹⁰ But in the next breath Pap makes the remarkable comment:

> What I am suggesting is that the word "unconscious" cannot appear in any genuine causal explanation, whether rigorously deterministic or probabilistic, whether in terms of the postulates of a rigorous theory of human behavior or, more modestly, in terms of pragmatically reliable empirical generalizations, because its function is only to *mark*, not to *solve*, a problem of explanation.¹¹

---

⁶ Heinz Hartmann, *Die Grundlagen der Psychoanalyse* (Leipzig, 1927), p. 11. This sentence was translated by Muller-Braunschweig in a review of Hartmann's book in *International Journal of Psychoanalysis*, 10, 1929, pp. 451-465.
⁷ MacIntyre, *op. cit.*, p. 67.
⁸ *Ibid.*, p. 69.
⁹ Pap, *op. cit.*, p. 287.
¹⁰ *Ibid.*
¹¹ *Ibid.*, p. 288.

on do not appear in the definition of the term "wish." So, if a dictionary definition is what is meant by the "ordinary meaning" of "wish," then we find that the expression "unconscious wish" is not analogous to "shapeless cube" as Pap has claimed, for the latter expression is, in fact, a contradiction according to the dictionary.[14]

If we are to accept the actual verbal practices of people as determining the ordinary meaning of an expression then, by Pap's own admission, the expressions "unconscious wish" or "unconscious hatred" are commonly used to refer to some efficacious mental states of an individual. Pap has admitted that "a good many people," "some professional psychologists" and "some educated laymen" use expressions such as "He really hates him, though he is not aware of it; he is not lying when he denies this emotion, he is just unconsciously repressing it."[15] But, according to Pap, these people are somehow in error because this use of the expression makes no "sense" in the "ordinary sense" of "wish." One begins to wonder if Pap is the one who has the extraordinary meaning of "wish," or if he is not just stipulating, as he did when he excluded hypothetical constructs from immature sciences.

To be perfectly accurate, Pap does not claim that the *actual* awareness of e.g., hatred, is part of the ordinary meaning of "hatred," but rather that the potential awareness of the hatred is, i.e., if one were to introspect, then one would be aware of the hatred. Pap says that "awareness of one's hatred" of somebody denotes "an act of introspection which need not, and often does not, accompany the introspectable state." This means that "one can hate a person at a time when, oblivious of the enemy, one is in a relaxed, even loving mood," so that "emotions and desires may occur without any [actual] awareness of them."[16] But Pap insists that the *possibility* of the introspective awareness is part of the meaning of "hatred."

So, as far as one can tell, Pap believes that there are some mental states of a person of which the person is aware and some mental states of the person of which the person is not aware, but of which he can become aware by ordinary introspection. It is remarkable how much Pap's account corresponds to Freud's description of the mental systems Cs (consciousness) and Pcs (pre-consciousness) in his essay *The Unconscious*.

> But the fact that it [an idea] so belongs [to the system Cs] does not unequivocally determine its relation to consciousness. It is not yet conscious, but it is certainly *capable of entering consciousness*, according to J. Breuer's expression, that is, it can now, without any special resistance and given certain conditions, become the object of consciousness. In consideration of this capacity to become conscious we also call the system Cs the "preconscious."[17]

For the sake of argument, let us assume that Pap is correct in maintaining that "part of the ordinary meaning" of, e.g., "hatred," is either that the hatred is conscious or is capable of becoming conscious by means of ordinary introspection. But surely this does not exclude Freud from extending the meaning of the term, for the process of redefining the ordinary meaning of terms is a respectable part of the scientific enterprise. Thus Hempel has noted:

---

[14] *O.E.D.*, 1933, XII, pp. 196-197; II, p. 1233.
[15] Pap, *op. cit.*, p. 293.
[16] *Ibid.*, p. 294.
[17] S. Freud, "The Unconscious," *Collected Papers* (New York: Basic Books, 1959), IV, p. 106.

II

5. MacIntyre's Criticism of the Unconscious. MacIntyre has maintained that the unconscious, like the electron, may well be a hypothetical construct. He argues:

> Certainly the unconscious and its contents are *ex hypothesi* unobservable, and if philosophy were still at the stage when positivism was waging a war to the death against unobservables no doubt the whole conception of the unconscious would have to be rejected. But the positivism that rejected unobservables in so wholesale a fashion was not merely too *a priori* in its framing of criteria by which concepts were to be judged legitimate or the reverse; it was also profoundly in error as to the character of scientific theorizing. For in such theorizing concepts which refer to unobservables have a legitimate, important and necessary place. And in elucidating the nature of the concept of the unconscious the possibility that it is a concept of this kind must be taken very seriously.[22]

MacIntyre believes, however, that not all theories containing terms which refer to unobservable entities are legitimate in science. Some theories containing terms which refer to unobservables have great explanatory value, e.g., the modern theory of subatomic particles, but other theories containing terms which refer to unobservables have no explanatory power at all, e.g., the theory of the ether. The important question, therefore, is "whether the unconscious is to be classed with the electron as a notion of great explanatory power or with the ether as a bogus and empty theoretical concept . . ."[23]

MacIntyre suggests two distinct requirements for the admissibility of theories in science containing terms which refer to unobservables. Presumably, MacIntyre intends his requirements to distinguish theories with explanatory power, such as the theory of subatomic particles, from theories with no explanatory power, such as the theory of ether.

(1) A theory T, containing some terms that refer to unobservable entities, is admissible in science if some empirical phenomena can be explained by T that are distinct from the phenomena T was originally introduced to explain.[24]

(2) A theory T, containing some terms which refer to unobservable entities, is admissible in science if the elimination of T would result in a loss of predictive power.[25]

MacIntyre judges Freud's theory of the unconscious by these requirements and concludes that the theory has no explanatory power. Briefly, he argues as follows.

The real significance of Freud's theory of the unconscious is that it purports to explain why certain childhood events are correlated with certain adult experiences. However, "from the supposition of such an entity [the unconscious] what consequences

---

[22] MacIntyre, *op. cit.*, p. 46.

[23] *Ibid.*, p. 48.

[24] "The theory must not merely be such that statements concerning the regularities which it was originally introduced to explain are deducible from it. We must also be able if the explanation of the regularities with which we were originally concerned is correct, to deduce further statements of a testable kind, the verifying of which constitutes the confirmation of the hypothesis." *Ibid.*, p. 47.

[25] "Concepts which refer to unobservables will have a place on the higher steps of the deductive ladder if by using them we can formulate assertions from which observation statements can be deduced which are true and which could not be deduced from the theory unless such assertions were included." *Ibid.*, pp., 47-48.

flow that could not otherwise be predicted? Freud's hypotheses as to the infantile origin of adult traits and disorders can all be formulated without reference to it."[26]

It should be noticed, first of all, that it is not completely clear whether MacIntyre's criticism of Freud's theory of the unconscious turns on his first or second requirement. (Indeed, it is not altogether certain that MacIntyre realizes he has set forth two distinct requirements.) By his question "From the supposition of such an entity what consequences flow that could not otherwise be predicted?" he could mean (1) that Freud's theory of the unconscious entails nothing more than what it was originally introduced to explain, (his first requirement), or (2) that elimination of the theory of the unconscious would not result in a loss of any predictive power (his second requirement).

It must be emphasized that these are *different* requirements. This can be seen from a simple example. Consider a theory T_1 containing some terms that refer to unobservable entities. T_1 is introduced to explain only one empirical phenomenon described by an observation statement 0_1; hence T_1 entails 0_1. But T_1 also entails 0_2 where this observation statement describes a different phenomenon. Hence this meets MacIntyre's first requirement. Assume that T_1 entails only 0_1 and 0_2. T_1 can then be replaced by a theory T_2 made up solely of the conjunction $0_1.0_2$. This replacement would contain only observational terms and yet would entail everything T_1 entailed. Hence T_1 would presumably not meet MacIntyre's second requirement although it met his first.

6. *MacIntyre's Requirement* (1). Let us consider MacIntyre's first requirement. This requirement is often proposed in order to eliminate *ad hoc* hypotheses that are used to explain a phenomenon but which no further evidence could refute. It is not strictly correct to say that such hypotheses are not disconfirmable since they do have empirical consequences, i.e., statements describing the phenomenon they were originally introduced to explain follow from the theory. But these hypotheses become disconfirmable, as it were, on just one move, since no further consequences can be derived.

Now depending on how one interprets MacIntyre, his claim that Freud's theory of the unconscious fails to meet his first requirement is either (i) false or (ii) unjustified.

(i) Sometimes MacIntyre writes as if he were interested only in what Freud claims and not in the truth of Freud's claims. In particular he seems to be concerned with Freud's claim that there are correlations between certain specific childhood experiences and certain specific aspects of adult personalities and Freud's further claim that such correlations can be deduced from the theory of the unconscious. On one reading of MacIntyre, he seems to be asking what more is *claimed* to follow from the theory. MacIntyre's answer is nothing, hence the theory of the unconscious is "empty" and "bogus."

But if we are talking about what is *claimed* to follow from the theory, the answer to MacIntyre's question is "almost everything significant in human behavior." Latter-day psychoanalysts have claimed to find anal eroticism in all manner of apparently innocent behavior. Indeed, as any reader of *Imago* must know, new "verified consequences" of unconscious anal eroticism are reported in art, literature and legend in each issue. Not only are all *these* things supposed to be accounted for by consequences of the theory, but contemporary psychoanalytic journals report the "finding" of *new* correlations between childhood oral and genital behavior and adult behavior in every issue. That such correlations obtain is also an alleged consequence of the theory. Moreover, later developments in psychoanalytic ego psychology claim to deduce

[26] *Ibid.*, pp. 71-72.

accounts of all rational behavior, at least in part, from the theory of the unconscious.[27] Instead of nothing following from the theory of the unconscious except what it was originally introduced by Freud to explain, if we take the *claims* of latter-day analysts seriously, an account of practically *all* human behavior is supposed to follow from it. Indeed, the alleged "new verified consequences" of the theory reported by Freud's followers make Freud's claims of correlations look modest in comparison.

(ii) MacIntyre may, on the other hand, be interpreted as talking not about what is *claimed* by psychoanalysts to follow from the theory, but about what consequences, besides the original correlations which *did in fact follow* from the theory, do follow from it. MacIntyre's thesis, on this interpretation, is that no more consequences follow from it. To determine this, however, is surely not an easy task. MacIntyre seems to assume that the empirical consequences (if any) of a vaguely and metaphorically stated theory such as psychoanalysis should be obvious at a glance. But surely, to determine if anything follows from Freud's theory of the unconscious aside from what it was originally introduced to explain, requires not only a close examination of the relation of the unconscious to other Freudian concepts, but also a close examination of the alleged inferences drawn from the theory by contemporary analysts, ethnologists,[28] experimental psychologists,[29] and so on. One can hardly know the further consequences of psychoanalytic theory without endeavoring to examine the arguments of those who purport to derive further consequences from it. Indeed, one of the major tasks in evaluating experimental and anthropological studies of psychoanalytic theory is to determine whether they do, in fact, test consequences of the theory. MacIntyre argues independently of all recent work purporting to draw testable inferences from the theory of the unconscious; hence it is hardly surprising that he fails to find any further consequences of the theory. This is not to say that MacIntyre is incorrect in his conclusion that nothing else follows from the theory, but only that he has failed to give good reasons in support of this conclusion.

7. *MacIntyre's Requirement* (2). As far as MacIntyre's second requirement is concerned, it would be a mistake to suppose that it would serve to eliminate theories which postulate unobservable entities such as the unconscious, but not theories which postulate unobservable entities such as electrons. A purely logical finding of William Craig[30] shows that *any* theory T_1 containing some terms which refer to unobservable

---

[27] See Heinz Hartmann, "Ichpsychologie und Anpassungsproblem," *Internat. Zeitschrift Fur Psychoanalyse und Imago*, 1939, 24, pp. 62-135.

[28] See for example John W. M. Whiting and Irvin L. Child, *Child Training and Personality* (New Haven: Yale University Press, 1953); Herbert Barry "Relationship Between Child Training and Pictorial Arts," *Journal of Abnormal and Social Psychology*, 1957, pp. 380-383; M. A. Straus, "Anal and Oral Frustration in Relation to Sinhalese Personality," *Sociometry*, 20, 1957, pp. 21-31; M. Spiro and R. G. D'Andrade, "A Cross-Cultural Study of Some Supernatural Beliefs," *American Anthropologist*, 60, pp. 456-466.

[29] See for example W. Sewell, "Infant Training and the Personality of the Child," *American Journal of Sociology*, 58, 1952-1953, pp. 150-159; Stanley M. Friedman, "An Empirical Study of the Castration and Oedipus Complexes," *Genetic Psychology Monographs*, 46, pp. 61-130; Gerald S. Blum, "A Study of the Psychoanalytic Theory of Psychosexual Development," *Genetic Psychology Monographs*, 39, 1949, pp. 3-103; J. R. Thurston and P. H. Mussen, "Infant Feeding Gratification and Adult Personality," *Journal of Personality*, 1950-1951, pp. 447-457.

[30] William Craig, "On Axiomatizability Within a System," *Journal of Symbolic Logic*, XVIII, 1953, pp. 30-32; see also William Craig, "Replacement of Auxiliary Expressions," *Philosophical Review*, LXV, 1956, pp. 38-55.

entities can be replaced by some theory T_2 which contains no terms that refer to unobservables and yet has the same empirical deductive consequences as T_1. So, according to MacIntyre's second requirement, not only can "Freud's hypothesis as to the infantile origin of adult traits and disorders" be formulated without the unconscious without loss of deductive power in this precise sense, but all the empirical generalizations which the theories of subatomic particles are supposed to explain can also be formulated without reference to these theories *without loss of deductive power*. The theory of the electron is as unexplanatory, on MacIntyre's second requirement, as the theory of the unconscious and for the same reason; namely any theory which contains such expressions can be replaced by another theory which does not without loss of deductive power relative to the theory's observable consequences.

But as Craig has pointed out, and several noted philosophers of science have argued,[31] Craig's results do not show that theories which postulate unobservable entities are unnecessary in science. Indeed, a Craigian replacement of such theories is done at a great loss.

(1) A Craigian replacement is in general an unwieldy and cumbersome theory with an infinite set of postulates. Theories with terms that refer to unobservables, on the other hand, may preserve deductive simplicity allowing a few postulates to have as their consequences a large body of empirical propositions.

(2) More importantly, however, a Craigian replacement does not preserve in all cases the inductive systematization of the original theory.

(3) Moreover, the history of science suggests that theories couched solely in terms of observables do not have the heuristic value of theories that are not couched solely in terms of observables.

Whether psychoanalytic theory does in fact provide deductive simplicity and inductive systematization and does possess heuristic value is another matter. The point is that MacIntyre neglects these *possible* values of the theory of the unconscious and judges it on grounds such that all theories in science containing terms which refer to unobservable entities are unwittingly excluded. Indeed, MacIntyre unwittingly excludes from science those theories he considers to have the highest explanatory value.

To sum up: MacIntyre has suggested two requirements for the admissibility of theories in science containing terms which refer to unobservable entities. If we take Freud's followers at their word, then a great deal more "follows" from the theory of the unconscious than the behavior it was originally introduced to explain. Thus MacIntyre's first requirement is met. On the other hand, if we don't take them at their word, then a close examination must be made of the inferences that are supposedly drawn from the theory both in the clinical situation and elsewhere. MacIntyre has not done this, hence his conclusion that nothing more follows from the theory is not justified and he has not shown that his first requirement is not met. MacIntyre's second requirement is too strong. It turns out to make all theories in science that refer to unobservables inadmissible and, moreover, to overlook the possible values a theory

---

[31] See C. G. Hempel, "The Theoretician's Dilemma," *Minnesota Studies in the Philosophy of Science*, II, ed. H. Feigl, M. Scriven and G. Maxwell (Minneapolis: University of Minnesota Press, 1958), pp. 57-81; Ernest Nagel, *The Structure of Science* (New York: Harcourt Brace and World Inc., 1961), pp. 134-137; I. Scheffler, "Theoretical Terms and a Modest Empiricism," *Philosophy of Science*, ed. A. Danto and S. Morgenbesser (New York: Meridian Books, 1960), pp. 167-173.

like Freud's might have. We may conclude, therefore, that MacIntyre has not done what he set out to do; namely to show that Freud's theory of the unconscious lacks explanatory power.

III

8. *Conclusion.* Our examination of Pap's and MacIntyre's criticism of the unconscious points up what *not* to do when critizing psychoanalytic theory. The question remains, however, whether the psychoanalytic theory of the unconscious is explanatory. I will not attempt to answer this question here; instead I will briefly outline what one must do in order to answer it.

In the first place, it is necessary to examine carefully the relation between the theoretical and observational terms of psychoanalysis. This would enable us to determine whether psychoanalytic theory really has any clear empirical implications. In particular, we would be able to determine whether the theory of the unconscious is connected with overt behavior in a way that permits it to be confirmed or disconfirmed. If it were found that the psychoanalytic theory of the unconscious could not be confirmed or disconfirmed, the theory could hardly be considered explanatory.

But to determine whether the theory is capable of confirmation or disconfirmation is not any easy task. One way to determine this would be to make a detailed and careful examination of the writing of Freud and other psychoanalysts in order to determine whether there is a clear relationship between the theoretical and observation language of psychoanalysis. One such investigation of Freud's writing has been attempted,[32] but more are needed. Another fruitful approach would be to make an empirical study of the theoretical and observational language used by psychoanalysts in their clinical practice. A third approach would be to examine the writings of ethnologists, experimental psychologists, and others who purport to draw testable inferences from psychoanalytic theory. Here it would be crucial to determine if these investigators are really deriving empirical implications from psychoanalytic theory, as they claim, or if they are actually *reformulating* psychoanalysis into a testable theory before beginning their empirical studies.

In the second place, since psychoanalytic theory in general and the theory of the unconscious in particular purport to explain certain correlations that are alleged to hold between certain childhood events and certain adult behavior, it is necessary to determine whether such correlations actually exist. Obviously psychoanalytic theory would not be explanatory if the subject matter it purports to explain was nonexistent. It would be necessary, therefore, to evaluate those studies which test these alleged correlations.

Finally, if it is established that the psychoanalytic theory of the unconscious is capable of confirmation and disconfirmation and that the correlations which the theory purports to explain actually hold, then more subtle investigations into the scope, simplicity and systematizing power of the theory can be attempted.

It should be obvious that the undertaking outlined above is a difficult one, but it is precisely what is needed and one should not settle for less. Indeed, one major weakness in both Pap's and MacIntyre's criticisms of the theory of the unconscious is that they are attempts to dispose of the theory in some too quick and easy ways.

---

[32] P. Madison, *Freud's Concept of Repression and Defense, Its Theoretical and Observational Language* (Minneapolis: University of Minnesota Press, 1961).

MR. FARRELL AND THE REFUTABILITY OF PSYCHOANALYSIS

by

Michael Martin

Mr. B. A. Farrell has argued that psychoanalysis is refutable, without clarifying different senses of 'refutable'. Once this clarification is done and the relevant literature examined, however, it is seen that psychoanalysis is not refutable in several important senses of 'refutable', although it is refutable in a sense that is quite uninteresting.

In a recent article Mr. B. A. Farrell[1] examined the question 'Can psychoanalysis be refuted?' After pointing out that psychoanalysis is not a unified theory but is composed of several different loosely related parts, Farrell argued that these parts can be refuted.[2] The crucial question, according to Farrell, is to determine what one *means* by 'refutable'. But although he does consider this to be crucial, it is never completely clear what he means by 'refutable' in his article. In any case, I will argue that Farrell's arguments are far from persuasive and that in several relevant senses of 'refutable' there is good reason to think that at least some of the parts of psychoanalysis which Farrell argues are refutable are in fact not refutable.

The Meaning of 'Refutable'

When we ask whether a theory T is a refutable theory, we may be asking any of the following questions:
(1) Are people who are advocates of theory T willing to specify what evidence could count against theory T?
(2) Are people who believe in theory T willing to accept some of the evidence brought forth to refute theory T instead of explaining it all away?
(3) **Is** the relation between the theoretical language and the observational language of theory T clear and unambiguous?

(4) Is it possible to give theory T, in which the relation between the theoretical and observational language is extremely vague and ambiguous, a clear and unambiguous formulation?

It should be obvious that these questions, although closely related, are not identical. Consider questions (1) and (2). People who are not willing to specify what evidence could count against their theory usually try to explain away evidence that is claimed by their opponents to be negative. But this need not be so. People could simply refuse to accept any evidence offered as negative evidence without making any attempt to 'explain it away'. Consider questions (2) and (3). If a theory is vaguely and ambiguously formulated, it is easy for people who believe in the theory to 'explain away' any evidence that is offered as negative evidence. But, again, this need not be so. One can imagine people upholding a vaguely and ambiguously formulated theory and yet accepting some of the evidence which is offered as negative evidence.

Of course, it does not follow that just because a theory is precisely formulated its advocates would give it up in the light of evidence offered as negative. One can well imagine a precisely stated theory being upheld by its advocates in the light of any *prima facie* negative evidence. In this case it is not clear what one could or should say. One might be inclined to say that these people are irrational, or at least that they do not understand their own theory. Or one might be inclined to say that it is *we* who do not understand their theory. Or perhaps, these people might have chosen to change some other theories in order to save their theory, e.g., to change some physical theory about the instruments used in gathering the purported negative evidence against their theory.

Question (4) is the most important question for our present purpose and we must take some care in relating it to the other questions. In an obvious sense the answer to question (4) is 'yes' no matter what theory T is. It is always possible to give any theory T a clear and unambiguous formulation as long as one is willing (a) to modify the theory as it is originally stated and (b) to ignore the protests of the advocates of the theory.

Let theory T be a paradigm case of an irrefutable theory: Absolute Idealism. We can well imagine an empirical investigator fixing upon some vague reference to the self-development of the Absolute in history.[3] In an attempt to give the theory a more determinate empirical meaning he might argue that since the Absolute is perfect and is developing in history we should expect to see an increase of perfection in the 'empirical world'. He might further postulate that if there were a decrease of perfection in the empirical world in the next hundred years, this theory would be refuted. He might take as indicators of decreased perfection, decay of civilization, increase of disease, mass atomic wars, and so on.

Now this reformulation of Absolute Idealism would undoubtedly be unacceptable to advocates of the theory; they would argue that it is not what they meant by the Absolute developing in history. Moreover, they would probably explain away any negative evidence presented by the investigator and would be unable to say what evidence would count against their theory. In short, the answers to questions (1), (2), and (3) above, where theory T is Absolute Idealism, would be 'no'. But the answer to question (4) would be 'yes'; the theory can be reformulated and can then be tested. It should be obvious, however, that this sense of 'refutable' is uninteresting since theories that are usually considered irrefutable are refutable in this sense.

The same thing can be said about the theory that there is an all-good, all-powerful God. This theory also is considered to be a prime example of an irrefutable theory, yet non-religious people have often attempted to give it a clear empirical meaning. They have argued that if God is all-powerful and all-good, then we should expect a world without evil. But since there *is* evil, the theory that an all-good, all-powerful God exists is refuted. In short, where T is the theory that an all-good, all-powerful God exists, the answer to question (4) is 'yes'. But it is well known that theists have ways of explaining the existence of evil away; that they are unwilling to specify what sort of evidence could count against their theory; and that the relationship between the theistic theory in its original form and empirical phenomena is vague and ambiguous. In other words, the answers to questions (1), (2) and (3), where theory T is the theistic theory, are 'no'.

Now let us relate what we have said to psychoanalysis. Consider the following possible situation (how far this situation corresponds to the actual world will be determined later): Psychoanalysts are unwilling to specify what evidence will count against their theory. Moreover, they tend to discount any evidence that is offered as counting against their theory. Furthermore, a close examination of Freud's writings reveals a complete lack of observational language for certain aspects of psychoanalysis, and for other aspects an observational language and rules of correspondence which are vague, ambiguous, and impressionistic. Finally, psychoanalysts use this vaguely formulated theory to their advantage in the face of proposed negative evidence.

Suppose also that experimental psychologists and anthropologists publish experiments which purport to test psychoanalysis; that many of these experiments have produced negative results; and that psychoanalysts reject this evidence. Upon examining these studies we find that some experimenters say explicitly that psychoanalysis as it was originally formulated is untestable; they then go on to make psychoanalysis testable. Other experimenters, however, put psychoanalysis into a testable form without any explicit acknowledgment of the fact that they are reformulating the original theory. Moreover, on further examination we discover that these experimenters could have reformulated psychoanalysis in a variety of ways, and we see that whether or not the results of their experiments tend to refute psychoanalysis depends on the particular reformulation they happened to choose.

What should one say if this situation were true?

Should one call psychoanalysis refutable or not? It makes very little difference what one says as long as one knows what the situation actually is. Certainly in several interesting senses of 'refutable' psychoanalysis could not be said to be refutable. That is to say, where theory T is psychoanalysis, the answers to questions (1), (2) and (3) would be 'no'. But in another sense, that of question (4) above, it could be said to be refutable: empirical investigators have in this imagined situation *given* certain aspects of psychoanalytic theory a clear, unambiguous formulation and have tested it despite the fact that psychoanalysis, by hypothesis, in its original form does not have a clear meaning, and despite the fact that psychoanalysts, by hypothesis, tend to reject these reformulations and the alleged negative evidence they produce. In other words, the answer to question (4), where theory T is psychoanalysis, is 'yes' even though the answers to (1), (2) and (3) are 'no'. But as we have seen, the answer to question (4) is 'yes' even in the case of theories commonly considered to be irrefutable; hence *this* sense of 'refutable' is quite uninteresting.

In the remainder of this essay I will show that the hypothetical situation outlined above very probably corresponds to the actual state of affairs, and that nothing Farrell says in his article has shown that it does not.

The Refutability of Psychoanalysis

Let us now turn to Farrell's question 'Can psychoanalysis be refuted?' and consider it in the light of the four questions listed above.

(1) Farrell says 'Analysts have been challenged to show that it [psychoanalysis] is refutable and they have been slow to meet the challenge'.[4] This suggests that, although analysts have been slow in saying what evidence could refute psychoanalysis, they have eventually done so. It is significant, however, that Farrell never says who these analysts are or what possible negative evidence they have specified.

A survey of psychoanalytic literature suggests that analysts are not merely slow in saying what evidence would count against their theory, but that they are, in general, unable to do so. To be sure, a complete and systematic study of the responses of psychoanalysts to questions about what evidence would count against their theory has never been attempted. But an unsystematic investigation by Sydney Hook of a group of psychoanalysts suggests that in general they are unable to specify what evidence would count against a boy's having an Oedipus complex.[5]

(2) Psychoanalysts have often denied in their writings that studies purporting to refute different aspects of psychoanalytic theory actually do so. Psychoanalysts typically explain away the evidence brought forth in these studies by saying that the studies have not been subtle enough or that the experiments performed do not really test psychoanalysis.[6] Typical is the statement of Hartmann and Kris:

> The limits of current experiments in the verification of psychoanalytic hypotheses become apparent when we realize that, at the present stage of investigation, the lack of experimental verification rarely, if ever, implies invalidation of the propositions. It proves rather that the ingenuity of the experimenter has not been able to master the translation from the area of life where the proposition was gained into that of the controlled situation where the experiment is performed.[7]

This sort of objection to studies, such as Sears's,[8] which purportedly produce evidence refuting certain aspects of psychoanalysis would be permissible, of course, if psychoanalysts went on to specify the sort of experimental design which would really test psychoanalysis, the sort of experiment that *would* be subtle enough. But I have yet to find a psychoanalyst who, after dismissing studies purporting to refute psychoanalysis, actually specifies what sort of study would be relevant to its refutation. In particular, Hartmann and Kris never say what sort of experiment would satisfy them.

It is interesting to note that the very studies reported by Sears, and cited by Farrell in an earlier article[9] as disconfirming psychoanalysis, are denied by psychoanalysts to have any relevance to their theory. If past experience in this area is a reliable guide to the future, then we can reasonably infer that the alleged negative evidence cited by Farrell in his recent article in order to show that various aspects of psychoanalysis are refutable would also be rejected by psychoanalysts. It is on the basis of bitter experience that William Sewell, an experimentally-minded sociologist interested in testing psychoanalytic theory, has remarked:

> I can assure you that its [psychoanalysis's] proponents will be ready to point out such weaknesses [of experimental design] — whether they exist or not — if the results are against the theory.[10]

(3) It has been noted by several philosophers of science that in order for a theory to be confirmable or disconfirmable it must have clearly formulated 'rules of correspondence' linking its theoretical structure to its observational base.[11] Without these rules a theory is incapable of empirical investigation. The important question for our purposes is not simply whether psychoanalysis has such rules, but how one is to find out whether it does or does not have them. One way to find out would be to examine carefully psychoanalytic writing, trying one's best to separate the observational basis of the theory from the theoretical structure, and to extract rules of correspondence from the context of the uses of the two languages.

Fortunately an attempt has been made recently to do this. Peter Madison, by a systematic and scholarly investigation of Freud's writings, has attempted to separate the observational and theoretical languages of Freud's theory and to extract rules of correspondence for the theory.[12] It should be clear that his results must be carefully studied by anyone who wishes to argue that psychoanalysis is or is not refutable.

Madison shows that certain crucial aspects of psychoanalysis, e.g., primal repression, cannot be disconfirmed since Freud specifies no observational language and rules of correspondence. For other aspects of Freudian theory Madison believes that he has found an observational language and rules of correspondence. But a close examination of Madison's actual findings reveals that his last contention is not strictly correct. What Madison has actually found are the rudiments of an observational language and rules of correspondence. Madison takes these rudiments and reformulates them into a clearer and more precise form. In other words, some of Freud's language has suggested to Madison the path that a testable reformulation of the theory might take. Unfortunately, however, Madison does not usually distinguish Freud's original statement from his own clarified version of it.

For example, Madison maintains that one empirical indicator of adult repression given by Freud is 'periods of silence' in the therapeutic session. Naturally, unless it is further specified what a 'period of silence' is, such an indicator is worthless. Freud, it should be pointed out, does not do this; we are left in the dark as to what exactly constitutes a period of silence, e.g., a minute, a second, etc. Madison does, however, give a clear meaning to Freud's suggestion. Madison argues that a 'silence ratio' can be devised which consists in the amount of silence in a fifty-minute therapeutic session. This is surely an improvement over Freud's vague statement, but whether it captures what Freud meant is not at all clear. Unfortunately, Madison sometimes seems to suggest that the 'silence ratio' is what Freud meant all along.

In any case, the silence ratio is not usable as an indicator of adult repression until we determine the amount of silence that is supposed to occur in a therapeutic session when a person is *not* repressing. Again Freud is no help on this point and even Madison does not seem to realize the need for this further specification. Moreover, it is never really clear from what Freud says whether the absence of the indicators of repression he vaguely suggests shows that a person is not repressing. We still do not know, in other words, whether it would be possible to say that someone was repressing no matter what the evidence. Until we know this we do not know if we have a refutable theory. Madison presumably takes Freud to be saying that the absence of these indicators *would* show that a person was not repressing. But I can find no justification in what Freud says for such an interpretation. In other words, a great deal of elaboration, clarification, and specification must be provided before Freud's vague statements about adult repression can be said to constitute a refutable hypothesis.

It is impossible to go into a detailed analysis and evaluation of the behavioral indicators of other hidden psychic processes that Madison finds scattered throughout Freud's writings. It must suffice to say that when a behavioral indicator is hinted at by Freud it is always stated in such a manner that without further clarification and specification it remains unacceptable as an observational basis for psychoanalysis. Madison's efforts to clarify and reformulate some of Freud's statements are both ingenious and worth while, for without such clarification and reformulation psychoanalysis, as it is revealed in Madison's study, would remain forever beyond empirical investigation.

Most of Madison's suggestions are not, however, reformulations of Freud's statements, but rather suggestions about how reformulations might proceed. We must not confuse this *program* for a reformulation of psychoanalysis with an *actual* reformulation of psychoanalysis, let alone with the *original* theory. Madison's work, in other words, does not show that psychoanalysis is refutable in its original form; indeed it shows just the opposite. What it does show is that an imaginative investigator can reformulate psychoanalysis or at least suggest the lines that a reformulation might take.

(4) Our discussion of Madison's recent work brings us naturally to the last question. Now no one, as far as I know, has ever denied that psychoanalysis can be reformulated so that it is testable. Surely if this were all that was at issue, there would be no objections raised to the scientific status of psychoanalysis. The question is, rather, whether psychoanalysis in its *original* form can be tested. The citing of empirical studies that are supposed to test psychoanalytic theory is quite irrelevant in answering the question whether psychoanalytic theory as originally stated is refutable, unless it is shown that these studies have been performed *without* a considerable amount of clarification and reformulation of psychoanalytic theory. I do not think this can be shown; indeed, a survey of the empirical literature strongly suggests[13] that clarification and reformulation are the rule.

Some empirical investigators of psychoanalytic theory have explicitly stated that psychoanalysis cannot be tested in its original form. Thus Sewell has argued:

> A precise formulation of these ideas into a theoretical statement capable of direct empirical testing is not found in psychoanalytic literature.[14]

This, of course, does not prevent Sewell from reformulating psychoanalysis and performing an interesting experiment on the effects of childhood training on personality.[15]

Child has remarked:

> The concept of anal character, suggestive though it is about possible dimensions of generalizations, is not really associated with any precise hypothesis about antecedent consequent relationships.[16]

Once again this does not prevent Child, in collaboration with Whiting, from testing the effects of toilet training on adult behavior.[17] We must remember, however, that Child and Whiting spend several pages reformulating psychoanalysis so that it is testable.

Again Bergin has remarked:

> The relationship between concepts and events is ambiguous enough so that an experimenter can select variables to test suitable to his own biases; and for the same reason, the psychoanalyst need feel no compulsion to accept the experimenter's test as adequately representing the proposed relationships regardless of which variables are related.[18]

But this does not stop Bergin, after he has given the theory a precise meaning, from performing an experiment to determine the influence of the therapist on the patient's acceptance of his interpretation.[19]

To be sure, not all empirical investigators have been so explicit about their reformulations as have Sewell, Child and Bergin. But it takes very little effort to see that in other studies which purport to test psychoanalysis a similar process of reformulation has taken place. Consider, for example, a study by Friedman.[20]

Friedman, in an elaborately designed experiment, has attempted to meet the objection that most studies purporting to test psychoanalytic theory are not subtle enough. In particular, he is concerned with the claim that most experiments do not test the *unconscious* motivation of people. Friedman argues that unconscious Oedipal feelings would be manifested only in projective tests and he uses such tests in his experiment. One of his projective techniques consisted in showing a series of pictures to boys and girls. The boys and girls were asked to make up stories about the pictures. One of the pictures shown to the boys was of a boy standing in a room by an open door; in the room also, facing the boy and seated at a table, was a woman (the mother-figure). A similar picture was shown to the girls except that a girl was standing by the door instead of a boy. Now according to Friedman, one can 'predict' from psychoanalytic theory (combined with certain principles of Lewin's field theory)[21] that, in general, in telling stories about the picture, because of their 'Oedipal needs', boys will produce more fantasies in which the child moves *toward* the mother-figure than will girls. The results of Friedman's study were positive and Friedman concluded that psychoanalysis was confirmed.

It is literally false, of course, that one can make a 'prediction', in the sense of drawing any logical conclusion of the kind Friedman mentions from psychoanalytic theory (even combined with Lewin's field theory). What Friedman means, surely, is that it seems 'reasonable' to him to draw this sort of conclusion from psychoanalytic theory. It seems plausible to him that boys would express a desire for their mothers in the symbolism of their fantasies and that, in the light of field psychology, this desire would be manifested in their stories about the picture by movement *toward* the desired object. But why is it not just as reasonable or plausible to suppose that boys, because of the 'castration threat', would produce fantasies in which the child moved *away* from the mother-figure? Again, why is it not plausible to suppose that girls would produce fantasies in which the child moved toward the mother-figure as much as, or more than, boys, on the grounds that girls would unconsciously wish to identify with their mothers to 'obtain' their father's penis? Moreover, certain passages in Freud's writing suggest that the normal children used in Friedman's experiment would not show *any* repressed 'Oedipal needs'.[22]

In any case, we must not be led to believe that Friedman made a 'deduction' from the theory that boys would tell a particular kind of story about the picture in question. Rather, Friedman specified a clear and unambiguous rule of correspondence that was lacking in the theory and that seemed to him to be reasonably in accordance with the theory as it was vaguely stated originally. But that other rules of correspondence are just as much 'in accordance' with the theory should not be overlooked — rules of correspondence that could account for all *possible* combinations of evidence, e.g., stories told by boys in which the child moved forward or backward, stories told by girls in which the child moved forward just as much as the child in boys' stories, etc. If we accept Friedman's rule of correspondence, this enables us to make a clear and unambiguous inference from the theory which it was impossible to make in its original form. The rest of Friedman's 'predictions' are of the same kind.

Naturally, it is impossible to examine here the various ways in which psychoanalysis has been reformulated by empirical investigators in order to make it testable; however, such an examination is available elsewhere.[23] It must suffice to say that I have yet to discover an experimental investigation of psychoanalytic theory that does not involve either an explicit or an implicit reformulation of psychoanalysis into a clearer and unambiguous form — a reformulation that was necessary before the *originally* stated theory could be tested.

In sum, there is good reason to think that in the first three senses of 'refutable' specified above psychoanalysis is not refutable. In the fourth sense of 'refutable' psychoanalysis is refutable, but, as we have seen, in *this* sense so is any theory, even ones that are commonly accepted to be irrefutable.

Farrell's Arguments

The first thing that one should note about Farrell's argument that psychoanalysis is refutable is that he does not clearly separate different senses of the term. With only a few exceptions (one of which we shall consider below) he does not appear to be concerned with questions (1) and (2) discussed above. He appears, rather, to be concerned with questions (3) and (4), although he does not seem to realize clearly the important distinction between these two questions. In any case, it should be emphasized that even if he established that any part of psychoanalysis was refutable in the senses of questions (3) and (4) this would not show that it was refutable in the senses of questions (1) and (2).

Farrell's arguments for his thesis that psychoanalysis can be refuted are of two kinds:

(1) He states a certain part of Freudian theory and then argues that certain evidence could refute the theory.

(2) He cites empirical studies that purport to test certain aspects of psychoanalysis and argues on the basis of these studies that these aspects of psychoanalysis are open to empirical investigation.

Let us consider some examples of each kind of argument in detail.

(1) (a) Farrell argues that Freud's theory of instincts is refutable because:

> On Freud's view, an instinct or drive has a 'source'. This is a 'somatic process', but 'we do not know whether this process is regularly of a chemical nature or whether it may also correspond with the release of other, e.g. mechanical, forces.' Now when we do come to uncover relevant physiological processes, it is possible

that we shall discover that whereas some of the ego instincts (e.g. thirst and hunger) have 'a source', others (e.g. flight from danger) have not. Or, what is more likely perhaps, we shall discover that the whole notion of 'a source' is far too naïve to cover the complex facts about the bodily organs of instinctual activity. If we discover either of these things we will succeed in forcing analysts to modify the theory. So, it could be said, it is possible in principle to refute this generalization of the Instinct theory.[24]

This argument is extremely puzzling. How can we refute the view that an instinct has 'a source' unless we know what 'a source' is supposed to mean and what is to count against an instinct's having a source? Farrell surely begs the question when he says 'when we come to uncover relevant physiological processes . . .', for the whole question is what is to *count* as 'relevant'. It is significant, I think, that Farrell does not say what sort of evidence would be 'relevant' in refuting the theory.

Indeed in one sense of 'source' it is difficult to see how this theory could be refuted, i.e., if it means only that an instinctual drive is causally connected with some physiological process or other. What exactly Freud meant by 'a source' is unclear.[25]

Recent statements by contemporary psychoanalysts, presumably the official interpreters of the Freudian corpus, have tended to argue that Freud was not suggesting a physiological hypothesis at all. Consider these statements coming from a New York conference of some of America's leading psychoanalysts.

> When he [Freud] spoke of special chemistry or processes . . . I do not believe that he did so as a physiologist or neurologist, but he was using what today would be called physiological models. There is a considerable difference between using physiological models and being physiologically oriented in the sense that one must measure things physiologically and correlate them.[26]

Again:

> However, in his paper *On Narcissism* he saw the difficulties arising from attempting to distinguish one small group of instincts from another small group on the basis of specific chemical, endocrinological, or physiological functional apparatus and, therefore, he proposed to dissociate the concept of libido from any kind of particular chemistry. . . . Freud . . . thus reformulated the libido theory as entirely separate from sexual chemistry.[27]

In the face of statements of this sort, Freud's vagueness, and the apparent unwillingness of psychoanalysts to accept negative evidence, what real force has Farrell's statement that 'If we discover either of these things we will succeed in forcing analysts to modify the theory?' How are we going to 'force' analysts to 'modify' their theory when from all indications they will not accept evidence purporting to count against their theory?

We might compare Farrell's argument to the following argument: 'Since religious people believe that God was the creator of life, when science demonstrates that life evolved from inorganic matter we shall force these people to modify their theory'. We shall indeed if these people accept our evidence as counting against their views. But it is well known that many religious groups who hold such views would not be disturbed by our evidence. We have only to recall the past moves of fundamentalist sects to explain away the findings of evolutionists.[28]

(b) Another of Farrell's arguments falling under this first category is the following:

> 'All little girls have penis envy and wish to be boys.' It seems clear that the direct observation of little girls fails to support this generalization, as most observant parents will agree. Orthodox analysts will probably reply that this negative evidence is not conclusive, because girls who do not show overt signs of penis envy have concealed it from view or repressed it. Their evidence for saying this stems from their use of psychoanalytic method in the analysis of adults and in play therapy with children. To assess the weight of this evidence we have to determine the validity of psychoanalytic method. In the absence of such an enquiry, the truth-value of the generalization will remain uncertain. But have we any grounds for asserting that it is not refutable *in principle?* Surely none whatever. Of course, it may be difficult to refute it in practice, and for reasons connected with the difficulty of doing satisfactory research in this field. But part of the business of scientific workers is to overcome the practical difficulties in their way.[29]

There are many things one might say about this statement. In the first place, psychoanalysts do not merely regard the evidence obtained from 'direct observation' as 'inconclusive'; they regard it as irrelevant. 'Penis envy' is a repressed unconscious desire manifested in the most subtle ways; it is not something that parents might notice.[30] In the second place, it is not clear what Farrell means when he says that generalization is not irrefutable *in principle*. If he is using 'refutable' in the sense of questions (1) or (2) above, then, as we have seen, there is good reason to think he is mistaken. If he is using 'refutable' in the sense of question (3), he seems mistaken also. The hypothesis of infant and childhood repression is one of the vaguest and most ambiguous in Freud's writings.[31] It seems probable from his references to 'scientific workers' overcoming 'practical difficulties' that he is using 'refutable' in the sense of question (4). If he is, then this seems hardly interesting. I don't know of anyone who would wish to deny that a 'scientific worker' could *reformulate* the theory of penis envy so that it would be testable.

(c) A third argument of Farrell's is the following:

> 'A second pregenital phase is that of the sadistic-anal organization (of sexual life).' Let us express part of this generalization in a more usual and convenient form. 'All children go through an anal-sadistic stage.' What this means, at least in part, is that all children go through a state when their chief sexual interest is anal pleasure.
>
> Is this refutable? One hesitates because it is so vague. What is a 'stage'? How does one decide that their interest in faeces is 'sexual'? How does one discover that what a child is really interested in, in expelling its faeces, is anal pleasure? How does one set about determining the relative strengths of the oral, anal-sadistic and phallic interests? It is tempting to conclude that the generalization is *so* vague as to be irrefutable. But is there much point in falling for this temptation? For if we do fall for it, are we doing much more than advertising our personal decision to put a generalization with this degree of vagueness beyond the limits of the refutable? And is not such a decision a bit arbitrary in view of the fact that all sorts of empirical considerations obviously do have a bearing on the truth or falsity of this generalization? Would not a careful programme of Gesell-like observation on a large sample, from different home-training regimes, do *something* to support or upset the generalization? And can we not imagine a programme of investigation, the results of which could make us inclined to say that the generalization *had* been refuted? I think we can imagine such a programme.[32]

Again Farrell's argument is very puzzling. First, he seems to admit that the generalization is extremely vague and unclear, and that it is not certain what evidence would be relevant to its confirmation or disconfirmation. But then he goes on to say that a program of observation on a large scale would tend either to support or refute the generalization. I must confess I find these two statements hard to reconcile. If we are really unclear about what a 'stage' is, when interest in faeces is supposed to be 'sexual', what evidence is supposed to show when anal experience is 'pleasurable', and so on, what are we to look for in the 'Gesell-like observations on a large scale'? Again, it is significant that Farrell does not say what we are supposed to look for; he avoids this crucial problem with a series of rhetorical questions. Moreover, it is not clear to whom the 'us' who would be 'inclined' to say that the generalization has been refuted in the light of this unspecified evidence refers. Does the 'us' include psychoanalysts? If it does, then, as we have seen, there is good reason to think that they would not accept this evidence, whatever it might be, as counting against their theory.

Furthermore, Farrell's statement that there would be no point in saying that this generalization is so vague that it is irrefutable is quite misleading. If he means merely that Freud's statements can be given a clearer meaning and put to empirical test, then he is quite correct. Indeed, Freud's vague statements have served and continue to serve an important heuristic function in psychological investigations. But if he means that Freud's statements are capable of being tested in their original form, he is mistaken. Far from being arbitrary in saying that psychoanalysis cannot be refuted in its *original* form we are making a crucial distinction between the original theory and reformulations of it which Farrell does not even take into account.

(2) Farrell cites (usually uncritically) many empirical studies purporting to test psychoanalysis. As I have already mentioned, the mere existence of such studies is not sufficient for determining that psychoanalysis is refutable in the sense of the first three questions mentioned above. In particular it is not sufficient for calling it refutable in the sense of the third question. For this it is necessary also to show that these studies have been performed without a great deal of clarification and reformulation. Farrell makes no attempt to show this and hence he has not shown that psychoanalysis, in its original form, is capable of refutation. Indeed, at one point he seems to admit that certain aspects of psychoanalysis must be clarified before research is possible:

> It is apparent, however, to the discerning eye that fruitful work on identification may only be possible after further clarification of the concept itself. In recent years psychologists have turned their attention to this logical task on several of the concepts concerned, including that of identification. This gain in

clarity is one of the undoubted benefits that has occurred from the attempts of psychologists to investigate the generalizations of psychoanalysis.[33]

One can only agree with this statement. But Farrell does not seem to realize the significance of it. If it is really necessary to clarify the concept of identification before investigation, and if Freud does not provide this necessary clarification, then we must say that the theory as it is originally stated cannot be subjected to empirical investigation.

One experiment which Farrell cites in order to show that psychoanalysis is open to empirical investigation is Feshbach's:

> 11. 'Unsatisfied wishes are the driving power behind phantasies; every separate phantasy contains the fulfilment of a wish, and improves on unsatisfactory reality.'
> Suppose we give this statement a strong interpretation as a universal generalization. The kernel of it is that 'All phantasies are wish fulfilling.' We may be tempted to say two different things about this statement. That it is obviously true, being only a matter of common sense; and that it is obviously not the sort of thing we can investigate scientifically at all. But the fact is that not all people have believed it, and it is open to scientific enquiry. Thus, Feshbach argued that if a social situation were to arouse hostility in people, then the expression of their hostility in phantasy should reduce somewhat the hostility they felt towards this situation. On investigation Feshbach found this hypothesis was correct. It is natural to say that this finding supports generalization 11, and that if the contradictory finding had been made, it would have counted against the generalization. It is hardly necessary to say that, and why, Feshbach's work is not conclusive. The inconclusive outcome of a single experiment is a common feature of work in science, and not one restricted to psychology alone.[34]

Let us examine Feshbach's study in detail to see if it does test psychoanalysis as originally stated, or if it tests a reformulation of the theory.

First of all, it is not clear just what the relationship is between Freud's statement about fantasies and Feshbach's hypothesis[35] that expression of hostility in fantasy is drive reducing. Is Feshbach's hypothesis a deductive consequence of Freud's statements? Farrell's use of the word 'argue' suggests that it is, or at least that Feshbach has deduced his hypothesis from Freud's statement about fantasies along with other statements of Freud. But a check of Feshbach's paper does not support this view. Feshbach apparently got his hypothesis not from Freud's writings but from the writings of P. M. Symonds, a professor of education.[36] Now, although Symonds writes from an admittedly psychoanalytic point of view, he does not say that he derived this idea from Freud's writings. In short, the step between Freud's statement and Feshbach's hypothesis is a long and uncertain one.

Secondly, even if Feshbach did derive his hypothesis from Freud's writings, it is still a further long step to its being a testable hypothesis. What, for example, is to count as an expression of hostility in a fantasy situation? What is to count as an expression of hostility in a non-fantasy situation? What is to count as an increase or decrease of hostility in either situation? Feshbach, it must be emphasized, spends several pages specifying and clarifying his hypothesis in order to put it into testable form.

Once we realize fully that the relationship between Freud's original statement and Feshbach's initial hypothesis is unclear, and that the gap is wide between this initial hypothesis and Feshbach's final testable statement of the hypothesis, do we *still* find it 'natural' to say that his study supports Freud's statement? Surely another source of the inconclusiveness of Feshbach's study, besides the fact that it is a single experiment, is that it is simply not clear what relevance, if any, it has to what Freud said.

In sum, Farrell has not shown that psychoanalysis is refutable in any interesting sense of 'refutable'. At best he has shown that psychoanalysis can be reformulated into a testable form. But, as far as I can tell, no one has ever denied this, and in *this* sense any theory commonly regarded as irrefutable is refutable.

Conclusion

I must conclude that there is good reason to think that there are several relevant and interesting senses in which psychoanalysis is not refutable. There is, of course, another sense of 'refutable' in which psychoanalysis is a refutable theory, namely, the sense in which psychoanalysis can be put into a testable form despite its original vagueness and ambiguity and despite the protests of psychoanalysts. Farrell has not shown that psychoanalysis is refutable in any other sense than this. But any theory can be reformulated in this way and thereby made testable. If this is all Farrell intended to show, his thesis is quite true but quite uninteresting.

NOTES

[1] B. A. Farrell, 'Can Psychoanalysis be Refuted?' *Inquiry*, 1961, pp. 16–36.

[2] Farrell believes that (a) the theory of instincts, (b) the theory of development, (c) the theory of psychic structure when the words 'id', 'unconscious', etc., are used as adjectives, (d) the theory of mental economics, and (e) the theory of symptom formation, are refutable. He believes that the theory of psychic structure should be construed as a model when the words 'id', 'unconscious', etc., are used as nouns; that it is misleading, therefore, to ask whether it can be shown to be true or false; that the proper question to ask is whether this model is useful or not useful. We will not be concerned with this aspect of Farrell's argument here.

[3] 'It is also the energizing power realizing this aim; developing it not only in the phenomena of the Natural, but also of the Spiritual Universe — the History of the World. That this "Idea" or "Reason" is the *True*, the *Eternal*, the absolutely *powerful* essence; that it reveals itself in the World . . .' G. W. F. Hegel, *The Philosophy of History*, Dover Pub., New York 1956, pp. 9–10.

[4] Farrell, op. cit., p. 16.

[5] S. Hook, 'Science and Mythology in Psychoanalysis', *Psychoanalysis, Scientific Method, and Philosophy*, New York University Press, New York 1959, pp. 212–24. Hook reports that although he has asked this question 'innumerable times' over a period of forty years he has received only two coherent answers to his question from psychoanalysts.

[6] See for example, R. Ekstein, 'Ideological Warfare in the Psychological Sciences', *The Psychoanalytic Review*, 36, 1949, pp. 144–51; S. Escalona, 'Problems in Psycho-Analytic Research', *International Journal of Psycho-Analysis*, 33, 1952, pp. 11–21; F. Alexander, 'Evaluation of Statistical and Analytical Methods in Psychiatry and Psychology', *The American Journal of Orthopsychiatry*, 4, 1934, pp. 433–48; H. Hartmann and E. Kris, 'The Genetic Approach in Psychoanalysis', *The Psychoanalytic Study of the Child*, I, 1945, pp. 11–30.

[7] Hartmann and Kris, loc. cit., p. 16.

[8] R. R. Sears, *Survey of Objective Studies of Psychoanalytic Concepts*, Social Science Research Council, New York 1943.

[9] B. A. Farrell, 'The Scientific Testing of Psycho-analytic Findings and Theory', *British Journal of Medical Psychology*, 24, 1951, pp. 35–41.

[10] W. Sewell, 'Some Observations on Theory Testing', *Rural Sociology*, 21, 1956, p. 9.

[11] See for example, Ernest Nagel, *The Structure of Science*, Harcourt Brace and World, New York 1961, Ch. 5; F. S. C. Northrop, *The Logic of the Sciences and Humanities*, Macmillan Co., New York 1947, Ch. 7; C. G. Hempel, 'Fundamentals of Concept Formation in Empirical Science', *International Encyclopedia of Unified Science*, II, 7, pp. 23–39.

[12] P. Madison, *Freud's Concept of Repression and Defense, Its Theoretical and Observational Language*, University of Minnesota Press, Minneapolis 1961.

[13] See Michael Martin, 'Psychoanalysis and Scientific Method', unpublished doctoral dissertation, Harvard University.

[14] Sewell, op. cit., p. 5.

[15] W. Sewell, 'Infant Training and the Personality of the Child', *American Journal of Sociology*, 58, 1952–3, pp. 150–9.

[16] I. L. Child, 'Socialization', *Handbook of Social Psychology*, ed. G. Lindzey, Addison-Wesley Pub. Co., Cambridge 1954, II, p. 667.
[17] J. Whiting and I. L. Child, *Child Training and Personality*, Yale University Press, New Haven 1953.
[18] Allen E. Bergin, 'Comments on Psychoanalytic Theory', unpublished paper.
[19] Allen E. Bergin, 'Personality "Interpretations" as Dissonant Persuasive Communications', *American Psychologist*, 16, 1961, p. 428.
[20] S. M. Friedman, 'An Empirical Study of the Castration and Oedipus Complexes', *Genetic Psychol. Monogr.*, 46, pp. 61–130.
[21] Ibid., pp. 106–7. According to Lewin, an object with 'positive valence' in one's psychological field will draw the person toward the object. The opposite would be true of an object with 'negative valence'. See K. Lewin, 'Behavior and Development as a Function of the Total Situation', *Manual of Child Psychology*, ed. L. Carmichael, Wiley, New York 1946, pp. 805–6.
[22] See S. Freud, *New Introductory Lectures on Psychoanalysis*, Norton, New York 1933, pp. 126–7.
[23] Martin, op. cit.
[24] Farrell, 'Can Psychoanalysis be Refuted', *Inquiry*, 1961, p. 18.
[25] See S. Freud, 'Instincts and their Vicissitudes', *Collected Papers*, Basic Books, New York 1959, IV, pp. 60–83.
[26] Nevitt Sanford, 'Discussion of Szasz's Paper', *Conceptual and Methodological Problems in Psychoanalysis*, ed. L. Bellak, Annals of the New York Academy of Science, Vol. 76, art. 4, p. 996.
[27] Mortimer Ostow, 'Discussion of Szasz's Paper', loc. cit., p. 997.
[28] See Martin Gardner, 'Geology Versus Genesis', in *Fads and Fallacies in the Name of Science*, Dover Pub., New York 1957, pp. 123–39.
[29] Farrell, 'Can Psychoanalysis be Refuted?' *Inquiry*, 1961, p. 21.
[30] See for example, C. Thompson, 'Penis Envy in Women', *Psychiatry*, 6, 1943, pp. 123–5.
[31] See Madison, op. cit., pp. 176–9.
[32] Farrell, 'Can Psychoanalysis be Refuted?' *Inquiry*, 1961, p. 20.
[33] Ibid., p. 29.
[34] Ibid., p. 30. The quotation at the beginning is from Freud's 'The Relation of the Poet to Day-Dreaming', *Collected Papers*, IV, p. 176.
[35] S. Feshbach, 'The Drive-Reducing Function of Fantasy Behaviour', *Journal of Abnormal and Social Psychology*, 50, 1955, pp. 3–11.
[36] P. M. Symonds, *The Dynamics of Human Adjustments*, Appleton-Century-Croft, New York 1946, Ch. 22.

ARE COGNITIVE PROCESSES AND STRUCTURE A MYTH?

By Michael Martin

NORMAN Malcolm has argued that cognitive processes and structure are a myth, that psychologists explain nothing by their theories of cognitive processes and structure since there are no such processes or structures.[1] In this paper we will show that Malcolm's arguments for this position are unsound.

The Alleged Myth of Cognitive Processes

Malcolm argues:

> There is a real difficulty . . . in our understanding what a psychologist is talking about when he says, for example, that he wants to explain "the processes of pattern recognition" or to construct a model for it. In recognizing patterns, shape, colors and people there is usually or often no *process* of recognition. So *what* is the model a model of?

For example, there is often no process involved in recognizing someone's face. You see a friend's face in a crowd. 'You smile at him and say "Hi John". You do not think "Where have I seen that face before?"' The same thing is true of remembering. Sometimes one does go through a process of *trying* to remember, according to Malcolm. For example you may "review in your mind" the places you went on the way home in order to recall where you left your briefcase. But in most cases there is no review. We just remember where, for example, we have left the pliers or where our clean shirts are.

It is important to note that Malcolm admits that sometimes there are cognitive processes, e.g. in the case of trying to remember. He maintains, however, that these cases are rare. Now, in the cases of cognitive processes Malcolm acknowledges, he seems to be talking about cognitive processes that are easily accessible to introspection. In his example you review in your mind where you went on the way home. The processes that psychologists are talking about, however, need not be processes like that.[2] Psychologists might well admit that processes of the kind Malcolm is talking about occur only sometimes. This admission would be perfectly compatible with the thesis that processes that are unconscious or subconscious always or at least often occur. Moreover, whether the

---

[1] Norman Malcolm 'The Myth of Cognitive Processes and Structures', *Cognitive Development and Epistemology*, ed. Theodore Mischel (New York: Academic Press, 1971), pp. 385-392. Malcolm's paper is in part a response to P.C. Dodwell's 'Is a Theory of Conceptual Development Necessary?', which also appears in this volume (pp. 365-388). Dodwell's response to Malcolm is in a postscript. Dodwell's response, although correct, does not attempt to evaluate Malcolm's specific arguments.

[2] For some typical work in cognitive psychology see J. Bruner, J. Goodnow and G. Austin, *A Study of Thinking* (New York: John Wiley, 1956) and J. Bruner *et al.*, *Contemporary Approaches to Cognition* (Cambridge: Harvard U. Press, 1957).

cases Malcolm acknowledges are as rare as Malcolm seems to suppose is not clear. Certainly Malcolm gives no evidence to support his thesis on this point. Even if these cases are as rare as Malcolm says, some do by his own admission exist. Such processes can hardly be myths in the cases where they do exist, and psychologists surely in these cases have a subject for their theories and models. At most, then, Malcolm has shown that psychologists' models of cognitive processes do not have as wide an application as they are thought to have, not that they have no application and hence are models of nothing. However, as I have suggested, psychologists have in general not been talking about conscious or introspectible cognitive processes.

Malcolm does not just lean on introspective evidence to establish his thesis. He argues that appeal to inner processes is a *philosophical* mistake. For the supposition that there is an inner process of recognition is based on an incorrect view of mind. The correct view does not appeal to inner processes; yet it is not strictly speaking behaviouristic. For example, recognition of John's face is not an inner process. To be sure, there may be all sorts of images, feelings, thoughts that are associated with recognizing a face. However, even if there are not, recognition is still possible. The criterion of whether someone has recognized a face is not in terms of the person's images, feelings or thoughts. This does not mean that recognition consists just in the behaviour of saying 'Hi John'.

> Imagine an eccentric who smiles at and says 'Hi John' to every tenth person he passes; and who has never seen this John before. Given those facts, his smile and utterance on this occasion would not be an expression of recognition. On the other hand, it is easy to imagine a situation in which such a smile and greeting would be an expression of recognition. Thus, it is the facts, the circumstances surrounding that behavior, that give it the property of expressing recognition. This property is not due to something that goes on inside.[1]

Thus, according to Malcolm, recognizing John's face is *appropriate behaviour in certain circumstances*.[2]

Several critical points can be raised about Malcolm's analysis. First, one might want to make a distinction between the achievement and process meaning of terms.[3] The term 'learning', for example, sometimes refers to certain achievements of people and sometimes to the process leading up to such achievements. It might be argued that 'pattern recognition' and 'remembering' also have an achievement and a process sense. Malcolm might then be interpreted as claiming that pattern recognition and remembering in the *achievement sense* refer only to certain behaviour in certain contexts, and he might well be correct. But this would show nothing about what remembering and pattern recognition

[1] Malcolm, *op. cit.*, p. 387.
[2] Malcolm is, of course, indebted to Wittgenstein for this view.
[3] I am indebted to David Marion for this point.

are in the *process sense*. In this sense inner processes might indeed be relevant for the analysis.

But let us suppose that there is no process sense of 'pattern recognition' or 'remembering', or, perhaps, that the analysis of the process sense of 'pattern recognition' or 'remembering' does not refer to anything inside the person who recognizes the pattern or who remembers. Still one might want to know *why* Jones' face was recognized and the explanation of this may refer to inner processes. Thus there is an important distinction to be drawn between two theses:

(1) A philosophical analysis of the terms 'pattern recognition' and 'remembering' in either the achievement or process sense involves inner process terms.

(2) A scientific explanation of the phenomena of pattern recognition and remembering involves reference to inner processes.

Malcolm seems to blur the distinction between (1) and (2). Once these theses are distinguished it is clear that Malcolm has at most refuted (1); his argument does not even seem to touch (2). Furthermore, it seems unlikely that psychologists are particularly interested in (1), if (1) is understood as giving a philosophical analysis of the commonsense or ordinary meaning of 'pattern recognition' or 'remembering'. Psychologists, like all scientists, redefine terms to suit their theoretical purposes. Cognitive psychologists have of course advocated (2). But, since Malcolm's argument does not touch (2), even if it is valid it seems to have little relevance to psychology.

The Alleged Myth of Structure

Malcolm criticizes social scientists like Chomsky and Lenneberg who appeal to systems of rules of abstract structures that explain the learning of language and other types of learning. Again he argues that appeal to such rules or structures is mythological.

Malcolm first quotes a linguist R. A. Hall who disagrees with Chomsky. However, such recourse to authority is hardly cogent unless the authority has good reason for *his* disagreement. Unfortunately the quotation from Hall used by Malcolm indicates that Hall's reasons are very weak indeed. For example, Hall says:

> As anyone can see by direct observation of ordinary people's normal every-day speech-activity, people simply do not talk according to rules, whether they be aware of the rules' existence or not. There are too many instances of normal speech which cannot be accounted for by any generative rules at all—which constitute, in fact, all kinds of "violations" of rules—but which cannot be neglected or whose existence cannot be denied in that account.[1]

[1] R. A. Hall, 'Some Recent Developments in American Linguistics', *Neuphilologische Mitteilungen*, 70, 1969.

It is as absurd to say that the existence of the rules Chomsky postulates can be refuted by 'direct observation' as it is to say that the existence of electrons can be so refuted. The postulation both of electrons and of these rules is based upon very indirect evidence. Ultimately the acceptance or rejection of these rules and also the acceptance or rejection of electrons will be in terms of their predictive capacity and their explanatory power. To suppose otherwise is to miss the entire point of their postulation.

Furthermore, to suppose that the existence of violations of grammatical rules in everyday speech counts against the theory is to misunderstand the theory completely. Chomsky wants to explain linguistic competence, not actual linguistic performance. Chomsky's theory purports to explain 'the behaviour of an ideal speaker, having perfect command of syntax and morphology, and free from . . . . memory lapses, slips of tongue and other irregularities'.[1] As is well known, idealization is an acceptable and crucial part of scientific theorizing. To argue against Chomsky in the way Hall does is thus to miss the point. One might as well argue against the laws of falling bodies by pointing out that a feather and an iron ball released from a second storey window will not hit the ground at the same time. These laws and Chomsky's theory apply only under certain idealized conditions.

Clearly then Malcolm's appeal to Hall as a linguistic authority lends no support to his thesis that cognitive structure is mythological. However, Malcolm has another argument, one which purports to show that the assumption of cognitive structure leads to 'an infinite regress, or else it leaves one with the same sort of "mystery" that led to postulating of a system or structure in the first place'.[2] His argument seems to be this: Cognitive psychologists postulate a system of rules R_1 to explain why people know how to perform some activity A_1 (speak a language, recognize a pattern). However, this does not explain how people know how to A_2 (use this system of rules R_1). Hence either (a) another set of rules R_2 needs to be postulated to explain why people know how to use A_2 and so on *ad infinitum*, or (b) people "just know how" to A_2. But if (b) one might as well say that they just know how to A_1.

The first thing to notice about Malcolm's argument is that it is not strictly speaking an infinite regress argument. We are not forced by the argument to go back and back forever. There is an important distinction to be drawn between two schemata:

(1) In order to explain why X knows how to A_n one must postulate a set of rules R_n that X knows how to use, where this using is symbolized by 'A_{n+1}'.

---

[1] Max Black, 'Comments on Noam Chomsky's Problems of Explanation in Linguistics', *Explanation in the Behavioural Sciences*, ed. Robert Borger and Frank Cioffi (Cambridge University Press, 1970), p. 453.
[2] Malcolm, *op. cit.*, p. 391.

(2) In order to explain why X knows how to A_n in terms of a set of rules R_n one must explain why X knows how to use R_n i.e. how to A_{n+1}.

Substituting in schema (1) does not lead to an infinite regress; what it leads to is an infinite series of explanations of the same sort (rule explanation).[1] However, in order to explain why X knows how to A_1 it is not necessary to *explain* why X knows how to use a system of rules R_1 (A_2) and so on. On the other hand, in schema (2) this is precisely what one has to do. One is forced into the position of not being able to explain one activity A_1 unless one can explain another activity A_2 and so forth *ad infinitum*. Clearly cognitive psychologists need not be committed to schema (2) in their explanatory activity.

Indeed, it is clear that they are not even committed to schema (1). They need not suppose that the explanation of why people know how to use certain rules postulated by them (in order to explain why people know how to recognize patterns, etc.) is itself explained by further postulation of rules people know how to use. Nor do psychologists have to say that people just know how to use such rules. Malcolm's argument here is based upon a false dichotomy: Either (a) an explanation of why people know how to do something is in terms of rules they know how to use, or (b) an explanation of why people know how to do something is 'They just know how'. Psychologists might attempt to explain why people know how to use such rules by neurological theories.[2] Such an explanation is presumably neither a rule explanation nor a 'They just know how' explanation.

Furthermore, psychologists might say that at the present time they don't know why people know how to use the rules they postulate. There is nothing scientifically suspect in this move. Any explanation in science that answers some question may raise another question that may be impossible to answer at that time, e.g. the question what is the explanation of this explanation. However, this does not show that no progress has been made. So long as the explanatory hypothesis meets the standard methodological requirements of testability, non-ad hocness, predictive power and so on and withstands critical test, progress has been made. Whether the explanatory hypotheses of the cognitive psychologists meet these standards is a big question.[3] However Malcolm's paper does not even attempt to answer this question.

[1] For an extended account of infinite regress arguments where this distinction is made, see John Passmore, *Philosophical Reasoning* (London: Gerald Duckworth and Company, 1961), Chapter 2.
[2] To be sure Malcolm has argued against these types of explanation. See Norman Malcolm, 'The Conceivability of Mechanism', *Philosophical Review*, 1968, pp. 45-72. However, his argument seems to have little merit. See Michael Martin, 'On the Conceivability of Mechanism', *Philosophy of Science*, 1971, pp. 79-86.
[3] For an illuminating critique of cognitive theories, see Robert Schwartz's review of J. Bruner, R. Oliver and P. Greenfield *et al.*, *Studies in Cognitive Growth*, in *Journal of Philosophy*, 65, 1968, pp. 172-179.

We may conclude, I think, that although cognitive processes and structure may be myths, Malcolm has not shown that they are.

Boston University

THEORETICAL PLURALISM

MICHAEL MARTIN

In recent years a number of philosophers of science have advocated a position that has been called Theoretical Pluralism. In this paper I will attempt to clarify what Theoretical Pluralism is, the claims made for it, and the problems involved in evaluating it.

THE ADVOCATES

Theoretical Pluralism has received its most articulated formulation in recent years from Karl Popper and his pupils. The name "Theoretical Pluralism" has been most often associated with Paul Feyerabend,[1] a pupil of Popper's, who explicitly acknowledges his debt to Popper.[2] Theoretical Pluralism has also been advocated by Noretta Koertge who acknowledges her debt to Feyerabend and Popper.[3] Some form of Theoretical Pluralism has also been advocated by Imre Lakatos, a student of Popper's.[4]

This is not to say that there are not great methodological differences between these Popperians. Popper and Koertge, for example, stress the possibility of comparing theories. Feyerabend stresses the impossibility of doing this. Nevertheless, despite these differences in methodological points of view, they agree on Theoretical Pluralism. This suggests that Theoretical Pluralism is a methodological position that might be held by people with other important methodological differences between them.

Indeed, despite the close association between Theoretical Pluralism and Popperianism there does not seem to be any necessity in this association. Theoretical Pluralism is perfectly compatible with positions that would be considered inductivist or justificationist by Popperians. Thus there does not seem to be anything in the nature of Theoretical Pluralism abstractly stated that would have prevented it from having been embraced by Carnap, the archenemy of Popperian philosophers. In this regard it is significant that Feyerabend maintains that he is indebted to Popper as well as to philosophers not in the Popperian tradition for Theoretical Pluralism.[5]

THE STATUS OF THE CLAIM

Sometimes it is unclear if the advocates of Theoretical Pluralism are putting forth a historical claim or a methodological position or both. Lakatos seems to be doing both. He says, "the history of science has been and should be a history of competing research programmes..."[6] In this paper we will assume that the claim is a purely methodological one. Thus Theoretical Pluralism will not be interpreted as a claim about the history of science. Rather it will be interpreted as a claim about what science should do in order to achieve certain aims.

To be sure, it may be necessary to examine the history of science in order to gather evidence to support or refute the methodological claim. For the history of science may show that science does not achieve the desired aim if it does what Theoretical Pluralism, methodologically interpreted, says it should. But although certain historical evidence may be relevant in evaluating Theoretical Pluralism when interpreted methodologically, it does not follow that Theoretical Pluralism is a historical thesis.

For our purposes, then, it will be convenient to state Theoretical Pluralism in the form of a maxim or a directive. Now as we have seen, advocates of Theoretical Pluralism have supposed that Theoretical Pluralism will bring about certain results. Thus Theoretical Pluralism may be interpreted as a hypothetical imperative of the following form:

(1) If you want result R, then do X.

It will be more convenient, however, to state Theoretical

Pluralism in categorical form:
 (2) Do X!
However, it should be understood that (2) is implicitly hypothetical; its fruitfulness is relative to certain results R that are supposed to be achieved by following (2).

We will consider in a moment what X is and what result R is supposed to be.

LAKATOS' METHODOLOGY OF SCIENTIFIC RESEARCH PROGRAMS

So far the most sophisticated account of Theoretical Pluralism has been that of Lakatos in "Methodology of Scientific Research Programs." Lakatos characterizes a scientific research program as consisting of three parts. First, a hard core of theory. Second, a negative heuristic. This consists of methodological rules which have two purposes:
(1) they protect the hard core from refutation by directing us to modify auxilliary hypotheses rather than change the hard core;
(2) they rule out radically different sorts of explanatory attempts.
Third, a positive heuristic. This consists of rules that guide the improvements in the theory's explanatory models. Following this research program generates a series of theories each one with the same hard core but different from the earlier theory because of variation in the auxilliary hypotheses.

Now according to Lakatos, all research programs have the above characteristics. However, only some research programs will be in a "progress phase." A research program is in a progress phase if each successive member of the series can make interesting new predictions which are corroborated. Thus progress for a research program is defined completely in terms of ability to make interesting new corroborated predictions.

Progress so characterized is quite compatible with a series of theories that are increasingly more complex, *ad hoc*, and unwieldy. Hence, it has been suggested by Koertge that Lakatos' requirements of progress might be strengthened by adding a requirement of simplicity.[7] In a progress phase each new theory would have to make new corroborated predictions but also be more coherent and unified than the preceding one. It will be convenient for our purposes to accept Koertge's suggestion, and we will assume in what follows that progress in a research program is characterized both by increased corroboration and increased unity and coherence.

EXTREME THEORETICAL PLURALISM AND ITS ALTERNATIVES

Given Lakatos' characterization of a scientific research program, we can characterize two methodological positions. The one we will call Theoretical Monism (TM) and the other Extreme Theoretical Pluralism (ETP).

TM: Do not develop alternative research programs in any science at any stage of development if the prevailing research program is progressive!

Now advocates of Theoretical Pluralism have argued that following TM will not lead to the greatest amount of scientific progress. They have argued that alternative research programs are essential for maximal scientific progress. The result R mentioned above is thus maximal scientific progress. We shall interpret Theoretical Pluralism in its most extreme form as follows:

ETP: Develop as many alternative research programs as possible in all sciences at all stages of development whether the prevailing research program is progressive or not!

Now it should be noted that even if acting on ETP were to bring about maximal scientific progress, it would not follow that ETP should be acted on. Suppose, for example, that a side effect of developing as many alternative research programs as possible in all branches of science were the loss of individual liberty or unacceptable state intervention. In short, suppose that scientific progress occurred at a maximum rate only when an undesirable political situation existed, e.g., a political regime which forced people to develop as many alternative research approaches as possible. This unacceptable political situation might outweigh any advantages that resulted from maximal scientific progress. Therefore, even if following ETP were to bring about maximal scientific progress, this would not show that maximal scientific progress was on balance desirable.

In order not to complicate the argument we will suppose that this supposition is true. Thus we will ignore for the sake of simplicity all possible undesirable ethical and political side effects of following the methodological maxims.

Now it is clear that ETP is not the only alternative to TM. Indeed, there are at least three ways in which alternative methodological maxims could be specified.

(1) There might be certain branches of science where many alternatives would not be necessary for maximum progress although in other branches many alternatives would be necessary. Perhaps in the natural sciences many alternative research programs would be most fruitful, whereas in the social sciences many alternative research programs would not be most fruitful.

(2) Furthermore, alternative research programs might be of great methodological advantage for scientific progress at certain periods and not at other periods. Thus, one might argue that for certain periods in the development of a science what is needed is consolidation of existing theories and not alternatives. What exactly these periods might be is a question we need not go into now, but they might be periods shortly after major conceptual innovation and revolution. Whatever the historical problems connected with Kuhn's periods of normal science where alternatives to accepted paradigms are not supposed to exist, there may be some methodological advantages for the growth of science in such periods. Thus, even if Kuhn is wrong and there are no periods of normal science as he describes them, it might be a good idea to create them so as to further the development of science.

(3) It might not be any more methodologically fruitful to have as many alternatives as possible as to have some lesser number. Perhaps several alternative research programs or even one or two is enough for maximum progress. Indeed, concentrating on developing many alternative research programs may in

fact hinder critical testing, since so much time and energy would go into developing alternatives that there would be little time or energy left to critically test and compare them.

Thus there might be an equilibrium point in developing alternative research programs, which has a maximum effect on the growth of science. Any more or any fewer alternatives would decrease scientific progress. Furthermore, such an equilibrium point might vary from science to science and from period to period in the development of science.

We can see that there are many different methodological maxims depending on the combinations of the three variables considered above. For example,

(1) Develop in advanced sciences (but not an immature one) after long periods without major conceptual innovations (but not immediately after such innovations) as many alternative research programs as possible, whether the prevailing research programs are progressive or not!

(2) Develop in all branches of science after a long period without major conceptual innovations (but not immediately after such innovations) a few alternative research programs (but not as many as possible), whether the prevailing research program is progressive or not!

THE EVALUATION OF ALTERNATIVES

Could such alternative methodological maxims be evaluated? I assume that they could but it would be difficult.

Historical evidence is often indecisive unless some sort of comparative study is made. Thus, showing that physical science progressed rapidly when many alternative research programs were used does not show that such progress could not have been achieved or even surpassed with only a few alternatives. What is needed, it seems to me, is more comparative historical research and less citing of isolated cases. One might compare the growth of some sciences during periods where few alternative research programs were used, periods where many alternatives were used, and periods where no alternatives were used. As far as I know no historical research of this kind has been done.

Another suggestion would be to compare the different research traditions in different countries during the same time. Does Russian social science have fewer alternative research programs than Western social science? If so, has its social science shown less growth? If it has not shown less growth, this might tend to eliminate some alternative methodological maxims. However, even here alternative explanations are possible.

Another possibility is that of setting up something like a controlled experiment. Let several groups of scientists work on a particular, rather esoteric branch of science. Encourage one group to develop as many research approaches as they can, another group to develop only a few alternative research approaches, and the third group only to refine the one they start with. Try to isolate each group from the other and from the scientific community as a whole. After a certain length of time compare the results of each group's activity. To be sure, such a study has large methodological problems, but something like it is possible in principle and might well give us much more reliable knowledge than we have now.

In testing these alternative maxims we have presupposed that we have a clear idea about what scientific progress means. But this is by no means so. To be sure we have a fairly clear idea of what progress means relative to a research program: new corroborated predictions and increased coherence. But what would progress mean when we are not talking about some particular research program? Certainly we would have to characterize the progress of science independently of the development of many research programs. For unless such an independent characterization was given, the progress of science would necessarily involve the development of many alternative research programs. No possible evidence would be counted as negative evidence in respect to Theoretical Pluralism.

One suggestion is this: We might use the criteria we have already specified for progress in particular research programs: new corroborated predictions and coherence. To say that a period P_1 of a science S shows more progress than some other period P_2 of S is to say that there is at least one research program RP in P_1 that is more progressive (in the sense defined above) than any RP in period P_2.

Such a characterization would not beg any questions concerning Theoretical Pluralism. It would be possible to have a period of science with only one research program that was more progressive than some other period with more than one research program.

A similar sort of definition could be used to characterize the progress shown among two groups of scientists. For example, group G_1 of scientists shows more progress during some particular period P than group G_2 if and only if there is at least one research program RP used by G_1 during P that is more progressive than any research program used by G_2 during P. Again, this definition prevents any questions from being begged with respect to Theoretical Pluralism. It would be possible for G_1 to use only one research program whereas G_2 might use several.

Still there is something not completely satisfactory about such an account. One supposes on intuitive grounds that a research program in one period P_1 might be more progressive (in the sense of increased corroborated content and coherence) than any other research program in another period P_2 and yet that more scientific progress would have been made in P_2. What is the basis of this intuitive feeling? Two suggestions come to mind.

(1) Perhaps progress for a period of science cannot be defined completely in terms of coherence and corroboration. Other more elusive criteria, for example the depth of the problems solved by the hard core of theory, may be relevant.[8] Thus, for example, one period P_1 may be more progressive in the sense of corroborated predictions and coherence than some other period P_2 and yet on intuitive grounds not be as progressive as the other period in some more important sense in which "deeper" problems are solved. It is unclear, however, just how the notion of deeper problems should be analyzed.

(2) There might be another basis for the dissatisfaction with the above characterization. The progress of science in a given

period may not be a function of just the most progressive research program in the period. Progress may be the function of the combined progress of several research programs. How such combinations could be clearly articulated is not obvious. There does not appear to be any readily available general way of "adding" the progress of research program RP_1 and research program RP_2 in period P_1 and getting a "sum" that is greater than the progress of research program RP_3 in period P_2.

Still there are obvious cases in which such comparative judgements could be made. Suppose there is only one research program PR_3 in period P_2, whereas there are two research programs RP_1 and RP_2 in period P_1. Now suppose that RP_1 is just as progressive as RP_3 and RP_2 is just as progressive as RP_3. Suppose furthermore that the theories in RP_1 can make corroborated predictions which the theories in RP_2 cannot make and vice versa. In short, suppose that the predictive ability of the theories in RP_1 and RP_2 complement each other. In this case it would seem plausible to suppose that there was more progress in period P_1 than P_2 despite the fact that no single research program in P_1 was more progressive than any in P_2. Other clear cases where comparative judgments can be made come quickly to mind.

In any case, unless we have some clarification of what scientific progress means it is difficult to evaluate the claims of Theoretical Pluralism and to evaluate the fruitfulness for scientific progress of the alternative methodological maxims specified above. However, what is most unfortunate is that the advocates of Theoretical Pluralism do not seem to see the need for spelling out the variants and varieties of Theoretical Pluralism, or the need to evaluate these alternatives in any systematic way. Until this evaluation is done Theoretical Pluralism will remain little more than a methodological dogma.

BOSTON UNIVERSITY
BOSTON, MASSACHUSETTS 02215
USA

MICHAEL MARTIN

NOTES

[1] Paul Feyerabend, "Explanation, Reduction, and Empiricism," *Minnesota Studies in the Philosophy of Science*, Volume III, eds. H. Feigl and G. Maxwell (Minneapolis: University of Minnesota Press, 1962); Paul Feyerabend, "How to be a Good Empiricist," *Delaware Seminar in Philosophy of Science*, Volume II, ed. B. Baumrin (New York: Interscience Pub. 1963).

[2] Paul Feyerabend, "Reply to Criticism," *Boston Studies in the Philosophy of Science*, Volume II, eds. R.S. Cohen and Marx W. Wartofsky (New York: Humanities Press, 1965), pp. 252–253, note 5.

[3] Noretta Koertge, "Inter-Theoretic Criticism and the Growth of Science," paper read at the *Philosophy of Science Association* meeting, Boston, Massachusetts, October 24, 1970. See also Noretta Koertge, "Theoretical Pluralism, Criticism, and Education," paper read at a conference on New Directions in Philosophy of Education, held at the Ontario Institute for Studies in Education, Toronto, in May 1970.

[4] Imre Lakatos, "Falsification and the Methodology of Scientific Research Programmes," in *Criticism and the Growth of Knowledge*, eds. Imre Lakatos and Allan Musgrave (Cambridge University Press, 1970), pp. 91–195.

[5] Feyerabend finds similar ideas in Naess and Boltzmann. See Feyerabend, "Reply to Criticism," *op. cit.*

[6] Lakatos, *op cit*, p. 155. For some unexplained reason Koertge in "Inter-Theoretic Criticism and the Growth of Science" interprets Lakatos as not advocating theoretic pluralism. But the above quotation and many others that could be cited indicate that she is quite mistaken.

[7] Koertge, *op cit*.

[8] This criterion is suggested by some remarks of Koertge, *op cit*.

PART II: OBJECTIVITY AND VALUE JUDGEMENTS

Methodologists have sometimes claimed that there are fundamental differences between the methodology of the social sciences and the methodology of the natural sciences. One alleged difference is this: natural science methodology is objective and furthermore the results of using this method are objective; social science methodology is subjective and the results of using this method are subjective.

By "subjective" and "objective" two things could be meant. First, the subjective-objective contrast might be simply the contrast between inner mental phenomena and other kinds of phenomena. The claim that social scientific findings are subjective would mean that social scientific findings are about inner mental phenomena; the claim that social scientific methodology is subjective is harder to interpret, given this understanding of "subjective," but it might simply be the claim that the methodology of the social sciences results in findings about inner mental phenomena.

Given this understanding of "subjective" there is some truth to the view that social science findings are subjective. Some psychological research, for example in psycho-physics and clinical psychology, does result in findings about inner mental phenomena. Since these findings result from the use of social science methodology, social science methodology is subjective. However, not all social science findings are subjective in this sense. For example, much research in macro-economics and demography has little to do with establishing facts about inner mental events and processes. So it is not true that all social scientific research findings are subjective in this sense.

In any case, this psychological sense of subjectivity is usually not what people have in mind when they say that social science is subjective and natural science is not. What is usually meant is that the findings of social science are biased and unreliable and, since the methodology of social science leads to such results, this methodology is biased and unreliable as well. This claim would be a very serious one if it could be shown to be true and there have been numerous attempts to do precisely this. In four of the five papers in this section I consider critically various arguments which attempt to show that social science is subjective in this second sense.

A popular view maintains that the scientist qua scientist does not make value judgements. On this view scientists establish laws and theories into which no value judgements enter. To be sure, once these laws and theories are established, value judgements may enter into the process of deciding how to apply the laws and theories for social good or ill. But such value judgements are not made by scientists; rather they are made by politicians, planners and citizens, some of whom may be scientists but, if they are, they are not acting in that capacity during this decision process.

This view of scientific objectivity has been challenged. Indeed it has been maintained that some value judgements enter into the very fabric of social scientific research. Thus it is argued that social scientists qua social scientists make value judgements and, since value judgements have no objective basis, subjectivity is an essential part of social scientific research.

The contention that scientists are committed to certain value judgements in accepting a scientific hypothesis, hence that acceptance is not just a function of the evidence at a scientist's disposal, but is partly a function of the values to be realized in accepting the hypothesis, is considered in "Value Judgements and the Acceptance of Hypotheses in Science and Science Education."[1] This essay makes it clear that the contention under examination is completely general: it holds for the natural sciences as well as the social sciences. No difference between the two can be shown by its argument.

In "Description and Objectivity" the argument that social scientists via their descriptions of phenomena are committed to certain value judgements and, since such value judgements are subjective, the social sciences are also subjective is considered. After careful analysis this argument is refuted. It is shown that social scientists are not in any important sense committed to value judgements by their descriptions and that, even if they were, the objectivity of the social sciences would not be seriously impaired.

In "Causal Importance and Objectivity"[2] the argument that the objectivity of the social sciences is compromised by the judgements of causal importance which social scientists make is evaluated. According to this argument, such judgements presuppose value judgements. In this paper several strategies are outlined which can be used to maintain the objectivity of the social sciences in the face of this argument.

Not all arguments against the objectivity of the social sciences turn on the use of value judgements by social scientists qua social scientists. The alleged lack of objectivity in the social sciences is sometimes attributed to experimental bias: an experimenter expects certain results, this expectation influences the results of the experiment; consequently the results of the experiment are biased and unreliable. The phenomenon of experimental bias has been studied extensively by Robert Rosenthal. In "The Philosophical Importance of the Rosenthal Effect" the problem of the objectivity of the social sciences is considered in the light of Rosenthal's work. I maintain that Rosenthal's studies do not show that the social sciences are necessarily subjective. Indeed Rosenthal's work has shown how objectivity is possible.

In the fifth and last paper of this section a different type of problem is considered. So far I have only hinted at the nature of the objectivity of scientific methodology. A rigorous and elaborate analysis of the objectivity of scientific methodology has been given by Richard Rudner and in "The Objectivity of Methodology" Rudner's views are critically evaluated.

Footnotes

1. See Alex C. Michalos, "Values in Science and Science Education," Philosophic Exchange, 1, 1973, 103-106 and K. Thomas Finley "Some Problems in Communication Between Philosopher and Scientist (An Asymptomatic Approach to Truth)" Philosophical Exchange, 1, 1973, 109-112, for comment on this paper.

2. This paper has been criticized by R.G. Frey in "Judgments of Causal Importance in the Social Sciences," Philosophy of the Social Sciences, 6, 1977, 245-248. My reply, "Judgements of Contributory Cause and Objectivity," Philosophy of the Social Science, and Frey's rejoinder, "Contributory Causation and the Objectivity of the Social Science," are forthcoming in Philosophy of Social Science.

Description and Objectivity

One crucial attack against the objectivity of the social sciences is by means of an argument that purports to show that the objectivity of the social sciences is compromised by the descriptions social scientists give of social phenomena. In this paper the attack will be critically considered. This argument can be stated as follows:

(1) If social science is objective, then the descriptions social scientists give of social phenomena do not commit them to value judgments.

(2) But the descriptions social scientists give of social phenomena do commit them to value judgments.

---

(3) .˙. Social science is not objective.

Now critics of the objectivity of the social sciences have held premise (1) because they have supposed that value judgments are not objective; that such judgments are not capable of rational defense. We will examine this assumption as we proceed. The evaluation of premises (1) and (2) will turn on the meaning of "commitment to value judgments." Consequently we will consider various interpretations of this expression.

First, however, an ambiguity should be noted in premise (1). The phrase "the descriptions social scientists give of social phenomena" could refer to descriptions social scientists give any social phenomena or it could refer to the descriptions social scientists give some particular social phenomena, say social phenomena of type T. Once this ambiguity is made explicit we have two different arguments with different first premises:

(1a) If social science is objective, then the descriptions social scientists give of any social phenomena do not commit them to value judgments.

(1b) If social science is objective, then the descriptions social scientists give of social phenomena of type T do not commit them to value judgments.

This ambiguity would affect the second premise of the argument and would yield:

(2a) But the descriptions social scientists give of any social phenomena do commit them to value judgments.

(2b) But the descriptions social scientists give of social phenomena of type T do commit them to value judgments.

Clearly an argument containing premises (1a) and (2a) would be much more challenging than an argument containing premises (1b) and (2b). For even if (1b) were true, it would still be possible for (2b) to be defeated: social scientists could simply elect not to describe social phenomena of type T. Consequently (2b) would be false. There would be no commitment to value judgments since there would be no description of social phenomena of type T. However, such a result is achieved at a certain price. Phenomena of type T would be put beyond the pole of scientific investigation. Whether objectivity is worth this price is an open question.

An analogous move is hardly open to us in the case of (2a). Social scientists do not have the option of not describing any social phenomena unless they are willing to give up doing social science.

Commitment to Value Judgments

In order to evaluate the two arguments some spade work is necessary. What does it mean to be committed to a value judgment?

One thing it might mean is that a sentence used by a social scientist describing some phenomenon entails a value judgment. Suppose a social scientist S describes social phenomenon X as having property P. This could be stated as follows:

(A) X is P.

And suppose that (A) entails the value judgment:

(3) X is good.

Then one can say that S's description of X commits S to a value judgment. Let us call this "the abstract logical sense of value judgment commitment."

In general, descriptive statements of the form (A) do not entail value judgments of the form (B) unless it is implicitly or explicitly assumed that the descriptive terms used stand in some particular semantic relation with certain evaluative terms, e.g. "is good." For example, one might assume that "is P" and "is good" are identical in meaning, i.e. one might assume as a premise:

(C) "is P" means the same as "is good."

Or one might assume

(D) "All P's are good" is analytic.

If one assumes premises like these, (B) follows from (A); otherwise the move from (A) to (B) is logically illegitimate.

However, the abstract logical sense of value commitment is not the only sense in which social scientists might be said to be committed to value judgments. Let us say that a social scientist S has an actual cognitive commitment to a value judgment J because of a descriptive statement M where S's belief that M influences S (in combination with S's other beliefs and attitudes) to believe that J. It is important to see that a social scientist can be committed to a value judgment in the abstract logical sense without an actual cognitive commitment. Thus M may entail J and yet for various reasons S may believe that M and not believe that J. In such a case S would have an abstract logical commitment to J because of M, but not an actual cognitive commitment. The converse is also true. M may not entail J and yet S's belief that M may influence S to believe that J.

There is another type of value commitment a social scientists might have on the basis of descriptive statements. Let us say that a social scientist S has an actual affective commitment to a value judgment J when S's belief that M influences S (in conjunction with S's other beliefs and attitudes) to have a feeling of approval or disapproval toward what the value judgment J is about. As in the case of actual cognitive commitments a social scientist can have an abstract logical commitment to a value judgment J on the basis of his belief that M and yet have no actual affective commitment. The converse is also true.

Now some cases in which a social scientist has an actual cognitive or affective commitment to a value judgment because of a descriptive statement are cases of rational commitment and some cases are not. For example, suppose a social scientist S is committed in the abstract logical sense to (B) because of (A). Suppose further that S believes that (D) as well as (A). Then S should have on rational grounds a feeling of approval towards X. If S does, then we can say that S has an actual cognitive and affective commitment to (B) which is rational; if S does not, we can say that S has no actual cognitive or affective commitment to (B) but S has both a <u>rational cognitive commitment</u> to (B) and a <u>rational affective commitment</u> to (B).

A social scientist S might not be committed to a value judgment in the rational commitment sense and still have an actual cognitive and affective commitment to the value judgment. Suppose that S's belief that (A) combined with S's other beliefs and attitudes influences S to believe that (B) and to have a strong feeling of approval toward X. However, let us suppose that in terms of (A) and S's beliefs about (C) or (D) there is not any reason for S to believe that (B). Then S is not committed in the abstract logical sense and yet has an actual commitment in the cognitive and affective sense.

For our purposes the abstract logical sense of commitment is the most important.

First, consider commitment in the actual cognitive and affective sense. Commitment in this sense is a purely psychological phenomenon. Whether social scientists are committed to value judgments in this sense is a result of their particular psychological make-up -- whether they are rational, whether they have certain beliefs about the semantic relation between descriptive and evaluative terms and so on. If we understand premises (1a) and (1b) to be about all social scientists, the truth of these premises becomes very dubious given this interpretation of commitment. Furthermore, even if (1a) and (1b) are true, commitment in this sense is subject to change. Given different social scientists, or the same social scientist trained or conditioned in certain ways the premise might be false. It is quite conceivable that with proper training no social scientist would be committed to value judgments in this sense.

But such an implication seems quite foreign to the spirit of the argument. Critics of the objectivity of the social sciences surely want to maintain that the lack of objectivity of the social sciences is not a function of the psychological make-up of social scientists; that objectivity is possible with different training. No, the problem according to the critic is much deeper. We can then ignore commitment to value judgments in the actual cognitive or actual affective sense of commitment in our discussion.

Next consider the rational sense of commitment in either the cognitive or the affective sense. This sense of commitment does not refer merely to psychological phenomena: it is concerned with what people should believe and what attitudes they should have. However, this sense of commitment is dependent on the abstract logical sense. For, as we have seen, whether a social scientist S should believe that (B) given that S believes (A) is dependent in part on whether S is committed to (B) in the abstract logical sense, that is, whether (A) entails (B) given premises like (C) or (D). Thus, if we can show that there are serious problems with either (1a) or (1b), as interpreted in the abstract logical sense, we will have shown that there are serious problems with (1a) or (1b) when interpreted in the rational commitment sense.

However, whether social scientists are committed to value judgments in the abstract logical sense depends to a certain extent on what sort of value judgment one is talking about. For example, a social scientist who describes a legal system may be committed to certain judgments of legal obligation. But such a description would not necessarily commit him to any judgment of moral obligation. For, in general, judgments of legal duty entail nothing about moral duty. Moreover, a description of a particular act may commit a social scientist to a judgment of _prima facie_ moral obligation without the social scientist being committed to a judgment of actual moral obligation. In order to derive statements of actual duty from statements of _prima facie_ duty one must also assume that other things are equal. Furthermore, the description of an institution as having such and such a function may entail that it is a good institution for a certain purpose, i.e. that it has instrumental value in producing such and such results. But there is nothing in this description which entails that the institution is intrinsically good. Hence, a social scientist who uses such a description would not be committed to a judgment of intrinsic value. A social scientist may be committed to a hypothetical value judgment without being committed to a categorical one. For example, he might be committed to the hypothetical value judgment "If gratuitous suffering of animals is wrong, then vivisection is wrong" without being committed in the abstract logical sense to either the categorical judgment that vivisection is wrong or gratuitous suffering of animals is wrong.

The importance of the above point to our discussion of objectivity is this: What sort of value judgment one is talking about is crucial for the question of whether the judgments are capable of rational defense. For example, I will argue later that judgments of instrumental value are capable of rational defense even though arguments of intrinsic value may not be; I will argue that judgments of legal obligation are capable of rational defense even though judgments of moral obligation may not be. I will maintain that certain hypothetical value judgments are capable of rational defense even though categorical judgments of moral obligation may not be. Thus, although a social scientist is committed in the abstract logical sense to a value judgment this does not by itself show that he is committed to a judgment that is rationally indefensible and consequently subjective. One must determine what sort of value judgment the social scientist is committed to.

One of the few philosophers of science to discuss the possibility that social scientists are committed to value judgment <u>via</u> their descriptions is Ernest Nagel. Nagel distinguishes between two types of value judgments. He argues that there are "two quite different senses of the term 'value judgment': the sense in which a value judgment expresses <u>approval or disapproval</u> either of some moral (or social) ideal, or of some action (or institution) because of a commitment to such an ideal: and the sense in which a value judgment expresses <u>an estimate</u> of the degree to which some commonly recognized (and more or less clearly defined) type of action, object, or institution is embodied in a given instance."[1] The first type he calls an appraising value judgment; the second type a characterizing value judgment.

According to Nagel appraising judgments entail characterizing judgments but not conversely. Thus if one uses "X is P" as a characterizing value judgment one does not express one's approval or disapproval of X, that is, one does not use "X is P" as an appraising value judgment. However, if one uses "X is P" as an appraising value judgment, one also uses "X is P" as a characterizing value judgment.

Nagel's distinction is no doubt a useful one. However, it does not show, as he seems to think it does, that the use of descriptive statements (what he calls characterizing value judgments) by social scientists does not commit them to value judgments. For Nagel's major point seems to be that a social scientist can use a characterizing value judgment without thereby expressing any feeling of approval or

---

[1] Ernest Nagel, <u>The Structure of Science</u> (New York: Harcourt, Brace and World, 1961) p. 492.

disapproval (without using an appraising value judgment). This, as we have seen, is certainly correct. A social scientist can use any descriptive statement without having -- let alone expressing by the use of this statement -- any feeling of approval or disapproval towards what he describes. However, once this is admitted it is still possible that a social scientist might be committed to value judgments by the use of his descriptive statements. As we have seen, a social scientist can use a descriptive statement (what Nagel call's a characterizing value judgment) and be committed to a value judgment in the abstract logical sense, in the rational cognitive sense and in the rational affective sense. This is perfectly compatible with the social scientist's not expressing approval or disapproval by the use of a statement; that is, with his not making what Nagel calls an appraising value judgment.

An Argument For Premise (2a)

So far we have considered a general argument that purports to show that social scientists are not objective because their descriptions of social phenomena commit them to value judgments. Under analysis this argument became two arguments depending on how one interpreted the premises. On the strongest interpretation of the argument, social scientists were committed to value judgments by their descriptions of any social phenomena. Thus, premise (2) of the argument becomes under this strong interpretation:

(2a) But the descriptions social scientists give of any social phenomena do commit them to value judgments.

An argument for (2a) can be derived from an example used by Max Black.[2] Consider the premise:

(4) Vivisection causes gratuitous suffering.

This surely is a purely descriptive statement. Yet one can deduce from (4):

(5) If nothing that causes gratuitous suffering ought to be done, vivisection ought not to be done.

[2] Max Black, "The Gap Between 'Is' and 'Should,'" Philosophical Forum, LXXIII, 1964, pp. 165-181; for more examples of this kind see David R. Kurtzman, "'Is,' 'Ought' and the Autonomy of Ethics," Philosophical Review LXXIX, 1970, pp. 493-509.

It should be stressed that (4) entails (5) (unlike the examples we considered above) without the addition of any hidden premises about the semantic relation between descriptive terms and evaluative terms; the entailment depends entirely on the form of the statement. Consequently any social scientist using a statement of the form "All actions A are actions B" is committed in the abstract logical sense of commitment to a statement of the form "If all actions B ought not to be done, then all actions A ought not to be done."

It is important to notice that by the same sort of argument one can deduce from (4):

(6) If anything causing gratuitous suffering ought to be done, vivisection ought to be done.

Consequently any social scientist using a descriptive statement of the form "All actions A are actions B" is also committed in the abstract logical sense to a statement of the form "If all actions B ought to be done, then all actions A ought to be done."

Indeed, a more general result is inferable. A social scientist who uses a sentence of the form "All A's are B" is committed in the abstract logical sense to a sentence of the form "If all B's are G, then all A's are G" where G is any evaluative term at all.

One might suppose that social scientists could avoid this abstract logical commitment by not using statements of the form "All A's are B" and restricting themselves to singular statements. However, this is not so. Consider a singular statement which says that some particular item a has property P. It can be shown that this statement entails "If all things which are P are G, then a is G" where G is any evaluative term at all. A similar result can be demonstrated for existential statements and statistical statements.

Thus Black's argument does establish premise (2a), for presumably any descriptive statement a social scientist makes will be either a singular statement, an existential statement, a general statement, or a statistical statement and all of these statements commit social scientists in the abstract logical sense to value judgments.

Black uses his example to show that, despite Hume's pronouncement to contrary, some ought-propositions can be derived from is-propositions. But he does not attach much importance to the particular example cited above, for he appears to think that the derived value judgment is trivial. The significance of Black's example for the traditional philosophical question of whether ought-propositions can be derived from is-propositions will not be at issue here. We will show, however, that Black's example and the general result extracted from it have very little significance for the question of the value-free nature of the social sciences and the question of the objectivity of the social sciences.

First, although Black's argument shows that natural scientists as well as social scientists are committed in the abstract logical sense to certain hypothetical value judgments by any descriptive statement they make, the results generalized from Black's example are completely neutral with respect to what the descriptive statements are about. Consider the following descriptive statement from the natural sciences.

(7) Object a weighs three grams.

This statement entails:

(8) If everything that weighs three grams is intrinsically good, then object a is intrinsically good.

Thus, Black's example and the results generalized from it cannot be used to show any difference between the social sciences and the natural sciences with respect to freedom from value judgments.

Secondly, given Black's argument it is difficult to see how premise (1a) of the argument could be upheld. This premise is stated as follows:

(1a) If social science is objective, then the descriptions social scientists give of any social phenomenon do not commit them to value judgments.

There seems to be no good reason why the objectivity of social science would necessarily mean not being committed in the abstract logical sense to the sort of hypothetical value judgments involved in Black's argument. In the natural sciences it would surely be implausible to suppose that propositions like (8) are not rationally defensible since they follow directly from propositions like (7) which surely are rationally defensible. There is no _a priori_ reason to suppose that the situation would be any different in the social sciences than it is in the natural sciences.

What is needed in order to establish premises (1a) and (2a)

is some argument that would show that social scientists by
their description of <u>all</u> social phenomena are committed to
value judgments which are not rationally defensible whereas natural scientists by their descriptive statements are
either not committed to value judgments or committed to
value judgments which are rationally defensible. As we
have seen, Black's argument does not show this and it is
doubtful that any argument could. At least I know of no
argument that attempts to do so. The usual procedure is to
argue that descriptions of particular social phenomena commit social scientists to value judgments that cannot be
rationally defensible. Certainly this sort of argument
seems much more plausible.

Arguments for Premise (2b)

These considerations take us to premise (2b) which is
stated as follows:

(2b) But the description a social scientist gives social
phenomena of type T does commit him to value judgments.

It has been argued that the following sorts of descriptions commit social scientists to value judgments:

(a) Jones is authoritarian.

(b) Smith knows that Jones believes that he has been unjustly
treated.

(c) Evans is president of the B- Club.

(d) Jones uttered the words "I hereby promise to pay you,
Smith, five dollars."

It is alleged that the commitment is due to the particular
nature of the phenomenon involved. In what follows the arguments used to show that descriptions like (a) - (d) commit
social scientists to value judgments will be critically considered. If any of these arguments are sound, they would
seem to establish premise (2b). For any of the sorts of phenomena that (a) - (d) describe could be considered social
phenomena of type T.

Strauss' Argument

The political scientist Leo Strauss seems to be arguing

for a premise like premise (2b) when he says: "We must not overlook the invisible value judgments which are concealed from undiscerning eyes but nevertheless most powerfully present in allegedly purely descriptive concepts. For example when social scientists distinguish between democratic and authoritarian habits or types of human being, what they call 'authoritarian' is in all cases known to be a caricature of everything they, as good democrats of a certain kind, disapprove."³

Strauss' argument seems to be as follows:

(11) If a social scientist describes a person or trait as authoritarian, then the social scientist disapproves of the person or trait.

(12) If the social scientist disapproves of a person or a trait of a person, then his description of that trait or person as authoritarian commits him to the value judgment that the trait or person is bad.

---

(13) If a social scientist describes a trait or a person as authoritarian, then he is committed to the value judgment that the trait or person is bad.

There is some serious question about the soundness of this argument. First, the truth of premise (11) is surely dubious. It is certainly not obvious that all social scientists who describe a trait or person as authoritarian disapprove of the trait or person. Certainly if one includes social scientists from countries (something that Strauss does not seem to consider) in which democracy is not the established form of government, indeed where democracy is frowned upon, it is unlikely that they would disapprove of authoritarian phenomena when they use the term "authoritarian."

Secondly even if all social scientists did disapprove of authoritarian traits or persons it would not follow that when they said "X was authoritarian" they were thereby committed to the value judgment, "X is morally bad or un-

---

³Leo Strauss, "The Social Sciences Cannot be Value Free," *The Nature and Scope of Social Science: A Critical Anthology*, ed. Leonard Krimerman (New York: Appleton Century-Crofts, 1969), p. 738.

desirable" in several important senses of "committed."

Consider the abstract logical sense of commitment. It is dubious that:

(A') X is authoritarian

as it is used in scientific contexts entails the judgment of moral value:

(B') is morally bad.

There is nothing obviously contradictory in saying "X is authoritarian and X is not morally bad." There does not seem to be any clear semantic link between an ethical term like "morally bad" and a descriptive term like "authoritarian."

To see this in greater detail let us take what social scientists mean by authoritarian and one common definition of morally bad. Social scientists distinguish between "authoritarian submission" and "authoritarian aggression." A person is authoritarian submissive when he has a submissive uncritical attitude towards the idealized moral authorities of the in-groups; a person is authoritarian aggressive when he has a "tendency to be on the look out for, and to condemn, reject and punish people who violate conventional values."[4] A common account of morally bad is a mixed denotological account. On this account to be morally bad would mean roughly "having the tendency to be either unjust or not benevolent."[5] It is not obvious that one can infer from the mere fact that something is authoritarian submissive or authoritarian aggressive that it is morally bad in this sense. Such an inference could only be made with the added - presumably moral premise - that an authoritarian tendency as so defined is unjust or not benevolent. One might argue, for example:

(C') A tendency to be on the look out for, to condemn, reject and punish people who violate conventional values is not benevolent.

[4]H. J. Eysenck, Uses and Abuses of Psychology, Penguin Books, 1959, p. 270.

[5]William Frankena, Ethics, (Englewood Cliffs, New Jersey, Prentice-Hall, 1963), pp. 37-42.

Such a premise or one similar to it seems to be absolutely essential for the inference to succeed. However, this is just to say that (A') does not by itself entail (B') unless it is combined with a moral premise. Furthermore, premise (C') does not seem to be analytic. There does not seem to be any contradiction in saying that the tendency to be on the look out for, to condemn, reject and punish people who violate conventional values is benevolent.

Consider now the rational cognitive sense of commitment. There is nothing in the nature of the case that would suggest that a social scientist who believed that X is authoritarian would fail to be rational if he did not believe that X is morally bad: For example, he might believe that there is no semantic link between "is authoritarian" and "is morally bad."

The same thing is true about the rational affective sense of commitment. A social scientist who believed that X is authoritarian would not necessarily be irrational if he did not disapprove of X. For example, he might not believe that there is any semantic link between "is authoritarian" and "is morally bad." Consequently, he would not believe that X is morally bad and thus not disapprove of X. Moreover, even if a social scientist did have a feeling of disapproval toward X, there might be nothing in his belief that X is authoritarian that made his feeling of disapproval a rational outcome of his particular belief. Consequently, it is not inconsistent for a social scientist who disapproves of an authoritarian trait or person to say "X is authoritarian; however, nothing I have said so far indicates whether I should believe that X is morally bad or whether I should feel disapproval toward X."

To be sure, if someone disapproves of X because X is authoritarian, then by definition he is actually cognitively or affectively committed to the value judgment "X is bad." But, as we have seen, this may be a function of his peculiar psychological make up and there may be no rational reason at all for him to be committed to this value judgment.

Strauss' Argument thus fails as an attempt to establish (2b) in any significant sense.

Krimerman's Argument

A different argument for premise (2b) has been given by Krimerman when he says: "To know whether Jones believes he

has been treated cruelly or kindly requires that I know
what cruelty is - have some standard or paradigm to go by.
But then to know whether Jones believes he has been treated
unjustly requires that I know what just treatment is, i.e.
have some standard or paradigm to go by. But employing
such standards is clearly an instance of making or being
committed to certain value judgments."[6] Krimerman's argument at first blush does not seem to be directly related
to our concern, namely whether a social scientist's use of
a descriptive statement commits him in the abstract logical
sense to a value judgment, for Krimerman's argument is that
X's knowledge of Y's psychological state, i.e. what Y believes, presumes X's knowledge of a value judgment. However, Krimerman's argument can be construed as an argument
that a social scientist's descriptive statement commits him
in the abstract logical sense to a value judgment. Thus,
Krimerman can be interpreted as saying that

(14) Smith knows that Jones believes that Jones has been
treated unjustly.

entails

(15) Smith knows what justice is.

However, (15) combined with a purely psychological description of what Smith believes justice is would entail some
statement of the form

(16) Justice is.....

Consequently (14), presumably a descriptive statement combined with another descriptive statement, entails a value
judgment. Hence a social scientist who uses these descriptive statement is committed in the abstract logical sense
to a value judgment. But if so, then (2b) seems to be established.

The trouble with Krimerman's argument construed in this
way is the move from (14) to (15). I see no reason why
Smith cannot know that Jones believes that Jones has been
treated unjustly without knowing what just treatment really
is, i.e. without Smith accepting any standards or paradigms

---

[6]Leonard Krimerman, The Nature and Scope of Social Science, p. 696.

of justice. Krimerman's argument has the absurd implication that a moral skeptic or a Socrates who is ignorant of what justice is could not know that other people thought they were unjustly treated.

Now there is another way of understanding the first premise of Krimerman's argument which does not make it seem so implausible. One might substitute the following for (14).

(14a) Smith knows that Jones believes Jones has been treated unjustly in terms of Jones' concepts of injustice.

Then one might argue that (14a) entails:

(15a) Smith knows that Jones means "......." by the term "unjust treatment."

One might argue for this inference by saying that in order to know that a statement is true one must know what the terms in the statement mean. Whether (15a) is entailed by (14a) is not obvious. It does not seem to be contradictory to say that "Smith knows that Jones believes that Jones has been treated unjustly in terms of Jones' concept of unjust treatment but Smith does not know what Jones means by "treated unjustly." In any case, interpreted in this way premise (15a) does not entail any value judgment. It merely entails

(16a) Jones means "....." by "treated unjustly."

But (16a) is not a value judgment on any plausible account.

Mackenzie's Argument

A different argument is given by Mackenzie. He argues that when one describes someone as president of B Club -- a club for collecting butterflies -- this entails that the person described has certain rights and obligations and this in turn commits the person who is describing to certain value judgments: "For to say that Jones is the president is to imply that Jones has certain rights and obligations since this is partly how the office of president is defined. And to say by implication, that one has rights and obligations is assuredly to make a statement that has value content."[7]

[7] P.T. Mackenzie, "Fact and Value," Mind 76, 1967, p. 229.

Mackenzie's argument more formally stated is this:

(17) If a social scientist says "Jones is president of Club B," then the social scientist is committed to the sentence "Jones has certain rights and obligations."

(18) If the social scientist is committed to the sentence "Jones has certain rights and obligations," the social scientist is committed to a certain value judgment.

∴ (19) If a social scientist says "Jones is president of Club B," then the social scientist is committed to a certain value judgment.

The important question in this argument is what sort of value judgment is being referred to in the premises. What one strongly suspects is that the value judgment is of a quasi legal obligation. However, as we have seen, nothing follows from this as to whether Jones has certain moral rights and obligations. Thus a social scientist who describes Jones as president is not committed thereby in an abstract logical sense to any statement of the form: "Jones has an actual moral obligation to ....."

Now one might argue that being described as president of a club does at least entail certain *prima facie* judgments of moral obligation. One might argue in particular that

(20) Jones is president of Club B

entails

(21) Jones has a *prima facie* moral obligation to carry out the (quasi legal) duties and fulfill the (quasi legal) obligation created by the position of president.

That this is not so can easily be seen if one imagines that Club B is a club - not for collecting butterflies - but for torturing old ladies. Surely in this case no *prima facie* obligation is created to carry out the duties of the office. Such *prima facie* obligation is inferable only with the addition of some other moral premise, e.g.

(22) The purposes of the Club are not morally forbidden.

Thus (20) does not by itself entail any judgments of moral obligation - actual or *prima facie* - unless combined with other moral premises. Hence, the use of (20) does not commit social scientists in the abstract logical sense to any judgments of moral obligation. To be sure, use of (20) may commit the social scientist to value judgments of quasi-legal obligation. But as we shall see later there is no problem in rationally defending these judgments.

Searle's Argument

Another argument that can be used to show that the descriptions given by social scientists of social phenomena commit them to value judgments is that of John Searle.[8] Searle argues that the statement:

(23) Jones uttered the words "I hereby promise to pay you, Smith, five dollars."

combined with only factual and analytic statements entails:

(27) Jones ought to pay Smith five dollars.

Searle first argues that (23) entails

(24) Jones promised to pay Smith five dollars

when combined with certain alleged purely factual statements about conditions prevailing at the time Jones made his utterance. For example, one must assume that Jones understands what he is saying, that he is not under the influence of drugs, and so on. Let us call these factual premises (23a). Thus, Searle claims that (23) and (23a) entail (24).

(24), according to Searle, in turn entails:

(25) Jones placed himself under an obligation to pay Smith five dollars.

since, according to Searle, the following statement is analytic:

(24a) All promises are acts of placing oneself under an obligation to do the thing promised.

and (24) and (24a) entail (25). (25) in turn entails

(26) Jones is under an obligation to pay Smith five dollars.

[8] John Searle, "How to Derive 'Ought' from 'Is,'" Philosophical Review LXXIII, 1964, pp. 43-58.

given the alleged factual premise

(25a) Other things are equal.

and the analytic premise

(25b) All those who place themselves under an obligation, other things being equal, are under an obligation.

Now (26), combined with the alleged factual premise

(26a) Other things are equal,

and the analytic premise

(26b) All those who are under an obligation, other things being equal, ought to perform their obligation,

entails (27). Consequently, Searle argues that (23) entails (27) when combined with only factual assumptions and analytic premises.

Doubts can be cast on this argument: The Thompsons have argued that Searle does not establish that (26a) when given a strong enough interpretation to entail (27) in combination with (26) and (26b) is a purely factual statement.[9] The Thompsons claim that Searle interprets (26a) in the following way: Other things are equal when one knows no reason why Jones need not pay. They argue that on this interpretation (26a) does not entail (27) when combined with (26b) and (26a). This is because (26), (26a) and (26b) might be true and (27) false if there was some unknown stronger obligation that Jones had which conflicted with Jones' obligation to pay.

According to the Thompsons, what is needed to carry off the deducation of (27) is a stronger interpretation of (26a), namely: If other things are equal, then there is no conclusive reason to think that it is false that Jones ought to pay. But on such an interpretation of (26a), (26a) is not a purely factual statement; for there is no conclusive reason to think that it is false that Jones ought not pay just in case Jones has no stronger obligation that conflicts with his obligation to pay. However, to say Jones has no

---

[9] James and Judith Thompson, "How Not to Derive 'Ought' from 'Is,'" <u>Philosophical Review</u> LXIII, 1964, pp. 512-516.

stronger obligation is to make a value judgment. Thus (26a) must not be interpreted in a purely descriptive way in order to deduce (27).

The Thompsons' argument is correct. But it does not show that some value judgments cannot be derived from (23). For example, their argument does not show that the prima facie obligation stated in (26) cannot be derived from (23). However, one can show by a different argument that (27) cannot be deduced from (23) combined only with factual statements and analytic statements.[10] To see this, consider another case of promising. Suppose:

(23') Goebbels uttered the words "I hereby promise you, Hitler, that I will murder five million Jews."

By an argument similar to Searle's one could presumably deduce:

(26') Goebbels is under an obligation to kill five million Jews.

But such a result is surely absurd. Neither Goebbels nor any one else could have a prima facie obligation to commit an outrageous immoral act. This suggests that Searle's deduction of (26) goes through only with the tacit assumption that paying Jones five dollars is not an outrageously immoral act. However, once made explicit, this premise is surely not analytic: whether paying Jones five dollars is morally outrageous will depend in part on the consequences of so doing and these consequences are not know a priori.

Hence, Searle's argument fails to show that statements of prima facie duty can be deduced from purely descriptive statements.

The Avoidance of Value Commitments

Suppose we grant all of the above arguments. Perhaps value commitment could still be avoided.

As we suggested earlier there is no a priori reason why social scientists need to describe certain particular phenomena, e.g. the phenomenon of promise-making. Of course,

---

[10]This argument was developed at greater length in my paper "The Deduction of Statements of Prima Facie Obligations from Descriptive Statements," Philosophical Studies 25, 1974, pp. 149-152.

if social scientists avoid such phenomena they do it at a
price. They can no longer describe certain phenomena and
this seems to conflict with an important maxim of scientific
practice.

M_1 All phenomena should be open to scientific investigation.

Nevertheless, maxim M_1 seems to be in conflict with another
reasonable maxim.

M_2 Avoid procedures which result in lack of scientific objectivity.

M_1 seems to urge that, e.g. promise-making behavior not be
avoided in social science investigation. M_2 urges that it
should be. If one does not avoid certain investigations one
forsakes objectivity, if one does avoid these investigations
one seems to forsake the spirit of free inquiry. Neither
course of action seems desirable. The question seems to come
down to which alternative is the least undesirable. But
this question, it should be noted, is a value question.
Whether it admits of any rational answer will depend on
whether value judgments can be rationally defended.

However, so far we have taken it for granted that the
only way to avoid value commitment in the abstract logical
sense was to avoid description of certain kinds of phenomena,
e.g. the phenomena of promise-making. Indeed, the above
discussion of the price involved in avoiding this commitment presumed this. However, this presupposition seems to
be mistaken. For one is not committed in the abstract logical sense for example simply because one describes a particular kind of phenomena. Rather one is committed because
one describes it in a certain way, using one mode of description rather than another, words in one sense rather than in
another and so on.

Consider, for example, the phenomenon of promise-making.
Searle himself points out that an anthropologist "observing the behavior and attitudes of the Anglo-Saxons" might
use language in the inverted comma sense, in what he calls
<u>oratio obliqua</u>. Instead of saying "Jones promised to pay
Smith five dollars," he might say, "Jones did what they call
promising Smith five dollars" and instead of concluding with
"Jones is under an obligation to pay Smith five dollars" he
could say "According to them, Jones is under an obligation
to pay Smith five dollars."

Searle argues that this point fails to damage his argument (that one can derive ought from is) because "what it says is only that the steps in his argument can be reconstructed as <u>oratio obliqua</u>..."[11] Searle is correct. But this point although irrelevant to Searle's argument is not irrelevant to the present thesis that commitment to value judgments can be avoided by alternative description. Indeed, Searle's example of alternative description shows how one can describe the phenomenon of promise-making (or rather what is called promise-making) and avoid value commitment.

Some of the examples considered above could be handled in a similar way. The description that Smith is President of Club B could be reformulated in <u>oratio obliqua</u>: "Smith is what is called president of Club B." One could conclude that according to their concept of president Jones has certain rights and obligations or what they call certain rights and duties.

To be sure, the use of the <u>oratio obliqua</u> way of describing may have certain disadvantages. But if the alternative is to use language that commits one to certain value judgments and thus to lack of objectivity the disadvantage may be worth the price. In any case, using this mode of description certainly seems preferable to not describing the phenomena at all in order to avoid lack of objectivity.

The use of <u>oratio obliqua</u> is not applicable to all cases where value commitment threatens. Consider the description Jones is authoritarian. One does not want to say that Jones or his peer group calls Jones authoritarian. On the contrary, Jones and his peer group do not call Jones authoritarian; it is social scientists who have used this terminology. And it would surely be perverse for a social scientist to say "Jones is what social scientists call authoritarian."

Nevertheless, other alternative ways are open to social scientists to avoid value commitment. Instead of using the <u>oratio obliqua</u> way of describing social phenomena, social scientists can use the standard way of describing social phenomena but change the meaning of the terms they use. For example, we argued above that the use of <u>oratio obliqua</u> could not be plausibly used with the description "Jones is authoritarian." However, social scientists could change the meaning of authoritarian so that "Jones is authoritarian" does not entail "Jones is morally bad."

Now, it may be objected that although this move is

[11] John Searle, "How to Derive 'Ought' from 'Is,'" <u>Philosophical Review</u> LXXIII, 1964, pp. 51-52.

possible it is made at a great price. For if social scientists change the meaning of the term "authoritarian" in order to avoid value commitment this means that they cannot talk about what they want to talk about; they must necessarily be referring to different phenomena from those which they usually refer to when they use the term "authoritarian." However, this objection is mistaken. A change in the meaning of a term does not necessarily entail a change in the referent of the term. It is possible to change the meaning of "authoritarian" yet keep the same referent the term had before the change.

For example, suppose "authoritarian aggressive" is redefined as having a score in the 80th percentile or above on test T. Suppose that the referent of authoritarian aggressive so defined is co-extensive with the referent of authoritarian aggression given earlier, i.e. the tendency to be on the lookout for, to condemn, reject and punish people who violate conventional values. Presumably under the new definition "Jones is authoritarian" would not entail "Jones is morally bad" and yet by hypothesis it would have the same referent as the original statement. It is an empirical question whether such a test T could be constructed. But if it could, and there seems to be no a priori reason to suppose it could not, the objectionable value commitment of "Jones is authoritarian" is avoided.

In any case, the above considerations suggest that (2b) as it stands is false and needs to be changed. (2b) should be replaced by:

(2b') But the descriptions social scientists give of social phenomena of type T commit them to value judgments if they describe this sort of phenomena in a certain way.

One can escape from value commitment not only by avoiding the description of certain social phenomena but by avoiding certain ways of describing them, avoiding certain meanings of terms, and so on. This suggests that the price that one pays for value freedom and hence objectivity may be much less than we originally supposed. For objectivity is not necessarily bought at the price of forsaking M_1. One can investigate all social phenomena without fear of value commitment in any important sense of commitment if one uses only certain modes of expression and terms understood in certain ways. Thus principle M_1 and principle M_2 are compatible. One can avoid procedures that lead to lack of objectivity and still be able to investigate all scientific phenomena so long as one describes them in certain ways.

The Rational Defensibility of Value Judgments

So far we have considered ways in which a social scientist might avoid commitment to value judgments. As a result we have seen how premise (2b') can be defeated by different descriptions. The time has come to challenge premise (1b). As suggested earlier this premise rests on the supposition that value judgments are not capable of rational defense. We need not argue here that value judgments are always rationally defensible. Our argument will pose a dilemma for the advocates of the argument considered in this paper. Social scientists either are or are not committed in the abstract logical sense to certain value judgments because of their descriptions: If they are committed, the value judgments are rationally defensible; if they are not committed, then even if the value judgments cannot be rationally defended, the objectivity of the social sciences is not affected. In other words, I will argue that the critics cannot have it both ways. They cannot maintain that social scientists are committed to value judgments *via* their descriptions and also maintain that these value judgments are not rationally defensible.

Certain types of value judgments can be easily shown to be rationally defensible. For example, consider judgments of legal obligation and quasi-legal obligation. Someone might argue that the descriptive sentence:

(29) Jones signed a contract to do the job.

commits the social scientist who uses the description to the judgment of legal obligation.

(30) Jones has a legal obligation to do the job.

However, as long as (29) is rationally defensible, (30) is also since (30) follows directly from (29). Moreover, there is every reason to think that (29) is a rationally defensible statement. Whether it is defensible to claim that Jones signed a contract will depend on various legal factors, e.g. the number of witnesses, whether Jones has not been drugged, the age of Jones and so on. But all of these factors are capable of rational determination and indeed are arguable in courts of law.

The same sort of thing is true in quasi-legal contexts. Recall that Mackenzie argued that

(20) Jones is president of Club B.

entails

(21) Jones has certain duties and obligations.

because being president is partly defined in terms of having certain rights and obligations. If Mackenzie is right, one can establish whether Jones has certain obligations merely by determining whether Jones is president. There may be nothing difficult about this. How someone becomes president of a club is often specified in the by-laws of the club. Suppose that Club B's by-laws state that someone is president of Club B if he is elected by a majority of the members of the Club who are present at the Summer meeting of the Club. Then we could well claim that Jones has certain obligations connected with being president of Club B if we had good grounds to suppose that Jones was elected in the manner specified in the by-laws.

Judgments of instrumental value seem to pose no particular problem either. For these kinds of value judgments are really empirical statements: they say that something X is good for a certain end Y. This can be translated to mean (and hence is directly derivable from) X is helpful in doing Y or X brings about Y. But whether something is helpful in bringing something else about or whether something brings about something else seems to be a straight-forward factual question which can be answered by appeal to evidence, argument and the like. For example, the claim that a particular psycho-therapy is good presumably means good with respect to getting cures, given some definition of cure. The person who makes such a claim need not suppose that cures are good or desirable or even that cures when defined in this way are good or desirable. But this claim is just to say that this psycho-therapy is helpful in bringing about cures. Whether it is or not is a difficult but rationally determinable question.

It has been argued in recent years that functional statements in the social sciences commit social scientists to certain value judgments, in particular, that functional statements commit social scientists to the desirability of the status quo, the present make-up of society. The analysis of function statements is a difficult topic.[12] Fortunately,

---

[12] For a general discussion of functional statements see Larry Wright "Functions," Philosophical Review LXXXII, 1973, pp. 139-168; for a discussion of functional statements in social science see Carl Hempel, "The Logic of Functional Analysis," Symposium on Sociological Theory, ed. L. Gross (New York: 1959).

it will not be necessary to discuss this here. For functional statements, whatever they mean, at most only entail judgments of instrumental value.

To say that the function of magic is to preserve tribal harmony may entail

(31) Magic is good for preserving tribal harmony.

Furthermore, it might be argued that when correctly understood, (31) may entail

(32) Preserving tribal harmony is good for maintaining the status quo.

But neither of these judgments presumes that preserving tribal harmony is intrinsically good or that the status quo is intrinsically good. They only say that magic and preserving tribal harmony are useful for bringing about certain ends. Whether these ends are good intrinsically or even instrumentally good for other ends is not presumed.

However, the traditional concern about the rational defensibility of value judgments has not focussed on judgments of legal obligation or judgments of instrumental value. The crucial question has always been the rational defensibility of judgments of moral value, judgments of intrinsic nonmoral value and judgments of moral obligation - especially the latter two types of judgments.

Traditionally, the dominant objective position in ethics has been naturalism, the view that value judgments, e.g. judgments of moral obligation and judgments of intrinsic value are derivable -- usually *via* definitions -- from factual descriptive statements.[13] Critics of naturalism have admitted that if these sorts of value judgments *could* be derived from factual descriptive statements, they would be rationally defensible and objective. But critics of naturalism have argued that such statements could not be so derived.

One of the major ironies of the present discussion is that the critique of objectivity in the social sciences under consideration seems to be committed to a form of naturalism in ethics. The claim is that social scientists are committed to value judgments *via* their descriptive

---

[13]Frankena, *Ethics*, Chapter 6.

statements; it is concluded from this that social science is not objective. Naturalists in ethics, on the other hand, concluded that because value judgments can be derived from factual ones, ethics is objective.

When viewed in this way there seems to be something very strange about the basic argument against objectivity in the social sciences that we have just been considering. How can the traditional and seemingly plausible view of naturalism have become so inverted as to show that social science is not objective?

One explanation is this: Two different and incompatible views of value judgments are being conflated. One traditional view -- a view coming down from at least Max Weber -- is that value judgments are subjective and arbitrary and are not derivable from factual statements. This is surely the view presumed in premise (1b). The other view coming down from Mill, Dewey and other naturalists in ethics is that value judgments are rationally defensible since they are a type of empirical descriptive statement. This latter seems to be the view assumed in premise (2b') -- if one interprets "commit" in the abstract logical sense. However these two views are incompatible. One cannot suppose them both to be true.

One might still attempt to defend premise (1b) in the following way. Although judgments of moral obligation and intrinsic value are derivable from descriptive statements such judgments are not defensible because the descriptive statements from which they are derived are not rationally defensible.

The trouble with this move is that it must be shown that the descriptive statement from which the value judgments supposedly are derived are not rationally defensible. But this is difficult to show. Consider, for example, some of the descriptive statements we have considered so far.

There does not seem any particular problem in establishing whether a person is authoritarian either in the submissive or aggressive sense used by social scientists. It seems to be a question of observing the person's behavior under certain conditions, asking the person certain questions and so on. To be sure, although in any particular case one's judgments about whether someone is authoritarian may be wrong, the judgment is defended or refuted by empirical evidence.

The same thing seems to be true in the case in which someone utters the words "I hereby promise to pay you, Smith, five dollars." Again, establishing this statement seems to be a matter of empirical evidence -- not whim or caprice. This is so also for the other descriptive statements which are alleged by Searle to be needed to derive a judgment of *prima facie* moral obligation or a judgment of actual obligation. For example, (26a), one of the "other things are equal" premises, as interpreted by Searle is a descriptive statement. Although (26a) is open ended and the things included under this premise are not completely specifiable the sort of things Searle has in mind are straight-forwardly empirical. For example, other things are not equal if Smith says "I hereby release you from your promise, Jones" provided Smith is not drugged, knows what he is saying and so on.

As we have seen, there is serious doubt about whether Searle can derive either a judgment of actual obligation or a judgment of *prima facie* obligation from the description he considers. However, the question now is: *if* he can, is there any particular problem involved in establishing these descriptive premises such that one might be inclined to say that they were not rationally defensible? The answer to this question seems to be "no."

Conclusion

We may conclude (a) that the usual arguments given to show that social scientists are committed to value judgments *via* their descriptions are unsuccessful; (b) that even if these arguments were successful, value commitment could be avoided; (c) that even if value commitment could not be avoided the objectivity of the social sciences would not be compromised thereby. Thus, premise (2b) can be defeated and premise (1b) is false.

Michael Martin
Philosophy Department
Boston University
Boston, MA 02215

VALUE JUDGEMENTS AND THE ACCEPTANCE OF HYPOTHESES IN SCIENCE AND SCIENCE EDUCATION

by

Michael Martin

Introduction

The relevance of philosophy of science for science education has too long been neglected. By and large philosophers of science have failed to help science educators and most science educators have failed to profit from the insights of philosophy of science. In some recent publications this unhappy tendency has to some extent reversed itself.[1] However, the full potential of philosophy of science for science education has yet to be realized. In this paper I will not fight for ground already won; instead I will endeavor to suggest new paths that philosophy of science may open up for science education, new insights that philosophy of science may provide.

Philosophy of science as it will be conceived of here has two basic tasks: (1) the analysis, clarification and critique of certain concepts, methods and problems found in all or nearly all science, e.g. the concepts of definition, observation, explanation, the methods of experimental inquiry, the problem of the comparability of scientific theories; (2) the analysis and clarification of concepts, methods and problems found in more restricted parts of science, e.g. the concept of operational definition of length in physics, the method of participant observation in anthropology, the problem of the objectivity of social science. Philosophy of science in this sense might be called *analytic philosophy of science.*

There are at least two contributions that analytic philosophy of science can make to science education. First, analytic philosophy of science may suggest new pedagogical insights and perspectives for science education, new ways of looking at and examining traditional approaches, new research problems and goals. Let us call the value that philosophy of science may have in suggesting new approaches and problems the *heuristic value* of philosophy of science for science education.

Secondly, analytic philosophy of science provides clarification and analysis of some of the major concepts in science education—namely, the concepts of science itself. Let us call the value that analytic philosophy of science has for science education in clarifying some of the concepts of science education the *analytic value* of analytic philosophy of science for science education.

As we shall see, the analytic value and the heuristic value of analytic philosophy of science go hand in hand. Philosophical analysis and clarification reveals distinctions, analogies, and ambiguities that are suggestive for science education.

Analytic philosophy of science should be contrasted with a more traditional view of philosophy of science.[2] Traditionally 'philosophy of science' was used to refer to the construction of a scientific world view. The philosophy of science in this sense would attempt to construct a systematic and unified picture of the world as presented by the particular sciences. This enterprise—which might be called *speculative philosophy of science*—would attempt to answer questions about the origin of the universe (cosmology) as well as questions about the ultimate make-up of the universe (ontology). I cannot consider here the possible value of speculative philosophy of science for science education. However, I have argued elsewhere that it may have value.[3]

Analytic philosophy of science, as we have seen, clarifies and evaluates the concepts, methods and problems of science. Such analysis and criticism can enter into science education in at least two ways:

(1) Students of science could learn the analysis and criticism of scientific concepts, methods and problems.
(2) Science educators could learn the analysis and criticism of scientific concepts, methods and problems.

Now although I do not deny that the study of analytic philosophy of science may be useful for science students,[4] I will concentrate here on the value of the study of analytic philosophy of science for science educators. I will discuss briefly some of the roles that value judgments play in connection with science and will then examine the recent controversy in philosophy of science over the acceptance of hypotheses. I hope to show that the clarification and analysis of the roles that values play in connection with science has both heuristic and analytic value for science educators.

Values and Science

There is no doubt that values and science are connected. First, science seems to be committed to certain general values, e.g. truth, knowledge and objectivity. Indeed, it would seem that without such commitment science would be impossible. Secondly, scientists normally are committed to the value of particular theories, techniques, approaches. Such commitment can lead to problems and, indeed, seems at times to conflict with the commitment of science itself to objectivity.

Scientists are human; like everyone else their behavior and even their perceptions are sometimes affected by their value commitments. They believe that certain things are good or bad, and have strong feelings about this. Their beliefs and attitudes may induce them—either consciously or unconsciously—to overlook evidence or to misconstrue evidence that might go against their well-entrenched views and commitments. As a result they may produce work which is biased. For example, a medical researcher with a strong liking for things oriental may tend to overlook negative evidence for the curative powers of acupuncture. Consequently his research report may be biased.

This insidious influence of value commitment on the results of scientific research is something that ideally should be excluded from science. It is at least in part a scientific question how the biasing of results can be prevented; what techniques and procedures scientists can use to prevent their value commitments from causing them to overlook evidence and misread the data. However, the problem is partly an educational one as well. What pedagogical procedures are best for training scientists to be sensitive to negative evidence, to data that conflicts with their most cherished views? I have suggested elsewhere some pedagogical procedures for decreasing the insidious influence of theory laden observation.[5] Other procedures, for example having science students subject their own value commitments to self-criticism, also need to be considered.

Now scientists may not only have value commitments which result in biased findings; they may also be called upon to answer value questions. For example "Is science worth engaging in?", "Is a particular scientific problem worth studying?", "Should a particular scientific finding be given practical application?" It may be argued however that these questions, whatever their importance, are not questions a scientist *qua* scientist answers; that they are not questions *within* science. The question of whether it is worth engaging in science, it may be argued, is a *pre*-scientific question as is the question of whether a particular scientific problem is worth studying. The question of whether certain scientific findings should be applied, it may be maintained, is a *post*-scientific question.

I for one find this argument too pat. For the question of whether a certain problem is worth studying seems to be something that a scientist has special competence to answer since the answer to it should be based, at least in part, on the consequences of studying this problem for the growth of science. Similarly the answer to the question of whether a certain scientific finding should be applied to solve a practical problem should be based in part on the probability of success.

Now it may be argued that answering the question about the desirability of studying certain problems scientifically and the question about the desirability of applying the results of science also depends on value judgments, e.g. the value judgment that the growth of science is desirable or that the solution of a practical problem is desirable. These value judgments, it may be argued, are surely beyond the competence of the scientist.

Whether or not value judgments are beyond the competence of the scientist depends on what view of ethics is correct. On a naturalistic interpretation, for example, value judgments are equivalent to scientific judgments. The question of the desirability of engaging in science is, then, on a naturalistic interpretation, a question that could be answered by science.

Now given a naturalistic interpretation one might still want to call the above questions pre and post scientific, thus distinguishing them from the more typical questions arising *within* science. But on a naturalistic interpretation the distinction between pre and post scientific questions on the one hand and questions falling within science on the other clearly could not be made on the grounds that the scientist has no special competence to answer the former sort of question. There would be no basic difference between the methodology used to answer typical scientific questions. Consequently the scientist *qua* scientist would on a naturalistic interpretation answer these post and pre questions as well as questions falling within science.

Given a non-naturalistic interpretation of value judgments there would be basic methodological difference between questions within science and pre and post scientific questions. Whether a scientist *qua* scientist should be expected to answer pre and post questions of the sort we have been discussing would then be problematic. However, the important point to note is that the neat separation on methodological ground of these pre and post scientific questions from questions arising within science does seem to presuppose a particular meta-ethical position, namely non-naturalism. Without this presupposition the role of the scientist *qua* scientist is not so narrowly circumscribed.

Suppose my suspicions are groundless and a scientist *qua* scientist should not answer what I have called pre and post scientific questions. Suppose that naturalism is untenable. A pedagogical issue of great importance can be raised. One can still ask: How should science education be conceived? Should science education be conceived of as an education designed to train a scientist *qua* scientist—an individual who has no training in answering pre and post scientific questions? One might well opt for science education more broadly conceived in which science students are trained not only *qua* scientists but in answering these pre and post scientific questions as well. Or one might argue that science education can be narrowly conceived so long as students of science are at some point given an education in problem solving in pre and post scientific questions.

In any event, a case can be made for an education call it a scientific education or not—which is concerned with value questions about the desirability of science, the desirability of studying certain problems rather than others, the desirability of the application of certain scientific results. Indeed, it is just these sorts of questions that relate science to humanistic concerns and traditions and illuminate science as a social institution.

Now in recent years the major controversy among philosophers of science about the role of value judgments in relation to science has been over the question of whether scientists *qua* scientists should answer a rather different type of question, namely "Should a particular hypothesis be accepted?" It has been argued by some that this is a value question arising within science, that it is a question a scientist *qua* scientist answers. The basic argument for this position is this: No scientific hypothesis is ever certain; hence in the acceptance of a scientific hypothesis there is always the possibility of error. Consequently, whether a scientist accepts a scientific hypothesis or not will depend on the seriousness of the mistake of accepting the hypothesis if it is false. However, an answer to the question of whether a mistake is serious or not is certainly based on value judgments held by the scientist. But since the scientist *qua* scientist accepts hypotheses, value judgments are an essential part of science, they are found *within* science. On this view the value judgments connected with the acceptance of scientific hypotheses are legitimate and indeed indispensible in science.

This view has not gone unchallenged. It has been argued that scientists *qua* scientists do not accept hypotheses and hence the value judgments connected with acceptance are not part of scientific practice. Put in the terms introduced earlier, the argument is simply that the question of whether a hypothesis should be accepted or rejected is a post scientific question. As we have seen if naturalism is correct, post scientific value questions are questions that a scientist *qua* scientist can answer. So the value questions connected with the acceptance of a hypothesis would be value questions a scientist *qua* scientist can answer. Thus this view must be committed to some form of non-naturalism. In any case, on this view scientists *qua* scientists gather evidence and specify how probable hypotheses are relative to the evidence, it is said. But as scientists they do not accept or reject such hypotheses. The acceptance of scientific hypotheses is left to others or to the scientist in some other role than that of scientist. This view, sometimes called "the odds maker view of science," has been advocated by such philosophers as Carnap[6] and Jeffreys.[7]

However even among those who argue that scientists *qua* scientists accept hypotheses there is controversy. The controversy is over what sort of value judgments are relevant to the acceptance of a hypothesis. On one view the acceptance of hypotheses depends on considerations of epistemic or theoretical value, i.e. values associated with achieving truth, simplicity, explanatory power and so on. This view has been advocated by Hempel[8] and Levi.[9] We will call it "the theoretical acceptance view." Another group of methodologists, namely Rudner,[10] Braithwaite,[11] Churchman[12] and Leach,[13] maintain that the values involved in the acceptance of scientific hypotheses are not completely epistemic or theoretical but also involve non-theoretical or practical values, values associated with human life, the saving of time and energy, and so on. Let us call this view "the practical acceptance view."

Evaluation of the Controversy

In order to evaluate this controversy it is necessary first to clarify the notion of acceptance and then to clarify the nature of the claims of the parties to the controversy.

Two different concepts of acceptance can be distinguished.[14] In one sense of "acceptance" to accept a hypothesis is to believe that it is true. Let us call his sort of acceptance, acceptance$_B$—the subscript$_B$ to remind us that this sense of acceptance has to do with the belief that the hypothesis is true. In science, of course, such a belief would be a tentative one subject to change in the light of new evidence and argument.

In another sense of "acceptance" to accept a hypothesis is not necessarily to believe that the hypothesis is true; rather it is to be disposed to act as if the hypothesis is true in a given context because it is believed that the hypothesis is a useful working hypothesis in that context. Let us call this sense of acceptance, acceptance$_U$—the subscript$_U$ to remind us that acceptance refers to the usefulness of the hypothesis as a working hypothesis in a certain context. Again, in science acceptance of this sort is tentative, subject to change in the light of the evidence.

It is important to see that these two senses of acceptance are logically independent of each other in that one could accept$_B$ a hypothesis H without accepting$_U$ H in a given contest and not accept$_B$ H. For example, the evidence that a certain drug can cure cancer may be weak, so weak that it does not warrant our acceptance$_B$ that the drug is effective; yet, since there is some evidence, albeit meager, for the effectiveness of the drug and good evidence that the drug has no damaging side effects, a medical therapist may accept$_U$ the hypothesis, i.e. he may be disposed to act as if it is true in the context of medical therapy. Conversely, there may be strong evidence that a drug can cure cancer and yet some evidence that the drug has lethal side effects. One might therefore accept$_B$ that the drug is a cure for cancer and yet not accept$_U$ that the drug is a cure for cancer in the context of therapy; that is one would not proceed on the assumption that the drug was effective and start using it on cancer patients.

Once the distinction between acceptance$_B$ and acceptance$_U$ is made there are several different things that the adversaries in the above-mentioned controversy could be saying. Let us consider some of the possibilities connected with the odds maker view of science:

(1) A scientist *qua* scientist can not accept$_B$ any scientific hypothesis.
(2) A scientist *qua* scientist can not accept$_U$ any scientific hypothesis.
(3) A scientist *qua* scientist does not accept$_B$ any scientific hypothesis.
(4) A scientist *qua* scientist does not accept$_U$ any scientific hypothesis.
(5) A scientist *qua* scientist should not accept$_B$ any scientific hypothesis.
(6) A scientist *qua* scientist should not accept$_U$ any scientific hypothesis.

Consider (1) and (2). The "can not" is to be understood as a logical "can not" in the sense that a brother can not be a female. Interpreted in this way (1) and (2) certainly seem to be dubious if "scientist *qua* scientist" is interpreted in its usual sense. It does not seem to be part of the ordinary meaning of "scientist *qua* scientist" that a scientist *qua* scientist can not accept scientific hypotheses in either of the senses of acceptance.

Of course, the claim may not be a claim about the ordinary meaning of "scientist *qua* scientist." Rather a proposal may be implicitly being made about how "scientist *qua* scientist should be understood. In short, (1) and (2) may be implicitly normative. We will consider the odds maker view as a normative claim in a moment.

What about (3) and (4)? If (3) and (4) are factual statements they certainly seem dubious. Scientists *qua* scientists as a matter of fact certainly seem to accept some scientific hypotheses in both senses of "accept." It would seem that the most plausible way to interpret the claim of the odds makers view of science is not as a factual claim about what scientists *qua* scientists do not do or logical claim about what they can not do but as a normative claim about what they should not do—that is as (5) and (6). Given this interpretation the theoretical acceptance and the practical acceptance views can then be interpreted as claiming that (5) and (6) are mistaken although advocates of the theoretical acceptance view and the practical acceptance view have different reasons for claiming that they are.

But is there any reason to suppose that these normative claims made by advocates of the odds maker view of science are correct? What might be the rationale for (5) and (6)?

It is not completely clear what rationale methodologists have for making these claims. But one plausible guess is this. Since they maintain that acceptance involves value judgments, they might well believe that acceptance of scientific hypotheses introduces an element of subjectivity into science. The odds maker view keeps this subjectivity out. Since subjectivity is thought to be undesirable in science, (5) and (6) are advocated. Furthermore, advocates of (5) and (6) think that the practical acceptance view is the only alternative to their view: they think that either one does not accept scientific hypotheses as a scientist or one accepts them in terms of practical values. One may guess that they believe that judgments about practical values are particularly subjective and rationally indefensible.

This argument for the odds maker view of science seems to me to be a very weak one. First, as we have seen the practical acceptance view is not the only alternative to the odds maker view. There is also the theoretical acceptance view. Even if judgments about practical values are subjective and not capable of rational defense or criticism, judgments about theoretical values may not be subjective. Thus, if the acceptance of scientific hypotheses is based on theoretical values there might be nothing subjective in the acceptance of scientific hypotheses.

Secondly, even if the practical acceptance view were the only alternative, it is not clear why judgments about practical values would necessarily be subjective. The idea that they are rests perhaps on a particular brand of non-cognitivism, i.e. the view that certain value judgments are expressions of emotion that are without rational basis. However, there is no good reason to embrace such a view and, indeed, such a view has serious problems. It is important to see that naturalism in ethics is not the only alternative to the sort of crude non-cognitive view that would make judgments of practical value irrational and subjective. A naturalistic interpretation but also certain sophisticated non-cognitivist interpretations of value judgments would entail that value judgments are rationally defensible or criticizable and hence objective.[15] Consequently, non-cognitivism in ethics, a rejection of the odds maker view of science, and the objectivity of science are logically compatible.

Now whether naturalism or some sophisticated type of non-cognitivism is a correct meta-ethical position is a long story, a story we cannot go into here. But there does certainly seem to be much more reason to embrace one of these meta-ethical positions than to embrace the crude non-cognitivism that seems to be presupposed by the odds maker view. There may, of course, be other reasons than the ones I have rejected here for accepting the odds maker view, but until they are brought forth there is good reason for rejecting that view of science. This does not mean, however, that the odds maker view may not be useful in science education. Indeed, I shall argue later that the odds maker view may in certain pedagogical contexts be very appropriate.

So far I have rejected the odds maker view of science. Two views remain: the theoretical acceptance view and the practical acceptance view. Let us interpret these two positions not as descriptive claims about how science does in fact operate but as claims about how science should operate. Interpreted in this way we can distinguish two variants of each position depending on which meaning of acceptance is at issue:

(7) For a scientist *qua* scientist the values which determine acceptance$_B$ or rejection$_B$ of scientific hypotheses should be epistemic values only.
(8) For a scientist *qua* scientist the values which determine the acceptance$_U$ or rejection$_U$ of scientific hypotheses should be epistemic values only.
(9) For a scientist *qua* scientist the values which determine the acceptance$_B$ or rejection$_B$ of scientific hypotheses should be, at least in part, practical values.
(10) For a scientist *qua* scientist the values which determine acceptance$_U$ or rejection$_U$ of scientific hypotheses should be, at least in part, practical values.

Consider now an argument of Rudner's for the practical acceptance view. Rudner argues:

Obviously our decision regarding the evidence and respecting how strong is 'strong enough' is going to be a function of the importance, in the typical ethical sense, of making a mistake in accepting or rejecting the hypothesis. Thus to take a crude but easily manageable example, if the hypothesis under consideration were to the effect that a toxic ingredient of a drug was present in lethal quantity, we would require a relatively high degree of confirmation or confidence before accepting the hypothesis—for the consequences of making a mistake here are exceeding grave by our moral standards.[16]

Undoubtedly Rudner assumes here that the drug will be given to human beings for presumably if the drug were given to monkeys the consequences of making a mistake would not be "exceeding grave" by our moral standards. Rudner's argument is an excellent argument for (10), that is, it is an argument for the advisability of taking practical values into account if one accepts$_U$ or rejects$_U$ a hypothesis. Thus if one were to act as if the hypothesis that the drug was not toxic were true in the context of medical therapy the danger to human life would have to be taken into account. But this says nothing about whether one should accept$_B$ or reject$_B$ the hypothesis and with respect to acceptance$_B$ or rejection$_B$ of the hypothesis, only epistemic values seem to be relevant. Thus Rudner's argument does provide good reason for maintaining that (10) is correct and that (8) is not correct but it provides no reason for maintaining that (9) is correct and that (7) is not.

Leach gives another argument for the practical acceptance view.[17] The strategy of Leach's argument is to show that what I have called acceptance$_B$ involves acceptances$_U$ and that despite my attempt to separate these two senses of acceptance there is a close connection between them. Leach admits, of course, that one can not straight-away identify acceptance$_B$ and acceptance$_U$.

To say that one believes that the hypothesis is true is not to say that one would act on the hypothesis in a given context, that one believes that the hypothesis would be a useful working hypothesis in this context. Leach does argue however that there is a more indirect connection between them.

He maintains that if some person P believes that H, then P has as a matter of fact a disposition to act on that hypothesis relative to some specific goal or other and that if a person P does have such a disposition, he will act on the hypothesis in certain circumstances. In this way Leach argues that there is a link between what I have called acceptance$_B$ and acceptance$_U$. The link is a contingent one however. There is no logical necessity that if a person P believes that H, then P has a certain disposition to act.

Consider a medical researcher who accepts$_B$ that a drug does not have a toxic agent present in lethal quantity. I have suggested that despite his acceptance$_B$ the researcher might not accept$_U$ this hypothesis in the context of medical therapy with human beings. For because he is dealing with human beings the researcher might believe that although the evidence warrants acceptance$_B$ the hypothesis does not warrant acceptance$_U$ in this context.

Leach's point, as I understand it, is that despite what I have just maintained, if the medical researcher believes that the drug does not have a toxic agent in a lethal amount, then he has as a matter of fact a disposition to act as if the hypothesis is true relative to some specific goal or other and would act on the hypothesis given certain circumstances. Leach may well be correct in this. For the researcher may have a disposition to act on the hypothesis relative to the goal of curing monkeys and given appropriate circumstances would try the drug on the monkeys.

Leach seems to believe that once he has shown that acceptance$_U$ is connected in the way he suggested with acceptance$_B$ practical values are relevant for determining whether someone should accept$_B$ some hypothesis. But it is difficult to see why this is so. Consider the above case. The fact that the researcher's belief that the hypothesis is true is contingently connected with his disposition to act on the hypothesis in some practical context does not mean that practical values should determine whether he should accept$_B$ the hypothesis. It is still possible that his acceptance$_B$ of the hypothesis that the drug has a toxic agent is something that should be a function of the evidence and epistemic values only; and that his acceptance$_U$ of the hypothesis, i.e. his disposition to act in a certain way in a given context is something that should in part be determined by practical goals. The fact (if it is a fact) that his disposition to act and his belief are contingently related may be of great psychological interest. However, it seems to have dubious relevance to the normative question of what sort of values are relevant to acceptance$_B$ and acceptance$_U$.

To make this clearer consider an analogous case. Suppose there were a contingent relation between aesthetically pleasing actions and actions that are morally obligatory such that X is a morally obligatory action if and only if X is an aesthetically pleasing action. If such a relation held, one could use moral criteria as reliable signs of aesthetic worth and vice versa. This is because the presence of moral criteria such as benevolence and justice would be reliable indicators of aesthetic criteria such as form and harmony, and conversely. However, this would not mean that aesthetic criteria were moral criteria or vice versa. Benevolence and justice would still be the relevant moral criteria and harmony and form would not be; harmony and form would be the relevant aesthetic criteria while justice and benevolence would not be.

In a similar manner if there is a close contingent relation between acceptance$_B$ and acceptance$_U$, a criterion used to evaluate whether one should accept$_U$ a hypothesis, e.g. the criterion that acting on the hypothesis will adversely affect human life, might be a reliable indicator of whether one should accept$_B$ this hypothesis. But this might be the case simply because practical consequences were a reliable indicator of the criteria relevant for acceptance$_B$, e.g. simplicity and explanatory power. If so it would no more mean that practical values are relevant to what one should accept$_B$ than that moral criteria in the above example are relevant to what is aesthetically pleasing.

I conclude that Leach's argument gives no support for (9) and does not refute (7). Indeed, it seems to me that the above considerations suggest that (7) is correct and that (9) is incorrect. I find it difficult to see how practical consequences of my acting on a hypothesis could be relevant to whether I should believe that a hypothesis is true unless acceptance$_B$ and acceptance$_U$ are logically related in a very strong way.

If for example "X is disposed to act as if p is true" entails "X believes that p," then if one should be disposed to act as if p is true because of certain practical consequences resulting from one's action, one should believe that p is true because of these consequences. Again if "X believes that p is true" entails "X is disposed to act as if p is true," then if one should not be disposed to act as if p is true because of bad practical consequences resulting from one's action, one should not believe that p is true because of these consequences. But these logical relations do not hold between acceptance$_B$ and acceptance$_U$, between belief and the disposition to act as if. Any contingent relation of the kind specified by Leach is not strong enough to show the relevance of practical values for acceptance$_B$. As we have seen this does not exclude the presence of practical values being a reliable sign of the presence of epistemic values. But if they are, it does not mean that practical values are relevant for acceptance$_B$.

Who is correct then: advocates of the practical acceptance view or advocates of the theoretical acceptance view? The answer to this depends on what sense of "acceptance" one is talking about. For we have seen that Rudner's argument has established (10) and refuted (8). So if we are talking about acceptance$_U$ the practical acceptance view is correct. My criticism of Leach's argument suggests that practical values are irrelevant for acceptance$_B$ unless certain unplausibly strong connections are supposed to hold between acceptance$_B$ and acceptance$_U$. So if we are talking about acceptance$_B$ (7) seems to be correct and (9) to be incorrect. However if this is so, it follows that the practical acceptance view is correct when acceptance is restricted to acceptance$_U$ and that the theoretical acceptance view is correct when acceptance is restricted to acceptance$_B$. Thus with respect to what hypothesis a scientist should accept$_B$, i.e. believe is true, epistemic values are the only relevant ones while with respect to what a scientist accepts$_U$, i.e. what he should be disposed to act on in a particular context, practical values should come into play.[18]

Science Education and Acceptance

What relevance has the above analysis for science education? Let us consider its relevance with respect to four types of science educators: (1) science teachers, (2) science curriculum planners, (3) science textbook writers, and (4) researchers in science education.

Science Teachers

Philosophy of science has analytic value and heuristic value for science teachers. For example, a science teacher explaining the rationale for theoretical physicists rejecting Newtonian mechanics might find it useful to keep in mind the distinction between acceptance$_B$ and acceptance$_U$. Although theoretical physicists reject$_B$ Newtonian physics, engineers and applied physicists accept$_U$ Newtonian physics in some of their work. Indeed without this sort of distinction clearly in mind a science teacher might not be able to explain to his class (or get them to discover) the different value commitments of theoretical scientists and applied scientists and the different roles of Newtonian theory in theoretical and applied disciplines.

Furthermore, the knowledge that value judgments are involved in the acceptance of hypotheses may enable the teacher to bring out to his class important similarities and perhaps differences between different branches of study. Thus bringing out the similar epistemic values involved in the acceptance$_B$ of theories in physics, biology and chemistry may provide unity and coherence in science courses that is too often lacking and even perhaps suggest important similarities and differences with the humanities and the arts.

We have seen that the odds maker view of science seems an implausible view of how a scientist *qua* scientist should operate. But it may be very suggestive for how science teachers should operate. Should science teachers maintain that certain scientific theories which are well supported by the evidence should be accepted relative to certain values? Or should science teachers become odds makers, presenting theories and the evidence for them, perhaps discussing the epistemic and practical values involved and then letting the student decide whether to accept or reject the theories without any recommendation from the teacher? In short, should the science teacher advocate the acceptance or rejection in either of the senses discussed of any scientific theories?

I do not believe that any general answer can be given to this question. Much will depend on what the teacher is trying to do in the class, the level and maturity of the students and the type of material investigated. In small classes with mature and self-reliant students the odds maker approach may be stimulating and productive; in large classes with naive and slow students the odds maker view approach may be too heady and anxiety provoking. But in any case the odds maker approach to teaching science is an approach that is well worth considering in some contexts.

Science Curriculum Planners

Analytic philosophy of science has special relevance to science curriculum planners. This is because of the profound changes that have occurred in science curriculum theory in the last several years. Although a coherent articulation of this new movement is not complete, even now one can discern two important facets. First, recent science curriculum theorists have stressed that science should not be taught as an inflexible and unchanging body of doctrine. The tentativeness and revisionary character of science should be stressed in science education; science should be taught as a flexible, everchanging method of inquiry. Thus Schwab has argued:

> What is required is that in the very near future a substantial segment of our public become cognizant of science as a product of *fluid enquiry*, understand that it is a mode of investigation which rests on conceptual innovation, proceeds through uncertainty and failure, and eventualizes in knowledge which is contingent, dubitable and hard to come by.[19]

In the area of social studies curriculum Massialas and Cox have maintained that social studies courses in the public school should have as one of their goals teaching the individual a method of inquiry which allows him to "reconstruct his system of beliefs and values in the process of inquiry."[20]

Secondly, recent science curriculum theorists have stressed that the structure of science should be taught. What exactly 'structure' means is not exactly clear but people who emphasize structure in science education seem to have in mind the basic concepts and methods of particular sciences and perhaps of all or most sciences. Thus Jerome Bruner, who has done so much to popularize the notion of structure in science education, illustrates the idea of structure by citing the concept of function as an "organizing concept" in biology[21] and argues for the importance of this concept in the teaching of biology. Bruner also suggests that operational definition is a "recurrent idea that appears in virtually all branches of science."[22] Here Bruner seems to be suggesting that structure sometimes refers to concepts basic to all or most sciences and he goes on to argue that structure in this sense may play an essential role in at least general science courses.

Schwab advocates the structural approach to scientific education also. He distinguishes three senses of structure that play an important role in science education.[23] In one sense, to say that one should teach the structure of science is just to say that one should teach the interrelations between scientific disciplines. Under this heading would fall the relations between formal sciences, e.g. mathematics, and non-formal sciences as well as the relation between physical sciences and social sciences. In another sense to say that one should teach the structure of science is to say that one should teach the basic concepts and theories of a scientific discipline. For instance, one might teach the theory of universal gravitation in physics. Schwab calls this substantive structure. In a third sense, to teach the structure of science one would teach the canons of proof and evidence in scientific disciplines. This Schwab calls syntactical structure.

Whatever the merits of the inquiry and structure approach to science education—and we believe they are many—analytic philosophy of science has great relevance. First it is analytic philosophy of science—in particular inductive logic—that investigates the logic of scientific inquiry.[24] Secondly, analytic philosophy of science, as we have already mentioned, investigates the basic concepts of sciences. Analytic work has already been done by philosophers on the notion of function in biology,[25] and on operational definitions.[26] Philosophers of science have discussed at length the relation between formal and non-formal sciences[27] and the relation between the natural and the social sciences.[28] Particular concepts of physics, biology, anthropology, psychology and so on have been analyzed by philosophers of science. The canons of proof and evidence in science have been analyzed by analytic philosophers of science and inductive logicians.[29]

It would seem, therefore, that a science curriculum construed in terms of inquiry and structure would be illuminated by the work of analytic philosophers of science, and that curriculum planners who utilized the notions of inquiry and structure in their work would benefit from the study of analytic philosophy of science. Indeed, it would not be too far wrong to say that the educational potential of the inquiry and structure approach to science education will not be fully realized until science educators realize the need for the analysis and clarification of the key notions of inquiry and structure.

One of the key notions in scientific inquiry and the structure of science is the notion of acceptance. Part of scientific inquiry—except on the odds maker view of science, a view which we have found no reason to embrace—is the tentative acceptance and rejection of hypotheses. Acceptance also seems to be one of those general notions that Bruner has in mind when he talks about the structure of science. Schwab's syntactical structure is concerned with the canons of proof and evidence in scientific disciplines. But as we have seen the canons of evidence and proof are closely connected with the gains and losses involved in accepting or rejecting hypotheses in terms of practical and theoretical values. It seems obvious that curriculum theorists who would teach science as inquiry and who would teach the structure of science can profit from the philosophical analysis of the relation between acceptance and values.

Science Textbook Writers

Analytic philosophy of science has both analytic and heuristic value for science textbook writers. The science textbook writer often deals with general concepts in his work that have been analysed and discussed at length by analytic philosophers of science. The textbook writer is usually ignorant of these analyses and the textbook which is the result of his work suffers accordingly.

That the scientist *qua* scientist may make value judgments in the acceptance of scientific hypotheses is something that is usually overlooked in the typical science textbook. Indeed, science textbook writers often present complex and difficult scientific theories along with the most simple minded views about the acceptance of these theories.

Consider for example a passage in ESCP *Investigating the Earth*. The authors say

> What is the difference between evidence and proof? . . . Evidence is observation that tends to support a conclusion. A *conclusion* is an interpretation or judgment based on the evidence. When there is a little evidence for it a conclusion is only probable. The conclusion becomes proved when there is sufficient evidence to support it.[30]

Now one plausible way of interpreting this passage is that when the authors say that the conclusion becomes proved when there is sufficient evidence to support the conclusion they mean that the conclusion should be accepted. Since no evidence ever makes the conclusion certain the question of when the evidence is "sufficient" for acceptance remains. The authors say nothing about this and indeed do not even seem to realize there is a problem. However, it is here, as we have seen, that value judgments enter into the picture. The question is what is at stake either epistemologically or practically, what gain and losses might accrue, in accepting a hypothesis that is less than certain.

Consider, for example, acceptance$_B$ and suppose the hypothesis at issue is the hypothesis that some particular individual has ESP. Now the acceptance$_B$ of this hypothesis may have grave repercussions on the whole scientific framework since it is not implausible to suppose that ESP can not at the present time be easily assimilated into our scientific framework. To assimilate this hypothesis without radical change in our basic assumptions may involve the acceptance$_B$ of a variety of *ad hoc* hypotheses which may seriously affect the over-all simplicity of the scientific world view. Since simplicity is one epistemic value sought in science, what will be considered sufficient evidence for the acceptance of the ESP hypothesis may have to be different from more typical cases of acceptance$_B$ where this simplicity is not in question.

Supposing acceptance$_U$ is at issue, then practical values enter into the picture. Suppose the hypothesis is that a drug is a cure for cancer and has no toxic side effects. As we have seen much would depend here on the context of the acceptance$_U$ e.g. whether it involved human or animal subjects. What would be sufficient evidence in the one case would not be sufficient in the other.

There is no discussion of these points in *Investigating the Earth*. This is especially unfortunate since students using this book are asked by the authors whether certain data is evidence or proof that the earth is round. Interpreted in the way we have suggested this comes down to asking whether certain evidence is sufficient for accepting the hypothesis that the earth is round. It is unclear how students could possibly answer such a question unless the authors clarified the values which are at stake in the acceptance of the hypothesis and what sort of acceptance is at issue. For example, in the context of a long ocean trip it might make some difference if acceptance$_U$ or acceptance$_B$ was at issue. For Magellan certain practical values were at issue e.g. the value of his life and his crew in the acceptance$_U$ of the hypothesis. If only acceptance$_B$ were at issue one might want to know how the hypothesis that the earth is round, if it were accepted$_B$, would affect certain epistemic values such as the simplicity of the scientific framework.

Knowledge of the philosophy of science could have had analytic value for the authors of *Investigating the Earth*. It takes little imagination to see how such knowledge might also have suggested different approaches to the material, i.e. have had heuristic value. For example, some clear idea that values enter into the acceptance of hypotheses in science might have suggested to the authors a number of new examples to utilize in the text, ones that bring out some of the epistemic and practical values that operate in the acceptance of hypotheses in science. Moreover, knowledge of the importance of values in the acceptance of scientific hypotheses might have suggested that different epistemic values operate in the context of pseudo-science than in science. The "flat earthers" for example can accept$_B$ that the earth is flat so long as certain complex auxiliary hypotheses are accepted. A discussion of whether flat earthers with their strange beliefs and modes of reasoning can be committed to the epistemic value of simplicity that scientists are committed to might provide an illuminating contrast with scientific epistemic values.[31]

Researchers in Science Education

Analytic philosophy of science has analytic and heuristic value for researchers in science education. We have already mentioned in passing one question that might be pursued in such research, namely: What affect does a science teacher who adopts the odds maker view have on his students? We have suggested earlier that a science teacher might adopt the odds maker view in certain contexts. Whether this approach would be fruitful is something that the educational researcher can help decide. In any case, a number of hypotheses suggest themselves. For example, since on the odds maker approach to science teaching the teacher never advocates the acceptance of any hypotheses and the student is left entirely on his own whether he accepts or rejects a hypothesis the following hypothesis H is suggested:

H Science teachers who teach science as odd makers tend to produce students who are less dogmatic than do science teachers who do not teach science as odd makers.

Whether H is true is something that only educational research can decide.

Educational researchers in their work accept$_U$ or reject$_U$ hypotheses e.g. hypothesis H suggested above, in the light of the evidence and certain practical values.

To use a recent example from educational psychology: Should educational researchers accept$_U$ the hypothesis that Whites as a group have a higher I.Q.

than Blacks as a group the difference between I.Q. being due to genetic factors? Whether educational researchers should accept$_U$ this hypothesis should involve the consideration of the practical values involved in doing so. One effect of educational researchers accepting$_U$ this hypothesis in their work might be serious racial unrest. Whether this effect is likely is an open question but if it is the value of domestic peace and human brotherhood must be weighed against any epistemic values that such research might achieve.

Perhaps part of the controversy between Jensen and his critics is over just this point. Jensen in some of his writing plays down the question of whether people should accept$_B$ his hypothesis about White genetic superiority.[32] He may be interpreted as advocating, rather, that scientists should take his hypothesis seriously; that they should consider it a fruitful working hypothesis in the context of empirical research at least, that the hypothesis should be accepted$_U$. Either Jensen seems not to consider the practical values involved in doing this or else he seems to believe that no practical considerations could outweigh the epistemic values. His critics, on the other hand, take the practical values involved very seriously and play down any possible epistemic values that might be the result of scientists accepting$_B$ his hypothesis.

It is difficult to say who is correct in this controversy. But two points need to be stressed. First, accepting$_U$ Jensen's hypothesis in the context of genetic research does not entail that one should accept$_U$ this hypothesis in the context of educational policy making. Secondly, accepting$_U$ Jensen's hypothesis in the context of educational policy making does not entail that the traditional goal of educational equality should be given up. Indeed it might be plausibly argued that far from Jensen's hypothesis justifying giving Blacks an inferior education it suggests that Blacks should be given an intensive and superior education not for environmental deprivation but for genetic deprivation.[33]

Perhaps if these points were clearly understood the acceptance$_U$ of Jensen's hypothesis in the context of empirical research would not be thought to have such drastic practical consequences. In any case some understanding of the practical and epistemic values involved in the acceptance of scientific hypotheses may bring some illumination to this controversy.

Conclusion

I have argued that a recent controversy in the philosophy of science concerning the acceptance of scientific hypotheses is illuminating for science education; that clarification and analysis of this controversy provides insights useful to science educators. I have tried to sketch in what some of these insights might be for various types of science educators. It is my hope that science educators will take these suggestions seriously; I hope even more that philosophers of science will take science education seriously enough to make other suggestions and criticize the ones I have made.

FOOTNOTES

[1] See for example Michael Martin *Concepts of Science Education: A Philosophical Analysis* (Glenview, Ill: Scott Foresman, 1972); James T. Robinson *The Nature of Science and Science Teaching* (Belmont, Calif.: Wadsworth Pub. Co. 1968); Martin Levitt *Philosophy of Science and Problems of Education* (Urbana, Ill.: University of Illinois Press 1972).
[2] For a similar contrast see I. Scheffler *Anatomy of Inquiry* (New York: Alfred Knopf, 1963) Chap. I; May Brodbeck "The Nature and Function of the Philosophy of Science," *Readings in the Philosophy of Science*, ed. H. Feigl and M. Brodbeck (New York: Appleton-Century-Crofts, 1953).
[3] Michael Martin, "Philosophy of Science and Science Education," *Studies in Philosophy and Education* 1972 pp. 210-225.
[4] See for example Barney M. Berlin and Alan M. Gaines, "Use Philosophy to Explain the Scientific Method," *The Science Teacher* 1966 p. 52; see also Merritt E. Kimball, "Understanding the Nature of Science: A Comparison of Scientist and Science Teachers," *Journal of Research in Science Teaching*, 1967-1968, pp. 110-120, Kimball's study showed that philosophy majors scored higher on *The Nature of Science Scale* than science majors.
[5] Martin *Concepts of Science Education* pp. 124-126.
[6] Rudolf Carnap *Logical Foundations of Probability* (Chicago: University of Chicago Press 1960).
[7] R. C. Jeffrey "Valuation and Acceptance of Scientific Hypotheses" *Philosophy of Science*, 23, 1956, pp. 237-246.
[8] Carl G. Hempel "Inductive Inconsistencies" *Synthese*, 12, 1960, pp. 439-469.
[9] I. Levi "Must the Scientist Make Value Judgements?" *Journal of Philosophy*, 57, 1960, pp. 345-357; I. Levi *Gambling with Truth* (New York: Knopf 1967).
[10] Richard Rudner "The Scientist Qua Scientist Makes Value Judgements" *Philosophy of Science*, 20, 1953, pp. 1-6.
[11] R. Braithwaite *Scientific Explanation* (New York: Harper 1953).
[12] C. W. Churchman "Science and Decision Making", *Philosophy of Science*, 23, 1956, pp. 248-249.
[13] J. Leach "Explanation and Value Neutrality" *British Journal for the Philosophy of Science*, 19, 1968 pp. 93-109.
[14] For a similar distinction see I.Scheffler *Science and Subjectivity* (Indianapolis: Bobbs-Merrill, 1967) p. 86.
[15] See for example Wm. Frankena *Ethics* (Englewood Cliffs, N.J.: Prentice-Hall 1963) Chapter 6.
[16] Rudner, *op. cit.* p. 2.
[17] Leach, *op. cit.*
[18] We have not considered in this paper how exactly values should enter into the acceptance of scientific hypotheses. In particular we have not considered whether a cost-benefit or a expected utility analysis is more desirable. For a defense of the cost-benefit approach which I find very persuasive see Alex Michalos "Cost-Benefit vs. Expected Utility Acceptance Rules" a paper read at the PSA meeting in Boston in 1970.
[19] Joseph J. Schwab, "The Teaching of Enquiry" *The Teaching of Science* (Cambridge: Harvard University Press, 1964) p. 5.
[20] Byron B. Massialas and C. Benjamin Cox, *Inquiry in Social Studies* (New York: McGraw-Hill, 1966) p. 46.
[21] Jerome S. Bruner, *The Process of Education* (Cambridge: Harvard University Press, 1961) p. 28.
[22] *Ibid.*, p. 26.
[23] Joseph J. Schwab, "Structure of the Disciplines: Meaning and Significance," *The Structure of Knowledge and The Curriculum* (ed.) G. W. Ford and Lawrence Pugno (Chicago: Rand McNally, 1964) pp. 1-30.
[24] See for example Carl G. Hempel *Philosophy of Natural Science* (New Jersey: Prentice-Hall 1966) Chapters 2, 3, 4.
[25] Hugh Lehman, "Functional Explanation in Biology," *Philosophy of Science*, 32, 1965, pp. 1-19.
[26] See for example Carl G. Hempel, "Operationism, Observation and Scientific Terms," *Philosophy of Science* (ed.) A. Danto and S. Morgenbesser (New York: Meridian Books, 1960) pp. 101-120.
[27] See for example Rudolf Carnap, "Formal and Factual Science," *Readings in the Philosophy of Science*, (ed.) H. Feigl and M. Brodbeck; Karl Popper, "Why are the Calculi of Logic and Arithmetic Applicable to Reality?" *Conjectures and Refutations* (New York: Basic Books, 1962).

[28] See for example Nagel *op. cit.*; Richard Rudner *Philosophy of Social Science* (New Jersey: Prentice-Hall, 1966); Karl Popper *The Poverty of Historicism* (Boston: Beacon Press 1957).
[29] See for example M. Foster and M. Martin, *Probability, Confirmation and Simplicity* (New York: Odyssey Press, 1966); R. Carnap, *The Logical Foundations of Probability* (Chicago: University of Chicago Press 1960); Wesley Salmon, *The Foundations of Scientific Inference* (Pittsburg: University of Pittsburg Press 1966); Karl Popper, *The Logic of Scientific Discovery* (New York: Basic Books, 1959).
[30] Earth Science Curriculum Project, *Investigating the Earth*, (Boston: Houghton, Mifflin Co., 1967) p. 61. For a critique of this passage along different lines see Martin *Concepts of Science Education* pp. 36-38.
[31] For an interesting discussion of flat earthers see Martin Gardner, *Fads and Fallacies in the Name of Science* (New York: Dover Pub., 1957) Chapter 2; for a discussion of the use of pseudo-science see Martin *Concepts of Science Education* p. 40-42.
[32] See for example Arthur E. Jensen "The Ethical Issues" *The Humanist*, 32, 1972, pp. 5-6.
[33] Michael Martin "Equal Education, Native Intelligence and Justice" unpublished.

Causal Importance and Objectivity

MICHAEL MARTIN

In this paper I will consider an argument against the objectivity of the social sciences. The argument will be called 'the argument from causal importance'. First, I will state the argument. Secondly, I will distinguish different senses of objectivity that might be involved in the claim that the argument shows that social science is not objective. Thirdly, I will consider different strategies to avoid the argument.

The argument from causal importance

In order to understand the argument from causal importance against the objectivity of the social sciences it is necessary to distinguish three different types of causal judgements.[1] First, there are judgements about the total cause of some social phenomenon. In this type of judgement one says that the total cause of a social phenomenon P is X. X would normally consist of several logically independent factors $X_1, X_2, \ldots X_n$ which jointly constitute a nomologically sufficient condition for P. Secondly there are judgements about the contributory cause of some social phenomenon. In this type of judgement one says that some causal factor X_i is a contributory cause of P. Now X_i would be a contributory cause of P just in case X_i is one of the factors $X_1, X_2, \ldots, X_n$ making up the total cause X of P; that is X_i is part of a nomologically sufficient condition of P. Thirdly, there are judgements of causal importance. In this type of judgement one says that some causal factor X_i (which is a contributory cause of P) is the most important cause of P. For example, a sociologist might say that the social position of a man's parents is the most important causal factor in determining his social position; a clinical psychologist might argue that his patient's divorce was the major cause of the patient's suicide attempt; an anthropologist might maintain that the decisive cause of cargo cults in New Guinea was the influx of Western religion.[2]

Judgements of the total cause and judgements of the contributory cause seem to raise no particular problem about the objectivity of the social sciences among philosophers of the social sciences. When we come to judgements of causal importance, however, the situation changes. For it has been argued[3] that the choice of the most important cause in a given situation is capricious and arbitrary. When the sociologist, clinical psychologist or anthropologist selects from a number of contributory causes one contributory cause and designates it as *the* major or most important cause of the particular phenomenon under study, it is argued that such a judgement is completely subjective.

For example, the clinical psychologist could have designated his patient's unstable psychological condition as the major cause of his attempted suicide, and the anthropologist could have cited the magical beliefs of the natives as the major cause of cargo cults. It seems then that one social scientist can claim that one thing is the major cause of some social phenomenon while another can claim that something else is and there can be no objective way to decide between them so long as both factors are contributory causes, that is so long as both factors are part of the total cause of the phenomenon.

Three types of subjectivity

The argument from causal importance sketched above is ambiguous. For there are at least three things people might be saying when they say that causal judgements lack objectivity.

In the first place, they might be saying that judgements of causal importance are neither true nor false. On this interpretation of objectivity, when one says that X_1 is the most important cause of P one is not stating a fact but is recommending, persuading, advising, etc. In short, on this interpretation judgements of causal importance are value judgements and value judgements are interpreted in a noncognitive way.

But the lack of objectivity attributed to judgements of causal importance need not be based on the noncognitive character of such judgements. Those who say that causal judgements are not objective might admit that judgements of causal importance are either true or false, but argue that these judgements are relative. To say that such a judgement is relative is just to say that certain relativizing phrases must be used in the analyses of the judgement, phrases like 'at time t', 'in culture C', 'from point of view m'. Thus when social scientists S_1 says that the magical beliefs of the natives are the most important cause of cargo cults and social scientist S_2 says that the influx of Western religious ideas is the most important cause of cargo cults they are not really disagreeing. They may be both making different empirical claims. For example, suppose one analyses 'is the most important cause' in terms of the relativizing phrase, 'is the most interesting contributory cause from point of view m'. Then S_1 is making the claim that magical belief is the most interesting contributory cause from point of view m_1, i.e. from S_1's point of view and S_2 is making the claim that the influx of Western religious ideas is the most interesting contributory cause from point of view

Causal Importance and Objectivity

m_2, i.e. from S_2's point of view. Both of these claims, it might be argued, can be tested empirically and both may be true.

Thirdly, those who say that judgements of causal importance are not objective might be referring not to the relativizing of judgements of causal importance but to the impossibility of rationally deciding which point of view should be preferred. In this sense of objectivity there would be no problem about the objectivity of judgements of causal importance even if they were relative so long as there could be some reason for preferring one point of view to another. The claim that judgements of causal importance are not objective is on this interpretation just the claim that there is no privileged point of view. In the above example there would be no objective way of saying whether social scientist S_1's point of view is to be preferred to S_2's point of view. Clearly, the third sense of objectivity is more important than the second. For there is nothing particularly disturbing about the relativity of judgements of causal importance if one relative position is preferable to another. Indeed if there were such a preferable position, judgements of causal importance would be relative only at a superficial level. At a deeper level there would be nothing relative about them.

Furthermore, the first sense of objectivity does not seem too important either unless it is supplemented with a particular metaethical view, the view that such judgements are unjustified. For even if judgements of causal importance are neither true or false, they may still be capable of being rationally justified. Consequently, judgements of causal importance may not be objective in the sense of not being true or false and yet be capable of being rationally debated and decided. However, if they are capable of being rationally debated and decided,[4] they are objective in much more interesting and important senses than the first sense of objective. That such judgements are neither true nor false would not matter.

Some strategies to avoid the argument

There are several different strategies that one might use to defeat the argument from causal importance. First, one might avoid all judgements of causal importance in the social sciences. Secondly, one might analyse judgements of causal importance in such a way that makes only some of these judgements relative, and then avoid these relative judgements in social sciences. Thirdly, one might analyse judgements of causal importance in such a way that makes them rationally defensible either if they are interpreted non-cognitively or if they are interpreted cognitively. In this latter case no judgements of causal importance need to be avoided to avoid subjectivity.

Let us consider each of these strategies in turn.

Michael Martin

Avoiding all judgements of causal importance
Consider the following somewhat radical approach to the argument from causal importance. One might say that even if the argument from causal importance does succeed in any of the senses of objectivity just considered it does not show that objectivity in the social sciences is impossible. What it shows is that objectivity is impossible *if* judgements of causal importance are made. Consequently, if judgements of causal importance are eliminated from the social sciences the non-objectivity of judgements of causal importance cannot be any hindrance to the objectivity of the social sciences. There seems to be no *a priori* reason why such judgements must be made in the social sciences. One could conceive of social scientists sticking to the specification of contributory causes and total causes. A similar view has some advocates.[5]

Many would feel that such a recommendation, although it would save the objectivity of the social sciences from attack, has too great a price. Social scientists do make such judgements and to forbid them their usual habits seems too confining. There is some force to this objection and it certainly would be advisable to canvass other less radical alternatives in order to preserve the objectivity of the social sciences before this extreme course of action is recommended. Nevertheless, it still needs to be stressed that this course of action is open to us if we are willing to pay the price: the thesis that the social sciences are objective would not be refuted by the argument if certain common practices are changed—namely that no judgements of causal importance are made.

Avoiding relativized judgements of causal importance
However, perhaps it is not necessary to avoid completely judgements of causal importance in order to preserve the objectivity of the social sciences. Perhaps if such judgements were correctly understood they would not lack objectivity. Much will depend on what is meant by 'the most important cause'. One possible analysis mentioned above in passing is the following:

> Definition 1: X_i is the most important cause of phenomenon P from point of view m if and only if X_i is the most interesting contributory cause of P from the point of view of the social scientist who regards his subject in manner m.

Now it is important to notice that this analysis does not make judgements of causal importance non-objective in the sense that they are neither true or false, for they are either true or false. But they are relative, hence they are not objective in the second sense: their analysis contains the relativizing clause, 'from point of view m'.

Causal Importance and Objectivity

In any case, perhaps Definition 1 is not correct; perhaps a non-relativistic analysis is possible. In recent years an analysis of judgements of causal importance has been argued by Morton White that is significantly different from Definition 1.

On this analysis some judgements of causal importance are relative and some are not. White argues that the most important cause of a phenomenon is the abnormal contributory cause. However, what is abnormal is often relative to the point of view one takes. Consider an example used by White. The wife of a man who has an ulcer might identify the most important cause of his indigestion as his eating parsnips, since from her point of view his eating parsnips was the abnormal contributory cause. The doctor, however, might regard the man's ulcer as the most important contributory cause, since from his point of view this is an abnormal contributory cause. Thus White defines 'the most important cause' in this way:

Definition 2: X_1 is the most important cause of phenomenon P from point of view m if and only if: (1) X_1 is a contributory cause of P; and (2) X_1 is the abnormal cause—from the point of view of the social scientist who regards the subject of inquiry in manner m.[6]

White illustrates his theory with the following schema. Suppose we have the general causal law

Whatever is P and R is Q

This combined with

a is P
a is R

explains

a is Q

Now the question is: Is the most important cause of a's being Q, a's being P or a's being R? From one point of view one asks why a has property Q when a is R and most R's are not Q. Looking at it from this point of view, a's being P is the abnormal factor—the difference maker—hence the most important cause. On the other hand, one can ask from another point of view, why does a have property Q when a is P and most P's are not Q? Looking at it from this point of view, a's being R is the abnormal contributory cause and hence the major cause.

White denies, however, that his view leads to complete relativity; he would argue that his view is significantly different, therefore, from the analysis presented in Definition 1 above. He maintains that it is not always possible to conceive of a contributory cause as abnormal and hence as the most important cause. Suppose, for example, that most R's are Q and most

P's are not *Q*. In this case one could ask, why does *a* have the property *Q* when *a* is *P* and most *P*'s are not *Q*? Thus *a*'s being *R* would be the abnormal contributory cause. But one could not ask why does *a* have property *Q* when *a* is *R* and most *R*'s are not *Q*. In this case *P* could not be cited as the abnormal contributory cause.

However, White insists that this sort of statistical asymmetry does not happen in many cases and in the cases where it does not occur the contributory cause that is chosen cannot be decided by statistical evidence; the decision is rather determined by the social scientist's interests which in turn rest on value judgements. While value judgements are not logically implied by judgements of causal importance, whether a social scientist chooses to look on the subject under investigation in manner *m* rather than in some other manner may reflect or rest upon a value orientation. White argues that such a value orientation is not rationally debatable.

White argues that although his abnormalism gives an account of most social scientists' usages of 'the most important cause', it does not give an account of all. Sometimes the most important cause is not identifiable with the abnormal or difference-maker contributory cause, but with some action that is morally praiseworthy or blameworthy. Thus White argues that sometimes when a social scientist says that a man's failure to act heroically was a major cause of a certain social event, he means merely that the man should not have acted that way and should be held responsible for the event. White argues that this use of causal language is unfortunate and should not be used. It is the philosopher's prerogative, according to White, to recommend that the social scientist use two distinct linguistic expressions, 'one that signalizes that this selection of *the* cause has been made on wholly empirical grounds and another that signalizes that the selection has been made on moral grounds'.[7]

As we have argued above, one could avoid the lack of objectivity in the making of causal judgements by barring all judgements of causal importance from the social sciences. However, as we have seen, this may be too high a price to pay for the prevention of subjectivity. Less stringent recommendations might be considered. White's analysis suggests an alternative: restrict judgements of causal importance to cases where there is a statistical asymmetry. Judgements of causal importance which are completely relative and which depend on social scientists' interests and value judgements would excluded. In the example we used above if there was no statistical difference between the relation of someone's unstable psychological state and a suicide attempt and the relation of someone's getting a divorce and a suicide attempt, neither his unstable psychological state nor his getting a divorce could be singled out as the most important cause.

Causal Importance and Objectivity

The present recommendation would (unlike the recommendation to bar all judgements of causal importance) allow some judgements of causal importance but exclude others. There certainly would be some definite advantages to this proposal. A social scientist who argued that X_1 rather than X_2 was the most important cause of social phenomenon P would be able to appeal to objective (non-relative) statistical evidence. People who disagreed could attempt to refute his claim by appeal to statistical evidence. It would not be a matter of interest or preference.

White, as we have seen, recommends two separate linguistic expressions to distinguish judgements of causal importance that are empirically testable from moral judgements that are disguised judgements of causal importance. He suggests that causal language be used only in the former case. My recommendation carries White's programme further. I recommend two separate linguistic expressions that distinguish between judgements of causal importance that are based on objective statistical facts and judgements that are relative to some point of view and ultimately based on interest. I recommend that causal language be restricted to the former. In the latter case a social scientist may say, for example, X_1 is the most interesting contributory cause from my point of view. He would not say X_1 is the most important cause of P, as he would in the former case. Such a linguistic separation, if White's analysis is correct, makes the basis of choice in social investigation clearer and more explicit.

Making value judgements and points of view objective

So far we have argued that two moves are open to defenders of the possibility of objectivity in the social sciences against the argument from causal importance. First, all judgements of causal importance can be excluded from the social sciences. Secondly, all relative judgements of causal importance can be excluded from the social sciences.

However, both of these moves may be unnecessary if value judgements are rationally defensible. Consider first the more radical view. Suppose that abnormalism is wrong (and indeed that all cognitive interpretations of judgements of causal importance are mistaken) and that judgements of causal importance are disguised value judgements interpreted noncognitively. It would surely not follow from this that such judgements were neither correct nor incorrect nor incapable of rational defence. As we suggested above not all noncognitivist value theories entail irrationality. For example, one might argue that in making a value judgement one is not making a statement that is true or false; one is not describing. Rather one is recommending, advising, assessing and so on. However, in recommending, advising, assessing and so on one purports to be unbiased, factually informed, conceptually clear and imaginative. In making a value judgement one is making a judgement that if correct, would be agreed to by other people who were unbiased, well-informed, conceptually clear and imaginative. One is claiming not an actual consensus but an ideal consensus. Let us call this position a 'noncognitivist ideal observer theory of value judgements'.[8]

Now it might be argued that this is not how value judgements in fact function in social science. However, it is difficult to know exactly how value judgements do function without more empirical studies than we have now. In any case, whether they do in fact function in this way or not, one might recommend that they *should* function in this way at least in the social sciences. If this recommendation were followed, one could have judgements of causal importance that were neither true nor false but nonetheless rationally defensible and absolute. In this case, the lack of objectivity of judgements of causal importance, in the sense that they were neither true, nor false, would be innocuous.

However, suppose that White is correct and that judgements of causal importance are true or false but sometimes relative to a point of view. There might be one point of view that is more rational to adopt than any other. White argues that judgements of abnormality sometimes rest upon one's interests and these in turn rest upon value judgements. He seems to suppose that value judgements are irrational and not debatable. But there is no good reason to suppose that this is so; there is good reason, if we want to preserve the objectivity of the social sciences, to adopt a different account. This account has already been outlined above in another context.

One might plausibly maintain that the point of view from which judgements of abnormality should be made is that of an ideal observer, an observer who is unbiased, fully informed, imaginative and so on. Given this point of view as privileged one could maintain that X_1 is the abnormal cause of P from point of view m_1 and X_2 is the abnormal cause of P from point of view m_2, but that m_1 is the point of view one should take for it is an unbiased, fully informed, imaginative view, i.e. the point of view of an ideal observer. There certainly seems to be good reason to take such a point of view as privileged. A person who is unbiased, well-informed, etc., is to be relied upon and trusted; the attributes of an ideal observer define a reliable and trustworthy judge.[9] Thus White's definition might be amended along the following lines:

> Definition 3: X_1 is the most important cause of P if and only if: (1) X_1 is a contributory cause of P; and (2) if there were an ideal observer, X_1 would be the abnormal cause from his point of view.

Thus a social scientist who claims that X_1 is the most important cause is assuming an ideal consensus—a consensus among fellow scientists who are

Causal Importance and Objectivity

also unbiased, informed and so on. If such a consensus does not in fact occur, one must assume that some ideal attribute is missing—not all the scientists are unbiased, not all are fully informed, etc. Arguments and research would proceed until a consensus was achieved or at least approximated.

Again it need not be claimed that Definition 3 is a completely reportive definition of 'the most important cause', that is that this is the way 'the most important cause' is used by social scientists. The claim need only be that adopting Definition 3 enables one to preserve objectivity of the social sciences against the argument from causal importance. Given this definition, one can at the same time maintain that judgements of causal importance, although not themselves value judgements, rest upon value judgements but (*pace* White) that these value judgements are rationally defensible and non-relativistic.

Abnormalism and radical social science

In his book *The Politics of History*,[10] Howard Zinn argues against White's analysis of causal importance and his argument may be used by other radical social scientists against White's position and those similar to it. It is important to see how the modifications suggested above relate to Zinn's critique.

Zinn's basic argument against White's position is that the most important cause should be determined by the most useful social policy. For example, he argues that it would not be socially useful to pick out Rap Brown's speech as the abnormal cause—and hence decisive cause—of the riots in Cambridge, Maryland. He recommends instead that the conditions of the Black communities—discrimination plus poverty—be considered as abnormal and hence the decisive cause. Taking discrimination and poverty as the decisive cause, Zinn argues, might lead to action against those conditions. Thus Zinn seems at least implicitly to suggest the following definition of the most important cause:

Definition 4: X_i is the most important cause of P if and only if: (1) X_i is a contributory cause; and (2) X_i is the abnormal cause—from the point of view of radical social policy.

Now condition (2), as Zinn understands it, entails: (3) X is capable of being changed by human effort. White, Zinn points out, rejects the view that the abnormal cause is always identified with the contributory cause that is manipulatable. White rejects this view because this is simply not how historians use causal language. Naturally, Zinn is not too impressed with this reason. Historical and social scientific language generally reflects a conservative or apathetic orientation. Zinn recommends a change in language

Michael Martin

and his implicit definition of causal importance should be construed as part of this recommendation.

The position taken in this paper has important similarities with and differences from the point of view taken by Zinn. First I believe with Zinn that there is nothing sacred about the language that historians and social scientists use. One may well recommend changes in their languages. (Indeed, as we have seen, even White recommended some changes.) Thus I agree that it is a very weak argument simply to point out, as White sometimes does, that historains do not use causal language in a certain way. The question is how they *should* use it.

Secondly, I recommend changes in White's analyses (although I am more explicit in exactly what I am recommending than Zinn is). I want to show how social science can become objective; Zinn wants to radicalize social science and history—to make them relevant to social change. Consequently our recommendations differ in their purpose. Nevertheless, there may be nothing incompatible with some of the things I recommend and what Zinn recommends.

If the goals of a radical social science are to be rationally justified, they may have to be justified by appeal to conditions which define an ideal observer. Indeed, it is not an implausible interpretation of Zinn to say that he assumes that what he recommends will also be recommended by a person who is clear-headed, well-informed, impartial, and imaginative. Thus the two modifications of White's definition—one made by me and one made by Zinn—may in fact pick out the same contributory cause as the most important cause, that is the two definitions may be materially co-extensive.

Whether they are or not is a question for further research.

Standards of comparison and objectivity

So far we have considered White's abnormalism and certain modifications that might be made in his analysis in order to defeat the argument from causal importance and yet not avoid judgements of causal importance in the social sciences. However, White's emphasis on the abnormal has not gone unchallenged. It has been argued that in a statistical sense of abnormal the most important cause does not have to be abnormal[11] and that if abnormal is used in some non-statistical sense the thesis that the most important cause must be abnormal is unclear.[12] Consequently, alternative analyses have been proposed and refined. Thus Samuel Gorovitz[13] has proposed an analysis of the most important cause not in terms of abnormal contributory cause and this analysis has been refined and deepened by Robert Shope.[14]

The basic idea in Gorovitz's analysis is that the most important cause is not necessarily selected by comparing it with some normal situation but by

Causal Importance and Objectivity

comparing it with some situation or other that is used as a standard of comparison. The most important cause is the difference-making factor relative to this contrast situation. The details of Gorovitz's analysis and its refinements need not concern us here. However, the basic idea is captured by the following partial analysis:

Definition 5: X_i is the most important cause of P relative to standard of comparison S only if: (1) X_i is a contributory cause of P; and (2) X_i is the difference-making factor relative to standard of comparison S.

The problem for the objectivity of social science raised by this analysis is how a standard of comparison is to be chosen. An indefinite number of standards of comparison can be chosen and, depending on what standard is chosen, various contributory causes can be the most important cause. We seem in danger of slipping into radical subjectivity again. Gorovitz suggests[15] that perhaps different standards of comparison are used in different areas of causal inquiry, e.g. psychology, history and law. And although this may be so this does not completely solve the problem. First, the mere fact that the use of some standard of comparison is the usual and accepted practice in some domain is no justification for its use. Secondly, within some domain of inquiry there can be disagreement over what is the most important cause (e.g. the disagreement over the most important cause of cargo cults within anthropology). Subjectivists might well argue that in the final analysis the standard of comparison is based upon scientific interest which in turn is determined by arbitrary and irrational value judgements.

However, as we have seen, value judgements are not necessarily arbitrary or irrational. There might be good reason why one standard of comparison is chosen over another. Indeed there is no reason to suppose that such a choice needs to be relativistic. Again one might incorporate an ideal observer analysis into the present analysis and define the most important cause in the following way:

Definition 6: X_i is the most important cause of P if and only if: (1) X_i is a contributory cause of P; (2) X_i is the difference-making factor relative to contrast situation S; (3) if there were an ideal observer, he would use contrast situation S in selecting X_i.

Again one need not suppose that Definition 6 completely captures the ordinary meaning of the most important cause, as this is used by social scientists. It is supposed only that such a definition enables one to preserve the objectivity of the social sciences against the argument from causal importance, given an analysis of causal importance suggested by the approach taken by Gorowitz.

Michael Martin

Conclusion

I have recommended several strategies for defeating the argument from causal importance. Following any of these strategies presumably would either defeat the argument from causal importance or else make it innocuous. Thus social science can be objective despite judgements of causal importance. Which one of these strategies is the most acceptable is a question for another paper, and whether the objectivity of the social sciences can be defended from other arguments is a topic for a book.

Boston University

NOTES

1 Cf. Morton White, *Foundations of Historical Knowledge*, New York 1965, Chapters 3 and 4.
2 For an interesting discussion of cargo cults, see I. C. Jarvie, *The Revolution in Anthropology*, New York 1964, Chapter 2.
3 See, for example, Max Weber, *The Methodology of the Social Sciences*, New York 1949, pp. 49-112. For a discussion of Weber on judgements of causal importance, see May Brodbeck (ed.), *Readings in the Philosophy of the Social Sciences*, New York 1968, pp. 82-4.
4 For a discussion of objectivity along these lines, see Israel Scheffler, *Science and Subjectivity*, Indianapolis 1967, Chapter 1; see also Karl Popper, *The Logic of Scientific Discovery*, New York 1959, p. 44, n.1.
5 See John Stuart Mill, *A System of Logic*, London 1961, p. 214.
6 See White, op. cit., p. 126. Although White's discussion is in the context of history, there is no reason not to suppose that he takes his analysis to have wider application and we will so interpret it here.
7 Ibid., p. 177.
8 See William Frankena, *Ethics*, Englewood Cliffs 1963, pp. 94-6. For the cognitivist version of the ideal observer theory, see Roderick Firth, 'Ethical Absolutism and the Ideal Observer', *Philosophy and Phenomenological Research*, 12, 1951-2, 317-45.
9 See Bruce Kuklick, 'The Mind of the Historian', *History and Theory*, 3, 1969, 313-31, for an application of the ideal observer theory to historical objectivity.
10 Howard Zinn, *The Politics of History*, Boston 1970, pp. 352-8. Zinn, as does White, writes from the context of historical research. But there seems to be no reason to restrict his views to history and we will not do so here.
11 Paul J. Dietl, 'Abnormalism', *Theoria*, 35, 1970, 93-9.
12 Samuel Gorovitz, 'Causal Judgements and Causal Explanation', *Journal of Philosophy*, lxii, 1965, 697-711.
13 Ibid.
14 Robert Shope, 'Explanation in terms of "The Cause"', *Journal of Philosophy*, lxiv, 1967, 312-20.
15 Samuel Gorovitz, 'Aspects of the Pragmatics of Explanation', *Nous*, 3, 1969, 61-72.

The Philosophical Importance of the Rosenthal Effect*

MICHAEL MARTIN

Robert Rosenthal and his colleagues have performed psychological experiments the philosophical importance of which has yet to be seriously considered. The purpose of this paper will be to describe briefly Rosenthal's work and its importance for philosophical issues connected with social sciences.

Rosenthal's experiments

Rosenthal's early experimental studies were connected with the effect an experimenter's expectancy about the results of an experiment have on the outcome of the experiment. He claimed to have shown in experiments with human and animal subjects that the expectancy an experimenter has about the outcome of an experiment unwittingly affects the outcome of the experiment in the direction of the expectancy. In later experiments Rosenthal claimed to have shown that the expectancies of teachers affect their student's behaviour in the direction of the expectancies. This effect on behaviour (of both experimenter and teacher) has come to be known in the literature as the Rosenthal effect. Let us consider three experiments.

One experiment was concerned with the effect that an experimenter's expectancy has on subjects' ratings of photographs.[1] Two groups of subjects, group G_1 and group G, were asked to rate photographs of people on a scale from -10 to $+10$ in terms of whether the people in the photographs had recently experienced success or failure. (The photographs actually had been chosen so that on the average the people should be seen as neither successful nor unsuccessful, but as neutral.) The experimenters who administered the test to the subjects in group G_1 were told that their group should average about $+5$, while the

* I would like to thank Robert Rosenthal and George Romanos for their comments on an earlier draft of this paper.

experimenters who administered the test to the subjects in group G_2 were told that their group should average -5. Aside from this difference the instructions to the experimenters for both groups were the same. The experimenters read exactly the same instructions to their subjects. Nevertheless, the results of the experiment for the two groups were different: group G_1 averaged $+0.40$ while group G_2 averaged -0.08 in their ratings. The experiment with minor variations was replicated several times.

Another experiment was concerned with the effect experimenter expectancy has on the performance of animals.[2] One group of experimenters was given rats which they were told were 'Maze bright' rats; a second group of experimenters was given rats which they were told were 'Maze dull' rats. (In reality the rats were randomly assigned to the two groups and were not bred for maze learning.) The two groups of rats were taught to run a T-maze by the two groups of experimenters. It turned out that the rats designated as Maze bright learned to run the maze better than the rats designated as Maze dull. In a similar experiment similar results were obtained with rats learning Skinner-box problems.[3] Rats thought by experimenters to be 'Skinner-box bright' did better in their learning tasks than rats thought by the experimenters to be 'Skinner-box dull'. According to Rosenthal, the combined probability that the results of these two experiments could have occurred by chance was 0.0007.[4]

In another experiment the experimenter was, as it were, replaced by a teacher.[5] The experiment tested the effect of a teacher's expectancy on students behaviour (Rosenthal refers to this experiment as the Pygmalion experiment). At the beginning of the year children in an elementary school were given a non-verbal test of intelligence by their teachers. The teachers were not told the test was an intelligence test and were made to believe that the test would predict academic 'blooming'. In each class one group of children was selected as children who 'would show unusual academic development during the coming year'. The teachers thought these groups were selected by the test results; actually the children were randomly assigned to the groups by Rosenthal. Thus the teacher in each class was given the expectancy that some children in his or her class were 'late bloomers'. The children were tested again at the end of the year. Children whose teachers thought they were late bloomers gained significantly more in IQ than the control group, that is those children who were not designated as late bloomers. The Pygmalion experiment has been replicated many times.[6]

It is not known how wide-spread the Rosenthal effect is in the social sciences. Rosenthal suggests that one might assess the generalization of his findings by considering the similarity of the design of his experiments to the design of typical experiments in psycholgy.[7] Judged in these terms the generalizability of the experiments is impressive. To be sure most of the experimenters used by Rosenthal were graduate students. But this should not affect the generalizability of the results. First, there is good reason to suppose that professional, competent and higher-status experimenters would be more likely to bias the results of an experiment than would more amateur experimenters. Secondly, most of the experimenters in psychological experiments today who come into direct contact with the subjects of the experiment are graduate students; the typical highly competent professional psychological experimenter has graduate students gather his data.

As far as the subjects of the Rosenthal experiments are concerned they were very much like typical subjects of psychological experiments: thus the generality of the results would not be affected by non-representative subjects. Moreover, the situations in which the experiments were performed were varied, thereby increasing the generalizability of the results. The experiments were conducted in several universities, in different geographical areas, in different types of laboratories. The tasks included photograph rating, verbal learning and taking standardized and projective psychological tests; for animal subjects the tasks included learning in T-mazes and Skinner boxes. One might suspect then that the Rosenthal effect is indeed widespread.

Exactly how the experimenters influence their human subjects to conform to their expectancies is not well understood, but it is generally agreed that the way the influence occurs is very complex and subtle. ESP was actually considered a possible means of communication between experimenter and subject at one point in Rosenthal's studies.[8] However, the ESP hypothesis was tested and dropped and the hypothesis that subtle and complex auditory and visual cues are the means of influence is now favoured.[9] How these cues work is unclear but there is reason to think that they can to a certain extent influence the results of an experiment at a very early stage, even before the subjects have responded to the tasks set by the experimenter.[10]

The way experimenters influence their animal subjects is even more difficult to understand. Rosenthal cites evidence suggesting that the quality and quantity of the handling of the rats 'communicates' the experimenter's expectancy. He also suggests that the experimenters working with 'bright' rats watch their rats more carefully, thus reinforcing the desired responses.[11]

Michael Martin
Issues in the philosophy of the social sciences

The Rosenthal effect raises several closely related philosophical issues connected with the social sciences. First of all, there is the issue of self-fulfilling prophecy: can the Rosenthal effect be considered a type of reflexive prediction—what has been commonly called a self-fulfilling prophecy? We shall argue that the Rosenthal effect cannot be so construed but that it, as well as a self-fulfilling prophecy, is a special case of a broader notion, one that will be called a reflexive truth vehicle. Secondly, the Rosenthal effect raises questions about the objectivity of the social sciences. In particular it can be asked how the Rosenthal studies relate to the recent discussions of objectivity by philosophers of science such as Scheffler and Popper. We shall argue that Scheffler's argument leaves unanswered an important question raised by Rosenthal's work and that Popper's strategy to achieve objectivity in science is not adequate to overcome the problem raised by Rosenthal's work. Nevertheless, it shall be maintained that Rosenthal does provide a way of achieving objectivity in the social sciences, a way of eliminating the Rosenthal effect. Thirdly, there is the issue of the coherence of Rosenthal's thesis: Can Rosenthal consistently defend the widespread nature of the Rosenthal effect and the validity of his own work? Does not a Rosenthal effect affect Rosenthal's own studies, paradoxically calling them into question? We shall argue that the possibility of a meta-Rosenthal effect is indeed a problem but that there is a way of rationally defending Rosenthal's thesis against the charge of incoherence.

Reflexive prediction

Rosenthal certainly thinks that the Rosenthal effect is a type of self-fulfilling prophecy and often speaks of the effect of the expectancies of experimenters and teachers in these terms. There does indeed seem to be an interesting analogy between the Rosenthal effect and the standard examples of self-fulfilling prophecies discussed in philosophical literature, e.g., the public prediction that a bank will fail causing a run on the bank. On the other hand, there seem to be some disanalogies as well. Rosenthal's graduate student experimenters did not in any obvious sense make a prophecy or a prediction about the results of the experiment. (Although they might have made one if they had been asked.) Clearly one must proceed with caution here lest crucial distinctions be overlooked.

Philosophical Importance of the Rosenthal Effect

After all what is the definition of a self-fulfilling prophecy? Although many people speak of self-fulfilling prophecies there have been very few actual analyses of this notion. To my knowledge the first extended treatment of the problem of the definition of reflexive prediction (which would include self-fulfilling prophecies as well as self-defeating prophecies) was Roger Buck's.

Buck suggest that the following four conditions define the concept of a reflexive prediction:[12]

(1) Its truth value would have been different had its dissemination status been different.
(2) The dissemination status it actually had was causally necessary for the social actors involved to hold relevant and causally efficacious beliefs.
(3) The prediction was, or if disseminated would have been, believed and acted upon.
(4) Something about the dissemination status or its causal consequences was abnormal, or at the very least unexpected by the predictor, by whoever calls it reflexive, or by those to whose attention its reflexive character is called.

Buck argues that his analysis accounts for typical cases of reflexive prediction in the social sciences. For example, an economist makes a public prediction that a certain bank may fail. The truth of the prediction would have been different had the dissemination status of the prediction been different, e.g., had the prediction not have been made public. Making the prediction public caused the patrons of the bank to hold certain beliefs which they acted on causing a run on the bank; this in turn caused the bank to fail.

Construed in one way Buck's analysis certainly applies in the Rosenthal experiments. Compare the case of the bank's failure and the experiments of rats learning the T-maze. One can say that Rosenthal and his associates are analogous to the economist and the graduate student experimenters are analogous to the patrons of the bank. Rosenthal and his associates disseminated certain information to the graduate student experimenters who affected the behaviour of the rats. In this case it is not implausible to suppose that the experimenters (unwittingly) acted upon certain beliefs in affecting the rats' behaviour.

But construed in another way, Buck's analysis fails. Suppose graduate student experimenters are analogous to the economist; the rats are analogous to the patrons of the bank. The graduate student experimenters somehow 'disseminated the prediction' to the rats. Of course, it is at this point that the analogy breaks down, for it is surely implausible to suppose that the rats had certain beliefs and acted on these beliefs.

Which analogy should we appeal to in understanding the Rosenthal effect? No doubt both analogies are helpful in bringing out different aspects of the experiment. The first analogy is helpful in bringing out the effect of Rosenthal's statements on his experimenter subjects; the second analogy is helpful in bringing out the effect of the experimenter subjects' expectancy on the rats. However, the Rosenthal effect in this experiment, as Rosenthal conceives of it, is the effect of the experimenter subjects on the rats, not his effect on the experimenter subjects. Consequently when he says that the Rosenthal effect is a self-fulfilling prediction he has in mind the second analogy. But Buck's analysis, as we have seen, does not work in this case.

There is good reason, however, to suppose that Buck's analysis is inadequate. George Romanos has argued persuasively that Buck's argument attempting to justify his restriction to acting-on-beliefs is circular.[13] Romanos has suggested the following as an alternative analysis of reflexive prediction:

The formulation/dissemination style of the prediction must be a causal factor relative to the prediction's coming out true or false.

Is the Rosenthal effect a reflexive prediction given this new construal? To be able to tell we need to understand what a formulation/dissemination style is. According to Romanos the formulation style (F-style) of a prediction is the formal or syntactical properties of the prediction. Every prediction must be formulated in some way; there must be something like a sequence of sounds or inscriptions which are said to convey or express the prediction. This formulation need not be in some natural language which is spoken or written but 'may be constructed out of such things as electric impulses, bodily movements, puffs of smoke, or anything else which can be interpreted as expressing a prediction'.[14] According to Romanos, the dissemination style (D-style) of a prediction is the manner of reproduction and/or transmission of the prediction in a certain F-style.

It is not clear that the Rosenthal effect is a reflexive prediction in Romanos' view, either. First, there is a conceptual problem for it is not clear what should be counted as a syntax of a language. Even if Rosenthal is correct that the Maze bright rats were handled differently by the experimenters from the Maze dull rats, it is not clear that the experimenters' behaviour can be considered to have expressed a

Philosophical Importance of the Rosenthal Effect

prediction in, e.g., some syntax of bodily movement. One certainly does not want to say that *any* piece of behaviour causally related to a person's expectance expresses a prediction. Suppose there was a stock broker who, whenever he thought there was going to be a sharp rise in the market, broke out in hives. We would not want to say that the hives' outbreak expressed the prediction that the market would rise sharply. (Although someone might *use* this information to make a prediction about a rise in the market.) The behaviour of the graduate student experimenters and the behaviour of our hypothetical stock broker may not be very much alike. But still the graduate student experimenters' behaviour is a far cry from the behaviour of someone in the standard case of making a prediction. Hence our hesitation.

Secondly, there is an empirical problem. Experimental psychologists do not know with any certainty how the rats were affected by the experimenters. Rosenthal's suggestion that the two groups of rats performed differently because they were handled differently needs further testing before it can be accepted. One might suppose that the situation is different with the human subjects in the photograph-rating experiment. But again it is not well understood how the experimenters influenced the human subjects, and consequently it is not clear whether it is plausible to interpret the experimenters' behaviour as expressing a prediction. Rosenthal may have this in mind when he says:

> We cannot be sure, however, that these changes in experimenter behavior are themselves conveyors of information to the subjects as to how they should respond. Possibly, those subjects who later go on to confirm or disconfirm the experimenter's hypothesis affect the experimenter differently early in the experiment. The experimenter then behaves differently towards these subjects but without necessarily conveying response-related information to the subject. In other words, differential treatment by the experimenter may be quite incidental to the question of whether a subject goes on to confirm or disconfirm the experimenter's hypothesis.[15]

Given Romanos' analysis, there is another reason why the Rosenthal effect should not be interpreted as a reflexive prediction. In so far as one can legitimately speak of a prediction being made, strictly speaking in some of the Rosenthal experiments the prediction comes out false. Recall that the one group of experimenters had the expectancy that their subjects would on the average rate the photographs about +5. The actual result was +0.4. The other group of experimenters had the expectancy that the subjects would on the average rate the photos as −5. The result was −0.08. Consequently it hardly seems plausible to say that the F/D-style of the prediction was a causal factor relative to the truth

177

or falsehood of the prediction. At best the F/D-style of the prediction was a causal factor affecting the degree of approximation of the prediction to the true value.

The above points should not be taken as criticism of Romanos' analysis of reflexive prediction. Rather they are difficulties in interpreting the Rosenthal effect as a reflexive prediction. Only if one is inclined preanalytically to include the Rosenthal effect as a reflexive prediction will these problems incline one to reject Romanos' analysis.

One thing is clear. Even if one in not inclined to include the Rosenthal effect under reflexive prediction, reflexive predictions and the Rosenthal effect seem to belong to the same species of methodological problem. They both have a reflexive nature: one is a prediction, the other is an expectancy. In a reflexive prediction the truth or falsity is affected; in a reflexive expectancy only the degree of approximation to the truth may be affected. In a prediction the reflexive aspect is a function of the F- and D-style of the prediction; in an expectancy the causal factors affecting the reflexive aspect are not well understood.

What is needed is some larger category in which both reflexive prediction and reflexive expectancy are included as special cases. I would suggest that such a category be that of a truth vehicle. Let us understand a truth vehicle as anything that can legitimately be said to be true or false in the relevant sense of true or false, e.g., beliefs, predictions, statements and so on, but not friends. However, the terms 'belief', 'prediction', 'statement' are ambiguous. One could be referring to what is believed, predicted, stated; one could also be referring to the act or state of believing, predicting, stating. Clearly it is the former and not the latter that are truth vehicles. One must also distinguish between the generic act or state of believing, predicting, or stating. Thus, one must distinguish between the generic act or state of predicting that a bank will fail and the act or state of predicting that a bank will fail by a particular person at a particular time. We shall refer to the particular act or state of believing, predicting or stating as the instantiation of a truth vehicle.

Thus an instantiation of the belief that group G_1 will have an average score of $+5$ might be Bill Jones' belief (a particular psychological or neurological state) at noontime on 14 July 1970 that group G_1 will have an average score of $+5$. An instantiation of the prediction that the Bank of Douglas will fail might be Professor Smith's prediction (the act of uttering a sentence in a particular way) made to her class at the University of Arizona during the 18 May 1960 seminar on banking. An instantiation of the prediction that some particular missile will miss the target might be the prediction (the producing of a particular electrical impulse travelling along a certain wire) made by a particular IBM computer during training practice on 1 April 1955 at 9.00 AM. (It should be clear that although truth vehicles can be spoken of as true or false, instantiations of truth vehicles cannot be spoken of as true or false. Thus, it is wrong to speak of a neurological state or the producing of an electrical impulse as true or false.)

Let us call the various instantiations of some truth vehicle V_1, instantiation $I_1 V_1$, instantiation $I_2 V_1$, instantiation $I_3 V_1$, ..., instantiation $I_n V_1$. One can, then, define the reflexivity of an arbitrary instantiation I_i of an arbitrary truth vehicle V_i as follows: $I_i V_i$ is reflexive IF $I_i V_i$ is a causal factor either affecting the degree of approximation of V_i to the truth or affecting whether V_i comes out true or false. Given this analysis both the Rosenthal effect and reflexive prediction become special cases of the reflexivity of instantiated truth vehicles.

Reflexive instantiated truth vehicles are found in both natural and social science. Given a sufficiently liberal interpretation of reflexive prediction, reflexive predictions are found in the natural sciences. And reflexive instantiated truth vehicles that are not predictions are found in the natural sciences. It would seem possible that a physicist (because of an expectancy that his experiment would turn out in a certain way) would unwittingly set up experimental equipment in a way so as to speciously get the results expected. However, it may not be plausible to interpret the physicist's behaviour as expressing a prediction.

Objectivity

The Rosenthal effect and its prima facie generality seems to have serious ramifications with respect to the objectivity of the behavioural sciences for, if the expectancy of the experimenter in the behavioural sciences influences the result of the experiment, doubt seems to be cast on the objectivity of the results of the experiment. The results of behavioural experiments may all be biased and may not constitute reliable knowledge.

Some recent philosophers of science have used psychological experiments to bring into question the objectivity of the natural sciences. It may be useful to relate their arguments to the Rosenthal effect. Thomas Kuhn, for example, has argued that a scientist's theoretical orientation influences what the scientist sees. He argues that scientists tend to be blinded to negative evidence because of the influence of their theoretical orientation on their observations; they tend to see what they believe and to fail to see what they do not believe. He used Bruner and Postal's experiment with playing cards as evidence for this influence.[16] In the Bruner and Postal experiment subjects were shown playing cards. Many of the cards were normal but some of them were anomalous, e.g., a red six of spades. The subjects tended to identify the anomalous cards as normal, e.g., a black four of hearts as a black four of spades.

Some defenders of the objectivity of science have argued against Kuhn as follows. First, it is important to distinguish between the influence of the theoretical premises held by a scientist on his observations and the influence of the theoretical categories held by the scientist on his observations. Thus a scientist may see the world in Newtonian categories, e.g., mass, force, without necessarily having all his observations conform to the predictions of Newtonian theory. Secondly, although the influence of a scientist's theoretical premises on observation may be strong, it is not inevitable. As Scheffler has put it: 'Our expectations strongly structure what we see, but do not wholly eliminate unexpected sights. . . . There is no evidence for a general incapacity to learn from contrary observations, no proof of a pre-established harmony between what we believe and what we see.'[17] Even in the Bruner and Postal experiment some subjects were finally able to recognize the anomalous cards as anomalous.

One naturally wonders whether the same sort of strategy can be used to defend the objectivity of behavioural research against the attack of the Rosenthal effect. Before such strategy is attempted, however, it is important to see exactly what has been accomplished by defences like Scheffler's. I think it is fair to say that Scheffler has shown at most that a scientist's theoretical orientation does not necessarily make his observations confirm his theories; that specious confirmation is not inevitable. However, this establishes only that objectivity *via* observational testing is not logically impossible in science.

This result is, of course, extremely important since some philosophers have seemed to deny that objectivity is possible. However, it still might be true that as a matter of fact in the vast majority of cases the theoretical beliefs of scientists blind them to negative evidence. The extent of this influence may be so wide that the validity of most of our alleged scientific knowledge may be in question even though objectivity is possible.

Philosophical Importance of the Rosenthal Effect

I believe that a similar Schefflerian move can be made with respect to the Rosenthal effect and a similar reply can be given. Rosenthal has not shown that there is any pre-established harmony between experimenters' expectancies and the results of their experiments. After all, some experiments do seem to conflict with the experimenters' expectancies. But even granted this, it still may be true in the vast majority of experiments that the Rosenthal effect is very strong. Consequently the objectivity of the results of behavioural experiments can be called into question.

The Rosenthal effect also seems to call into question the way in which some philosophers of science have supposed objectivity can be achieved in science. Popper, for example, argues that the objectivity of science is not a function of the individual scientist but is a function of the essential social character of science. He argues that there are two important aspects to this social character of scientific objectivity: first, there is something approaching free criticism in that scientists put forth theories and other scientists criticize these theories; secondly, scientists avoid speaking at cross-purposes, for they state their conflicting theories in testable form and evaluate their theories by experience which is an impartial arbitrator. Popper says: 'when speaking of "experience" I have in mind experience of a "public" character like observations, and experiments'. He argues 'everyone who has learned the technique of understanding and testing scientific theories can always repeat the experiment and judge for himself'.[18]

Popper's two aspects of objectivity are no doubt important. Indeed, free criticism and testable theories may be necessary conditions for the objectivity of science. But in the light of Rosenthal's results they do not seem to be a sufficient condition. The results of an experiment may be the results of the experimenter's expectancy. Consequently experience may not be an impartial arbitrator at all, as Popper supposes.

This does not mean that objectivity cannot be achieved in behavioural research. However, techniques will have to be used to meet the particular problems raised by Rosenthal's research. Mere appeal to intersubjective criticism in terms of repeatable experiments is not enough. Rosenthal himself has suggested a number of strategies that go a long way towards meeting the problem. Let us briefly consider a few of these strategies.[19]

One important strategy to control the Rosenthal effect is to use a number of experimenters (say drawn randomly from a population of experimenters) each of whom would deal with a small number of subjects. Such a technique would have the effect of tending to eliminate experimental bias because there is reason to suppose that experimenters unintentionally learn from their subjects how to influence them. With fewer subjects the chance of this learning taking place may decrease. Also, with a number of experimenters it is likely that there will be experimenters with different biases; these biases would statistically tend to cancel one another out.

It may also be possible to learn the bias of the experimenter before the experiment takes place. Once a bias is learned it can be correlated with the results of the experiment. If the correlation is large, the experimental effect can be corrected by such well-known statistical methods as partial correlations or analyses of co-variance. If the experimental effect is insignificant, it can be ignored.

Another strategy to diminish the Rosenthal effect is to minimize and standardize contact between the experimenter and the subjects. It should be recalled that the Rosenthal effect is produced by experimenters dealing with different subjects in subtly different ways, e.g., in their instructions to the subject. One way of eliminating such differential treatment would be to have the instructions to a group of subjects prerecorded, e.g., on video-tapes. Both experimental and control groups would be shown the same tapes. In order that the subjects would not feel that the experimental situation was unrealistic they could be led to believe that their instructions were coming 'live' over closed-circuit TV. In order to further lessen the influence of the experimenter the subjects might (when this was feasible) record their own responses.

If an experiment required that the experimenter have direct contact with the subjects, techniques could be introduced which would reduce the cues available to both the experimenter and the subjects. There is good reason to suppose that visual and auditory cues were very important in producing the Rosenthal effect. Imposing a screen between the experimenter and the subject would eliminate visual cues; auditory cues could be eliminated by having the subjects and experimenter communicate by writing.

Still another technique that could be used to correct the Rosenthal effect is the so-called expectancy control group method. Suppose we were interested in whether some psychological treatment T was effective. Standard experimental studies using an experimental and control group would be unreliable for it would be unclear if the results of the studies were due to treatment T or to the Rosenthal effect. However, this problem could be overcome in the following way. One experimenter would be chosen with an expectancy that treatment T would be effective and would use treatment T on experimental group

E_1, and not on control group C_1. Another experimenter would be chosen with an expectancy that treatment T would not be effective and would use treatment T on experimental group E_2 and not on control group C_2. By a two-way analysis of variance a main effect attributable to treatment T, a main effect attributable to experimental effect, and an interaction to these two effects could be determined.

In conclusion, the impossibility of objectivity in the social sciences has not been established by Rosenthal's work but it is possible that most social science research is biased as a result of experimental expectancy. However, the same sort of thing may well be true in the natural sciences. Although there is no reason to suppose that objectivity in the natural sciences is impossible, most observations used in testing theories may as a matter of fact be biased by the theoretical commitment of the observer.

Furthermore, there is no reason to think that the Rosenthal effect must be overcome by certain methods or approaches unique to the social sciences, e.g., Verstehen, or wholistic-phenomenological orientation. As we have seen, the Rosenthal effect can be controlled by particular experimental techniques, e.g., certain types of control groups, statistical analyses of the results of experiments. Verstehen and other such methods, whatever their value and whatever they may involve, do not seem to be needed.

The meta-Rosenthal effect

So far we have not considered a problem that has been lurking in the background in much of our discussion of the Rosenthal effect. Rosenthal claims to have shown that an experimenter's expectancy influences the results of experiments and he maintains that such biasing of the results of experiments is widespread. But if this is so it seems paradoxically to apply to the results of his own experiments. For Rosenthal's experiments are also performed by experimenters, e.g., Rosenthal. These experimenters have a certain expectancy, namely, that experimental expectancy will affect the result of the experiment in the direction of the expectancy. This expectancy may affect the result of *their* experiments in the direction of *their* expectancy. Let us call the Rosenthal effect as it affects Rosenthal's own research the meta-Rosenthal effect.

There are three basic questions that one can ask about the meta-Rosenthal effect. We might wonder what a meta-Rosenthal effect would show. We might wonder if it would be coherent to maintain that the Rosenthal effect is widespread and yet deny that the meta-Rosenthal effect exists. We might ask whether there is a meta-Rosenthal effect.

With respect to the first question one can say at least that if there is a meta-Rosenthal effect it would tend to undercut our trust in Rosenthal's studies. Furthermore, it would seem to give comfort to defenders of the objectivity of the social sciences. For if the Rosenthal studies are untrustworthy because of the meta-Rosenthal effect, one could not claim that the social sciences lacked objectivity on the basis of the Rosenthal experiments. A similar argument was used by Scheffler in defending the objectivity of the natural sciences against critics like Kuhn who used psychological studies and historical evidence to show that natural science was subjective. Scheffler argued:

And indeed there is a striking self-contradictoriness in the effort to persuade others by argument that communication, and hence argument is impossible; in appeal to the facts about observation in order to deny that commonly observable facts exist, in arguing from the hard realities of the history of science to the conclusion that reality is not discovered but made by the scientist. To accept these claims is to deny all force to the arguments brought forward for them.[20]

In order to answer the second question one must distinguish two different positions. It would be contradictory to maintain the following theses:

(1) The meta-Rosenthal effect does not exist.
(2) The Rosenthal effect is found in every experiment.

Since Rosenthal's research is an experiment, by (2) the Rosenthal effect would influence his own experiment. But this is denied by (1). However, Rosenthal need not assert (1) and (2). Rosenthal can coherently maintain the following:

(1') The meta-Rosenthal effect does not exist.
(2') The Rosenthal effect is found in all experiments except the Rosenthal experiments.

Actually Rosenthal seems to believe something even weaker than (2'), namely:

(2'') The Rosenthal effect is likely to be found in many experiments but not in the Rosenthal experiment.

Philosophical Importance of the Rosenthal Effect

The question is whether Rosenthal and his colleagues have any justification for the last clause in (2′) and (2″). For it might be suggested that unless they do they escape incoherence only by an arbitrary restriction.

This brings us to the last question. Rosenthal would argue, I believe, that it is unlikely that the meta-Rosenthal effect exists because he and his colleagues (unlike most other experimenters) have taken the trouble to control for experimental expectancy in their research; they have instituted techniques that would tend to eliminate the bias that results from the Rosenthal effect. We have reviewed some of Rosenthal's techniques above. However, one technique we did not mention and the only technique explicitly mentioned[21] by Rosenthal in his own research is the technique of the total double-blind experiment.

In this experimental set-up, no one knows the experimental condition to which any subject is assigned. For example, in the photograph rating experiment ten experimenters were used. Each experimenter was assigned at random to ten different research rooms. Furthermore, ten sets of instructions were randomly assigned to the rooms (five inducing the $+5$ expectancy and five inducing the -5 expectancy). Subjects were also randomly assigned to the rooms. The experimenter read over the instructions when they arrived at the room thus creating the experimental expectancy. It was not until the end of the experiment that any one knew what instructions each experimenter had gotten.

Now although the total double-blind experiment may eliminate some aspects of the Rosenthal effect it is doubtful whether it could eliminate all. For just because Rosenthal and his colleagues did not know which graduate student experimenters would get which instructions, Rosenthal et al. still could have influenced the graduate student experimenters in a general way before they went to the research rooms. The graduate students might have been unwittingly influenced to influence their subjects' behaviour in the direction of their expectancy rather than not at all or in the opposite direction. The total double-blind situation would not seem to eliminate this problem.

However, Rosenthal could have eliminated this problem by other techniques which he suggests but apparently does not use. For example, Rosenthal-type experiments can be conducted by various experimenters—some sympathetic to Rosenthal, some with an expectancy that there would be no Rosenthal effect. The result of different expectancies would tend to cancel each other out in the final result.

I believe one can conclude that although the problem of the meta-

Michael Martin

Rosenthal effect is not completely eliminated by Rosenthal's experimental design, the problem could be in principle eliminated. Consequently, it is possible that with more research Rosenthal could claim (2″) with some certainty.

Conclusion

The methodological importance of the Rosenthal effect should not lead us to draw unwarranted inferences concerning it. The Rosenthal effect, despite its similarity to phenomena of self-fulfilling prophecy, is not easily assimilated to this phenomena. Furthermore, it would not be warranted to dismiss Rosenthal's position as self-refuting because of the meta-Rosenthal effect. For although the possibility of the meta-Rosenthal effect is not completely eliminated in Rosenthal's work it is in principle completely eliminable. Thus there is no paradox or arbitrary restrictions in maintaining that the Rosenthal effect is widespread but absent from Rosenthal's own studies. Finally, although the Rosenthal effect raises serious questions about the objectivity of social science research it would be a mistake to conclude that Rosenthal has shown that objectivity is impossible in the social sciences. Indeed, Rosenthal shows how the Rosenthal effect can be overcome and how objectivity is still possible.

Department of Philosophy, Boston University,
232 Bay State Road, Boston, Mass. 02215, U.S.A.

NOTES

[1] R. Rosenthal & K. L. Fode, 'Three Experiments in Experimenter Bias', *Psychological Reports*, 1963, 12, pp. 491–511; see also R. Rosenthal, *Experimenter Effect in Behavioral Research* (New York: Appleton-Century-Crofts, 1966), pp. 145–57.

[2] R. Rosenthal & K. L. Fode, 'The Effect of Experimental Bias on the Performance of the Albino Rat', *Behavioral Science*, 1963, 8, pp. 183–9; R. Rosenthal, *Experimenter Effect . . .*, pp. 158–65.

[3] R. Rosenthal & R. Lawson, 'A Longitudinal Study of the Effect of Experimenter Bias on the Operant Learning of Laboratory Rats', *Journal of Psychiatric Research*, 1964, 2, pp. 61–72; R. Rosenthal, *Experimenter Effect . . .*, pp. 165–76.

[4] *Ibid.*, p. 176.

[5] R. Rosenthal & L. Jacobson, *Pygmalion in Classroom* (New York: Holt, Rinehart & Winston, 1968).

Philosophical Importance of the Rosenthal Effect

⁶ For a review of this literature see R. Rosenthal 'On the Social Psychology of the Self-fulfilling Prophecy: Further Evidence for Pygmalion Effects and their Mediating Mechanisms', MSS Modular Publications, Inc., New York (1974), Module 53, pp. 1–28.

⁷ R. Rosenthal, *Experimenter Effect*..., Ch. 17. Not all psychologists have agreed that the Rosenthal effect is wide spread, and indeed some have challenged the statistical basis of Rosenthal's experiments. See Theodore X. Barber & Maurice J. Silver, 'Fact, Fiction, and the Experimenter Bias Effect', *Psychological Bulletin Monograph Supplement*, 1968, 70, pp. 1–29. It will be assumed in this paper that these statistical objections can be met. See R. Rosenthal, 'Experimenter Expectancy and the Reassuring Nature of the Null Hypothesis Decision Procedure', *Psychological Bulletin Monograph Supplement*, 1968, 70, pp. 30–47; T. X. Barber & M. J. Silver, 'Pitfalls in Data Analysis and Interpretation: A Reply to Robert Rosenthal', *Psycholgical Bulletin Monograph Supplement*, 1969, 70, pp. 48–62.

⁸ *Ibid.*, p. 282.

⁹ *Ibid.*, pp. 281–9. There is reason to think that expectancy can be communicated by auditory cues alone. See J. G. Adair & J. S. Epstein, 'Verbal Cues in Mediation of Experimenter Bias', *Psychological Reports*, 1968, 22, pp. 1045–53.

¹⁰ R. Rosenthal, *Experimenter Effect*..., pp. 289–93.

¹¹ *Ibid.*, p. 178; see also R. Rosenthal, 'On the Social Psychology of the Self-fulfilling Prophecy...', pp. 4–5.

¹² R. C. Buck, 'Reflexive Prediction', *Philosophy of Science*, 1964, 30, pp. 359–69; see also A. Grunbaum, 'Comments on Professor Roger Buck's Paper "Reflexive Predictions"', *Philosophy of Science*, 1963, 30, pp. 370–2; R. C. Buck, 'Rejoinder to Grunbaum', *Philosophy of Science*, 1963, 30, pp. 373–4.

¹³ George Romanos, 'Reflexive Predictions', *Philosophy of Science*, 1973, 40, pp. 97–109.

¹⁴ *Ibid.*, p. 105.

¹⁵ R. Rosenthal, *Experimenter Effect*..., pp. 300–1.

¹⁶ Thomas Kuhn, *The Structure of Scientific Revolutions* (Chicago: University of Chicago Press, 1962), p. 63.

¹⁷ See I. Scheffler, *Science and Subjectivity* (Indianapolis, Ind.: Bobbs-Merrill, 1967), p. 44.

¹⁸ Karl Popper, 'The Sociology of Knowledge', in (ed.) Philip P. Weiner *Reading in the Philosophy of Science* (New York: Charles Scribner & Sons, 1953), p. 362.

¹⁹ Rosenthal, *Experimenter Effect*..., Chs. 19–23.

²⁰ Scheffler, *op. cit.*, pp. 21–2.

²¹ Rosenthal, *Experimenter Effect*..., p. 373. Elsewhere Rosenthal has argued that in 185 studies of experimenters' expectation 63 of these studies showed the effect of experimental expectancy at the 5 per cent level of significance. He concludes from this that it is overwhelmingly likely that the Rosenthal effect exists. However, these results may be due to a meta-Rosenthal effect. See Rosenthal, 'On the Psychology of the Self-fulfilling Prophecy...', p. 5.

DISCUSSION

THE OBJECTIVITY OF A METHODOLOGY

MICHAEL MARTIN

Boston University

In this paper I consider critically Richard Rudner's account of the objectivity of a methodology. I show that Rudner's analysis provides neither a sufficient condition nor a necessary condition for one method being more objective than another.

1. Rudner's Account of Objectivity. 'Objectivity' can be predicated of people, sentences, methods, and so on. Rudner, in his book *Philosophy of Social Science*,[1] considers several of these different uses of 'objectivity' and gives an account of what it means to say that one method is more objective than others. A method, according to Rudner, is the logic or criteria of justification which provides the rationale by which sentences are accepted or rejected. According to Rudner one method is more objective than another if it is more reliable than the other and a method is more reliable than another if its continued employment is less liable to error than the continued employment of the other method. Rudner explains that one method is less liable to error than another if it is less likely to result in its users continuing to believe or coming to believe false sentences than is the other method.

Given this account of objectivity Rudner argues that a method is maximally reliable if it minimizes the likelihood of error more than the alternatives and a method is absolutely reliable if it makes error impossible. Now Rudner argues that no method of empirical inquiry is absolutely reliable in this sense. Consequently scientific method is not absolutely reliable. However he maintains that the course of history shows that scientific method is maximally reliable in terms of other methods. According to Rudner this is because of the self-correcting nature of scientific method: no hypothesis is ever immune from revision and the continued application of scientific method will make it likely that false hypotheses will be eliminated.

I do not want to question Rudner's contention that scientific method is the most objective method or his explanation of this objectivity. I will argue that Rudner's account of objectivity is not adequate. First, I will show that there are some methods clearly less objective than scientific method which turn out to be more objective on Rudner's account. Rudner's view at least needs supplementation. Hence, his account is not a sufficient condition for the objectivity of method. Secondly I will show that there are certain historical methods which may be more objective than other historical methods and yet do not meet his definition. Hence his account does not provide a necessary condition of the objectivity of method.

[1] Richard Rudner, *Philosophy of Social Science* (Englewood Cliffs, Prentice-Hall, 1966), pp. 73–83.

2. The Problem of Cautious Methods. Rudner's definition of objectivity with respect to methods is this:

> (1) A method A is more objective than a method B if and only if the use of method A is less likely than method B to result in its users continuing to believe, or coming to believe, false sentences.

Consider, for example, a methodology that would entail that one should not believe or disbelieve any synthetic sentence. Let us call this methodology, a method of extreme caution. This method would be more reliable than scientific method given Rudner's definition for users of this method neither continue to believe nor come to believe any synthetic statement. Hence they would not continue to believe or come to believe any false synthetic sentence. Consequently a method of extreme caution would be absolutely reliable and thus it would be more objective than scientific method. But that this method is more objective than scientific method is clearly absurd. Hence there must be something wrong with (1).

Now the above criticism may be thought to be unfair to Rudner. Clearly, it might be said, Rudner is thinking of a method in which people do believe or disbelieve some synthetic sentences. Undoubtedly he is, although this is not explicitly stated in his writing. Taking this supposition into account we can reformulate his definition thus:

> (2) A method A is more objective than method B if and only if (a) the use of A is less likely than method B to result in its users continuing to believe, or coming to believe, false sentences and (b) the users of method A continue to believe and come to believe some synthetic sentences and the users of method B continue to believe and come to believe some synthetic sentences.

But (2) still has problems. For consider a methodology which would entail that one should not believe any sentence except a sentence with a probability equal to or greater than 0.9999999. Let us call this methodology, a method of moderate caution. Suppose that there are sentences which meet this restricted requirement. This method would be more objective than scientific method for it is surely the case that a method of moderate caution would be less likely to result in its users coming to believe or continuing to believe false sentences than would scientific method which on any plausible formulation would allow belief in more speculative and less well established hypotheses. Consequently a method of moderate caution would be more objective than scientific method. But this again seems wrong and suggests that (2) is not an adequate account of the objectivity of method.

On Rudner's account of objectivity scientific method is less objective than more cautious methods. On these methods one should either believe no synthetic sentence or believe synthetic sentences only under the most stringent conditions. This suggests a way out of the problem. Popper and other methodologists have stressed the importance of bold speculative hypotheses in science. The cautious methods we have considered rule out belief in such hypotheses. Perhaps the objectivity of scientific method consists in the reliability of scientific method with respect to bold and speculative hypotheses. This consideration suggests the following definition:

> (3) Method A is more objective than method B if and only if (a) the use of A is less likely than method B to result in the users of A continuing to believe or coming to believe false sentences and (b) the users of A and B continue to believe and come to believe bold and speculative sentences.

This definition certainly has advantages over the others for it seems to eliminate both a method of extreme caution and a method of moderate caution as being more objective than scientific method since neither of these methods allow belief in bold speculative theories and hypotheses. Whether (3) provides a sufficient condition for the objectivity of method is another question which we will consider later. In any case, it is clear that Rudner's account must be supplemented to provide a sufficient condition for the objectivity of method.

3. The Problem of Distorting Omissions. Now condition (a) in definition (3) above is not a necessary condition for the objectivity of a methodology. For one method could be more objective than another and yet not be more reliable in Rudner's sense. Consider two historical methods HM_1 and HM_2 which provide criteria of evaluating historical accounts. Now these historical accounts can be thought of as complex sets of sentences about the past. HM_1 and HM_2 thus provide the rationale for accepting or rejecting these accounts.

Let us suppose that the two methods are used to evaluate different accounts of the histories of various countries. Let us also suppose that HM_1 is a little more reliable than HM_2 in Rudner's sense; it is slightly less likely that the use of HM_1 will result in historians believing or coming to believe false sentences contained in these histories than that the use of HM_2 will. However, although historians using HM_1 will be a little less likely to have false beliefs than historians using HM_2 it is possible that historians using HM_1 would be much *more* likely to believe accounts of history with gross omissions, accounts which leave out crucial social political movements, battles, people and dates; in sum, accounts which although perhaps containing all true sentences provide a distorted picture of history. On Rudner's account one seems to be forced into saying that HM_1 is more objective than HM_2, despite the gross bias that might result from HM_1 in contrast to HM_2 simply because HM_1 is a little more reliable than HM_2. However, the contrary seems to be the case. HM_2, although slightly less reliable than HM_1, would presystematically be considered more objective than HM_1 because its use resulted in less distorting omissions. Consequently, condition (a) in definition (2) above does not provide a necessary condition for one method being more objective than another.

Now it might be argued against the above criticism that so long as it is true and about the period under investigation what is included in a historical account can not be decided on methodological grounds. Clearly not all true sentences about, e.g. English history can be included in a history of England and selection according to one's purposes and interest is required. No doubt this is so. Selection is essential in what is included in historical accounts. But *given certain purposes* certain omissions are distorting while other omissions are not. For example a historian who wrote a history of England with a special emphasis on the courage of the English people during time of war which contained no sentences about the English people's reaction to the Nazi bombing of England during World War II would be guilty of a serious omission, an omission that is seriously distorting. Consequently a methodology whose use would result in a historian accepting this history may well be considered less objective than some other methodology. On the other hand a historian with the above purpose who wrote a history of England and did not include sentences describing the change in Englishmen's hats from 1800–1900 would not be guilty of a distorting omission and a methodology which resulted in the acceptance of historical accounts with such omissions would not because of this, at least, lack objectivity.

4. Rudner's Account Revised. The above criticism also shows that (3) above cannot provide a sufficient condition for the objectivity of a methodology. Historical method HM_1 can meet (a) and (b) in (3) but may not be as objective as historical method HM_2. Use of HM_1 may make it much more likely than the use of HM_2 that accounts with distorting omissions will be accepted although use of HM_1 is a little less likely than HM_2 to result in its users believing false sentences. Hence HM_1 would not be as objective as HM_2.

In the light of this criticism one might suggest a further modification in Rudner's definition of the objectivity of a methodology:

> (4) Method A is more objective than method B if and only if (a) the use of A is less likely than method B to result in the users of A continuing to believe, or coming to believe, false sentences and (b) the users of A and B continue to believe or come to believe bold and speculative sentences and (c) the use of A is less likely than the use of B to result in the users of A believing accounts with distorting omissions.

However, these modifications will not do and we have already seen why. Conditions (a), (b), and (c) may well provide a sufficient condition for the objectivity of a methodology. But (a) is not a necessary condition. For similar reasons (c) is not a necessary condition. Consequently (4) fails.

Whether a set of necessary conditions can be formulated for the objectivity of method is a question we will not consider. However, the above considerations suggest the difficulty in doing so.

PART III: EXPLANATION AND PREDICTION

Two activities that social scientists and natural scientists engage in are explaining and predicting. There are many interesting philosophical questions connected with both activities.

One question is whether one can abstract from these activities and formulate a model that shows the logical relation between the sentences used in both explanation and prediction. There is one philosophical theory that argues not only that this can be done but that what is revealed is that explanation and prediction have the same structure, the difference between prediction and explanation being merely pragmatic. According to this theory—sometimes called the deductive-nomological model—to explain some event e, one deduces a description E of event e from a set of general laws, L_1, L_2, L_3, ...L_n and a set of statements specifying initial conditions C_1, C_2, C_3,......C_n. The difference between explanation and prediction is simply that in explanation the event e has already occurred while in prediction the event e has not yet occurred.

As the name indicates, according to the deductive-nomological model the relation between laws, statements of initial conditions and the description of the event to be explained or predicted is a deductive one. Some methodologists have advocated an alternative model of explanation and prediction. In this model—sometimes called the inductive-statistical model—the event description does not deductively follow from laws and statements of initial conditions; rather the event description is probable relative to statistical laws and statements of initial conditions. The difference between explanation and prediction is again a pragmatic one because it turns on whether the event description refers to an event that has or has not already occurred.

These two models of explanation and prediction have been attacked in various ways. For example, it has been maintained that although the models provide an adequate account of explanation, they do not provide an adequate account of prediction. It has also been maintained that, although the deductive-nomological model provides an adequate account of explanation, the inductive-statistical model does not. It has furthermore been argued that, although explanations in the social sciences and history are deductive, they are not nomological. There can be no general laws of social behavior, it has been maintained, and what look like empirical laws are really analytic statements.

Advocates of the deductive-nomological and the inductive-statistical models of explanation and prediction have usually been committed to the view that explanation and prediction in the social sciences are not basically different from explanation and prediction in the natural sciencs. One could, of course, endorse these models in the natural sciences only; alternatively one could reject them entirely while maintaining that explanation and prediction are basically the same in both the social sciences and the natural sciences. In any case, the uniqueness of social scientific explanation and prediction has been a dominant theme in philosophical literature. Thus it has been maintained that social scientific explanations have special properties which distinguish them from natural scientific explanations. In particular, it has been argued that social scientific explanations must be based on the actor's desires and beliefs and that they must be based on Verstehen. It has also been argued that it is impossible for there to be prediction in the social sciences which is closely analogous to prediction in the natural sciences.

In the five essays that follow these and other problems connected with explanation and prediction are discussed. In "Explanation in Social Science: Some Recent Work"[1] books in which the theme of explanation in the social sciences plays a major role are reviewed. In a review of Explanation in the Behavioral Sciences, edited by Borges and Cioffi, various views of explanation in the behavioral sciences are critically evaluated. Alan Donagan's thesis that deductive, but not nomological, explanations are appropriate in history is critically evaluated in "Situational Logic and Covering Law Explanations in History"; Leonard Krimerman's interpretation of Verstehen is criticized in "A New Interpretation of Verstehen"; and in "Social Scientific Predictions and Open Concepts" MacIntyre's thesis that social scientists are not able to make the sorts of predictions natural scientists are able to make is examined.

Footnotes

1. One aspect of my argument in this paper—an aspect having to do with methodological individualism and reduction—is criticized by Michael Hyland and Martin Bridgstock in "Reductionism: Comments on Some Recent Work," Philosophy of Social Science, 4, 1974, 197-200. I reply to this critique in "Reduction and Typical Individuals," Philosophy of Social Science, 5, 1975, 307-308.

Explanation in Social Science: Some Recent Work

MICHAEL MARTIN

The philosophy of the social sciences, once a poor cousin of the philosophy of the natural sciences, has in recent years surely come into its own. Several new anthologies,[1] several recent textbooks[2] and three new journals[3] give evidence of the vitality of the field. In the present study four books in the philosophy of the social sciences and the first issue of a new journal with a strong interest in the philosophy of the social sciences will be reviewed. Three of the books are anthologies: *Sociological Theory and Philosophical Analysis*, edited by Emmet and MacIntyre; *Rationality*, edited by Wilson; *The Proper Study*, with an introductory foreword by Vesey. One is a textbook: *The Philosophy of the Social Sciences*, by Ryan. And the journal is the *Journal for the Theory of Social Behavior*, edited by Secord and Harré.[4]

The papers in the first two anthologies mentioned above are written by philosophers, e.g. Winch, Morgenbesser, Schutz; social scientists, e.g. Horton, Beattie, Turner, Leach; and some people who seem to bridge both fields, e.g. Gellner and MacIntyre. As might be expected, the papers in these anthologies having the most philosophical interest are those written by philosophers. The papers written by social scientists are nevertheless useful. For although they do not usually advance a philosophical thesis they often illustrate some philosophical point. Most of the papers in these two anthologies have appeared before but both volumes should nonetheless be welcome additions to the library of students of the philosophy of the social sciences.

The third anthology, *The Proper Study*, is rather different. For one thing all of the papers appear for the first time. Moreover, many of the papers are less in the philosophy of the social sciences than they are in political and social philosophy or in the philosophy of language. (For example the papers by Laslett, Bell and Mitchell are in political philosophy and Vendler's paper is in the philosophy of language.) Finally, those papers which are in the philosophy of the social sciences proper are presented as popular lectures and thus tend to be philosophically rather thin although some very interesting arguments are presented in them. (Although we shall not consider it in this review the paper by Cioffi should be especially noted.) All in all, however, the papers in this volume will play much less of a role in the present review than the papers in the other two anthologies.

The textbook by Ryan is a good one. It is very readable with numerous examples from the social sciences. As will become evident there is much in it with which to disagree. However, it is undoubtedly the best textbook available in the field of philosophy of social science at the present time.

The *Journal for the Theory of Social Behavior* welcomes contributions on theoretical methodological and philosophical problems of social science. In particular the editors wish to 'encourage philosophers to contribute to conceptual analyses of terms pertaining to social behavior, as well as to pursue more general questions of method in the light of current developments in the philosophy of science'. The first paper in the journal, 'Positivism, Naturalism, and Anti-naturalism in the Social Sciences' by Russell Keat, is on the philosophy of science. Other papers in this first issue of the journal will perhaps be of less interest to philosophers of the social sciences although they are all on more or less theoretical and methodological topics.

The philosophical perspectives represented in the works under review are rather diversified. For example, the Wittgensteinian ordinary language approach is represented by Winch, the phenomenological approach by Schutz, a strong Popperian influence is found in Jarvie and Agassi, a realistic point of view is utilized by Keat. Perhaps the only position not well represented (although it is constantly under attack) is the neo-positivistic view. For example, none of the anthologies has a paper by Hempel, Nagel, Rudner, or Brodbeck although there is, to be sure, a paper by Morgenbesser who is perhaps more easily classified in this camp than in any other.

It will be impossible in this study to consider all the major issues that are raised in the works under review or even to discuss all of the non-popular philosophy of social science papers to be found in the anthologies. However, a fairly broad range of topics and papers can be covered by concentrating on one central issue in the philosophy of the social sciences: explanation. We will consider various types of explanation and issues closely related to explanation that are discussed in these works.

Throughout our discussion we will concentrate mainly on what we believe to be the dubious philosophical theses or arguments concerning explanation that are advanced in these works. Although this concentration will make our topic manageable it may tend to create the impression that in our view nothing the authors say is correct or worthwhile. This impression would be incorrect. All of these books contain much that is valuable on the topic of explanation. Indeed, the reader will sometimes find us taking one thesis or argument and contrasting it with an argument found elsewhere in these works that shows it to be incorrect. However, we will not hesitate to point to sources and arguments not found in the works under review to back up our criticisms or to indicate other relevant literature.

1. *The deductive covering law model of explanation*

One of the central topics in philosophy of science and philosophy of history in recent years has been the status of the deductive covering law model of explanation. Some philosophers have defended this model in both the natural and social sciences; others have rejected its applicability in both areas. The most common view is perhaps to defend its applicability in the natural sciences and to reject it as applicable in the social sciences. If this latter thesis can be defended successfully, it has been argued, then there is a crucial methodological difference between the natural sciences and the social sciences.

Keat calls the position that the methodology of the natural sciences can be applied to the social sciences 'naturalism' and the position that the methodology of the natural sciences cannot be applied to the social sciences 'anti-naturalism'. Since the deductive covering law model has usually been associated with the

Explanation in Social Science: Some Recent Work

methodology of the natural sciences those who would oppose its application in the social sciences might well be called anti-naturalists. Keat raises the important question of whether the deductive covering law model is even applicable in the natural sciences.[5] This same question is also raised by Ryan in a chapter of his book devoted to the deductive covering law theory. Unlike Keat, Ryan attempts to answer it.

Ryan says that he does not believe, as some philosophers do, that this model has application in natural science but not in the social sciences. He maintains, rather, that its 'merits and demerits are visible more or less evenly across the scientific spectrum'.[6] Since the general outline of the deductive covering law model is very likely well known to readers[7] of this journal we may move on to what Ryan believes are the problems with this view. Ryan argues that the deductive covering law view has been associated with the view that causal laws are statements of *de facto* regularities but that causal laws are not *de facto* regularities. Now it should be noted that even if Ryan is correct, this would not affect the deductive covering law view. For there is no necessary connection between that view and any particular analysis of causal laws. At best Ryan's point would affect one particular interpretation of the covering law view.

Whether Ryan is correct in his rejection of the *de facto* regularity view of causal laws is another matter. In any case, his reasons for rejecting this view seem to be confused and wrong. He argues that (what he considers to be) the *de facto* regularity 'Night always follows day' does not explain 'the way day and night follow each other'.[8] Here he seems to be confusing two different theses: (*a*) *de facto* regularities do not explain cases falling under them, e.g. the occurrence of some particular day, and (*b*) a regularity itself needs explaining and a regularity does not, as it were, explain itself. Now, of course advocates of the deductive covering law view have never denied (*b*). Indeed, they have maintained that laws are explained by theories or by more general laws. However, the truth of (*b*) is quite independent of the truth of (*a*).

Ryan might have more plausibly argued that (*a*) is true. For it is true that 'Night always follows day' (combined with appropriate statements of initial conditions) does not explain the occurrence of some particular day. But of course 'Night always follows day' is not a *de facto* regularity. Night does not always follow day: night follows day only under certain conditions—the earth must turn, the sun must shine and so on. To put it another way, the correct form of the regularity at issue is:

(1) If night occurs, then day occurs if condition C holds

where C specifies the manifold conditions under which night follows day. But *de facto* regularities are not conditional in this way; they do not depend on some condition C. They have the form

(2) If A, then B

and not

(3) If A, then B if C.

One could, of course, put condition C into the antecedent of the conditional. Let $A' = A \& C$. Then

(4) If A', then B.

In the case at issue the conditional stating the *de facto* regularity would be

(5) If night occurs and the sun shines and the earth turns, etc. then day occurs.

However, in this case it is not so obvious that the *de facto* regularity combined with appropriate statements of initial conditions does not explain the occurrence of some particular day.

As we shall see in our discussion of the identity thesis—the thesis that explanaion and prediction have the same structure—there are indeed deductive arguments using general laws and intial conditions that are not explanatory. As Keat points out in his paper, some philosophers who advocate the deductive covering law view readily admit this. They seem only to hold that a necessary condition for explanation is the pattern specified by the deductive covering law theory.[9] In any case, it is clear that Ryan's example does not show what he thinks it does, namely that there are some deductive covering law arguments that are not explanatory. In particular, his argument against the *de facto* regularity view of causal laws is mistaken.

Independent of Ryan's criticism of the deductive covering law view of explanation via his critique of the *de facto* regularity view of causal laws is his own view of the nature of causal laws. Ryan's own view is that causal statements 'are not statements of *de facto* regularities, but recipes for constructing causal histories'.[10] Such statements offer rules for constructing an 'indefinitely large number of actual and hypothetical histories'.[11] For example, consider a causal statement from economics 'All firms which raise their output in a static market will have to lower their unit price'. This statement 'has its place' in the construction of causal histories in economics since in particular cases the statement allows us to construct causal histories of what firms would do under certain conditions.

This view has problems. First, taken quite literally it seems to be false. If causal statements *are* recipes or rules for constructing causal histories, such statements are not true or false, since rules and recipes are not true or false. Causal statements, however, do seem to be true or false. Secondly, taken in a non-literal way Ryan's view does not seem to distinguish causal statements from *de facto* regularities. Suppose we understand Ryan not to be saying that causal statements are rules but that causal statements are equivalent to rules in the following sense. Consider a statement of the form 'All A's are B'. This is a true causal statement (on the present interpretation) if and only if there is a valid rule of the form 'For every x, if x is A, then infer x is B'! However, this criterion does not distinguish causal statements from *de facto* regularities since for *any* true statement of the form 'All A's are B' there is a valid rule of the form 'For every x, if x is A, then infer x is B'! Thus Ryan's suggestion when construed in this way does not distinguish *de facto* regularities from causal laws. But this is precisely what it is supposed to do.

Now Ryan might argue that causal statements are equivalent, in the above sense, to rules that enable one to construct causal histories and that *de facto* regularities at best are equivalent to rules which do not enable one to construct causal histories. But unless one has some independent idea of what a causal history is, this suggestion will be to no avail. Unfortunately Ryan does not provide us with any independent criterion.

Ryan finds other problems with the deductive covering law account but some of them seem to be based on a misunderstanding of that account. For example, Ryan believes that the existence of theories poses a problem for the deductive covering law account of explanation. Theories pose a problem, he says, because they are not generalizations from evidence; they posit non-observable entities. But of course the deductive covering law account of explanation does not hold that theories are generalizations from evidence. Indeed, it need not even suppose that

Explanation in Social Science: Some Recent Work

the laws used in the explanation of particulars are generalizations from experience. The question of the *origin* of laws is quite irrelevant to the deductive covering law account.

A similar sort of misunderstanding is found in Wellmer's 'Some Remarks on the Logic of Explanation in the Social Sciences'. Wellmer argues that 'in contrast to the [Hempel-Oppenheim] model we can now differentiate between two different levels of explanation: that of the causal explanation of singular events and that of theoretical explanation of general phenomena'.[12] However, advocates of the deductive covering law model have distinguished these two levels of explanation.[13]

Ryan's chapter on the deductive covering law view and Wellmer's paper are really the only works under review in which the deductive covering law view is seriously discussed. Although the topic of the deductive covering law view is by no means exhausted by our remarks, these remarks represent quite fairly the discussions of the topic in the works under review.

2. *The logical identity of explanation and prediction*

According to Ryan closely associated with the deductive covering law theory of explanation is the *de facto* regularity view of causal law. According to Keat another thesis closely associated with that theory is the thesis that explanation and prediction have the same logical form.[14] Now this thesis, like the *de facto* regularity view of causal law, is logically independent of the covering law theory. One can quite consistently defend the deductive covering law view of explanation and reject the logical identity thesis.[15]

Ryan alone in the works under review seems to wish to defend the identity thesis. It is unclear how to reconcile his critique of the deductive covering law view of explanation with his apparent acceptance of the identity of deductive covering law explanations and predictions. In any case, he argues that this identity of explanation and prediction is 'unshakable'.[16] According to Ryan the difference between explanation and prediction is temporal. In an explanation one begins with the event to be explained, that is with the conclusion of the deductive argument, and finds the appropriate generalizations and initial conditions. In the case of prediction, one begins with the generalizations and initial conditions and then deduces the conclusion, a conclusion about some coming event.

This view, although a very popular one, is mistaken unless one restricts the meaning of prediction in a very drastic way. This is well pointed out by Morgenbesser in his paper 'Is it a Science?'[17] First, there is a pragmatic sense of prediction. In this sense one speaks of a person predicting. Predicting is an activity that people engage in. Now clearly in this sense of 'prediction' explanation and prediction are not logically identical if one means by explanation a deductive covering law explanation. For an explanation, according to the deductive covering law view, is not an activity but a certain logical relation between sentences. (There is of course a pragmatic sense of 'explanation'.[18] Whether prediction in the pragmatic sense is identical with explanation in the pragmatic sense is another question. Indeed whether it even makes sense to speak of logical identity here is unclear.) In any case, people sometimes predict without using general laws and initial conditions.

Secondly there is, according to Morgenbesser, a semantic sense of prediction. In this sense theories can be said to predict and people cannot be said to predict. In this sense 'predict' specifies a relation between sentences, not an activity of people. 'Predict' in this sense is used interchangeably with 'entail'. However, in this semantic sense the identity thesis is false. Just because a sentence E is entailed by the laws and statements of initial conditions, it does not mean that the event described by E is explained. Morgenbesser's example to illustrate this point is not as persuasive as other examples in the literature and the reader is referred to one first constructed by Bromberger.[19] From certain laws of geometrical optics plus statements of initial conditions, e.g. the length of a shadow, the angle from the end of the shadow to the top of a pole, we can deduce the height of a flag pole. But these laws and initial conditions do not explain the height of the flagpole.

Thirdly, there is what Morgenbesser calls an 'epistemological sense' of 'prediction' which he extracts from a passage written by Milton Friedman, the economist. In this sense a scientist uses a theory T predictively about E at time t if he presents the theory at time t and does not know at t whether E is true or false and E is deducible from T or at least T and E are compatible. Notice that in this sense E need not be about a future event but could be about past events. This sense of prediction includes what is often called postdiction. But in any case, prediction in this sense is not logically identical with explanation. Consider the example already given. Suppose someone does not know the height of the flagpole and uses the theories of geometrical optics and statements of initial conditions to deduce the sentence 'The height of the flagpole is 34 feet'. Suppose this sentence is true. The theories of geometrical optics and initial conditions would still not explain the height of the flagpole yet the height of the flagpole would have been predicted in this epistemological sense.

Again although much more could be said about the identity of explanation and prediction, not much more is said in the works under review.

3. *Methodological individualism*

One of the liveliest controversies in recent philosophy of social science literature is the controversy between those (methodological individualists) who believe that individualistic explanations are basic in the social sciences and those (methodological holists) who believe that holistic explanations are basic. Ryan in his book[20] and Lukes in his paper 'Methodological Individualism Reconsidered'[21] both agree that the controversy between methodological individualists and methodological holists has been largely based on confusions and unclarities. Let us consider Lukes' argument first.

Lukes distinguishes a number of different theses that might be confused with methodological individualism which is, he says, the view that no purported explanation of social (or individual) phenomena is to be counted as an explanation or at least as a rock bottom (basic) explanation unless it is couched wholly in terms of facts about individuals. This view may be confused with (*a*) the trivially true view that groups consist of people, that rules are followed by people, that roles are filled by people; (*b*) the view that every statement about social phenomena is either a statement about individual human beings or else is meaningless; (*c*) the view that only individuals are real and that social phenomena are mental constructions; (*d*) the view that laws about social wholes are impossible; (*e*) the view that society has as its end the good of individuals.

Now Lukes maintains that (*a*)-(*d*) are independent of the thesis of methodological individualism and that (*e*) is also, except on one interpretation of it which makes (*e*) identical with methodological individualism. The important question in relation to methodological individualism, according to Lukes, is what is meant by 'facts about individuals'.

Lukes distinguishes four different kinds of predicates that can be applied to individuals: (*i*) physiological type predicates, e.g. predicates about brain states, genetic make up; (*ii*) psychological predicates that presuppose no social context in their application, e.g. predicates about stimulus-response, gratification; (*iii*) predicates that presuppose a certain social context for their application but which do not presuppose any particular form of group or institution, e.g. predicates about power, cooperation; (*iv*) predicates which do presuppose some particular form of social institution or group, e.g. predicates about cashing checks, voting.

Once these different predicates are distinguished Lukes argues that methodological individualism will either be (1) obviously implausible or (2) unduly restrictive or (3) 'harmless but also pointless'.[22] For if we are talking about statements in terms of predicates of type (*i*) or (*ii*), then it is quite implausible to suppose that such statements could explain most social phenomena. If, on the other hand, we restrict explanation to type (*iii*) predicates we are being unduly restrictive since there may be valid and useful explanations which presuppose the existence of particular social institutions or groups. Finally, to restrict explanations to predicates of type (*iv*), predicates which do presuppose the existence of particular social institutions and groups, is harmless but pointless since, because of their presuppositions, references to social phenomena have not been eliminated but have only been 'swept under the carpet'.[23]

Now it is certainly clarifying and helpful for Lukes to have distinguished various sorts of individual predicates. However, it does not seem to me that the issue between methodological individualism and its rivals is thereby disposed of. First, a methodological individualist need not and should not maintain that theories, general laws and initial conditions containing only predicates about individuals explain social phenomena. It is a logical turth that such theories and statements of initial conditions could not entail sentences which contain holistic predicates unless they are combined with certain principles, e.g. bridge laws, that connect individual predicates and holistic predicates.[24] It is hardly surprising that it appears grossly implausible to Lukes that physiological theories, i.e. theories couched in (*i*) type predicates, could explain social phenomena; Lukes does not seem to be aware of the need for any connecting principles. Without the connecting principles it would indeed be implausible to suppose that methodological individualism using (*i*) type predicates could be correct. However, it does not seem so implausible to suppose that bridge laws connecting physiological variables may eventually be discovered.

Secondly, the methodological individualist need not maintain that explanation in terms of individuals can now be achieved, e.g. via bridge laws. He need only maintain that the goal of achieving such explanations is a desirable long range theoretical goal of science. He might admit that the attempt to achieve individualistic explanations is premature or undesirable at present. In particular, he need not restrict the sort of predicates that are permissible in explanation either now or in the foreseeable future. Nor need he restrict the sort of predicates that are permissible in non-basic explanations. The methodological individualist need only maintain that whatever non-individualistic explanations one comes up with in the

Michael Martin

future, acceptable though they may be for practical purposes, are not as basic as individualistic ones and should eventually be reduced to individualistic ones. The time at which such reduction should be attempted, he can claim, is a matter of judgement and depends on many factors including the state of the field. But even if the time is ripe for reduction, he need not place any restrictions on the type of predicates used in explanations that are non-basic.[25] It is difficult to see how, when interpreted in this way, Lukes' critical points are even relevant. Methodological individualists need not restrict the type of predicates used in their explanations in any harmful way nor need they deny that reduction to individualistic explanations at the present time is impossible and even harmful.

Thirdly, it is difficult to see why the methodological individualist who uses predicates of type (iv) should be concerned that such predicates presuppose social institutions or groups, or why methodological individualists who use type (iv) predicates have a pointless position. Perhaps Lukes supposes that if an individualistic explanation presupposes social institutions, then holistic *explanations* are presupposed. But this seems to me to be a logical blunder. Suppose Lukes is correct that sentence S_1 using predicates of type (iv) entails sentence S_2 which contains holistic predicates. Suppose further that S_1 (combined with bridge laws) entails S_3 which describes social phenomenon P which we are interested in explaining. Now these suppositions are perfectly compatible with there being no known sociological laws that when combined with S_2 entail S_3. In short, there may be no holistic explanation of some social phenomenon despite the fact that there exists an individualistic explanation of this phenomenon which presupposes sentences containing holistic predicates. So the methodological individualist might well grant Lukes' point and yet insist that methodological individualism is by no means pointless.

Let us now consider Ryan's position. Ryan argues that the controversy between methodological individualists and methodological holists is a 'sham battle'.[26] The controversy has been partly the result of a confusion between several different senses of 'reduction' and partly the result of a confusion between two senses of 'individual'. There are, according to Ryan, two distinct sorts of indivduals: actual and typical individuals. Actual individuals are presumably specified by proper names, e.g. John Q. Evans, or definite descriptions, e.g. the man who lives in the white house on Central Street. These individuals are not specified in terms of social roles or positions. Typical individuals are specified in terms of social roles or positions, e.g. British member of Parliament, bank teller. (One gathers that Ryan's typical individuals are similar to individuals characterized by Lukes' type (iv) predicates.) Now Ryan seems to suggest in places that when methodological individualists restrict basic explanation to explanation in terms of typical individuals there is no distinction to be drawn between individualistic and holistic explanation. This is because statements about typical individuals are logically interchangeable with statements about social wholes, i.e. institutions or groups. Furthermore, Ryan suggests that methodological individualists have usually had typical and not actual individuals in mind.

Unfortunately this suggestion which would seem so neatly to undercut much of the controversy between methodological individualists and their rivals is not correct. Now it might be the case that statements about typical individuals presuppose the existence of certain social institutions and groups: a bank teller presupposes a bank; a member of Parliament presupposes Parliament. (This point would be similar to the point made by Lukes in relation to type (*iv*) predicates.) But it does not follow from this and it does not seem to be obviously true that all statements about typical individuals are logically interchangeable with statements about institutions or groups. Consider the statement, presumably about a typical individual, 'The bank teller began to tell people who had accounts that everyone was withdrawing his money'. It is certainly not obvious that this statement is logically interchangeable (equivalent) with statements about banks although it might entail a statement about a bank. Thus it is not so obvious that individual explanations and holistic explanations are really the same.

At times Ryan seems only to suppose that *some* statements about typical individuals, namely statements about the individual's roles and duties, are logically interchangeable with *some* statements about groups, namely statements which specify group norms and roles. Surely this is true but it hardly shows that the battle between methodological individualism and holism is a sham since there are countless other statements about typical individuals that are not logically interchangeable with statements about groups. Not all statements about typical individuals are, presumably, about roles and duties despite the fact that typical individuals are identified in terms of their roles and duties.

Now one might understand statements about typical individuals to be *only* about their roles and duties. In this case the above statement about the bank teller would not be about a typical individual since it is not about a bank teller's roles and duties. However, if we understand statements about typical individuals in this way, then many individualistic explanations are not about typical individuals. Consequently the legitimacy of the controversy between methodological individualists and holists still holds at least in those common cases where non-typical individualist explanations are at issue.

Ryan also distinguishes three different kinds of reduction that he claims underlie the sham battle between methodological individualists and their rivals. However, I for one remain sceptical that these alleged ambiguities are at the basis of the controversy between methodological individualists and their rivals and that once these are cleared up the controversy will be seen to be a sham battle. After Ryan's distinctions between two kinds of individuals and three kinds of reduction are made, two crucial questions remain. (The same questions remain after Lukes' analysis.) Suppose we understand the reduction of holistic explanations to individualistic explanations in the following way: Laws couched in terms of individual predicates (interpreted in any of the ways specified by Ryan or Lukes) combined with bridge laws and with appropriate initial conditions entail all holistic laws used for explanatory purposes. Given this meaning of reduction: (1) Can all holistic explanations eventually be reduced to individualistic explanations? (2) Is it worthwhile to pursue the goal of individualistic reduction when this is interpreted as a long range theoretical and methodological commitment? The answers to these questions, despite all of Lukes' and Ryan's distinctions, are certainly not obvious.

As we have seen, one type of methodological individualism holds that all basic rock-bottom explanations of social phenomena must be physiological, that is individuals must be characterized by physiological predicates, i.e. predicates of type (*i*) to use Lukes' classification. Now such methodological individualism is identical with a programme of physiological reduction. We argued in our critique of Lukes that nothing he said was good reason for thinking that such a reductionist programme is unfeasible. Ryan, however, gives another argument which, if correct, might well prove to be a serious obstacle to such a programme.

It would seem that in order to explain social phenomena in terms of physiology one would have to explain psychological phenomena. However, Ryan argues that any attempt to reduce psychological phenomena to physiological phenomena assumes the identity of body and mind. In particular it assumes that psychological states or processes, e.g. thinking, feeling, are identical with certain physiological states or processes. But, argues Ryan, there are well known philosophical objections to such an identity. For example, it makes sense to ask for the spatial location of a physiological event but not of a thought. But if a thought *is* a certain physiological event it should make sense to ask the same question about both. Ryan also reviews other well known objections to the identity theory.[27]

Fortunately for psychologists interested in furthering the programme of physiological reduction there is no need to answer these philosophical problems related to the identity theory. For it is not the case that the reduction of psychology (in a variety of different senses of reduction) to physiology presupposes that psychological events or states are identical with physiological events or states. For example, in one sense of 'reduction' analysed by Nagel,[28] physiology would reduce psychology just in case the laws of psychology could be deduced from physiology given suitable connecting principles, e.g. bridge laws connecting physiological and psychological variables. However, such bridge laws do not presuppose any body-mind identity.

Thus the objection that Ryan raises to physiological reduction based on the problem of the body-mind identity, would not be a problem for this sort of physiological reduction. There are several other senses of reduction in which there is no problem either.[29] All this is not to say that the programme of physiological reduction is a plausible one. What it does mean is that Ryan's sort of philosophical objection, viz. that such reduction presupposes the dubious thesis of body-mind identity, will not work.

4. *Situational logic explanations*

As we have seen, there are several different varieties of individualistic explanation. One type is physiological. Another type, not easily placed into Lukes' scheme, is situational logic explanation. Crucial to situational logic explanations is the rationality of the action to be explained. One of the anthologies we are examining (*Rationality*, edited by Wilson) consists entirely of papers on various aspects of rationality and some of the papers in the other volumes are also concerned with this topic. There are several questions concerning rationality that need to be answered. First, what does rationality mean? Secondly, what is an explanation in terms of the rationality of the actor? Thirdly, do situational logic explanations have any privileged status in the social sciences? Closely connected with the last question is the problem of whether an assumption of rationality is in some sense a presupposition of the translation of native languages into our own, for if rationality is a presupposition of translation, then it may be a presupposition of explanation as well.

Several of the authors in the anthologies under review attempt to clarify what is meant by 'rational'. First of all one must distinguish between the rationality of action and the rationality of belief. According to Jarvie and Agassi in their paper 'The Problem of the Rationality of Magic'[30] a person has a rational belief when the person's belief satisfies some standard of rationality, e.g. when the belief is based on good evidence or is beyond reasonable doubt or is held open to criticism. On the other hand a person's action is rational when it is directed toward some goal. One must also distinguish the rationality of a belief or an action from the rationality of a person. Jarvie and Agassi distinguish a weak and a strong sense of the rationality of a person and define these in terms of the rationality of belief and action. A person is rational in the weak sense if his actions are rational in the above sense; a person is rational in the strong sense if his actions are rational in the above sense and are based on rational beliefs.

It should be evident that Jarvie and Agassi's definition of rational action is a very minimal one and hence that their weak sense of the rationality of a person is indeed a weak sense. A native who believed that action X was the only way to achieve Y and wanted Y and did Z believing $Z \neq X$ in order to achieve Y would be rational in this weak sense despite the fact that his action was out of keeping with his own belief. In their paper, however, Jarvie and Agassi seem to assume a stronger sense of rational action than the one they explicitly state: An action is rational if it is goal-directed *and* is in keeping with the belief of the actor about the best way to achieve the goal. Thus they argue that magic is believed by the natives to be instrumental to a certain end and that the use of magic by the natives is a rational action. They conclude that the natives are rational in the weak sense distinguished above. The natives are indeed rational in the sense the authors explicitly define but the natives would also be rational in this sense if they did not perform magic and did some other action which they did not believe was a good way to achieve their goals provided the action was directed towards achieving their goals. But presumably this is not what Jarvie and Agassi really want to say. One can only conclude that their explicit definition of rational action is not the one actually used in their paper.

Jarvie in another paper, 'Explaining Cargo Culture',[31] Lukes in his paper 'Some Problems of Rationality'[32] and Schutz in his paper 'The Problem of Rationality in the Social World'[33] all distinguish various senses of rationality. Given the various senses of rationality what would a situational logic explanation be? This type of explanation is one in which a person's actions are explained in terms of his beliefs, goals and rationality in some appropriate sense of rationality.

Perhaps the most important of the senses of rationality for explanatory purposes is the sense of rationality that seemed to be implicitly assumed by Jarvie and Agassi: an action is rational if it is believed by the actor to be the most efficient means to a given goal. In this sense one would explain someone's action, say a native performing some magic ritual, in terms of his goals (he wants his crops to grow) and his beliefs about the best way to achieve them (he believes that the magic ritual he is performing is the best way to achieve this goal).

However, sometimes this simple schema of rational action will not work. For example, suppose the native has several alternative goals which he values differently; suppose further that he believes that the means to achieving each of these alternative goals have different chances of success. In cases of this sort it is not so obvious which course of action is rational. Decision theorists usually specify rational action in this sort of case in terms of subjective expected utility (the subjective utility of the goal times the subjective probability of achieving the goal) and there are still more sophisticated cases. In general, the authors of the papers on rationality considered here seem either to be ignorant of or to ignore formal decision theory as a way of clarifying rational action and explanations in terms of rational action. However, it seems likely that in any extended discussion of rationality which illuminated the logic of explanation, considerations from decision theory would have to be introduced. Hempel's discussion of rational explanation still remains the best account of it and there concepts of decision theory are explicitly utilized.[34] Although Jarvie and Agassi seem to be aware of Hempel's work (they footnote him with approval)[35] they seem to have learned little from it. The other authors do not even seem to be aware of Hempel's work.

Whatever the relevance of formal decision theory to situational logic explanations, another question arises, namely: 'Do situational logic explanations have any privileged status in the social sciences?' Some of the contributors to the Wilson anthology seem to suggest that they do. For example, Jarvie and Agassi in their paper on the explanation of magic explicitly advocate situational logic explanations of particular phenomena, viz. magic. But their argument for this type of explanation in these cases seems easily capable of generalization and from what they say elsewhere[36] it seems clear that they wish to uphold a general thesis about the superiority of situational logic explanations.

What reasons are given for the superiority of situational logic explanations over other kinds? Jarvie and Agassi do not give any serious defense of their claim. Their major defense seems to be to try to refute views that (they claim) deny that natives are rational in their weak sense of rational or views that (they maintain) deny that beliefs and goals explain native behaviour. For example, a long section of the Jarvie and Agassi paper is devoted to a critique of Beattie's views on magic which Jarvie and Agassi interpret as denying that natives are rational in their very minimal sense of rational.

However, Beattie replies in his paper 'On Understanding Ritual', that he is not denying this.[37] What he is denying is that the actions of natives can be *completely* explained in terms of their beliefs, goals and rationality. However it is doubtful that Jarvie and Agassi believe that the actions of the natives can be completely explained in this way either.

As good Popperians they hold the deductive covering law view of explanation. Surely they would not maintain that a proffered law couched completely in terms of beliefs, goals and rationality could be formulated and stand up under empirical test. At least environmental factors, e.g. meteorological and geological ones, might have to be taken into account to explain the actions of the natives. (No magic ritual can be performed in the middle of a hurricane, for example.)

The difference between Jarvie and Agassi and Beattie seems to come down to precisely what other factors would have to be taken into account for a complete explanation. Beattie seems to be arguing that it is necessary to take into account the symbolic meaning of magic ritual in order to explain it. (Now by 'symbol' Beattie means some concrete entity, idea or pattern of behaviour which represents by some underlying rationale some more or less abstract notion to which social value is attached). This symbolic meaning would transcend the natives' categories. The anthropologist, not the natives, sees the natives' actions in these symbolic terms.

Would Jarvie and Agassi be opposed to the introduction of an explanatory concept that transcended the natives' categories—the explanatory concept of symbolic meaning? Beattie apparently thinks that they would but it is difficult to see why they should be. Concepts of meteorology and geology may go beyond the beliefs of the natives too and these might be quite necessary for a complete explanation.

In any case, there is a danger in giving preferential treatment to situational logic explanations of human actions unless this sort of explanation is given a very liberal interpretation. They, like Verstehen explanations which we will consider later, are too restrictive. Unless they are construed liberally, explanations that go beyond the beliefs, aims and rationality of the actors are ruled out.

But not only do situational logic explanations narrowly construed rule out *a priori* explanations like Beattie's; they seem appropriate only to certain types of problems. Situational logic explanations presumably are designed to explain human actions—what people do or do not do. But as MacIntyre points out in 'The Idea of A Social Science',[38] this is not all that social scientists are interested in explaining. They want to explain not only what people do but what happens to them and what they are. They are interested in explaining, for example, a person's being unemployed, and rates of population change. In these sorts of cases situational logic explanations are much less relevant than other types of explanations even if interpreted quite broadly. In light of cases of this sort Ryan argues[39] that explanations in terms of beliefs and motives are more appropriate in certain sciences than in others, for example they are more easily applied in cultural anthropology than in demography. It is significant that the examples used by Jarvie and Agassi are all from anthropology rather than from other social sciences.

Besides Jarvie's and Agassi's unsuccessful attempt to argue for the superiority of situational logical explanations over other kinds, there is a general consideration that may suggest that priority should be given to situational logic explanations. Hollis in his papers 'The Limits of Irrationality' and 'Reason and Ritual'[40] argues that an *a priori* assumption in the translation of native speech into our own is the assumption that the natives are rational. We must assume *a priori*, says Hollis, that most of the natives' everyday beliefs are true; we must assume *a priori* that the natives share our concept of 'being a reason for'; and so on. In general Hollis argues that there will always be better reasons for accepting rather than rejecting an anthropological translation of native language if the translation makes most of the native beliefs coherent and rational and most of their empirical beliefs true.

The first thing to notice about Hollis' claims is that even if they are correct they do not give any support to the superiority or priority of situational logic explanations. One might well argue for the need for *a priori* rational assumptions in translation and yet not maintain that situational logic explanations are to be preferred. One might maintain with perfect consistency that explanation in terms of physiological or environmental variables are to be preferred. If one grants the need for *a priori* assumptions of rationality in translation, one would only be committed to this: *If* one uses explanation in terms of beliefs and goals, *then* one must assume that most native actions in terms of their beliefs and goals are rational and perhaps that most of their beliefs and goals are rational. But this would not mean that one would have to explain their actions in terms of beliefs and goals and rationality.

Secondly, the need for *a priori* assumptions of the sort Hollis suggests is surely

Michael Martin

not obvious. A more plausible view is presented by Gellner in his paper 'Concepts and Society'.[41] According to Gellner the assumption of rationality is not one we *must* make but one that we can *choose* to make. If we choose not to assume that the natives are rational this brings with it certain costs and benefits. One benefit is that we will tend not to overlook the functional irrationality of certain beliefs and practices. Gellner argues that certain beliefs and practices may indeed be irrational and that such irrationality may have a definite cultural value. The question is whether the benefits of not overlooking these functional irrational factors in society outweighs the costs in translation, e.g. in having incoherent translations.

For Hollis it is not a matter of choice. Hollis maintains that without the assumption of rationality one cannot understand the translation of the native language. Indeed he seems to suggest that without understanding one would not really have a translation of the native language. But first of all, it is not obvious that understanding is a necessary condition for translation. Surely one can give a correct translation of some message in a foreign language which is in code and not understand the message. Secondly, it is not obvious that the assumption of rationality in Hollis' sense is a necessary condition for understanding the translation. Why, for example, it is necessary that most of the natives' empirical beliefs be true in order to understand a translation of sentences that states these beliefs? Surely the only thing that may be necessary is that one has a good hypothesis that explains why most of these beliefs are false if in one's translation they come out false. Much the same sort of objection can be raised to Hollis' other *a priori* assumption. It is not necessary that we assume that most of the natives' beliefs are coherent in order to understand a translation of their language. We may have a good hypothesis that explains why most of them are not coherent if in our translation they come out mostly incoherent. There seems to be no *a priori* reason why there could not be an explanatory hypothesis of this kind. One sort of hypothesis (although by no means the only kind) would be in terms of the beliefs that natives had about their own beliefs, that is certain meta-beliefs. We might postulate that the natives believe (falsely) on certain plausible grounds that their other beliefs are coherent. This hypothesis would enable us to understand (in at least one important sense) the translation. There is no reason why this sort of hypothesis could not be confirmed.

In particular, with respect to situational logic explanations *a la* Jarvie and Agassi, there is no need to make assumptions about the rationality of the actors in the sense presupposed (but not explicitly stated) by these authors. Suppose we translate some native discourse thusly: 'I think that performing magic ritual X is the best way to assure that my crops will grow. I will perform magic ritual X in order to make my crops grow and $Z \neq X$'. On Hollis' view such a translation would be ruled out *a priori* or at least this sort of translation could not become the general rule. But there is no reason why such translations should be ruled out. For one might have an explanatory hypothesis derived from psychology or neurology that would explain the natives' apparent lapses. It may be true that people under certain conditions e.g. hardening of the arteries in some portion of the brain, fail to see the implications of their beliefs with respect to plans for action and there may be independent evidence that the natives in question do have hardening of these arteries. Indeed, it may be the case that there is independent reason to suppose that most of the natives in this society have such a problem. This would explain why they have frequent lapses from rationality and it would give independent support to translations in which rationality is not presumed.

All in all the best approach seems to be to consider rationality as neither an *a priori* assumption nor a choice determined by benefits and costs but as an empirical hypothesis subject to empirical refutation and confirmation. And this seems to be the way in which anthropologists in general regard it. Thus Horton, in his paper 'African Traditional Thought and Western Science',[42] argues that traditional African thinking is very similar to Western scientific thinking, and hence more rational than has been supposed. African thought, according to Horton, is an attempt to formulate theories that give unity and meaning to everyday experience. In such theorizing, theoretical entities and causal sequences are postulated and abstractions and analogies are made that are striking in their similarity to Western scientific theorizing. The basic difference between Western thought and African thought is the existence of alternative theories in the former but not in the latter. It is clear that Horton puts his view forward not as an *a priori* assumption but as an empirical hypothesis that may be incorrect.

And according to Beattie[43] some of Horton's hypotheses are incorrect. Beattie points out what he takes to be crucial differences between African thought and Western thought and challenges Horton's view that the basic difference between the two is the lack of alternative theories in African thought and the presence of alternatives in Western thought. It suffices here to insist that the issues between Horton and Beattie will be settled by more anthropological evidence and not by transcendental deductions of *a priori* forms of understanding.

As we have seen situational logic explanations are in terms of the actor's rationality, beliefs and purposes. Explanations of this sort are linked in the literature with the idea of Verstehen but as we shall see Verstehen explanations and situational logic explanations are not in all cases identical.

5. *Verstehen explanations*

The doctrine of Verstehen has been the target of criticism of positivists and neo-positivists. Philosophers like Nagel,[44] for example, have argued that Verstehen is at best a useful heuristic technique in the context of discovery. Trying to empathize with social actors may enable one to generate hypotheses about their actions. But Verstehen is not a means of testing hypotheses; it has no use in the context of justification. However, according to Schutz, Winch and Ryan this standard positivistic critique of Verstehen is wide of the mark. Nagel and those who agree with him have not understood what Verstehen is.

Verstehen, according to Schutz in his paper 'Concept and Theory Formation in the Social Sciences', is not a method used by social scientists but 'the particular experiential form in which commonsense thinking takes cognizance of the social cultural world'.[45] What this seems to entail in relation to explanation is that an explanation of certain social behaviour in terms of Verstehen is an explanation in terms of the commonsense categories of the actors themselves. Furthermore, Schutz argues that such an explanation has a privileged status. He says: 'All scientific explanations of the social world *can* and for certain purposes *must* refer to the subjective meaning of the actions of human beings from which social reality originates'.[46] Thus the doctrine of Verstehen is not a method of how to test or generate hypotheses about social action (as Nagel wrongly thought) but—at

Michael Martin

least in relation to explanation—defines what an acceptable explanation of human behaviour will be. An acceptable explanation must be in terms of the commonsense categories of the actors themselves; an acceptable explanation in the social sciences must, then, be a Verstehen explanation.

Patrick Gardiner, in his paper 'The Concept of Man as Presupposed by Historical Studies', suggests that this sort of explanation is typical of historical explanation: 'The historian works and thinks, so to speak, as a vicarious agent, and strives for understanding in an agent's terms'.[47] However, little justification is to be found for restricting social science to Verstehen explanations either in the practice of social scientists or on general methodological grounds. On general methodological grounds such restrictions are surely harmful. Since the commonsense categories of actors may be imprecise and muddled, a re-formulation, an explication or even a replacement of the commonsense categories would certainly seem to be in order as it is in other scientific fields. Furthermore, scientific practice seems to belie such a restriction and indeed several papers by social scientists in the Emmet and MacIntyre volume illustrate this point well.

In his paper 'Sociological Explanation' Burns shows that in several sociological studies the explanations given of people's behaviour is in sharp contrast to those given by the actor.[48] Indeed, Burns argues that sociology has a critical function, namely that of exposing the falsehoods and deceptions of the commonsense ideas of the actor about his own actions. Turner in 'Symbols in Ndembu Ritual'[49] introduces theories and concepts based upon psychoanalytic and sociological theory that transcend the primitive thinking of the natives concerning the use of symbols; Levi-Strauss (although his work does not appear in Emmet and MacIntyre it is commented on by Leach and Worsley) introduces explanatory notions that go well beyond that of the natives whose behaviour he is attempting to account for. This, of course, is not to say that all these social scientific explanations have been successful. Far from it. Leach in his paper 'Telstar and the Aborigines or la Pensée Sauvage'[50] and Worsley in his paper 'Groote Eylandt Totemism and Le Totémisme Aujour d'hui'[51] point out serious problems with the theories of Levi-Strauss. The point is that the problems with his explanations do not lie in the fact that they depart from the commonsense thinking of the natives. Social scientists are perfectly justified in introducing new explanatory categories and theories that are quite foreign to the people whose behaviour they are interested in explaining.[52]

Now Schutz at times seems to identify explanations in terms of everyday commonsense categories with explanations in terms of motive, belief, emotion and the like. On this interpretation Verstehen explanations are explanations in terms of motives, beliefs, emotions and other commonsense psychological categories. Now although such an identification may be the correct one to make in our society and culture, it is not obvious that it is the correct one to make in all cases. For it is not implausible to suppose that some commonsense categories which are used to explain actions of some primitive tribes are not in terms of motives, beliefs, emotions, etc. A native might believe that Abuto has been possessed by an evil spirit and believe that this is why he is acting the way he is. He might not believe, what in fact may be the truth, that Abuto believes that he has been possessed by an evil spirit and because of this is acting in certain ways. A Verstehen explanation in this case would be an explanation in terms of evil spirit possession and not in terms

Explanation in Social Science: Some Recent Work

of beliefs about evil spirit possession. In any case, the problems that we raised against the doctrine that all social scientific explanation is to be Verstehen explanation are relevant whether Verstehen explanations are interpreted as explanations in terms of the common sense categories of the actors, whatever they may be, or in terms of the beliefs, motives and emotions of the actor. Social science has no need to stick to either.

It should be clear that some Verstehen explanations are situational logic explanations. This is because the concepts of belief, goal and rationality are sometimes concepts employed by actors to explain their own actions and those of others. However, there could be a group of people who acted rationally but who did not have the concept of rationality and hence did not explain their own actions or other's actions in terms of rationality. In this case situational logic explanations might well be unintelligible to the actor. Conversely not all Verstehen explanations are situational logic explanations since one might explain some action in terms of everyday concepts, e.g. devil possession, other than those of belief, goal and rationality. Even if one interprets Verstehen explanations as explanations in terms of belief, motive and emotion, situational logic explanations and Verstehen explanations are still not identical since the element of rationality so vital to situational logic explanations need not be present in such Verstehen explanations.

So far we have considered Verstehen explanations as explanations in terms of the commonsense concepts of the actor. However, a weaker (and perhaps more plausible) interpretation of the doctrine of Verstehen is possible. At one point Schutz says that the categories used by actors in social situations are 'the first level constructs' of the social sciences and that second level constructs must be 'erected'[53] on these. This suggests that explanatory concepts which are different from commonsense categories can be introduced so long as they are based in some unspecified way on the commonsense categories of the actor. The crucial question is exactly how these second order constructs must be related to the first order constructs. There is a clear danger here of making the relation either too restrictive or empty.

Ryan in defending Winch holds a position similar to this weaker interpretation of Schutz and runs into similar problems. Ryan believes that Winch is correct to maintain that whatever explanations we end up with 'we must root our story in that which is told by the agents themselves'.[54] Ryan links this restriction explicitly to the doctrine of Verstehen and argues that to construe Verstehen as a heuristic device is 'quite inadequate'.[55] The crucial question for Ryan is what he means by 'root'.

Ryan's meaning is clarified by the following quotation:

> For the point is that the identification of the events to be understood necessarily depends on understanding the rules which make them count as events of whatever kind it may be. Thus when we describe a set of actions as *praying*, this necessarily is to employ *religious* criteria, when we describe an act as that of *voting* this necessarily is to employ *political* criteria.[56]

From this one gathers that the commonsense categories of the actors are used to identify the subject matter to be explained. Once it has been identified, then explanatory theories and categories can be introduced that go beyond the actor's point of view.

However, even this restriction on social science is too much. Why must social scientists start by identifying their subject matter in terms of the categories of the

Michael Martin

actor? Suppose a social scientist wants to find out why a certain pattern of group behaviour occurs in a particular primitive society. Suppose further that the members of the group do not recognize this pattern and indeed do not even have terms for it. It would seem that Ryan's restriction would prevent the social scientist from explaining this pattern of social behaviour. But there does not seem to be any good reason for preventing him from doing so. Thus the doctrine of Verstehen on this weaker interpretation also seems too restrictive.

6. *Functional explanations*

We have seen that there is little reason given in the works under review to give situational logic explanations or Verstehen explanations a privileged status in the social sciences. Alternative types of explanation may be appropriate. One possible alternative we have not yet mentioned is functional explanation. Instead of explaining the working of some social institution, e.g. magic, in terms of the beliefs, goals and rationality of the actors in the society, or in terms of the actors' own concepts, in a functional explanation one would explain magic in terms of the function of magic in the society, e.g. bringing about tribal learning.

As we shall see in a moment, questions can be raised about the genuine explanatory value of functional accounts. However, even if functional explanations are problematic this still would not mean that one should prefer situational logic explanations or Verstehen explanation since functional explanations are not the only type of non-situational logic, or non-Verstehen explanation available.

Suppose that the function of magic is to preserve tribal learning. How does this explain magic? As Ryan points out, on some views of function to say that Y is the function of X is merely to say that Y is a useful unintended consequence of X.[57] Clearly if this is all that is meant, then citing the function of X does not explain X. Ryan attempts to clarify under what conditions a functional account would be explanatory. But his analysis is not satisfactory.

At one point he argues that functional explanations are 'only in place where an event or series of events is explained by showing that it was required for some goal or other *and* and this fact is a sufficient condition of the event's occurrence'.[58] Thus let X be the event to be explained and G be the goal at issue. Ryan's condition comes to this:

(1) If X is necessary for G, then X.

For example,

(1)' If magic is necessary for tribal learning, then magic occurs.

As we interpret Ryan he is saying that if (1)' is true, citing

(2) The function of magic is to preserve tribal learning

would explain

(3) Magic occurs.

Now it would seem that in order for Ryan's claim to be true one would at least have to assume

(4) If the function of magic is to preserve tribal learning, then magic is necessary for preserving tribal learning.

For given (4) and (2) and (1)' we could deduce (3), and (4) is necessary for the deduction of (3). However, it is dubious that (4) captures very well what social scientists have had in mind when they have made functional statements. Magic may have as its function preserving tribal learning without its being necessary to

Explanation in Social Science: Some Recent Work

preserve tribal learning for there may be functionally equivalent social practices. Thus Ryan's first analysis fails. Later however Ryan explicitly links the explanatory value of functional accounts to negative feedback mechanisms. To explain an event functionally is to explain its occurrence on the grounds that it is contributing to a goal or end state and the goal or end state is sought or maintained by the system in which the event to be explained takes place. 'The system in question has to possess some kind of negative feedback characteristics in the sense that a movement away from its goal is compensated for by some kind of correcting mechanism'.[59] Thus Ryan argues that in order to explain some institution e.g. magic, by citing that the function of magic is to preserve tribal learning we would have to show: (a) what goal the institution serves, e.g. preservation of tribal learning; (b) that wherever the institution declines some other form of behaviour functionally equivalent to it appears, e.g. religion; (c) that there is a process of feedback between the inability of the social system to meet whatever goal it has and its developing some substitute for the institution; (d) that such an explanation is the simplest available. It should be clear that this account is different from the one previously discussed. One basic difference is that on this account magic is not necessary for achieving tribal learning since there can be functionally equivalent conditions.

However, the sense in which magic is explained on this negative feedback model is not clear. Ryan is not very helpful here. He has no trouble in showing that it is dubious that proffered functional explanations of social institutions do not meet conditions (a)-(d) above. But what is unclear is why proffered functional explanations that do meet these conditions would explain.

One plausible answer is rejected by Ryan: Proffered functional explanations that meet conditions (a)-(d) presuppose some deductive covering law explanation and deductive covering law explanations of a certain kind presuppose functional explanations. Functional accounts are explanatory because they are equivalent to deductive covering law explanations of a certain type; functional explanations are thus reducible to a species of deductive covering law explanation. However, Ryan says that a functional explanation is not a 'mechanical [causal] explanation phrased peculiarly but a different kind of explanation'.[60] He admits that functional explanations may be replaced by non-functional explanations and that functional explanations may come in only in the beginning of inquiry. However, his point seems to be that nevertheless functional explanations can stand on their own; they can serve as explanations even if they can never be replaced by non-functional explanations. It is not clear that Ryan's contention is true for it is not clear just how functional 'explanation' explains in the first place.

Perhaps all that Ryans means is this: to say that a proffered functional explanation explains is just to say that conditions (a)-(d) hold. The fulfilment of these conditions defines what a functional explanation is. However it is unclear that this is what 'functional explanation' has traditionally meant. Ryan is free, of course, to stipulate some meaning. But then his thesis would have little interest.

Gellner does try to answer the question of how functional 'explanations' explain. He says:

All that is required is that each 'functional' explanation be as it were read backwards. The explanation of institution X is not really the proper, causal explanation of it, but of the manner in which it contributes to the society as a whole. The 'real' explanation of X is provided when the functional accounts of the other institutions is given—of all

Michael Martin

of them, or of a relevant subset of those of them which contribute towards the maintenance of X—which jointly make up a 'real' causal explanation of X itself (just as the 'functional' account of X figures in their causal explanation).[61]

In contrast to Ryan, Gellner does seem to maintain that functional explanations can be replaced by deductive covering law explanations of a certain kind. For example, suppose one truly says that the magic in society S is explained because the function of magic is to contribute to tribal learning. This functional explanation can be replaced by a deductive covering law explanation of the following sort. The covering law would specify other sets of practices found is S, e.g. economic, political, religious, which jointly constitute a sufficient condition for the practice of magic. In a similar manner the functional explanation of certain economic practices could be replaced by a covering law which specified other social practices (including magic) which would constitute a sufficient condition of the economic practice.

Indeed, not only *could* such replacements be made; Gellner seems to suggest that *unless* they could be made we would not have functional explanation. The explanatory value of functional explanations is on his view contingent on the existence of deductive covering law explanations which would explain the same thing. Furthermore, Gellner suggests that these causal explanations are the basic sort of explanation; functional explanation therefore can be reduced to another type of explanation.

Unfortunately, Gellner gives no argument for his view. As it stands it seems like a plausible but unproven thesis. Thus both Ryan's and Gellner's attempts to show how functional accounts are explanatory prove unsatisfactory.

Although many more topics than explanation are covered in the works under review, the above account may give the reader some idea of the philosophical problems connected with explanation in the social sciences. Although philosophy of social science has come into its own in the last few years there are many unexplored questions and problems that remain. The works under review should help to make the philosophy of the social sciences with its unexplored questions and problems more accessible to interested students.

Boston University

NOTES

1 In addition to the three anthologies under review in this paper, the reader is referred to May Brodbeck (ed.), *Readings in the Philosophy of the Social Sciences*, London 1968; Maurice Natanson (ed.), *Philosophy of the Social Sciences: A Reader*, New York 1963; Leonard I. Krimmerman, *The Nature and Scope of Social Science: A Critical Anthology*, New York 1969.
2 In addition to the textbook under review in this paper the reader is referred to Richard S. Rudner, *Philosophy of Social Science*, Englewood Cliffs, N.J. 1966; Quentin Gibson, *The Logic of Social Enquiry*, London 1960; Abraham Kaplan, *The Conduct of Inquiry*, San Francisco 1964.
3 In addition to the journal under review, *The Journal for the Theory of Social Behavior* and the journal in which the present paper appears, *Philosophy of the Social Sciences*, the reader is referred to *Theory and Decision*. Older philosophy journals occasionally having papers directly relevant to the philosophy of social sciences are: *Philosophy of Science*, *British Journal for the Philosophy of Science*, *Inquiry*, *Journal of Philosophy*, *Mind*, *Ethics*, *Theoria*, *Methodos*, and *History and Theory*.
4 For convenience of reference these works will be abbreviated as follows: (*a*) Dorothy Emmet and

Explanation in Social Science: Some Recent Work

Alasdair MacIntyre (eds.), *Sociological Theory and Philosophical Analysis* (London: MacMillan and Co., 1970. $3.50) = *STPA*. (*b*) Bryan Wilson (ed.), *Rationality* (Oxford: Basil Blackwell, 1970. £2.75) = *R*. (*c*) Royal Institute of Philosophy Lectures, *The Proper Study*, Vol. 4, 1969–70 (London: Macmillan, 1971. $16.00) = *TPS*. (*d*) Alan Ryan, *The Philosophy of the Social Sciences* (London: Macmillan, 1970. $3.50) = *PSS*. (*e*) *Journal for the Theory of Social Behavior*, Vol. 1, no. 1 = *JTSB*.
5 *JTSB*, p. 8.
6 *PSS*, p. 47.
7 Readers not acquainted with this model are referred to Karl Popper, *The Logic of Scientific Discovery* New York 1959, section 12, and Carl G. Hempel, *Aspects of Scientific Explanation*, New York 1965.
8 *PSS*, p. 59.
9 *JTSB*, p. 8.
10 *PSS*, p. 60.
11 Ibid.
12 *TPS*, p. 68.
13 See Hempel, op. cit.
14 *JTSB*, p. 8.
15 See I. Scheffler, *The Anatomy of Inquiry*, New York 1963, pp. 43–6.
16 *PSS*, p. 201.
17 *STPA*, pp. 29–35.
18 See Jane Martin, *Explaining, Understanding and Teaching*, New York 1970.
19 S. Bromberger, *The Concept of Explanation*, Ph.D. thesis, Harvard University 1960.
20 *PSS*, chapter 8.
21 *STPA*, pp. 76–88.
22 Ibid. p. 86.
23 *STPA*, p. 86.
24 Cf. Ernest Nagel, *The Structure of Science*, New York 1961, Chapter 11, pp. 535–47.
25 See Michael Martin, 'Methodological Individualism and the Reduction of Cultural Anthropology to Psychology', *Scientia*, 104, 1969, 489–502.
26 *PSS*, p. 173.
27 *PSS*, Chapter 5.
28 Nagel, *op. cit.*
29 See Michael Martin 'The Body-Mind Problem and Neurophysiological Reduction', *Theoria*, 37, 1972, 1–14.
30 *R*, pp. 172–93.
31 *R*, pp. 50–61.
32 *R*, pp. 194–213.
33 *STPA*, pp. 89–114.
34 Hempel, op. cit., pp. 463–89.
35 *R*, p. 179.
36 See for example I. C. Jarvie, *The Revolution in Anthropology*, London 1964; J. Agassi 'Methodological Individualism', *British Journal of Sociology*, 11, 1960, 244–70.
37 *R*, pp. 240–68.
38 *R*, pp. 112–30.
39 *PSS*, pp. 157–8.
40 *R*, pp. 214–20, pp. 221–39.
41 *R*, pp. 18–49; *STPA*, pp. 115–49.
42 *R*, pp. 132–71.
43 *R*, pp. 240–68.
44 Nagel op. cit., pp. 481–5.
45 *STPA*, p. 9.
46 Ibid., p. 15.
47 *TPS*, p. 28.
48 *STPA*, pp. 55–76.
49 Ibid., pp. 150–82.
50 Ibid., pp. 183–203.
51 Ibid., pp. 204–23.
52 For a criticism of Verstehen see Jane Martin, op. cit., Chapters 7 and 8.
53 *STPA*, p. 15.
54 *PSS*, p. 143.
55 Ibid.
56 Ibid.
57 Ibid., p. 189.
58 Ibid., p. 183.
59 Ibid., p. 184.
60 Ibid., p. 186.
61 *STPA*, p. 118; *R*, p. 21.

6

SITUATIONAL LOGIC AND COVERING LAW EXPLANATIONS IN HISTORY

Michael Martin

Boston University

Donagan has argued (a) that the covering law model of explanation does not apply in certain cases in historical explanations; (b) that situational logic explanations do apply, and (c) that situational logic explanations are fundamentally different from covering law explanations. It is argued that (b) is false as Donagan construes situational logic explanations. Once situational logic explanations are correctly construed they are similar to Hempel's rational explanations in covering law forms — hence (c) is false if situational logic explanations are correctly interpreted. Finally it is argued that one major reason Donagan gives for (a) is mistaken.

Critics of the covering law model of explanation in history have a twofold task: First, they must show that there are genuine problems with this model. As is well known many attempts to do this have failed because they were based on gross misunderstandings of the purpose of the model, as when it is criticized on the grounds that in their writings historians don't put their explanations in covering law form.[1]

But apart from the negative task of finding genuine problems with the model, its critics are faced with the positive one of giving an alternative account of the logic of historical explanations.

Alan Donagan[2] has attempted the latter by means of an account of explanation in terms of the logic of the situation. He argues that explanations in terms of the logic of the situation are fundamentally different from covering law explanations. In this paper I wish to challenge this thesis. I will try to show, first, that Donagan's characterization of situational logic explanations in history is seriously inaccurate and that once it is corrected it is not fundamentally different from a type of covering law explanation proposed by Hempel, and secondly, that the one major obstacle Donagan finds to accepting the covering law deductive model is non-existent.

I. The Logic of the Situation

Taking his cue from Popper, Donagan has characterized a type of explanation found in history in terms of what an agent does in 'a situation as he thinks it to be, rather than the situation as it is'.[3] Such explanations contain no general laws. Nevertheless they are deductive in form and they must be testable. Donagan gives an example of this type of explanation. An historian explains Brutus' joining Cassius' conspiracy 'by saying that Brutus had resolved to preserve the Republic at all costs, and judged that the logic of his situation was that only by his joining Cassius could the Republic be preserved'.[4] According to Donagan such a situational logic explanation has the following form:

(1) A was resolved to achieve the end E at all costs.
(2) A judged his situation to be C.
(3) A judged that E could only be achieved in C if he did x.
(4) $\therefore$ A did x.

Alternatively Donagan thinks that the form of such explanations could be construed in this way:

(1') A was resolved to achieve the end E at all costs.
(2') If A judged that E could only be achieved in C if he did x and A judged his situation to be C, A did x.
(3') A judged that E could only be achieved in C if he did x.
(4') A judged his situation to be C.
(5') $\therefore$ A did x.

In this alternative formulation (2') is supposed to follow from (1') as a corollary, and (2') combined with (3') and (4') is supposed to entail (5').

According to Donagan, situational logic explanations are to be sharply contrasted with Dray's rational explanations[5] as formulated by Hempel[6] in covering law deductive form as follows:

(1″) *A* was in a situation of type *C*.
(2″) *A* was a rational agent.
(3″) In situations of type *C* a rational agent will do *x*.
_____
(4″) ∴ *A* did *x*.

On Donagan's view there are two major weaknesses in the Hempel schema.

> First, there is no criterion of rationality which uniquely singles out one course of action as 'the thing to do'. Secondly, there is no reason to believe that all historical agents are rational in any of the several senses of 'rational' which Hempel has explored.[7]

In Donagan's schema there is 'no psychological assumption of rationality'; actions are intelligible but not necessarily rational.

II. Critique of Donagan's Evaluation

Donagan may believe that the Hempel analysis is committed to an assumption that all historical agents are rational. If so, he is clearly mistaken.[8] It is true that (3″) is in the form of a general law. But this no more commits Hempel's analysis to any universal assumption about the rationality of historical agents than does the law of falling bodies commit one to the assumption that all bodies are falling. As far as the truth of (3″) is concerned there need be no rational agent. To be sure, in any *application* of (3″) it is assumed that some particular agent is rational. But this is just to say that (2″) must be true in any correct application. On the other hand, if Donagan does not believe Hempel's analysis is so committed, it is difficult to see the relevance of his remarks. Is the point just that the schema has limited application; that sometimes it applies in historical explanatory contexts but sometimes it does not. This may well be admitted. However, it does not follow that the covering law model has limited application, since Hempel's schema of rational explanation does not exhaust covering law explanations of human action in history. Moreover it does not follow that Donagan's schema has wider applications than Hempel's schema of a rational explanation. Indeed, one may well suspect that historical agents are seldom resolved to pursue some end at *all* costs although historical agents may often be resolved to pursue some end at high cost. In particular, one may well wonder whether historical agents are not more often rational — in one or the other of the senses specified by Hempel — than resolved to pursue some end at all costs.

In any case, it should be noted that Hempel's schema can be easily modified to accommodate any particular sense of 'rationality' one wishes. Suppose one was interested in, say, sense y. One need only modify (2″) and (3″) to read:

(2″) A was a rational agent in sense y
(3″) In situations of type C a rational agent in sense y will do x.

Of course, even given one particular meaning of rationality, e. g. the Bayesian account, one unique course of action might not be prescribed. But (3″) does not prescribe one course of action, it *predicts* one course. It is a factual statement, not a normative principle. If several courses of action were all rational relative to a given definition of rationality this would not preclude predicting one unique course of action for a rational actor. Factors in the situation not having to do with the rationality of the actor in the specified sense would have to be taken into account, e. g. emotional preferences of the actor, his psychological tendencies and so on. It is quite clear that Hempel intended such factors to be included in his schema.[9]

I conclude that the two problems Donagan finds with the Hempel schema are illusory, and that so far he has given no reason to reject the Hempel model. More than that, however, Donagan's alternative schema has serious problems of its own.

III. Donagan's Situational Logic Examined

One basic shortcoming of Donagan's schema is that the conclusion (4) does not follow from the premises (1), (2), and (3); thus despite his insistence that situational logic explanations are deductively valid, as he formulates them they are not. If we consider his alternative formulation, (2′) is false and moreover (2′) does not follow from (1′). To see the invalidity of his argument consider an extreme case. Let x be leaping over the moon. A madman may be resolved to achieve a certain purpose at all costs and may believe that it is necessary for him to leap over the moon to achieve this purpose, yet he certainly will not in fact leap over the moon.

But it is not necessary to appeal to feats that conflict with laws of physics. Let x be memorizing a large dictionary by heart in one week. Clearly an ordinary man could not accomplish such a feat even if he believed it was necessary to achieve some purpose. Indeed, we need not even consider astonishing mental feats. Donagan's own example will do, namely Brutus' joining Cassius. Suppose members of the conspiracy had not allowed Brutus to join Cassius. Then, even though Brutus believed this was necessary to save the Republic, he would not have joined.

But even granting the above, could we not deduce a weaker conclusion?

(4a) A tried to do x.

No, for if Brutus had been assassinated in a counter-plot immediately after his resolve, he would not even have *tried* to join the conspiracy. Indeed, all sorts of factors — psychological, physiological, environmental — might have prevented Brutus from joining or from even trying to join Cassius despite his resolve and his belief.

I think it is fair to conclude that if situational logic explanations take into account *only* the agent's resolve and belief about the situation and not the situation itself, as Donagan suggests, these sorts of explanations can explain very little. It is significant that authors close to Popper,[10] Donagan's own inspiration for situational logic explanation, have stressed both the actual situation (let us call this C') and the situation-as-perceived, C, as necessary ingredients in situational logic explanations.

We might correct Donagan's schema as follows:

(1) A was resolved to achieve the end E at all costs.
(2) A judged his situation to be C.
(3) A judged that E could only be achieved in C if he did x.
(3a) A was in a situation of type C', i. e. the conditions were normal, factors $F_1 F_2 \ldots F_n$ were not present.

(4) $\therefore$ A did x.

But even the addition of (3a) does not allow the deduction unless we assume that Brutus had certain other beliefs. Consider the following cases:

(i) Donagan's language suggests that Brutus believed that joining the conspiracy was a necessary condition for saving the Republic. However, this is perfectly compatible with his belief that such action was not a sufficient condition and with his belief that saving the Republic had not the slightest chance of success. He might have believed, for example, that other things were necessary if the Republic was to be saved and that these things would never come to pass. This belief might well have influenced him not to join the conspiracy.

(ii) Suppose that Brutus thought that his joining the conspiracy was necessary to save the Republic and also that if he joined the conspiracy it would be likely that the Republic would be saved. He might still have refrained from joining because he believed that he would not be allowed to join or because he believed that his life would be taken if he tried to join.

(iii) Suppose Brutus believed he could join the conspiracy. But suppose he believed he could also perform some other action that was necessary for saving the Republic; moreover suppose he believed that this other action was likely to bring about the salvation of the Republic. Suppose also that he mistakenly believed that this other action was incompatible with his joining the conspiracy.[11] In this case what could we possibly infer about what Brutus would do?

Example (iii) illustrates quite clearly, I think, that a minimal sense of rationality must be assumed in Donagan's schema despite his insistence that his schema assumes no rationality. We must surely suppose that Brutus does not have logically incompatible beliefs to bring off the deduction of (4).

Moreover, it is only a little less obvious that the first examples (i) and (ii) presuppose that Brutus is rational in an even stronger sense than example (iii) does. For even supposing that Brutus had no incompatible beliefs and that he was resolved to save the Republic at all costs and that he believed that he could join the conspiracy without incident and that his joining the conspiracy was necessary to save the Republic and likely to succeed and so on, he might still not have drawn the inference 'I should join the conspiracy'. Temporary mental confusion, deep-seated irrationality, or a subtle self-deception may have prevented him from making this inference. It seems clear then that Donagan is not only committed to Brutus' not having logically incompatible beliefs but also to Brutus' being able to make certain logical inferences. Let us call an agent who is rational in these ways a rational agent in sense z.

Donagan's schema could be corrected in the light of the above considerations in the following way:

(1) A was resolved to achieve the end E at all costs.
(2) A judged his situation to be C.
(3) A judged that E could only be achieved in C if he did x.
(3a) A was in a situation of type C' (normal conditions).
(3b) A had certain other beliefs about his situation.
(3c) A was a rational agent in sense z.
(4) $\therefore A$ did x.

It should be noted that once Donagan's schema is corrected it begins to look like the Hempel schema. This is especially obvious when we realize that the agent's goals and beliefs are not explicitly stated in Hempel's schema but seem to be included either under C or under the rubric of 'rational agent'. Moreover, Donagan's implicit assumption of rationality seems to be simply a weaker sense of rationality than that considered by Hempel. Hempel's characterization of a rational actor seems to entail a rational agent in sense z.

IV. The Need for General Laws

The major difference between the Hempel and Donagan schemata now appears to be the absence of a covering law in the latter and its presence in the former. Where Donagan believes that (4) can be deduced without covering laws, Hempel believes it cannot be. Is Donagan right? Can the deduction of (4) proceed without a general law analogous to (3'')?

Consider the following statement analogous to (3'') in Hempel's schema.

L_1 In situations of type C' (normal conditions) a rational agent in sense z who has resolved to pursue goal E at all costs and judges that his situation is C and judges that E could be achieved in C if he did x and has certain other beliefs about his situation, does x.

If L_1 is analytic, then (1), (2), (3), (3a), (3b) and (3c) do entail (4). On the other hand if L_1 is a factual statement (1), (2), (3), (3a), (3b) and (3c) do not entail (4). Thus Donagan would have to maintain that L_1 is analytic.[12]

However, whether L_1 is analytic or not will surely depend on how one interprets the phrase 'normal conditions'. This phrase *could* be interpreted in such a way that L_1 becomes analytic. Such a course is always available even in the natural sciences. Consider a natural science law mentioned by Donagan:

L_2 In normal conditions a man who takes a large dose of arsenic will soon afterwards have burning pains in his throat.

The phrase 'normal conditions' could be interpreted in a way that *makes* L_2 analytic. Thus if someone did take a large dose of arsenic but did not get a burning pain we could suppose that he was not in normal conditions — no matter what the evidence. But 'normal conditions' need not be interpreted in this way; indeed, scientists do not in general interpret L_2 in this way. The phrase 'normal conditions' is vague. Normal conditions are not exhaustively specifiable. Nevertheless one has a more or less clear idea of what *sort* of conditions are excluded: e. g. the stomach is not pumped immediately, no antidotes of a certain kind are taken, the stomach and throat are not coated with some protective substance, etc. If a man had no burning pain in his throat after taking a large dose of arsenic and none of these conditions or conditions of a *similar* sort were present, then scientists would have a good case for saying L_2 was false.

There seems to be no *a priori* reason for supposing that L_1 could not be interpreted in a similar way, and I know of no *a posteriori* reason for supposing that historians would interpret L_1 as analytic. One knows more or less what *sort* of conditions are excluded by 'normal conditions' in L_1; e. g. the agent's becoming paralyzed, having his life taken by an assassin before he does x, and so on. And if normal conditions did prevail and (1), (2), (3), (3a), (3b), and (3c) seemed to be true and (4) was false, one might well suppose that L_1 was false. Surely any hesitation that we might have on this matter is not of a fundamentally different kind from the hesitation one would have in supposing L_2 to be false under similar circumstances.

Now if we interpret L_1 in this way, (4) would not follow from (1), (2), (3), (3a), (3b) and (3c) without L_1. However, Donagan's schema with L_1 added is a special case of the Hempel schema; thus there seems to be no essential difference between Donagan's account of situational logic explanation and Hempel's account of covering law rational explanation.

It would seem therefore that if we are to give a deductive explanation of why A did x by this modified schema, e. g. why Brutus joined the conspiracy, we must use some general law.

V. The Alleged Unavailability of Laws of Social Science

However, another problem arises. Are there any laws one can use in historical explanations? Donagan argues that there are no available general laws of the social sciences to explain human behavior. Thus he would presumably maintain that if L_1 is interpreted as a factual statement, it is false, and hence cannot be used to explain, e. g., why Brutus joined the conspiracy.

Donagan admits that there are laws of the natural sciences that can be used to explain historical events. For instance the statement:

L_3 All living creatures die when exposed to intense heat.

This is cited by Donagan as a law of natural science that may be used to explain Bruno's death at the stake. However, such laws cannot explain why Bruno was sent to the stake or why he defied his persecutors; laws of natural science cannot explain human action.

To refute the view that general laws of the social sciences are now available Donagan uses the following procedure. He cites some examples of alleged general laws of the social sciences and easily shows that counter-examples can be found to all of them. For example:

L_4 People who have jobs do not like to lose them.

Donagan's charwoman is cited as a case of a person who would not mind losing her job; thus either L_4 is false or else it is a disguised statistical generalization:

L_5 People who have jobs do not usually like to lose them.

According to Donagan L_5 cannot explain a human action or event, e. g. why Jones does not want to leave his job, because it is statistical. We need not consider Donagan's claim that statistical laws cannot explain particular actions or events. It suffices to say that such a claim is answered elsewhere.[13] We will only consider his view that although there may be social scientific general laws none are yet known.

What is curious about Donagan's argument on this point is that the very procedure he uses to refute proposed general laws of the social sciences could be used to refute general laws of the natural sciences — the very ones mentioned by Donagan. Consider L_3. Without serious qualification and modification L_3 is false. Firemen and forest fire fighters are exposed to intense heat and sometimes do not die although it is true that they are injured severely and often die. Thus either L_3 is false or L_3 is a disguised statistical generalization:

L_6 Living creatures who are exposed to intense heat usually die.

On Donagan's showing L_6 could not explain Bruno's death.

SITUATIONAL LOGIC AND COVERING LAWS

The specific qualification that would have to be made to make L_3 *both* a true general law *and* applicable to Bruno is certainly unclear. But in general such precise qualification is neither possible nor necessary. As Brown has pointed out,[14] laws as they are actually used in science are accompanied by 'texts' that indicate the meaning of the key terms and the intended range of application of the law. As I have already argued, it is generally impossible to specify exactly what this range is, and some general terms like 'under normal conditions' or 'other things being equal' are often used to indicate that certain qualifications are needed. Nevertheless, the *sort* of factors in the situation that would make the law inapplicable are known. This is true in L_3. Thus, correctly stated, L_3 becomes

L_7 Under normal conditions people who are exposed to intense heat die.

Stated in this way and rightly understood L_7 is true.

Now is it really the case that there are no available laws of the social sciences for which similar claims can be made? This seems to be doubtful. L_1 seems to be true. And there are other examples. Consider for example:

L_8 Under normal conditions a person who is mentally retarded will not graduate *summa cum laude* from an accredited university.

L_8 is true. But the phrase 'under normal conditions' is important, for it is conceivable that college boys might play a prank, or fraud or conspiracy might occur to enable a mentally retarded person to graduate from a university with highest honors: other students could take his exams, his records could be tampered with, bribery could be used. All these factors and more are intended to be excluded by the phrase 'under normal conditions' and these factors can no more be exhaustively enumerated than can the abnormal conditions under which a man will not feel a burning sensation in his throat after taking arsenic. It is significant that Donagan uses such a qualifying phrase in his statement of the natural law of poisoning but not in his examples of social scientific laws.

But is L_8 analytic? No more than L_7 or L_2 is. It is surely not logically impossible that a mentally retarded person could graduate with highest honors from an accredited university under normal conditions.

Were L_8 shown to be false there would be ramifications throughout social science: serious modifications would have to be made in our beliefs about mental retardation or about the standards at institutions of higher learning or about how much motivation can overcome, etc. But in the same manner a falsifying instance of L_2 would have serious ramifications: wide ranging modifications would have to be made in our beliefs about poisons and human physiology and so on. Moreover, L_1 and L_8 are by no means the only laws of social science.[15] Again it is important to judge these social scientific laws with standards which are no stricter than those appropriate to the natural sciences.

VI. Conclusion

One can sympathize with Donagan's desire to preserve the scientific status of historiography 'as it is' rather than to force it into a natural science mold. However, one may well wonder whether the scientific status of historiography is as he has characterized it. First, as I have shown, his schema of situational logic explanations is seriously inadequate. Once corrected it seems quite close to Hempel's deductive covering law model of a rational agent. Secondly, his belief that general laws of social science are not now available seems to be based on a double standard. The standard he applies to the proposed social science laws to show that they are false would also show that some well-established laws of the natural sciences are false. When the actual standards used in natural science contexts are applied to proposed laws of the social sciences some proposed social science laws are left intact.

NOTES

1. For Hempel's account of the status of the model see C. G. Hempel, *Aspects of Scientific Explanation*, The Free Press, New York 1965, pp. 412–15.
2. Alan Donagan, 'The Popper–Hempel Theory', in William Dray (Ed.), *Philosophical Analysis and History*, Harper & Row, New York 1966, pp. 127–59.
3. Ibid., p. 147.
4. Ibid., p. 150. At one point Donagan speaks as if the task is to explain Brutus' decision to join. I take it that this is a temporary slip and that the actual problem is to explain why Brutus actually joined.

5. William Dray, *Laws and Explanation in History*, Oxford University Press, 1957, Ch. 5.
6. See, for example, C. G. Hempel, 'Explanation in Science and in History', *Philosophical Analysis and History*, pp. 95–126.
7. Donagan, op. cit., p. 155.
8. Hempel seems to explicitly repudiate any such assumption. See Hempel, *Aspects of Scientific Explanation*, p. 477.
9. Ibid., p. 472.
10. See, for example, I. C. Jarvie, *The Revolution in Anthropology*, The Humanities Press, New York 1963, p. 113.
11. Thus suppose Brutus held the following inconsistent set of beliefs:
    (i) If the Republic is saved, I join the conspiracy.
    (ii) If the Republic is saved, I do action y.
    (iii) I join the conspiracy if and only if I do not do action y.
    (iv) The Republic will be saved.
12. Hempel meets a similar argument against (3''); see Hempel, 'Explanation in Science and in History', p. 119; see also Hempel, *Aspects of Scientific Explanation*, p. 461.
13. Hempel, *Aspects of Scientific Explanation*, p. 391; I. Scheffler, *The Anatomy of Inquiry*, Knopf, New York 1963, pp. 31–43.
14. Robert Brown, *Explanation in Social Science*, Aldine Publishing Co., Chicago 1963, pp. 145–56.
15. For more examples see ibid., pp. 133–65.

OPEN CONCEPTS AND SOCIAL SCIENTIFIC PREDICTION

In this paper I evaluate an argument of A.C. MacIntyre[1] that purports to show that predictions of the kind typical of the natural sciences are impossible in the social sciences. I will call this argument "The argument from open concepts." I will maintain that MacIntyre fails to show by this argument that predictions typical of those made in the natural sciences cannot be made in the social sciences.[2]

The Argument from Open Concepts

MacIntyre maintains that a necessary condition of being able to predict in the natural sciences is being able to identify unambiguously the items one wishes to predict through time. Thus in predicting the behavior of gas via gas laws and statements of initial conditions one must be able to identify gas through time; in predicting the behavior of planets via Kepler's laws and statements of initial conditions one must be able to identify planets over time. By "identify a particular planet or gas over time" MacIntyre means that the concept of a planet or the concept of a gas must enable one to pick out a planet or a gas at different times.

According to MacIntyre this is precisely what one is unable to do in the social sciences. For example, consider social classes and political parties:

> The identification of these particulars by the social scientist is made via the identification made by agents who engage in the relevant activities. The social scientists' concepts attempt to capture phenomena which are partially constituted by and in terms of the concepts of social and political agents. But in the activities which embody their concepts agents extend, reinterpret and reshape those concepts...Thus at any given point in the history of such particulars as classes and parties there is an openness toward the future which involves an openness towards the future application of the concept.[3]

This openness is not to be confused with the openness of the concepts of the natural sciences:

> To say that the concept of gold has open texture is to say that we cannot determine completely in advance any set of necessary and/or sufficient conditions for its application in particular circumstances. To say that the concept of party is open is to say that debate as to the character and application of the concept of party is inherent in the activities of those to whom in their organized political life the concept applies.[4]

MacIntyre does not wish to deny that predictions are sometimes possible in the social sciences. What he maintains is that natural science type predictions are impossible. In a natural science type prediction prima facie counter-examples to a prediction can be handled in certain ways. Suppose in natural science we predict from a tentatively accepted law and statements of initial conditions and auxiliary hypotheses that something will occur and it does. The natural scientist has, according to MacIntyre, four moves open to him: (1) rejecting the law, (2) modifying the content of the law, (3) modifying the scope of the law, (4) keeping the law in tact and modifying one or more of the auxiliary hypotheses.

MacIntyre can be interpreted as arguing that in the social sciences there is another possibility. Suppose one has a law-like hypothesis of the following form: If x is a social class and x has property A, then x has a property B. Now suppose some entity a is alleged to be a social class and to have property A. But suppose that a does not have property B. One might not be able to handle the prima facie counter-example in any of the four ways specified above, ways that are characteristic of the natural sciences. For the concept of social class may have changed; that is the members of the social class may have extended, reinterpreted and reshaped the concept of a social class so that the social scientist's concept of social class used in the statement of the initial conditions (which is based on the social actors' concept at time t + n) is different from that found in the law used in the prediction (which is based on the social actors' concept at time t). In other words it seems as if the form of the prediction is this:

(1) (x) (Sx.Ax ⊃ Bx)
(2)   Sa.Aa
―――――――――――――――
(3) ∴   Ba

Let us call this pattern A.
In fact, the prediction rests on an equivocation:

(1') (x) (S_1x.Ax ⊃ Bx)
(2') S_2a.Aa
―――――――――――――――
(3') ∴   Ba

Let us call this pattern B.

In pattern A if (3) is false, one can assume that there is something wrong with the law or initial condition. But in pattern B if (3') is false no such inference can be made since the notion of social class in (1') and (2') is different.

Since the extension, modification, and reshaping of concepts in the social sciences by social agents is always possible and is itself unpredictable, according to MacIntyre, social scientific concepts have an openness not characteristic of natural science concepts: social scientific particulars cannot be identified unambiguously through time hence social scientific predictions are impossible.

Critique of the Argument

The Alleged Importance of the Concepts of Social Actors

One of the major assumptions of MacIntyre's argument is that the concepts of social science are partly determined by the concepts of the social actors. Consider social classes: Social classes are often specified by social scientists in terms of income and education and other objective indices. Now MacIntyre seems to be saying that social scientists' concept of social class is modeled after the concept of social class held by the members of social classes.

However, it is unclear that people in the social classes specified by social scientists have a concept of social class very similar to that of the social scientists. Furthermore if they do have a concept of social class, it is unclear if this similarity is due to the social scientists trying to capture this common sense notion of social class. Indeed, in some cases one might wonder whether the influence is just the opposite of what MacIntyre supposes. Rather than social scientists basing their concepts on the concepts of the social actors, social actors seem to base their concepts on the concepts of social scientists. Taking courses in sociology, for example, may influence people to have a concept of social class they did not have before.

We do know that people in one class often do not judge correctly what class they are in, given a social scientist's view of class. Thus lower class people may not judge they are in the lower class.[3] This may be explained in a number of ways, e.g. that they refuse to admit their lowly position to themselves or at least to their interviewers. But another hypothesis is that they have a different concept of class from that of social scientists, one which social scientists choose to ignore.

Furthermore, it is worth noting that as social scientific theories get more abstract and formal the similarity of the concepts in them to the concepts of the social actors decreases; for example, concepts used in mathematical economics have little similarity to the concepts of social actors.

In any case, how much and in what circumstances social scientists desire to model their concepts in terms of the concepts of social actors is an empirical question belonging to the sociology of the social sciences. Without more evidence than we have any judgement is extremely hazardous. Consequently, MacIntyre's judgement based, as it seems to be, on his offhand impressions is dubious.

So far we have argued against MacIntyre's empirical claim that social scientific concepts are partially determined by the concepts of the social actors the social scientist is studying. However, implicitly at least, MacIntyre seems to be making the normative claim that social scientists' concepts should be partially based on the concepts of social actors. However, there is reason to doubt this normative claim. Social scientists have many goals—major and minor. Among the major goals are making accurate predictions and building unambiguous and systematic theories. These goals, it seems to me, should be primary. Any attempt to reflect the changing concepts of the social actor in the theories of social scientists that interferes with these primary goals must give way. In so far as the goals of accurate prediction and systematic theory are in conflict with basing the concepts of social science on the concepts of social actors the latter and not the former must go.

Consequently MacIntyre's argument, if successful, only shows that social scientists ought not to adopt certain techniques of concept formation that interfere with their goals of prediction and systematic theory building. It does not show that natural science type prediction is impossible.

MacIntyre at one point says that someone might object that

> All that my argument shows is that [social scientists ought not] make social classes, parties and the like the particular objects of their inquiry. But this negative remark has force only insofar as some alternative is formulated which is free from the kind of objection that I have set out.[6]

My present objection, however, is not that social scientists should not make social classes, parties and the like the objects of their inquiry. My objection is rather that social scientists should not use the concept of social class, parties and so on of the social actor if this use adversely affects predictability. Social scientists should formulate their own concepts of social class, party and so on so as to maximize certain scientific goals. One of these goals is predictability. So there is no burden on me to suggest some radically different way of doing social science. Indeed, social scientists sometimes do ignore the concepts of the social actors they are investigating and formulate their own concepts. Their reason for doing this is usually precisely the one suggested here. The concept of the social actors is not adequate to their scientific purposes.[7]

Unambiguity as an Auxiliary Hypothesis

Another crucial assumption in MacIntyre's argument is that pattern B described above cannot be construed in terms of how counter examples are handled in the natural sciences. For example, MacIntyre seems to suppose that if (3') is false, one cannot suppose that some auxiliary hypothesis is false.

The trouble with MacIntyre's thesis is, I think, that he takes too limited a view of the auxiliary hypotheses which a natural scientist relies on. Scientists not only assume certain substantive hypotheses but also certain procedural ones. A natural scientist, for example, may suppose that when he makes a prediction he has committed no fallacy or logical error in the deduction; in particular he may suppose that he has committed no equivocation in the terms used in the premises of his argument. Until this procedural auxiliary hypothesis is checked out no inference to the falsehood of the law or substantive auxiliary hypotheses used in the prediction can be made on the basis of the falsehood of the conclusion of the prediction.

.Thus the sort of failure of prediction that results from changing concepts (and consequently the ambiguity of language) is quite compatible with the natural scientist type of prediction proposed by MacIntyre so long as a more liberal view of auxiliary hypotheses is accepted, a view that is in fact used in the natural sciences themselves.

The kind of failure of prediction MacIntyre seems to have in mind is due to a particular procedural auxiliary hypothesis being false: terms in the premise are used ambiguously. However, this problem is not unique to the social sciences. Recent discussion of conceptual change in the natural sciences by Feyerabend,[8] Kuhn,[9] Scheffler[10] and others indicates that because of conceptual change predictions which seem to falsify a natural scientific theory do not. I have suggested elsewhere various ways of handling similar problems.[11] However, the important point to note here is that conceptual change in both the natural and the social sciences affect how prima facie counter examples are handled. This is true whether the conceptual change is based ultimately on the conceptual change of the scientists who are predicting (as it is in the natural sciences) or on the conceptual change of the social actors whose behavior scientists are trying to predict and whose concepts social scientists (according to MacIntyre) do or should adopt.

Conclusion

MacIntyre may be correct that the kinds of prediction typical of the natural sciences are not possible in the social sciences. However, his argument from open concepts is not sound and consequently fails to prove his case. Certain factual and normative presuppositions of his argument are dubious, and in any case, a more inclusive notion of auxiliary hypotheses shows that even on his view prediction in social science proceeds in the same way as in the natural sciences.

Footnotes

1. A.C. MacIntyre, "Predictability and Explanation in the Social Sciences," Philosophic Exchange, 1, 1972, pp. 5-13.

2. For a perceptive criticism of MacIntyre along a different line than mine see Paul G. Morrison, "Do Social Events Defy Scientific Prediction?", Philosophic Exchange, 1, 1972, pp. 23-31.

3. MacIntyre, op. cit., p. 7.

4. Ibid.

5. James West, Plainville, U.S.A. (New York: Columbia University Press, 1961), Chapter 3.

6. MacIntyre, op. cit., p. 13.

7. Actually there is reason to think that social scientists' concept of class is based primarily on theoretical concerns and changes according to changes in theory—not according to changes in the actors' concept of class. See R.C. Hinkle and A. Boskoff, "Social Stratification in Perspective," Sociological Theory, eds. H. Becker and A. Boskoff (New York: Holt, Rinehart and Winston 1957), pp. 368-395.

8. Paul K. Feyerabend, "Explanation, Reduction, and Empiricism," Minnesota Studies in the Philosophy of Science Vol. 3, eds. H. Feigl and G. Maxwell (Minneapolis: University of Minnesota Press, 1962).

9. Thomas Kuhn, The Structure of Scientific Revolutions (Chicago: The University of Chicago Press, 1962).

10. Israel Scheffler, Science and Subjectivity (Indianapolis: The Bobbs-Merrill Company, 1967).

11. Michael Martin, "Referential Variance and Scientific Objectivity," British Journal for the Philosophy of Science, 1971; Michael Martin, "Ontological Variance and Scientific Objectivity," British Journal for the Philosophy of Science, 1972; Michael Martin, Concepts of Science Education: A Philosophical Analysis (Glenview, Illinois: Scott, Foresman and Company, 1972), Chapter 3.

ON A NEW INTERPRETATION OF VERSTEHEN

The New Interpretation

Leonard Krimerman in his book, The Nature and Scope of the Social Sciences,[1] proposes a new interpretation of Verstehen. According to Krimerman Verstehen is correctly interpreted as the ability to use psychological concepts correctly. Verstehen gets its methodological importance, he holds, from the fact that psychological concepts are not reducible to non-psychological concepts hence hypotheses about people's psychological states cannot be verified by sense perception alone. Presumably sense perception can tell us whether Jones is behaving in a certain way in a particular circumstance. It can establish statements couched in physicalistic language. But sense perception alone cannot tell us whether, for example, Jones is acting out of revenge. In order to establish this we must appeal to Jones' objectives, expectations, hopes and so on, i.e., we must use psychological concepts. The necessity for using psychological concepts in the process of verifying a hypothesis about someone's psychological state is, according to Krimerman, the only respect in which the use of Verstehen is subjective. No subjective feeling of empathetic identification is necessary.

Krimerman's suggestion, then, seems to come to this: (1) Verstehen is simply the use of psychological concepts in the process of verifying a psychological hypothesis. (2) Verstehen is indispensible in social science because of what may be called the Verification Thesis:

    (I) No hypothesis of the form "X is P" where P is some psychological predicate can be confirmed or disconfirmed without using some psychological predicate.

The reason Krimerman seems to give for (I) is the alleged irreducibility of psychological language. This may be called the Irreducibility Thesis and may be defined as follows:

    (II) No psychological predicate P is definable in terms of some non-psychological predicate B, e.g., a predicate from physicalistic language.

Now (I) can be understood in two ways:

    (Ia) No hypothesis of the form "X is P" where P is some psychological predicate can be confirmed or disconfirmed without using some psychological predicate or other (this predicate may be identical with P).

    (Ib) No hypothesis of the form "X is P" where P is some psychological predicate can be confirmed or disconfirmed without using some psychological predicate logically independent of P.

233

Critique of the New Interpretation

Thesis (Ia) is surely true but trivial. In order to confirm the hypothesis

(1) Jones is in pain

one must use the predicate "is in pain" since one uses this predicate in stating (1). But this is hardly interesting since this would be true no matter what was predicted of Jones. In order to confirm the hypothesis "Jones is bald" one would have to use the predicate "is bald." Furthermore, the truth of (Ia) does not seem to have anything to do with the truth of (II). One can deny (II) and assert (Ia) with perfect consistency.

Suppose, for example, that the psychological hypothesis at issue is:

(1) Jones is in pain.

Now (1) can surely be verified relative to the following evidence statements without using further psychological concepts:

(2) Jones is grimacing and writhing on the ground after being hit by a car.

(3) Both of Jones' legs are broken.

(4) Jones has not received an anaesthetic.

(2), (3), and (4) confirm (1) but one does not need to suppose that the predicate "is in pain" is definable in non-psychological terms, i.e., one does not need to assume that (II) is true.

Now it might be argued that (2), (3), and (4) are not relevant to the confirmation of (1) unless we assume:

(5) In most cases when people are grimacing and writhing in pain on the ground after being hit by a car and have broken legs and have not received an anaesthetic they are in pain.

Now whether (5) is an empirical statement or an analytic statement we need not decide here. For in any case (5) does not use any other psychological concept than the concept of pain and does not presume that the predicate "is in pain" is reducible to non-psychological terms. Thus even if (5) is needed, (Ib) is still false.

It may be argued further that (2), (3), (4), and (5) do not confirm (1) unless one assumes a statement something like the following:

(6) Jones has never attempted to deceive anyone in the past about his being in pain.

But (6) utilizes psychological concepts, e.g., the concept of attempting to deceive. Now it is true that the assumption of (6) would increase the support of (1), relative to (2)-(5). But it is one thing to say that (6) when conjoined to (2)-(5) increases the confirmation of (1) and quite another thing to say that (2)-(5) lend no support at all, as Krimerman seems wrongly to suppose.

Much the same thing can be said about other psychological hypotheses. Consider Krimerman's own example, namely:

(1')   Jones did action A out of revenge.

The following evidence statements established by sense perception tend to confirm (1'):

(2')   Jones uttered the words "I did action A out of revenge."

(3')   Jones' demeanor was serious when he uttered these words.

(4')   Jones uttered these words in ordinary circumstances--e.g., not on a stage.

(2'), (3'), and (4') support (1') and yet do not use any psychological concept other than the concept of acting out of revenge. Now it might be argued that (2')-(4') do not support (1') unless it is assumed:

(5')   Usually when Jones utters the words "I did action A out of revenge" in ordinary circumstances with a serious demeanor he did action A out of revenge.

Whether this is so or not we need not decide here for in any case (5') uses only psychological predicates already used in the hypothesis. Consequently (Ib) is false although it does not follow that the predicate "acting out of revenge" is defined in terms of behavioristic or environmental predicates.

We have argued that Krimerman's new interpretation of Verstehen can be interpreted in at least two different ways--(Ia) and (Ib). On the first interpretation Krimerman's view is true but trivial; on the second interpretation his view is false. In neither case is the reduction of psychological terms relevant.

There is another possible interpretation. We have seen that one can confirm a psychological hypothesis by using evidence that does not contain psychological predicates other than those contained in the hypothesis. However, statements which do contain other psychological predicates might increase the confirmation of the hypothesis. This suggests the following interpretation:

(Ic)   Any hypothesis of the form "X is P" where P is some psychological predicate that is confirmed to a certain extent without using sentences containing other psychological predicates can be confirmed to a greater extent by using sentences using other psychological predicates.

Thus in the case of Jones acting out of revenge, although (2'), (3'), (4'), and (5') confirm (1'), the following sentences would make (1') even more probable:

(6)   Jones believes that doing A will hurt Z.

(7) Jones believes that Z did Jones a great injustice.

(8) Jones hates Z because of (7).

(6)-(8) all use psychological predicates not used in (1') and seem intuitively to increase the probability of (1'). However, whether it is always the case that the use of other statements containing different psychological predicates would have this confirming effect is another question. Suppose we know

(9) Jones has brain state of type S1.

(10) Whenever someone has brain state of type S1 he acts out of revenge.

Relative to (9) and (10), (1') is certain. Thus given (9) and (10), (6)-(8) do not increase the probability of (1'). Furthermore (9) and (10) do not use psychological predicates except those found in the original hypothesis. Thus (Ic) is false too. Moreover, (9) and (10) do not presuppose (1').

We may conclude, I believe, that the new interpretation given Verstehen by Krimerman under three possible readings is either false or else is true but without methodological significance.

FOOTNOTES

1. Leonard I. Krimerman, <u>The Nature and Scope of Social Sciences</u>, (New York: Appleton-Century Croft, 1969), pp. 353-361.

REVIEWS

Robert Borger and Frank Cioffi (eds.), *Explanation in the Behavioral Sciences*. Cambridge University Press, Cambridge, 1970, pp. xii + 520. $ 15.00

This volume consists of twelve original essays by well known philosophers and social scientists on various aspects of social scientific explanation. Each essay is followed immediately by critical comments by some other philosopher or social scientist and these comments are then answered by the author of the essay. This format is a useful one; the critical comments often bring to the surface important points and the replies enable the authors of the essays to clarify their positions. In what follows I will outline the major theses of the essays, some critical responses to these theses and replies to them; I will also introduce my own critical comments.

The first four papers in the volume discuss various aspects of the relationship between psychological (in particular psycho-neurological) explanation and purposeful explanation. Stephen Toulmin in 'Reasons and Causes' argues that although reasons are not causes, the having of reasons for an action is a cause of the action. Thus the citing of certain reasons may justify a person's action or it may signal his goal or it may describe his action. However the person's having these reasons may (partially at least) causally explain his action. All actions that are done for reasons are applications of procedures (methods of calculation, techniques, rituals or other formalized modes of behavior) that we have learned. Once this is understood, Toulmin says, the Kantian problem of the place of reason in a world of causes vanishes.

In his comments R. S. Peters objects that someone's having reasons for doing some action does not explain his action unless the person also wants or desires certain ends; he also argues that Toulmin's emphasis on learning is not relevant to his argument. Toulmin, correctly I think, points out that Peters is interested in a different question from his, viz. the Humean question of the causal efficacy of reason without passion rather than the Kantian question of the causal relevance of reason *at all* in a world governed by causal law. Consequently Peters' objection is not to the point. Furthermore given the Kantian problem learning *is* relevant since reasons for action become causally relevant only when people learn to operate in terms of them. Toulmin might have also mentioned that even citing someone's having reasons *and* passion is not always an adequate causal explanation of his action. Other factors might have to be taken into account for a complete causal story. However, this is compatible with the having of reasons being *part* of the cause of an action.

Toulmin's solution to the problem of the relation of reasons and causes is sound. However, one could have wished for some discussion of the arguments philosophers have given for supposing that having reasons and causes are fundamentally different. Why anyone should have thought that there is a fundamental difference is, after reading Toulmin's paper, a mystery.

Toulmin briefly considers the relevance of neurology to explanations of human action. This topic is taken up in detail in Charles Taylor's 'The Explanation of Purposive Behavior'. Taylor argues that whether purposive behavior will be ultimately explained by purposive explanations or by neurological mechanistic explanations cannot be answered by *a priori* arguments; it is an empirical question that has yet to be answered. Taylor maintains that the question of whether neurological mechanistic explanations are the basic type of explanation is not to be confused with another question, namely whether mental events or states, e.g. intention, have neurological correlates. For the latter thesis, according to Taylor, may be true and yet mechanistic explanations may not be the basic kind of explanation since neurological explanations of purposive behavior may themselves be purposive. (Purposive explanations, for Taylor, are distinguished by the *form* of the explanatory principles used rather than by their content.)

Robert Borger in his comment on Taylor's paper seems to assume that Taylor supposes that mechanistic explanations and purposive explanations are rivals and identifies Taylor's position with that of Norman Malcolm. Taylor in his reply maintains that his view is not to be identified with either Malcolm's or Borger's. Taylor, unlike Malcolm, believes that neurological mechanistic explanations can be basic. However, unlike Borger he does not think that neurological mechanistic explanations are necessarily basic. The question of which sort of explanation is basic is an empirical question. He does suggest that as far as short range research strategy is concerned purposive rather than mechanistic oriented research seems to offer the most promise.

The next paper in the volume also stresses the empirical nature of the question 'Can neurology explain all human behavior?' N. S. Sutherland in 'Is the Brain a Physical System?' argues that the brain is a physical system. The real import of the question for Sutherland seems to be this: Can the brain and other neurological factors completely determine human behavior? (The title of Sutherland's essay would perhaps have been less misleading if it had been 'Can Neurology Explain All Human Behavior?') Sutherland argues that all philosophical *a priori* arguments that purport to show that neurological explanations are impossible are fallacious and that existing empirical evidence supports the view that neurological explanations of all human behavior will be possible. Moreover, he argues that his thesis is in principle disconfirmable.

J. H. Grundy in his comment on Sutherland's paper maintains that Sutherland does not appreciate the importance of *a priori* considerations; in particular he maintains that *a priori* philosophical analysis is necessary to clarify the meaning of certain mental concepts, e.g. intelligence, before a neurological explanation of the behavior falling under the concept is attempted. Sutherland replies that he is skeptical of the importance of the philosophical analysis of mental concepts for neurological research since ordinary language may enshrine animistic thinking and other unscientific ideas. Real progress in understanding the meaning of mental concepts will come from neurology and not from philosophical analysis.

Now surely Sutherland and Grundy both have a point. Neuropsychologists might well profit from philosophical analysis. Grundy is thus correct. However, such analyses should not be so rooted in ordinary language that revisions and modifications of that language in the light of scientific inquiry is forbidden. After all philosophical analysis has often consisted in giving explications and rational reconstructions. Not all philosophical analysis is Oxford ordinary language analysis as Sutherland seems to suppose. On the other hand, Sutherland may be correct in that the explication of mentalistic concepts should perhaps be more neurologically oriented than it has been.

An entirely different view is presented in the next paper. In 'Conditioning and Behavior' D. W. Hamlyn argues that classical conditioning is a phenomenon which at best is rare and which possibly does not occur at all. Operant conditioning, according to Hamlyn, is not the same sort of thing at all and should not be subsumed under the concept of conditioning. Operant conditioning, unlike classical conditioning, has to do with human and animal actions and not with what happens to humans and animals. Indeed, Hamlyn argues that no mechanism that, for example, might be postulated in a conditioning theory or in a neurological theory can provide a sufficient condition of an action although it might provide a necessary condition.

A. J. Watson in his comment takes issue with Hamlyn's latter thesis. Hamlyn in his response to Watson seems to change his argument. He now seems to agree with Watson that a mechanism, e.g. a neurological mechanism, could be a sufficient condition for an action. However, he argues that since actions are identified in terms of the actor's intentions the intelligibility of the connection between the neurological state and the action is dependent on the intention. So a neurological mechanism could be a sufficient *condition* for an action but it could not be a sufficient *explanation* for the action; it is the intention which gives the action intelligibility.

Now Hamlyn may be correct that intentions are necessary in order to identify actions. But it does not follow that intentions and not neurological mechanisms make the action intelligible. There are many ways to make actions intelligible depending on one's point of view; one of these ways, but only one, is in terms of intentions. Another way is in terms of neurology. A neurologist, e.g. Sutherland, might plausibly argue just the opposite of Hamlyn's position: instead of the intention making the connection between a neurological condition and an action intelligible, the neurological condition makes the relation between the intention and the action intelligible.

The next two papers in the volume take up various problems having to do with rationality in the social sciences. In 'Understanding and Explanation in Sociology and Social Anthropology' I. C. Jarvie criticizes Winch's views on rationality and argues for a Popperian view. Jarvie maintains that for Winch standards of rationality are culture bound. For example, Winch holds that an Azande assertion that there are witches is rational in the Azande culture; in our culture it is not rational. However, Jarvie maintains that despite cultural differences there is a 'community of rationality' shared by all men but fostered by different societies in varying degrees. In all cultures at least the germs of criticism and change in the light of the criticism are present. (Criticism and change are the essence of Popperian rationality.) There are simply different degrees of the Popperian open society in different cultures; none is completely closed. The universal standards of criticism Jarvie appeals to are the logical incoherence of beliefs and the conflict of beliefs with the external world (empirical refutability). According to Jarvie modern science utilizes these standards to the highest degree.

In his comments on Jarvie's critique of his views Winch claims he has been misunderstood. However there does seem to be some genuine disagreement between Winch and Jarvie. Winch argues that someone who says "There are no witches" is (appearances notwithstanding) not denying that there are witches; he is expressing his lack of comprehension of the institution of witchcraft. According to Winch a westerner can raise questions about the institution of witchcraft but arguments against witchcraft cannot be made by appeal to western science. Science is not the paradigm of rationality in all cultures. Jarvie in his reply to Winch maintains that, on the contrary, when a westerner says that there are no witches he is not expressing his lack of understanding of the institution of witchcraft but is denying what the Zande assert about 'the furniture of the earth'. Furthermore, science is the paradigm of rationality and gives us good reasons for rejecting the Zande's claim.

Whether Jarvie is correct in his belief that modern science is the paradigm of rationality is unclear. In any case, one need not accept Jarvie's Popperianism in order to accept the fact that science does give us good grounds for supposing that the Zande are wrong about the existence of witches. However, Jarvie's way of arguing is open to question. Jarvie wants to establish the non-relativity of rationality by arguing that the elements of scientific rationality are as a matter of fact found in all cultures and societies. Hence scientific rationality is not relative. However, this naturalistic approach to the question will not do. For one can always ask: "Supposing scientific rationality is found in all cultures, should it be taken as the paradigm of rationality?" Perhaps scientific rationality is only appropriate in certain situations. Factual universality does not entail normative universality and the claims of scientific rational-

REVIEWS

ity are normative. What Jarvie needs to establish is the normative universality of scientific rationality and for this more than anthropological evidence is required.

Whatever the limitations of scientific rationality, the question still remains of the importance of rationality as an explanatory concept in social science. This topic is taken up by John Watkins in 'Imperfect Rationality'. Watkins contrasts the view of rationality as portrayed by decision theorists with a view of rationality he calls 'imperfect rationality'. In a decision theoretic model of rational action one must know all possible outcomes and have a complete preference ordering. In actual decision making great simplification and selection are involved. According to Watkins it is this imperfect rationality that plays a crucial role in historical explanation. Watkins suggests an Imperfect Rational Principle as a methodological rule concerning historical explanation. First one should attempt to provide conjectural explanations of past actions in terms of the actor's 'decision scheme' (the beliefs and goals of the actor explicitly or implicitly considered in making his decision) and the practical consequences which follow from the scheme. Secondly the conjectural explanation should be as little *ad hoc* and as well supported by the evidence as possible. In order to close the gap between the practical conclusion which follows from the actor's scheme and the actor's actual behavior historians need not believe that people always do act rationally but need only proceed on the assumption that they do. Using such a rule historians will discount apparent cases of irrational behavior and seek new evidence that indicates that the action was rational after all. Watkins gives as an example an apparent piece of irrational action from British naval history which under close historical scrutiny becomes rational.

Alan Donagan in his comment on Watkins' essay argues that no assumption of imperfect rationality needs to be made to bridge the gap between a conclusion drawn from someone's decision scheme and the person's actual behavior. For according to Donagan it is analytic that if an agent knowingly accepts a practical conclusion drawn from a decision scheme that calls for him to perform a certain action, then he performs the action or at least attempts to perform it. Watkins in reply to Donagan, correctly I think, argues for the implausibility of Donagan's view.

However, Watkins also says that accepting the rational principle as a synthetic proposition enables one to regard certain behavior as inconsistent and cites an example from literature to illustrate this. He argues that on Donagan's view this behavior could not be so regarded. The trouble with Watkins' reply is that his methodological rule would *not* allow for such inconsistency in human behavior. On Donagan's view such inconsistency would be logically impossible. On Watkins' view, although logically possible, it would be methodologically incorrect. For if Watkins' case from literature were a case from history, the rational principle would enjoin historians not to be satisfied until they had a rational non-*ad hoc* explanation of the *apparently* inconsistent behavior. Surely such a principle is too strong. Whether a weaker principle of rationality would be less objectionable is unlikely. For even on a weaker version historians would, presumably, be enjoined at least to give *preference* to rational explanation. This would seem to have the result of making many social scientific and psychological explanations less desirable than rational ones. However, such explanations may be very fruitful in historical inquiry. For example Festinger's cognitive dissonance theory, explicitly mentioned with approval by Watkins, does not in any obvious sense provide explanations in terms of the actor's decision scheme.

The next two papers deal with the long standing controversy between methodological individualists and methodological holists. J. O. Wisdom in 'Situational Individualism and the Emergent Group-Properties' argues against the adequacy of Popperian methodological individualism, which he calls situational individualism, and for transindividualism. Situational individualism is the view that all social wholes can be reduced to individual actions plus the unintended consequences of those actions. According to Wisdom, on Popper's view unintended consequences are consequences that could have become intended; they are the result of calculations which have gone wrong. However, Wisdom holds that there are consequences of human actions thay may be of an entirely different order of things; these are emergent properties – properties that cannot be deduced either from properties of individuals or from the unintended consequences of the actions of individuals without the aid of bridge laws. Wisdom argues that sub-acute depression, which he believes is manifested in British society, is an emergent property of this sort. This property is not an unintended consequence of human action in Popper's sense.

Robert Brown in his comments argues that it is unclear if Wisdom is maintaining (a) that certain properties are emergent relative to the known properties of individuals or (b) that certain properties are emergent in some absolute sense. He suggests that (b) is most likely Wisdom's view but that (b) is very difficult to maintain. With respect to the property of sub-acute depression Brown argues that Wisdom has not supplied enough information to determine whether or not this property is emergent in Wisdom's sense. Wisdom retorts that his thesis is (a) and not (b). Wisdom seems to agree with Brown's comments about sub-acute depression.

Whatever the status of sub-acute depression, another kind of emergent property, one not considered by Wisdom, is possible. A property may be emergent in the sense that it is not deducible from individual actions or from their unintended consequences even when combined with known bridge laws. In this sense a property such as sub-acute depression would be emergent not only relative to known facts about individuals and the unintended consequences of their actions but also relative to known laws connecting individual actions and their unintended consequences to social phenomena. This sense of emergent seems to me to be more in keeping with current discussions of methodological individualism and holism than Wisdom's; it is not implausible to suppose that at the present time there are some emergent social properties in this sense as well as in Wisdom's sense.

In 'The Relevance of Psychology to the Explanation of Social Phenomena', George C. Homans advocates methodological individualism. After adopting a deductive nomological account of scientific explanation he argues that any sociological generalization from which many features of social behavior can be derived can itself be derived from psychological propositions. The psychological propositions that he considers are borrowed from classical economics and behavioral psychology. These propositions, he believes, when combined with statements of initial conditions enable one to derive any sociological proposition that itself is explanatory of social phenomena. Functional statements, according to Homans, cannot be derived but since these are tautological they are not explanatory.

Peter M. Blau in his comments gives examples of sociological propositions which he believes do not meet Homans' criteria. They can only be derived from psychological propositions when these are combined with other sociological propositions. In his reply to Blau Homans seems to admit that other sociological propositions would be needed for the derivation of these sociological propositions but argues that such propositions in turn could be derived only with the 'help of' (p. 342) psychological propositions. Unfortunately this reply will not do. Just because psychological propositions are necessary in the explanation it does not mean that sociology is reduced to psychology. Blau's point is that sociological propositions cannot be eliminated; he need not claim that psychological propositions are not needed.

There are many claims both in Homans' paper and reply and in Blau's comment on Homans about some proposition being derived or not being derived from some other. It is unclear in most cases if such derivations can or cannot be made. No derivation is shown. The authors admit that such derivations are 'sketchy' and yet much of their argument depends on whether such derivations do or do not hold. Neither author seems to be aware of any need for bridge laws connecting psychological and sociological variables although Homans has apparently read Danto's *Analytic Philosophy of History* (incorrectly listed as *Anatomical Philosophy of History* in his bibliography, p. 328) in which the need for bridge laws is stressed.

The upshot of the discussion then is inconclusive. One thing is certain, however: Homans' strong claims about psychological reduction have not been shown. On the other hand Blau's thesis has not been demonstrated either.

In the next four papers special problems connected with explanation in fairly specialized areas of social research are discussed: learning theory, personality theory, linguistics and psychoanalysis. R. A. Boakes and M. S. Halliday in 'The Skinnerian Analysis of Behavior' defend at least in large part a Skinnerian approach to psychological research. In such an approach the search for behavioral variables that are related by simple and continuous functions is the primary goal; the basic units of analysis are rate of response and reinforcement; there is a distrust of physiologizing in advance of establishing behavioral facts; the emphasis is on tightly controlled experiments with animals. Boakes and Halliday admit that there are problems in extrapolating the Skinnerian approach to human beings. In particular, the creative aspect of human language acquisition is not illuminated by Skinnerian type studies of animals. However, they stress that Skinnerian analysis is "by far the most promising approach to the understanding of behavior."

REVIEWS

Karl H. Pribram in his comments agrees with Boakes and Halliday that behavioral science can function independently of physiology and that physiologizing is often not useful. However, Pribram appears to disagree with the authors over particular cases. Boakes and Halliday argue that physiology has little to say about learning – the concern of Skinnerians – as opposed to perception and that physiology can be avoided in the study of learning. Pribram argues that neurology can be useful in explaining learning and he cites as an example studies of memory storage. Boakes and Halliday do not directly answer Pribram's point about the relevance of neurology to learning except to stress again that physiology without behavioral analysis is unprofitable.

The editors of this volume, Borger and Cioffi, suggest that some of the disagreement found in the book is "due to divergent estimates of the heuristic promise of particular approaches" (p. v). This is certainly true in the present case; in particular the disagreement seems to come down to whether at the present time given what we know about the brain and human behavior a physiological approach to learning is more fruitful than a Skinnerian one. Surely no *a priori* answer can be given; moreover the evidence available at the present time makes any confident judgment suspect. Perhaps the best policy at the present time is to encourage a number of different research programs and to see what happens.

In 'Explanation and the Concept of Personality' H. J. Eysenck argues that 'explanation' in psychology should have the same meaning as in the exact sciences. Consequently Eysenck argues that explanation should be identified with description rather than understanding where the latter is used in a humanistic and ideographic sense. Eysenck argues against the neo-behaviorists who believe that personality should be explained solely in terms of S-R relations. Personality traits and types are also important in explaining personality and ultimately the explanation of personality will be found in a neurological reduction.

D. Bannister in his comments maintains that psychological problems should be solved on their own terms and not on the terms of neurology and that the exact sciences cannot be the model for psychology. There is at least one basic difference between psychology and physics, viz. reflexivity. By reflexivity Bannister appears to mean the explanation of the activities of a scientist in terms of the discipline of the scientist, e.g. psychological explanation of the research activities of psychologists.

REVIEWS

Eysenck counters that there is no reason why psychological problems may not be solved in neurological terms and that reflexivity is in general not a problem in psychological research.

Surely Eysenck is correct on the first point. It would be arbitrary to limit the solution of psychological problems to psychology. However, he dismisses the reflexivity objection too quickly. One thing Bannister closely connects with reflexivity is the sort of experimental bias pointed out by Rosenthal. The correct answer to the problem of experimental bias is not to deny that it occurs in much psychological research but to argue that it also may exist in some form in the exact sciences and that, in any case, there are ways of controlling it that are commensurate with natural science methodology.

One point that Bannister does not touch on should be mentioned. Explanation in the natural sciences is neither pure description nor does it involve humanistic ideographic understanding. Indeed, Eysenck considers with approval four types of explanation found in the natural sciences (deductive, probabilistic, functional and genetic) yet in none of these types of explanation is a scientist merely describing. So Eysenck's suggestion that explanation in the natural sciences and psychology is akin to description is surely misleading.

In 'Problems of Explanation in Linguistics' Noam Chomsky argues that one of the major problems in explanation in linguistics is that the phenomena to be explained are too obvious and familiar. Consequently one supposes that the explanation of the phenomena must be "transparent and close to the surface" (p. 426). On the contrary, Chomsky argues that in order to explain language acquisition one must postulate an internalized system of rules of a very abstract kind. These are the rules of grammar of the language. The supposition that people have internalized these rules explains their linguistic competence and knowledge of their language. At a deeper level the linguist explains the restricted choice of particular grammars by postulating a universal grammar – a system of innate structures and principles that limit the choice of particular grammar. Such innate structures also help explain how people are able to learn a language on the basis of restricted and degenerate data.

Max Black in his comments on Chomsky questions the need for postulating an innate structure of the mind. Black accuses Chomsky of pitting an old fashioned and unresourceful empiricism against his own

247

nativism. There is no reason, says Black, why given a less crude notion of induction and experience language learning cannot be explained in terms of experience. Furthermore, Black argues that the evidence usually cited for the existence of innate structure is inadequate since no neurological evidence is available. Moreover, the existence of linguistic universals may be the result of our criteria of what counts as a language; consequently Chomsky's thesis may be tautological. Chomsky counters Black's criticisms by arguing that the empiricist view of language acquisition that he has criticized is the most up to date view available; it is not old fashioned and he is not obligated to refute all conceivable varieties of empiricism. Furthermore, he argues that the hypothesis of innate structure is not tautological: it "can easily be refuted if wrong" (p. 467). But the little neurological evidence that is available supports the view that there are innate structures, he says.

The controversy exhibited here seems again to be due to divergent estimates of the heuristic promise of particular approaches; again there seems to be no way at the present time to decide between Chomsky and Black. Although Black's view that nativism as a stimulus to research is a 'dead end' is surely mistaken, Black may be correct that empiricism "suggest programmes of investigation that may be expected to uncover interesting data" (p. 459). Both positions should be encouraged as research programs until that time when more solid evidence and argument can decide between them.

Frank Cioffi in 'Freud and the Idea of a Pseudo-Science' argues that psychoanalysis is a pseudo-science. This is not because psychoanalytic propositions, due to some formal defect, cannot be tested empirically. (Indeed Cioffi seems to think that they can be.) Rather psychoanalysis is a pseudo-science because of pragmatic reasons. For Freud (and presumably his followers) psychoanalytic propositions did not function as testable hypotheses. Cioffi shows from a close examination of Freud's writings that by various shifts of meaning, evasions and other devices characteristic of pseudo-science Freud made it impossible for psychoanalysis to be refuted.

B. A. Farrell in his reply does not seem to have grasped Cioffi's major point: the pragmatic nature of pseudo-science. Farrell argues that philosophers of science have not been able to draw a sharp line between propositions that are testable and those that are not and thus that the notion of pseudo-science is unclear. But as Cioffi points out in his reply to Farrell this point, even if correct, is not too relevant to Cioffi's argument. Philosophers of science, although they have not clearly separated the pragmatic and formal in their analysis (Popper, for example, seems to blur the two) have in general not been talking about the pragmatic dimension of disconfirmation but about the syntactical or formal dimension.

What is not brought out by either Cioffi or Farrell is this. Cioffi's pragmatic analysis of pseudo-science makes pseudo-science a relative notion. Cioffi may be correct that psychoanalysis is a pseudo-science relative to psychoanalysts. However, it does not seem to be a pseudo-science relative to experimental psychologists and other social scientists. For these scientists psychoanalytic propositions function as hypotheses. Until this relative aspect of pseudo-science is noticed the question of whether psycho-analysis is a pseudo-science or not will be systematically ambiguous.

As the above comments should indicate philosophers of social science as well as social scientists interested in theory and methodology should find this volume of great interest. The wide range of topics, the variety of points of view, the lively interchanges make for fascinating and rewarding reading.

Boston University MICHAEL MARTIN

PART IV: REDUCTION

A fundamental question in the philosophy of science is whether one science can be reduced to another. In the social sciences the question arises primarily at two different levels. First, there is the question of whether sciences that deal with social wholes can be reduced to sciences that deal with individuals only. A special case of this question is whether anthropology—a science concerned with social wholes (cultures, societies, communities)—can be reduced to psychology. Second, there is the question of whether psychology can be reduced to neuropsychology. Closely related to this is the question of whether neuropsychology can explain all of human behavior; that is, whether mechanism is possible.

An important job of philosophy of the social sciences is to analyse the key concepts employed in these questions. For example, what does it mean for one science to be reduced to another? Until this question is answered the questions of whether cultural anthropology can be reduced to psychology and whether psychology can be reduced to neurology can hardly be answered. Another job of philosophy of the social sciences is to consider critically the arguments that are used to establish or refute claims that reduction is impossible or undesirable or conceptually problematic.

In the four papers included in this section both of these jobs are displayed. Three of the papers analyse different senses of "reduction" while the fourth distinguishes and clarifies different senses of "mechanism." In "Methodological Individualism and the Reduction of Cultural Anthropology to Psychology," A.L. Kroeber's well known argument that anthropology cannot be reduced to psychology is considered. In "The Body-Mind Problem and Neurological Reduction"[1] the argument that neurological reduction commits one to some controversial answer to the body-mind problem is examined. Jerry Fodor's argument that neurological reduction is impossible is evaluated in "Neurological Reduction and Psychological Explanation." Finally, in "On the Conceivability of Mechanism" Malcolm's interesting argument that, although mechanism is not logically impossible, if it is true it cannot be asserted or argued for, is criticized.

In all the papers listed above, the possibility of reduction or mechanistic explanations is defended against a priori arguments to the contrary. It is shown that there is no a priori way to prove that either the reduction of holistic sciences to individualistic sciences or the reduction of psychology to neurology is impossible; there is no a priori way to show that mechanistic explanations are impossible in psychology.

In the final analysis, philosophers of the social sciences can not decide the question of reduction. What they can do is to clarify the major concepts involved in the controversy and clear away the a priori arguments.

Footnotes

1. In a postscript to this paper, printed here, I comment on R.L. Barnette's criticisms published in "Comments on Neurophysiological Reduction," Theoria, 38, 1972, 143-144.

2. For a critique of this paper see Laurence F. Mucciolo, "Neurophysiological Reduction, Philosophy of Social Sciences 5,1975, 451-462. I reply to this critique in "Neurophysiological Reduction and Type Identity," Philosophy of Social Science, 7 1977, 91-93.

The body-mind problem and neurophysiological reduction

by

MICHAEL MARTIN
(Boston University)

Some psychologists have attempted to reduce psychology to neurophysiology; other psychologists, although they have not attempted such a reduction, have been in sympathy with neurophysiological reduction. However, both sorts of psychologists tend to ignore what philosophical commitments they might be making either in pursuing or in advocating neurophysiological reduction. In particular one might well wonder whether neurophysiological reduction commits psychologists to some traditional answer to the body-mind problem. It is well known that the traditional answers are debatable philosophical positions which raise subtle and difficult issues of semantics and logic. It might well be supposed that psychologists are incompetent to handle these issues or else that they would not take them to be within the domain of psychological and neurophysiological investigation. Nevertheless, neurophysiological reduction is a program with some support in the psychological profession. One might wonder whether psychologists are simply ignorant of what they are getting into or whether they think that neurophysiological reduction is worth the philosophical price.

I shall argue in this paper that psychologists interested in neurophysiological reduction are correct in ignoring the traditional body-mind question. Commitment to neurophysiological reduction does not necessitate any prior solution to that question. I will show that fortunately for psychologists who are inclined toward neurophysiological reduction no such prior solution is needed to this difficult traditional philosophical problem. In short, I will show that when psychologists ignore the body-mind problem in neurophysiological reduction they are on firm ground whether they know it or not.

To establish this thesis, I will first consider the possible scope of the science of psychology. Then I will consider several analyses of reduction found in the literature of philosophy of science and I will explicitly relate these analyses to the reduction of psychology to neurophysiology. I will then present five traditional answers to the body-mind problem and show that in each case the neurophysiological reduction of psychology is neutral with respect to each of these answers. Finally, I will suggest several different ways in which psychologists can be committed to neurophysiological reduction without taking any traditional stand on the body-mind problem.

The scope of psychological science

In order to consider the question of whether commitment to the neurophysiological reduction of psychology commits one to some particular answer to the body-mind problem we will briefly consider the scope of psychological science. For unless we are clear on what the scope of psychological science is it will be unclear what a neurophysiological reduction of psychology amounts to.

However, the scope of psychological science has been conceived of differently by different psychologists depending on their methodological and theoretical orientations. One way of understanding these differences in scope is to consider the sort of laws they have thought psychologists could not or at least should not find (Spence (1960)). Let us consider several different types of laws. With these different types of laws before us we can classify different methodological positions and define our problem in this paper.

(1) Laws relating environmental conditions to behavior.
(2) Laws relating behavior to other behavior.
(3) Laws relating behavior to neurological conditions.
(4) Laws relating environmental conditions to neurological conditions.

(5) Laws relating environmental conditions to mental states.
(6) Laws relating behavior to mental states.
(7) Laws relating neurological conditions to mental states.
(8) Laws relating mental states to other mental states.

Behaviorists of the Skinnerian variety seem to have limited the scope of psychology to (1) and (2); other behaviorists with a neurological interest have limited the scope to (1), (2), (3) and (4); classical psycho-physicists limited the scope to (5) or perhaps to (5), (6) and (7); classical associationists restricted the scope to (8); some psychologists who believe that psychology is a purely idiographic science argue that psychology cannot discover any laws; modern psychologists who are anti-behaviorist and antiidiographic have argued that psychology should try to establish laws of all these different kinds although they might admit that *their* research interests inclines them to one particular kind.

What can we do in the light of these diverse accounts of the scope of psychology? One thing to do would be to show separately for each view of the scope of psychology that the neurological reduction of psychology does not presume any particular answer to the body-mind problem. However, such a procedure seems unwise. First of all, for psychology conceived along idiographic lines the concept of neurological reduction hardly seems applicable. Secondly, even if we restrict our attention to non-idiographic, i.e., nomothetic, conceptions of psychology the alternatives seem too numerous to consider in one paper. We shall approach the problem in a different way.

It can be generally agreed, I think, that the more psychology includes laws containing mentalistic concepts, the more difficult it would be to reduce psychology to neurophysiology without presupposing some answer to the body-mind problem. Thus one generally supposes that if psychology is conceived along behavioristic lines, i.e., if the scope of psychology is limited to (1), (2), (3) and (4), then the argument that a neurophysiological reduction would commit one to some particular answer to the body-mind problem would not be so compelling.

We will, therefore, for the purposes of this paper suppose the *most difficult* case, namely, where psychological science is limited to (8). We do this with the full awareness that few modern psychologists hold such a position and that indeed psychology should not be considered in this way. However, if our argument succeeds when psychology is conceived in this way, it will surely succeed in other less difficult cases. If it can be shown that the neurophysiological reduction of psychology when psychology is limited to (8) does not presuppose any particular solution to the body-mind problem, then the neurophysiological reduction of psychology will not presuppose this in cases where psychology is conceived of differently.

Thus throughout the paper, unless otherwise notified, the reader should understand by psychology a discipline which attempts to discover laws of type (8) only and should understand by psychological science an organized set of such laws. We need not, however, presuppose any particular methodology for establishing such laws. For our purposes it makes little difference whether such laws are established by introspection, by inference from verbal or non-verbal behavior, or in some other way. Moreover, no particular view needs to be assumed about the content of such laws except that they relate mental states to other mental states: they need *not* be associative laws in the sense of "associative laws" used in traditional psychology; they need *not* relate mental states occurring at different times; and so forth.

The meanings of reduction

The meaning of reduction in scientific contexts is vague and ambiguous. Philosophers of science have attempted to clarify the notions of reduction and these attempts have resulted in several different analyses of the concept of reduction. We will consider some of the most well known of these analyses below and the way these analyses apply to the reduction of psychology to neurology.

(1) In one sense of reduction defined by Kemeny and Oppenheim (1956) a theory T_2 is reduced to a theory T_1 if and only if T_1 explains and predicts all that T_2 explains and predicts—and perhaps more besides—and T_2 contains terms not found in T_1, and T_1 is at least as well systematized as T_2. Now one branch of science B_2 is reduced to another branch of science B_1 at time t if and only if there is some theory T_1 in B_1 such that T_1 reduces T_2 at time t where T_2 is all the accepted theories of B_2.

The application of this account to the reduction of psychology to neurophysiology is obvious: Psychology is reduced to neurophysiology at time t if and only if there is some neurophysiological theory T_1 which (a) explains and predicts all the phenomena that the accepted psychological theories T_2 explain and predict, and (b) is at least as well systematized as T_2. (The condition that T_2 would contain terms not found in T_1 presumably would be automatically satisfied in the case of psychology and neurophysiology.)

(2) Hempel (1966) has suggested that one science B_2 is reduced to another science B_1 at time t if and only if (a) the laws and theories of B_2 are deduced from the laws and theories of B_1, and (b) the terms of B_2 are definable in terms of the vocabulary of B_1. (The definitions could be either analytic definitions, i.e., definitions specifying relations of synonymy, or extensional definitions.)

The application to neurological reduction is as follows: Psychology is reduced to neurophysiology at time t if and only if the laws and theories of neurophysiology entail the laws and theories of psychology, and the terms of psychology are definable in the terms of neurophysiology. (Since analytic definitions seem out of the question in the case of neurophysiological reduction the definitions would presumably be extensional ones.)

Now Hempel's characterization is logically a stronger one than Kemeny's and Oppenheim's: If science B_2 is reduced to science B_1 in Hempel's sense of reduce, B_2 would also be reduced to B_1 in Kemeny's and Oppenheim's sense of reduce so long as B_2 contained terms not found in B_1 and B_1 was as well systematized as B_2. However, the converse need not hold.

(3) A weaker sense of reduction than Hempel's can be derived from Hempel's account by dropping (b). On this version a science

B_2 is reduced to science B_1 if and only if the laws and theories of B_2 can be derived from the laws and theories of B_1. In general such a derivation could not be carried off without some principles that specify some relation between the terms of B_2 and B_1. This relation could take the form, for example, of extensional definitions as specified in Hempel's account by (b). But this relation could be logically weaker. For example, bridge laws, i.e., laws connecting the phenomena studied by B_2 to the phenomena studied by B_1 which specify sufficient conditions but not necessary conditions might enable the derivation to proceed. This sense of reduction is close—if not identical—with the sense of reduction specified by Nagel (1960, 1961).

The application to neurophysiological reduction is as follows: Psychology is reduced to neurophysiology at time t if and only if the theories and laws of psychology are derivable from the laws and theories of neurophysiology at time t. Without analytic or extensional definitions such a derivation might require bridge laws—which, for example, might specify sufficient conditions—connecting neurological phenomena with psychological phenomena as well as bridge laws connecting psychological phenomena with neurophysiological phenomena.

This sense of reduction—although it is weaker than the sense specified by Hempel—is stronger than the sense specified by Kemeny and Oppenheim: If psychology is reduced to neurophysiology in the present sense, then psychology would be reduced to neurophysiology in Kemeny's and Oppenheim's sense of reduce so long as psychology contained terms not found in neurophysiology and neurophysiology was as well systematized as psychology. However, the converse need not hold.

(4) Other philosophers—most notably Schaffner (1967)—have suggested that the notion of reduction be expanded to include "corrections" made by the reducing science B_1. The laws and theories of science B_1, it has been pointed out, may not entail the laws and theories of B_2—as in the Hempel and Nagel senses of reduction—but rather they may entail theories and laws of which the theories and laws of B_2 are close approximations. The theories and laws which are deduced from B_1 are more accurate than those

of B_2. In this sense the reduction of B_2 to B_1 provides a correction of B_2.

In neurophysiological reduction neurophysiological theories and laws might—when combined with, e.g., appropriate bridge laws—entail theories and laws of psychology that are more accurate than the theories and laws that are accepted. In this way, neurophysiology could correct psychology while reducing it.

The idea of "correction" in reduction could be expanded. First, in the Kemeny and Oppenheim sense of reduction the reducing science B_1 might explain and predict more accurately everything that B_2 explains and predicts. Put more precisely: B_1 might make predictions that are strictly speaking incompatible with the predictions made by B_2. Nevertheless, the predictions made by B_2 might closely approximate the predictions of B_1 and moreover the predictions of B_1 might be more accurate than those of B_2. Secondly, in Hempel's sense of reduction the definition of the terms of B_2 in the vocabulary of B_1 might allow for the terms of B_2 to be explicated or rationally reconstructed in terms of B_2. Strictly speaking, explications or rational reconstructions are neither analytic definitions nor extensional definitions since in a sense they "correct" or "improve" the definiendum (Hanna 1968).

Again the application to neurophysiological reduction is obvious: Neurophysiological theories could reduce and correct psychology in both of the following ways: (1) More accurate predictions could be made on the basis of neurophysiology than on the basis of psychology, and (2) neurophysiology could provide explications or rational reconstructions in neurophysiological vocabulary of psychological terms.

The neutrality of neurophysiological reduction to the body-mind problem

For our purposes here we can concentrate on Hempel's analysis of reduction. Hempel's analysis, as we have seen, is logically stronger than either Nagel's analysis or Kemeny and Oppenheim's analysis. Thus any conclusion we arrive at with respect to neurophysiological reduction and the body-mind problem will automatically apply to Nagel's analysis and Kemeny and Oppenheim's analysis. Furthermore, Schaffner's modified analysis of reduction in terms of correction can be safely ignored. Any conclusion we arrive at with respect to Hempel's analysis can with only slight modification be applied to Schaffner's analysis.

In order to see in detail what neurological reduction in Hempel's analysis involves, consider a schematic version of a typical law of psychology.

L_p. If someone has mental state M_1, then he has mental state M_2.

The reduction of L_p to neurophysiology can represent the general case, i.e., of the reduction of the science of psychology which consists in an organized set of laws like L_p, to neurophysiology. Now according to Hempel (a) L_p must be deduced from the laws and theories of neurology, and (b) the terms in L_p, i.e., "has mental state M_1" and "has mental state M_2" must be defined in terms of neurophysiology. Consider the two following extensional definitions:

DEFINITION 1. Someone has mental state M_1 if and only if he has neurological condition N_1.
DEFINITION 2. Someone has mental state M_2 if and only if he has neurological condition N_2.

It should be noted that such extensional definitions are in fact laws relating mental states to neurological conditions; thus they are laws of type (7) mentioned above. Although by our restriction of the scope of psychology to laws of type (8) these definitions or laws could not be part of psychological science they could be part of neurology. Thus condition (b) is fulfilled.

It should be noted that Definition 1 and Definition 2 specify that certain neurological conditions are nomologically sufficient and necessary conditions for certain mental states. For to say that N is a nomologically necessary condition for M is to say that N and M are lawfully related such that if M, then N; to say that N is a nomologically sufficient condition of M is to say that N and M are lawfully related such that if N, then M. However, to say all of this is not to presume that N and M are *causally* related. Causal relations are a proper sub-class of nomological relations. For example, if N is the total cause of M, then N is special type of nomologically sufficient condition of M. Definition 1 and Definition 2, therefore, leave open the question of whether the neurological conditions and mental states specified are causally related to one another. This point will prove important in our subsequent argument.

Now consider a schematic version of a typical law of neurology:

L_n. If someone has neurological condition N_1, then he has neurological condition N_2.

But L_n and Definition 1 and Definition 2 entail L_p, so condition (a) is fulfilled.

It remains to be shown that this reduction is neutral with respect to various traditional answers to the body-mind problem.

Traditional approaches

Basically there have been two approaches to the problem of the relation between body and mind: monistic solutions and dualistic solutions. We will consider two of the most popular monistic solutions first and then three of the most popular dualistic solutions. In each case we will show that neurological reduction is neutral with respect to each of these positions.

Monistic solutions

(1) Philosophical behaviorism

Some philosophers, most notably Ryle (1949), have argued that statements about people's mental states can be translated without loss of meaning into statements about people's behavior—either actual or potential. Thus to say that Jones is angry, on this view, is just to say that Jones is behaving in a certain way or is disposed to behave in a certain way. This position is sometimes called philosophical behaviorism in order to distinguish it from the type of behaviorism—called methodological behaviorism—commonly known to psychologists. The methodological behaviorism of the psychologist is not a view about the meaning of psychological terms as is philosophical behaviorism. Rather methodological behaviorism is a commitment to a certain research program in which psychology should be concerned only with overt behavior or else overt behavior and neurophysiological conditions; that is, with laws of type (1)—(4).

The above reduction of L_p to neurophysiological laws and definitions is quite neutral on the question of whether mentalistic terms like "has mental state M_1" or "has mental state M_2" can be analyzed in behavioristic terms. Such an analysis might be possible or it might not be. If such an analysis were possible, then L_p could be restated as a law connecting different behavior, i.e., as a law of type (2), and Definition 1 and Definition 2 would give extensional definitions of behavioral terms in terms of neurology. Thus, for example, suppose under semantic analyses (a) x has mental state $M_1 = x$ is disposed to behave in way B_1, (b) x has mental state $M_2 = x$ is disposed to behave in way B_2. Given (a) and (b) L_p would become L'_p.

L'_p. If someone is disposed to behave in way B_1 then he is disposed to behave in way B_2.

The reduction of L'_p would proceed as before.

(2) The identity theory

Some recent philosophers (Place 1962, Smart 1962) have argued that mentalistic language is not translatable into behavioristic language. Thus they are not philosophical behaviorists. However, they have argued that mentalistic language refers to the same thing as neurological language. Thus to say that "Jones has mental state M_1" is not the same thing as saying "Jones is in neurological condition N_1", i.e., the two expressions do not *mean* the same thing. Nevertheless, these philosophers do insist that mental state M_1 of Jones is the neurological condition N_1 of Jones. The 'is' in the last sentence is the 'is' of contingent identity, not logical identity. Logical identity is established by rules of logic or mathematics or semantics. For example, the identity of $4+4$ and 8, and the identity of being a brother and being a male sibling, is that of logical identity. A contingent identity is established by empirical considerations. For example, the identity of the morning star and the evening star, and Tully and Cicero, are examples of contingent identity. Thus mental state M_1 and neurological condition N_1 are identical in the present view in the way the morning star is identical with the evening star and not the way $4+4$ is identical with 8.

The above reduction, however, is neutral on the question of whether mental state M_1 is neurological condition N_1. Of course, if such an identity held it would explain why Definition 1 held. It would not be surprising that mental state M_1 is a nomologically necessary and sufficient condition for neurological condition N_1 if mental state M_1 is contingently identical with neurological condition N_1. However, as we shall see, Definition 1 could be explained along dualistic lines, and the identity theory is in no way uniquely presupposed.

Dualistic solutions
(1) Interactionism
Some philosophers have been opposed to the identity theory, i.e., that mental states and neurological conditions are identical, and have argued that there is causal interaction between mental states and neurological conditions. Descartes (Shaffer 1968, pp. 35—37, pp. 71—72) is perhaps historically the most famous advocate of this view.

However, the above analysis of reduction is neutral with respect to all forms of dualism including interactionism. Just as the above analysis could be interpreted in terms of the identity theory, so it could be interpreted in terms of interactionism. Thus Definition 1 and Definition 2 could be interpreted in this way: Mental state M_1 is the cause of neurological condition N_1, and neurological condition N_2 is the cause of mental state M_2. But mental state M_1 is a nomologically necessary condition for neurocal condition N_1, and neurological condition N_2 is a nomologically necessary condition for mental state M_2. This would explain Definition 1 and Definition 2.

(2) Epiphenomenalism
Some philosophers have maintained that although neurological

conditions cause mental states, mental states do not cause neurological conditions (Shaffer 1968, pp. 68—71). Mental states in this view are epiphenomena of neurological conditions with no causal efficacy.

It can be easily seen how the above reduction is compatible with epiphenomenalism. But as we have also seen, it is compatible with other views as well. Thus neurological condition N_1 could be the cause of mental state M_1, neurological condition N_1 could also be the cause of neurological condition N_2 which in turn could be the cause of mental state M_2. (Thus neurological conditions would cause, but not be caused, by mental states.) However, by hypothesis neurological condition N_1 is a nomologically necessary condition for mental state M_1, and neurological condition N_2 is a nomologically necessary condition for M_2. Thus Definition 1 and Definition 2 could be true on the epiphenomenalist view.

(3) Parallelism

On this traditional dualistic view neurological conditions and mental states do not causally interact at all: mental states do not cause neurological conditions, and visa versa; rather mental states and neurological conditions are always found together (Shaffer 1968, pp. 62—68).

The account of reduction presented above is also compatible with this view although it in no way presupposes it. Mental state M_1 and neurological condition N_1 are nomologically necessary conditions for each other but are not caused by one another; the same is true for mental state M_2 and neurological condition N_2. Thus Definition 1 and Definition 2 could be true on the parallelist view.

Ways of being committed

The argument so far has shown that in several senses of neurological reduction, neurological reduction does not presuppose any particular view of the body-mind problem. Thus psychologists can be committed in several ways to neurological reduction without being committed to any particular view of the body-mind problem.

First, psychologists can believe that the neurophysiological reduction of psychology is *logically possible* without any philosophical presuppositions about the body-mind issue. Belief in logical possibility of such reduction, it should be noted, does not mean that the psychologist must believe that such reduction is very likely to occur, or that it is fruitful to attempt such a reduction.

Secondly, psychologists can believe that in the light of the evidence neurophysiological reduction is *likely* to occur without any presuppositions about the body-mind problem. It is important to notice that if a psychologist believes that neurological reduction is likely he must, to be consistent, believe that it is logically possible. However, it is not necessary that he believe such reduction is fruitful or worth pursuing. Indeed, he may think that it is not.

Thirdly, a psychologist can believe that it is *fruitful* to attempt to reduce psychology to neurophysiology without presupposing any view of the body-mind problem. This belief is quite consistent with the belief that such a reduction is logically impossible. There might be beneficial side effects from attempting the impossible.

Now whether neurological reduction is logically possible, likely, or a fruitful research program we have not argued here. What we have shown is that commitment in any of these ways to neurological reduction need not be hindered by philosophical scruples, i.e., we have shown that these commitments are not indefensible commitments because of alleged unproven philosophical presuppositions about the mind-body relation. However, whether such commitments *are* defensible is another question—a subject for another paper.

References

HANNA, JOSEPH. "An explication of 'explication'." *Philosophy of science*, vol. 35 (1968), pp. 28—44.

HEMPEL, CARL G. *Philosophy of natural science.* (Englewood Cliffs, N. J.: Prentice Hall, 1969).

KEMENY, J. AND OPPENHEIM, P. "On reduction." *Philosophical studies*, vol. 7 (1956), pp. 6—17.

NAGEL, E. "The meaning of reduction in the natural sciences." In *Philosophy of science*, edited by A. Danto and S. Morgenbesser. (Cleveland: Meridan Books, 1960).
NAGEL, E. *The structure of science*. (New York: Harcourt, Brace, and World, 1961).
PLACE, U. T. "Is consciousness a brain process?" In *The philosophy of mind*, edited by V. C. Chappell. (Englewood Cliffs, N. J.: Prentice Hall, 1962).
RYLE, GILBERT. *The concept of mind*. (New York: Barnes & Noble, 1949).
SCHAFFNER, KENNETH. "Approaches to reduction." *Philosophy of science*, vol. 34 (1967), pp. 139—147.
SHAFFER, JEROME. *Philosophy of mind*. (Englewood Cliffs, N. J.: Prentice Hall, 1968).
SMART, J. J. C. "Sensations and brain processes." In *The philosophy of mind*, edited by V. C. Chappell (Englewood Cliffs, N. J.: Prentice Hall, 1962).
SPENCE, KENNETH. "Historical and modern conceptions of psychology." In *The structure of scientific thought*, edited by E. H. Madden. (Boston: Houghton Mifflin, 1960).

Received on January 13, 1971.

POSTSCRIPT (1977) ON
NEUROPHYSIOLOGICAL REDUCTION

In his "Comments on Neurophysiological Reduction," Theoria, 38, 1972 pp. 143-144, R.L. Barnette raises the following problem with my account of neurophysiological reduction: L_n and Definitions 1 and 2 entail L_p. But L_p and Definitions 1 and 2 also entail L_n. Given this symmetrical situation Barnette argues that L_p is not reduced to L_n, as I maintained. He suggests that I should "build in some reference to the scope of various theories and look to these factors when developing examples of alleged reduction."

Barnette is correct. I should have said that, in order for the reduction of psychology to neurophysiology to take place, all psychological laws must be deduced from neurological laws plus definitions and some neurological laws cannot be deduced from any psychological laws plus definitions. Given this specification neurophysiology has a wider scope than psychology.

Barnette goes on to suggest that the consideration of scope might tell against my claim that neurophysiological reduction is neutral vis a vis different answers to the body-mind problem, but does not develop this suggestion. However, I do not see how consideration of scope could tell againt my neutrality thesis except perhaps in the case of parallelism. In philosophical behaviorism, the identity theory, interactivism and epiphenomenalism there is no assumption that the scope of neurology is the same as the scope of psychology. Only in some versions of parallelism is the assumption made that for every neurological event there is a parallel mental event, and conversely. In most modern versions of paralellism it is only assumed that for every neural event there is a parallel neurological event; the converse need not hold. With this type of parallelism neurology could have a wider scope than psychology. Consequently, reduction could take place.

Neurophysiological Reduction and Psychological Explanation

MICHAEL MARTIN

In a recent book and paper Fodor[1] has argued that psychology cannot be reduced by neurophysiology. What makes Fodor's thesis so intriguing is that he admits that psychological states may be contingently identical with nuerophysiological states. However he argues:

> To claim that mind states and brain states are contingently identical need not be to hold that psychological theories are reducible to neurological theories.[2]

In this paper I will examine Fodor's argument. I will maintain that Fodor has not shown that psychology cannot be reduced to neurophysiology in several senses of 'reduce' used in the literature. In particular I will show that Fodor has not shown that psychology cannot be micro-reduced to neurophysiology—the sense of 'reduce' that Fodor seems to be concerned with. Finally I will indicate some problems with Fodor's views on psychological explanation that turn on his characterization of the relation between neurology and psychology.

1. *Fodor on the Relation between Psychology and Neurology*

Fodor argues that his account of the relation between psychology and neurology is to 'be distinguished from all varieties of reductionism'[3] and that his account if correct 'suggests that the reductivist view of the relation between psychological and neurological theories is seriously misleading.'[4]

To understand Fodor's position we must consider the distinction he makes between what he calls the "two phases" of psychological explanation. These phases should not be thought of as temporally preceding one another but only as analytically distinguishable.

In the first phase the psychologist produces psychological theories whose constructs have a functional characterization in the sense that these constructs 'are individuated primarily or solely by reference to their alleged causal consequences.' The hypothesis using such constructs must be complex enough to account 'for whatever behavioral capacities the organism can be demonstrated to possess' and the 'specific aspects of the character of the organism's behaviour must be explicable by reference to specific features of the hypothesized underlying states and processes or of their interaction.'[5]

The second phase of psychological explanation is concerned with the specification of the neurological mechanisms 'that do, in fact, exhibit the functional characteristics enumerated by phase-one theories.'[6] Thus the 'goals of physiological psychology are set by the attempt to find neurological mechanisms that correspond to certain [psychological] functions.'[7] In other words the psychological theories that articulate these functions 'determine the principle of individuation for the neurological mechanisms.'[8]

Given this two-phase account of psychological explanation Fodor argues against Oppenheim and Putnam who 'are explicit in referring to neurological theories such as those of Herb, as constituting "micro-reductions" of the corresponding psychological theories of memory, learning, motivation and so on.'[9]

Fodor's articulation of his main argument against the possibility of neurological micro-reduction relies heavily on certain analogies he draws from the operation of an internal combustion engine.

If I speak of a device as a 'camshaft' I am implicitly identifying it by reference to its physical structure, and so I am committed to the view that it exhibits a characteristic and specifiable decomposition into physical parts. But if I speak of the device as a 'valve lifter,' I am identifying it by reference to its function and I therefore undertake no such commitment. There is, in particular, no sense to the question 'What does a valve lifter consist of?' if this is understood as a request for microanalysis.... (There is, of course, sense to the question 'What does *this* valve lifter consist of?' But the generic valve lifter must be *functionally* defined, and functions do not have parts).... From a functional point of view, a camshaft is a valve lifter and *this* valve lifter (i.e. this particular mechanism for lifting valves) may be 'nothing but' a camshaft. But a mechanistic account of the operations of internal-combustion engines does not seek to replace the concept of a valve lifter with the concept of a camshaft, nor does it seek to 'reduce' the former to the latter.[10]

The relation of this example to neurological micro-reduction is as follows:

It is, then, conceivable that serious confusion could be avoided if we interpret statements that relate psychological and neurological constructs not as articulating microanalyses but as attributing certain psychological functions to corresponding neurological systems.... Drives, motives, strategies and such are, on the present view, internal states postulated in attempts to account for behavior, perception, memory and other phenomena in the domain of psychological theories. In complete accounts, they could presumably serve to characterize the functional aspects of neurological mechanism.... But this does not entail that drives, motives, and strategies have micro-analyses in terms of neurological systems any more than valve lifters can be micro-analyzed into camshafts.[11]

Neurophysiological Reduction and Psychological Explanation

2. *The Notion of Neurophysiological Micro-Reduction*

To evaluate Fodor's criticism of neurological micro-reduction we must determine what a micro-reduction is. Oppenheim and Putnam, who come under Fodor's attack, specify the notion of micro-reduction as follows:

> Under the following conditions we shall say that the reduction of B_2 to B_1 is a micro-reduction: B_2 is reduced to B_1; and the objects in the universe of discourse of B_2 are wholes which possess a decomposition into proper parts all of which belong to the universe of discourse of B_1.

They define a potential micro-reduction as follows:

> A branch B_1 is a *potential micro-reducer* of branch B_2 if the objects in the universe of discourse of B_2 are wholes which possess a decomposition into proper parts all of which belong to the universe of discourse of B_1.[12]

The application of their notion of micro-reduction to neurophysiological reduction is as follows: psychology is micro-reduced to neurophysiology at time *t* if and only if psychology is reduced[13] to neurophysiology at time *t* and the objects of the universe of discourse of psychology are wholes which possess a decomposition into proper parts all of which belong to the universe of discourse of neurophysiology.

Now whether the micro-reduction of psychology is a plausible supposition depends in part on what one takes to be the objects of the universe of discourse of psychology and neurology. If, for example, the objects of the universe of discourse of psychology consist of certain kinds of organisms, e.g. human beings and certain animals, and the 'objects' of the universe of discourse of neurology are neural entities, states or processes, then a micro-reduction of psychology to neurology is clearly impossible since obviously organisms are not completely decomposable into neurological entities, states or processes.

However, the universe of discourse of psychology could be construed in a different way. At least *part* of the 'objects' in the universe of discourse of psychology could be considered to be mental entities, states or processes. Now neurology would be a *partial* potential micro-reducer of psychology on this construal if mental events, states and processes could be completely decomposed into the entities, states, or processes that comprise the universe of discourse of neurology.

It should be clear that a necessary condition for this decomposition of mental entities into neurological entities is that mental entities are identical with complex neurological entities. Thus neurological micro-reduction of this kind must take a definite stand on the traditional body-mind problem. Since the identity between mental entities and neurological entities could

Michael Martin

hardly be a logical identity neurological micro-reduction would entail that mental entities were *contingently* identical with complex neural entities.

Now although Oppenheim's and Putnam's sense of micro-reduction—given the construal of the universe of discourse of psychology and neurology suggested above—does entail the contingent identity of mental entities and neurological entities, this account of micro-reduction is neutral on several other points. To see this let us state more precisely what on Oppenheim's and Putnam's account potential micro-reduction involves: B_1 is a potential micro-reduction of B_2 means:

> (x) (x is an entity in the universe of discourse of B_2. $\supset (\exists y)$ (y is an entity in the universe of discourse of B_1 & y is a proper part of x & (z) (z is a proper part of x. $\supset z$ is an entity in the universe of discourse of B_1))).

It is important to note that micro-reduction so construed is not committed to the view that any member of some particular class of entities in the universe of discourse of B_2 is decomposed into some particular type of entities in the universe of discourse of B_1. Consider one of Oppenheim's and Putnam's examples:

> Let us suppose that B_2 is a branch of science which has multicellular living things as its universe of discourse. Let B_1 be a branch with cells as its universe of discourse. Then the things in the universe of discourse of B_2 can be decomposed into proper parts belonging to the universe of discourse of B_1. If, in addition, it is the case that B_1 reduces B_2 at time t, we shall say that B_1 *micro-reduces* B_2 at time t.[14]

Now clearly in this example Oppenheim and Putnam do not assume that any multicellular animal of a certain type can be decomposed into cells of some particular type. Oppenheim and Putnam leave this as an open question. Thus, as far as their analysis is concerned, Rover and Fido—both members of the class of Boston terriers—might be decomposable into different types of cells; Rover might be decomposable into cells with genetic structure S_1; Fido might be decomposable into cells with genetic structure S_2.

Oppenheim and Putnam are also neutral on another question. Suppose that all members of the class of Boston terriers were decomposable into the same type of cells. The question remains open in Oppenheim's and Putnam's analysis how this class is to be characterized. The cells may be classified in terms of their genetic structure. But the cells may also be classified in terms of their function, their evolutionary origin and in other ways. The only restriction Oppenheim and Putnam seem to put on such a classification in order to avoid trivial micro-reduction is that the classification is one normally used in B_1.[15]

The implications for neurological micro-reduction of the above considerations are as follows: (1) The neurological entities of which mental entities are decomposed need not be neurological entities of any particular type; (2) If mental entities of a certain type are decomposable into neurological entities of a certain class, this class need not be any particular kind of class.

Does Fodor's argument refute neurological micro-reduction? From our discussions of Oppenheim and Putnam we see that it does not. Fodor seems to suppose that neurological micro-reduction entails that mental entities of a certain type, i.e. with the same behavioral consequences are decomposable into neural entities of a certain type, i.e. with the same anatomical characteristics. He argues that mental entities with the same behavioral consequences may be composed of neural entities with different anatomical characteristics; he concludes from this that micro-reduction is impossible. But neurological micro-reduction no more entails this, as we have seen, than the micro-reduction of a science of multicellular organisms to a science of cells entails that every organism of a certain type is decomposable into cells of a certain genetic structure. It is not uncommon in neurology to classify neurological states functionally as well as structurally.[16] Thus neurological micro-reduction is perfectly compatible with functionally equivalent neurological mechanisms that are anatomically different.

3. *Other Senses of Neurophysiological Reduction*

Fodor, as we have seen, argues that his account is to be 'distinguished from all varieties of reduction' and that his view if correct would 'suggest that the reductional view of the relation between psychology and neurological theories is seriously misleading.'

We have shown that Fodor's views are compatible with Oppenheim's and Putnam's account of micro-reduction. However, there are several other senses of reduction found in the literature. Let us consider these senses briefly.

(1) In one sense of reduction defined by Kemeny and Oppenheim[17] a theory T_2 is reduced to a theory T_1 if and only if T_1 explains and predicts all that T_2 explains and predicts—and perhaps more besides—and T_2 contains terms not found in T_1 and T_1 is at least as well systematized as T_2. Now one branch of science B_2 is reduced to another branch of science B_1 at time t if and only if there is some theory T_1 in B_1 such that T_1 reduces T_2 at time t where T_2 is the accepted theories of B_2.

The application of this account to the reduction of psychology to neurophysiology is obvious: Psychology is reduced to neurophysiology at time t if and only if there is some neurophysiological theory T_1 which (*a*) explains and predicts all the phenomena that the accepted psychological theories T_2 explain and predict and (*b*) is at least as well systematized as T_2. (The condition that T_2 would contain terms not found in T_1 presumably would be automatically satisfied in the case of psychology and neurophysiology.)

(2) Hempel[18] has suggested that one science B_2 is reduced to another science B_1 at time t if and only if (a) the laws and theories of B_2 are deduced from the laws and theories of B_1 and (b) the terms of B_2 are definable in terms of the vocabulary of B_1. (The definitions could be either analytic definitions, i.e. definitions specifying relations of synonymy, or extensional definitions.)

The application to neurological reduction is as follows: psychology is reduced to neurophysiology at time t if and only if the laws and theories of neurophysiology entail the laws and theories of psychology and the terms of psychology are definable in the terms of neurophysiology. (Since analytic definitions seem out of the question in the case of neurophysiological reduction the definitions would presumably be extensional ones.)

Now Hempel's characterization is logically a stronger one than Kemeny's and Oppenheim's: if science B_2 is reduced to science B_1 in Hempel's sense of reduce, B_2 would also be reduced to B_1 in Kemeny's and Oppenheim's sense of reduce so long as B_2 contained terms not found in B_1 and B_1 was as well systematized as B_2. However, the converse need not hold.

(3) A weaker sense of reduction than Hempel's can be derived from Hempel's account by dropping (b). On this version a science B_2 is reduced to science B_1 if and only if the laws and theories of B_2 can be derived from the laws and theories of B_1. In general such a derivation could not be carried off without some principles that specify some relation between the terms of B_2 and B_1. This relation could take the form, for example, of extensional definitions as specified in Hempel's account by (b). But this relation could be logically weaker. For example, bridge laws, i.e., laws connecting the phenomena studied by B_2 to the phenomena studied by B_1 which specify sufficient conditions but not necessary conditions might enable the derivation to proceed. This sense of reduction is close—if not identical—with the sense of reduction specified by Nagel.[19]

The application to neurophysiological reduction is as follows: psychology is reduced to neurophysiology at time t if and only if the theories and laws of psychology are derivable from the laws and theories of neurophysiology at time t. Without analytic or extensional definitions such a derivation might require bridge laws—which, for example, might specify sufficient conditions —connecting neurological phenomena with psychological phenomena as well as bridge laws connecting psychological phenomena with neurophysiological phenomena.

This sense of reduction—although it is weaker than the sense specified by Hempel—is stronger than the sense specified by Kemeny and Oppenheim:

if psychology is reduced to neurophysiology in the present sense, then psychology would be reduced to neurophysiology in Kemeny's and Oppenheim's sense of reduce so long as psychology contained terms not found in neurophysiology and neurophysiology was as well systematized as psychology. However, the converse need not hold.

(4) Other philosophers—most notably Schaffner[20]—have suggested that the notion of reduction be expanded to include 'corrections' made by the reducing science B_1. The laws and theories of science B_1, it has been pointed out, may not entail the laws and theories of B_2—as in the Hempel and Nagel senses of reduction—but rather they may entail theories and laws of which the theories and laws of B_2 are close approximations. The theories and laws which are deduced from B_1 are more accurate than those of B_2. In this sense the reduction of B_2 to B_1 provides a correction of B_2.

In neurophysiological reduction neurophysiological theories and laws might—when combined with, e.g. appropriate bridge laws—entail theories and laws of psychology that are more accurate than the theories and laws that are accepted. In this way, neurophysiology could correct psychology while reducing it.

The idea of 'correction' in reduction could be expanded. First, in the Kemeny and Oppenheim sense of reduction the reducing science B_1 might explain and predict more accurately everything that B_2 explains and predicts. Put more precisely: B_1 might make predictions that are strictly speaking incompatible with the predictions made by B_2. Nevertheless, the predictions made by B_2 might closely approximate the predictions of B_1 and moreover the predictions of B_1 might be more accurate than those of B_2. Secondly, in Hempel's sense of reduction the definition of the terms of B_2 in the vocabulary of B_1 might allow for the terms of B_2 to be explicated or rationally reconstructed in terms of B_1. Strictly speaking explications[21] or rational reconstructions are neither analytic definitions nor extensional definitions since in a sense they 'correct' or 'improve' the definiendum.

Again the application to neurophysiological reduction is obvious: neurophysiological theories could reduce and correct psychology in both of the following ways: (1) More accurate predictions could be made on the basis of neurophysiology than on the basis of psychology and (2) neurophysiology could provide explications or rational reconstructions in neurophysiological vocabulary of psychological terms.

The four senses of neurological reduction considered above seem quite compatible with Fodor's point that there are functionally equivalent but anatomically distinct neurological mechanisms and with Fodor's thesis about the two phases of psychological explanation. Thus Fodor is mistaken to suppose that his account is to be 'distinguished from all varieties of

Michael Martin

reduction' and that his view if correct would 'suggest that the reductional view of the relation between psychology and neurological theories is seriously misleading.'

It is important to realize that none of the four senses of neurophysiological reduction considered above entails neurological micro-reduction. So even if our critique of Fodor's argument against neurological reduction is in error and neurological micro-reduction is impossible this by itself does not show that any of the above four senses of neurophysiological reduction is impossible. Fodor, it must be stressed, has brought up no arguments against any sort of neurophysiological reduction except neurophysiological micro-reduction. None of his arguments are even relevant to these other types of neurophysiological reduction.

It should also be noted that none of the senses of reduction considered above, except micro-reduction, presupposes the identity of mental states and brain states. The only other sense of reduction considered above which looks like it might be committed to body-mind identity is Hempel's sense of reduction. In particular, the condition of definability specified in (*b*) might suggest that body-mind identity was assumed. But a closer examination indicates that this is not so. Extensional definitions of mental terms in neurophysiological terms do not entail the identity theory since such definitions are compatible with parallelism. Thus it is possible to maintain that psychology can be reduced to neurophysiology in several important senses of 'reduce' without taking any traditional stand on the body-mind theory.

4. *Phases of Psychological Explanation*

Fodor argues that his account of the relation between neurology and psychology 'is compatible with strong claims about the ineliminability of mental language from behavior theory'.[22] This is presumably because functionally equivalent neurological mechanisms must be characterized according to equivalent psychological functions. However, the importance of functionally equivalent neurological states in behavioral theory does not entail these states and must be characterized by using *psychological*, functional language.

Fodor's thesis is *also* compatible with very strong claims about the complete *eliminability* of mental language. One could speak of that class of neurological mechanisms which bring about the same behaviour as psychological state S. But one need not use this psychological characterization. One could also speak of the class of neurological mechanisms which bring about behaviour of type B. (Behaviour B would be specified independently of psychological state S.) These two classes of neurological mechanisms would be coextensive.

Neurophysiological Reduction and Psychological Explanation

This possibility of alternating characterizations of neurological mechanisms casts serious doubt on Fodor's account of the two phases of psychological explanation in so far as these two phases are supposed to constitute necessary aspects of all psychological explanations. Behavioural research *may* by-pass phase one—the mental phase—and move directly to phase two—the neurological phase. Psychologists could postulate a class of functionally equivalent neurological states to account for certain kinds of behaviour; no postulation of internal psychological states would be needed.

There is one further problem with Fodor's characterization of psychological explanations that should be mentioned. Fodor maintains, as we have seen, that the psychological states postulated in phase one of psychological explanation 'are individuated primarily or solely by reference to their causal consequences'. But this view seems mistaken.

As Hempel[23] and Scheffler[24] have pointed out, knowledge of a particular psychological state, e.g. knowledge of X's wish for a glass of water does not enable one to draw any inference about X's behaviour unless one postulates that X has other particular goals and beliefs. Moreover, the same behaviour of X is compatible with alternative sets of particular goals and beliefs of X. In short, the same behaviour could be caused by different sets of complex psychological states.

Thus there seem to be functionally equivalent but psychologically distinct complex psychological states—just as there are functionally equivalent but anatomically distinct complex neurological states. Since there are functionally equivalent but distinct psychological states it is hardly correct to suppose, as Fodor does, that such states 'are individuated primarily or solely by reference to their causal consequence'.

What effect will this have on Fodor's thesis? If the above consideration is correct, Fodor's characterization of the phases of psychological explanation may be seriously over-simplified. The task of psychological explanations—if phase one is not by-passed as suggested above—is not merely to match psychological states (postulated in phase-one) with functionally equivalent neural mechanisms (discovered in phase-two) but to match complex functionally equivalent but psychologically distinct states (postulated in phase-one) with functionally equivalent but perhaps anatomically distinct neurological mechanisms (discovered in phase-two). However, physiological psychology would also attempt to identify among these functionally equivalent neural mechanisms those neurological mechanisms that correspond to distinct complex psychological states. (One might call this aspect of psychological explanation phase-three.) These identifications might well be based on anatomical differences among the functionally equivalent neural mechanisms. Also physiological psychology would isolate neurologically the psychologically

Michael Martin

distinguishable aspects of complex psychological states: this would involve discovering the neurological mechanisms—characterized functionally or anatomically or in some other way—that correspond to, e.g. belief rather than motive in some complex psychological state that contains them both. (This might be called phase-four of psychological explanations.) These phases should not, of course, be considered as temporal stages but as analytically distinguishable aspects of psychological explanation.

The Center for the Advanced Study in Theoretical Psychology,
University of Alberta

NOTES

1 Jerry A. Fodor, *Psychological Explanation: An Introduction to the Philosophy of Psychology* New York 1968; Jerry A. Fodor, 'Explanations in Psychology', in Max Black, ed., *Philosophy in America*, Ithaca 1965, 161–79.
2 Fodor, *Psychological Explanation*, p. 107.
3 Fodor, 'Explanations in Psychology', 176.
4 Fodor, *Psychological Explanation*, p. 111.
5 Ibid., p. 108.
6 Ibid., p. 109.
7 Ibid., p. 110.
8 Ibid.
9 Ibid., p. 112.
10 Ibid., pp. 113–14.
11 Ibid., pp. 114–15.
12 Paul Oppenheim and Hilary Putnam, 'Unity of Science as a Working Hypothesis', in H. Feigl, M. Scriven and G. Maxwell eds. *Minnesota Studies in the Philosophy of Science*, vol. II, Minneapolis 1958, p. 6.
13 Although Oppenheim and Putnam partly define micro-reduction in terms of a sense of 'reduce' specified by Kemeny and Oppenheim, micro-reduction could be partly defined in any of the senses of 'reduction' we will consider below.
14 Ibid.
15 Ibid., 10.
16 See Peter Robinson, *A Philosophical Analysis of the Concept of Reduction in the Behavioral Sciences*, unpublished doctoral dissertation, Boston University, ch. 5, for a similar point against Fodor.
17 J. G. Kemeny and P. Oppenheim, 'On Reduction', *Philosophical Studies*, 7, 1956, 6–17.
18 C. G. Hempel, *Philosophy of Natural Science*, Englewood Cliffs 1966, pp. 101–10.
19 Ernest Nagel, *The Structure of Science*, New York 1961, pp. 336–97.
20 Kenneth F. Schaffner, 'Approaches to Reduction', *Philosophy of Science*, 32, 1967, 137–47.
21 Cf. Joseph F. Hanna, 'An Explication of "Explication"', *Philosophy of Science*, 35, 1968, 28–44.
22 Fodor, *Psychological Explanation*, p. 116.
23 C. G. Hempel, *Aspects of Scientific Explanation*, New York 1965, 472–7.
24 I. Scheffler, *Conditions of Knowledge*, Chicago 1965, 87–90.

DISCUSSION

ON THE CONCEIVABILITY OF MECHANISM

MICHAEL MARTIN

Boston University

In a recent paper Norman Malcolm has argued that mechanism is an inconceivable position.[1] By this Malcolm does not mean that mechanism is logically contradictory. Rather mechanism is a position which cannot be asserted or argued for. For, according to Malcolm, asserting a position and arguing for a position involve purposeful behavior and mechanism excludes all purposeful behavior. Thus mechanism may well be true, but *if* it is true, *then* it cannot be asserted or argued for.

The bulk of Malcolm's paper is an attempt to develop the thesis that mechanism excludes all purposeful behavior. This exclusion turns on another of Malcolm's theses, namely that a neurophysiological explanation and a purposeful explanation of the same bodily movements are impossible. If this latter thesis is shown to be false, Malcolm's argument for the inconceivability of mechanism collapses. Malcolm is quite aware of this and in his final paragraph he says:

> I must confess that I am not entirely convinced of the correctness of the position I have taken in respect of the crux of this paper—namely, the problem of whether it is possible for there to be both a complete neurophysiological explanation and also a complete purposive explanation of one and the same sequence of movements. . . . Perhaps the publication of the present paper will be justified if it provides a truly convincing defense of the compatibility of the two forms of explanation ([1], p. 72).

My paper perhaps will not provide a "truly convincing defense" of the compatibility of the two forms of explanation Malcolm mentions. However, it will show that Malcolm's uneasiness about his own argument is quite justified. I will show that Malcolm has given no good reason to suppose that neurophysiological explanations and purposeful explanations are not compatible and thus that his thesis that mechanism is inconceivable is unwarranted. I will also show that in one important sense mechanistic explanations could be more basic than purposive explanations.

1. Ambiguities in Malcolm's Definition of 'Mechanism'. As Malcolm initially introduces the concept of mechanism it refers to "A special application of physical determinism—namely to all organisms with neurological systems, including human beings" ([1], p. 45). This version of mechanism assumes a neurophysiological theory which is adequate to explain and predict all movements of human bodies except those caused by outside factors. The explanation provided by the theory would

---

[1] Norman Malcolm, "The Conceivability of Mechanism," *Philosophical Review*, 1968, pp. 45–72. For further criticism of Malcolm's paper see Alvin Goldman's paper in *Philosophical Review* 1969. The present paper was written before Goldman's article appeared.

state "sufficient conditions of movements and not merely necessary conditions" ([1], pp. 45–46). Let us call his version of mechanism M_1.

It is important to realize that as Malcolm characterizes M_1, M_1 provides some sufficient neurological condition as well as some necessary neurological condition for any bodily movement that is not caused by outside factors. This characterization is perfectly compatible with: (a) some necessary condition of some bodily movement (which is not caused by outside factors) being non-neurological and (b) some sufficient condition of some bodily movement (which is not caused by outside factors) being non-neurological. These non-neurological necessary or sufficient conditions could be certain psychological states, e.g. purposes or beliefs.

Later on in his paper Malcolm introduces—apparently without realizing it—a stronger notion of mechanism, one that is not entailed by M_1.

> Let us remember that the postulated neurophysiological theory is comprehensive. . . . It is a closed system in the sense that it does not admit, as antecedent conditions, anything other than neurophysiological states or processes. . . . If the neurophysiological theory were true, then in no cases would desires, intentions, purposes be necessary conditions of any human movement ([1], p. 56).

It is clear that in this passage Malcolm is at least suggesting that neurophysiological theory would provide some sufficient condition and some necessary condition for any bodily movement (not caused by outside factors) and moreover any necessary condition for any bodily movement would be a neurophysiological one. Let us call this version of mechanism M_2.

Malcolm does not distinguish M_2 from another even stronger version of mechanism suggested in the above passage by the phrase "it does not admit as antecedent conditions anything other than neurophysiological states or processes." On this version neurophysiological theory provides some sufficient condition and some necessary condition for any bodily movement (not caused by outside factors) and excludes any necessary condition other than a neurophysiological one for any bodily movement *and* excludes any sufficient condition other than a neurophysiological one for any bodily movement. Let us call this version of mechanism M_3.

It is important to realize that although M_3 entails M_2 and M_2 entails M_1, M_1 does not entail M_2, and M_1 does not entail M_3, and M_2 does not entail M_3. Once these three progressively stronger varieties of mechanism are clearly distinguished much of the force of Malcolm's thesis is lost.

2. The Argument for the Inconceivability of Mechanism. A neurophysiological explanation, according to Malcolm, would have the following form:

(1) Whenever an organism O of structure S is in neurophysiological state q, O will emit movement m, provided there are no countervailing factors.
(2) Organism O of structure S was in neurophysiological state q.
(3) There were no countervailing factors.

(4) ∴ Organism O emitted movement m.

Premise (1) in the explanatory argument is, according to Malcolm, a contingent proposition that could be refuted by empirical evidence. (1) is to be contrasted with some premises in purposive explanation. Purposive explanations have the following form:

(1') Whenever an organism has goal G and believes that movement m is required to bring about G, it will emit m provided there are no countervailing factors.
(2') Organism O had G and believed m was required.
(3') There were no countervailing factors.

(4') Organism O emitted m.

Now (1'), according to Malcolm, is not a contingent truth but an *a priori* principle; it is true because of the meaning of the terms 'goal' and 'believe.' Malcolm argues that because of the *a priori* nature of (1'), (1) cannot be more basic than (1'). According to Malcolm (1) would be more basic than (1') only if (1') was dependent on (1). But since (1') is *a priori* true, it cannot be dependent on any contingent statement like (1).

Malcolm points out, however:

> Someone might suppose that although purposive explanations cannot be dependent on nonpurposive explanations, they would be refuted by the verification of a comprehensive neurophysiological theory of behavior. I think this view is correct: but it is necessary to understand what it *cannot* mean. It cannot mean that the principles (the universal premises) of purposive explanations would be proved false.... Since the verification of a neurophysiological theory could never *disprove* any purposive principles, the only possible outcome of such verification, logically speaking, would be to prove that the purposive principles have no application to the world ([1], p. 51).

But to say that (1') has no application to the world would be to say that either (2') or (3') is false for *any* organism O. Malcolm rejects the suggestion that (3') would be false in every case and concludes that if mechanism is true, (2') is false for any organism O. But to say that (2') is false for any organism O is just to say that organisms do not ever have goals or beliefs about these goals. Thus mechanism excludes an organism asserting mechanism or arguing for mechanism since asserting and arguing presuppose goals and beliefs.

The crucial question is why Malcolm supposes that the confirmation of mechanism would make alleged *a priori* principles like (1') not applicable to the world and thus make (2') false for any organism O. It would seem that the only reason for supposing this to be true is that Malcolm is talking about mechanism M_3. Neither mechanism M_1 nor mechanism M_2 would exclude some non-neurological sufficient condition for some bodily movement (not caused by outside factors) and thus the confirmation of M_1 or of M_2 would not entail that organisms do not have purposes and beliefs that were sufficient conditions for their behavior. In short, on M_1 and M_2, (1') could apply to the world and thus M_1 and M_2 could be asserted or argued for.

The only passage I can find in which Malcolm tries to answer the sort of objection just raised is the following:

> It might be thought that there could be two different systems of causal explanations of human movements, a purposive system and a neurophysiological system. The antecedent conditions in the one system would be the desires and intentions of human beings; in the

other they would be the neurophysiological states and processes of those same human beings. Each system would provide adequate causal explanations of the same movements.

Generally speaking, it is possible for there to be a plurality of simultaneous sufficient causal conditions of an event. But if we bear in mind the comprehensive aspect of the neurophysiological theory—that is, the fact that it provides sufficient causal conditions for all movements—we shall see that desires and intentions could not be causes of movements. It has often been noted that to say B causes C does not mean merely that whenever B occurs, C occurs. Causation also has subjunctive and counterfactual implications: if B *were* to occur, C *would* occur; and if B has *not* occurred C would *not* have occurred. But the neurophysiological theory would provide sufficient causal conditions for every human movement, and so there would be no cases at all in which a movement would not have occurred if the person had not this desire or intention. Since the counterfactual would be false in all cases, desires and intentions would not be causes of human movements. They would not ever be sufficient causal conditions nor would they ever be necessary causal conditions ([1], pp. 56-57).

There are a number of problems with this passage. First, although it may be true that "B causes C" cannot be analyzed in terms of "Whenever B occurs, C occurs" and must be analyzed in terms of subjunctive and counterfactual conditionals it does not follow that "B causes C" entails "If B had *not* occurred, C would *not* have occurred." Malcolm is apparently confusing here nomologically sufficient conditions and nomologically necessary conditions: "Jones' taking poison caused Jones' death" entails "If Jones *would* have taken poison, Jones *would* have died" but not "If Jones would not have taken poison, Jones would not have died" since Jones might have been shot at the same time as he was poisoned.

Secondly, even if one assumes that causality involves both nomologically necessary and nomologically sufficient conditions, Malcolm's conclusion does not follow. If B is a necessary and sufficient condition for C, this does not mean that some distinct factor D could not be both necessary and sufficient for C. Thus the fact that neurophysiological factors are both necessary and sufficient for behavior does not mean that purposes and beliefs could not also be necessary and sufficient for the behavior. As we have seen, this possibility is allowed for in mechanism M_1.

Moreover, as we have seen, even if purposes and beliefs for behavior are ruled out as necessary conditions (as they are in mechanism M_2) they might still be sufficient conditions for behavior. And only mechanism M_3 seems to rule out this possibility.

We must conclude that Malcolm has not shown that on mechanisms M_1 and M_2 purposive explanations and neurophysiological explanations cannot be given of the same human behavior (where an explanation provides sufficient conditions) and thus he has not shown that mechanisms M_1 and M_2 are inconceivable.

3. **The Tenability of Mechanism M_3.** Thus far we have argued that at most Malcolm has shown that M_3 is inconceivable. But has he shown this? To decide the issue we must distinguish between two different versions of M_3. On the first version of M_3 all nomologically non-neurological sufficient conditions of human behavior (that is, not caused by outside factors) are excluded. Nomologically sufficient conditions are specified by contingent law-like propositions. On this version of mechanism M_3 all such contingent non-neurophysiological propositions which purport to explain

human behavior would be supposed to be either false or not applicable to the world, i.e. their antecedents would be false. Let us use 'M_{3a}' to denote this version of mechanism M_3.

On the second version of M_3, all sufficient conditions (nomological and logical) are excluded. By a logically sufficient condition I mean this:

A is a logically sufficient condition for B if and only if A entails B.

According to Malcolm

>   (a) An organism O has goal G and believes that movement m is required to bring about G and there are no countervailing factors

entails

>   (b) Organism O emits movement m.

Thus the goals and certain beliefs of an organism under certain conditions provide a logically sufficient condition for the organism emitting a certain movement. Indeed, it is because of this logically sufficient condition that (1') is supposed by Malcolm to be an *a priori* truth.

Now on this version of M_3 it is supposed that any logically sufficient condition for (b) that is not in neurophysiological terms is false. Put in a different way: any *a priori* true hypothetical proposition (not in neurophysiological terms) in which the consequent specifies that an organism emitted movement m would not apply to the world, i.e. the antecedent of the hypothetical would be false. Let us use 'M_{3b}' to denote this version of mechanism M_3.

Now clearly Malcolm has not shown that M_{3a} is inconceivable since all contingent non-neurophysiological law-like statements that purport to explain human behavior may be false. This would be perfectly compatible with the existence of purposes and beliefs and with allegedly *a priori* principles like (1') applying to the world.

At best Malcolm's argument has shown that M_{3b} is inconceivable. But what a strange position this is. Who has ever held it? For to advocate M_{3b} would be to advocate that any proposition (even a proposition which is completely innocuous to mechanists) that entails (b) would be false. Consider, for example:

>   (c) Organism O emitted movement m'.

Now let us define movement m' as a movement immediately preceding movement m. Then (c) entails (b) and thus (c) is a logically sufficient condition for (b). Therefore:

>   (1″) Whenever an organism emits movement m', then the organism emits movement m.

is a conceptual *a priori* truth analogous to (1') and by an argument analogous to Malcolm's (1″) could never apply to the world. Therefore (c) would be false. This would mean that no movement of an organism is preceded by any other movement.

It is far from obvious that any mechanist has ever embraced M_{3b}. But even if some mechanists have embraced M_{3b} with its absurd implications they would not need to. Weaker and less objectionable versions are open to them, e.g. M_1, M_2, and M_{3a}.

Now it may be objected that (c), unlike (a), does not specify a cause of the movement of the organism. This suggests still another version of M_3. On this version neurophysiological theory excludes all logically sufficient conditions for human behavior which could specify causes of the behavior. Let us call this version of M_{3b}, M_{3b1}. Consider however:

(d) Organism O receives external stimulus s.

External stimulus s can be defined as a stimulus immediately preceding organism O emitting movement m.

Now (d) entails (b) and it is not unusual to speak of a certain external stimulus that precedes behavior as a cause of the behavior. For example one might say "Jones' walking into the room caused Smith to fidget" or "The fumes from the fire caused Jones to cough." Now:

(1‴) Whenever an organism receives stimulus s then the organism emits movement m.

would be an *a priori* truth.

By an argument similar to Malcolm's (1‴) would not apply to the world. Thus (d) would be false. This would mean that organisms never receive stimuli immediately before they emit movements. As far as I know no mechanist has ever embraced a position with such absurd implications, and as we have seen there is no need for a mechanist to do so.

Instead of embracing M_{3b1} a mechanist would surely argue that if stimulus s is the cause of behavior B a neurophysiological explanation could be given of the causal relation; he would maintain that there is a neurological connection between the stimulus s and behavior B if s is the cause of B. It should be noted that neither the fact that (d) entails (b) nor the fact that (1‴) is an *a priori* truth prevents him from doing this.

This consideration also applies to purposes and beliefs. The fact that (a) entails (b) and the fact that (1′) is an *a priori* truth does not prevent neurophysiology from specifying a neurophysiological connection between purposes and beliefs and the behavior which results from these purposes and beliefs.

4. Mechanism and the Meaning of Terms. So far we have seen that a mechanist need not hold a position that entails that (1′) does not apply to the world. Moreover, we have seen that one mechanistic position that seems to be implicit in Malcolm's paper would have such absurd consequences that no sane mechanist would embrace it.

Let us suppose, however, that some particular version of M_{3b1} was formulated which would entail that (1′) does not apply to the world but which would not have the kind of absurd implications specified above. Let us call this version of mechanism M_{3b1}, M^*_{3b1}. Would Malcolm be correct? Would mechanism M^*_{3b1} be inconceivable in the sense that if M^*_{3b1} were true, it could not be asserted or argued for?

Let us grant Malcolm's thesis that (1') is true *a priori*. As Malcolm correctly notes the *a priori* nature of (1') could not be due to the form of the statement. Rather if (1') is true *a priori*, then it is because of the present meaning of the terms in it, in particular the meaning of terms like 'goal' and 'belief.'

Now although Malcolm is correct that M^*_{3b1} cannot be asserted or argued for given the present meaning of 'goal' and 'purpose,' it does not follow that M^*_{3b1} could not be asserted given some *other* meaning of 'goal' and 'purpose.'[2] If 'goal' and 'belief' meant something different in (1') from what they mean in (1'), then (1') might be found to be a false contingent statement. If it were, (2') need not be false and organisms could have goals and beliefs. Hence, M^*_{3b1} could be asserted.

Indeed, it is not implausible to suppose that the confirmation of a comprehensive neurophysiological theory would bring about changes in the ordinary meaning of psychological terms like 'purpose' and 'belief.' These changes might make it possible to assert M^*_{3b1} in the ordinary sense of assert, i.e. the sense of 'assert' that prevailed at that time in which the theory had gained great prominence.

It is also important to realize that if changes in the meaning of certain psychological terms were to occur due to the wide acceptance of M^*_{3b1}, this would not necessarily bring about any changes in the denotation or reference of these terms. Change in meaning or sense is compatible with fixed reference. Thus although 'purpose' and 'belief' might come to have different senses than they do now, they might still refer to some class of mental states, dispositions and the like. Thus one might assert M^*_{3b1} and in this activity be doing something that has always been *called* 'asserting,' i.e. the denotation of 'asserting' would be the same as it is now; the only thing that would have changed would be the meaning or sense of 'asserting.'

Thus M^*_{3b1} is conceivable given certain changes in the meaning of our psychological language which are compatible with invariance in the referent of such language.

5. The Primacy of Neurophysiology.

So far I have argued that Malcolm has not shown that several different versions of mechanism are inconceivable. Moreover, I have argued that there is implicit in Malcolm's paper another sense of 'mechanism' that is inconceivable but that this sense of mechanism has such absurd consequences that no sane mechanist could embrace it. Finally, I have argued that even if a definition of mechanism could be constructed which does not have these absurd consequences this purified version would still be conceivable given changes in the meaning of some of our psychological terms that are compatible with fixed references for these terms.

I have throughout defended the compatibility of purposive explanations and neurophysiological explanations. One question that remains is in what sense a mechanist could maintain that although purposive explanations and neuro-

---

[2] See Peter Robinson, *The Concept of Reduction in the Behaviorial Sciences*, unpublished Ph.D. Dissertation, Boston University, 1969, for a similar point.

physiological explanations are compatible neurophysiological explanations are more basic than purposive explanations.

It is clear that a mechanist could maintain that mechanistic explanations are more basic if the meaning of certain psychological terms changed. If the meaning of 'goal' and 'belief' changed, (1') could be a contingently true statement. The truth of (1') might be dependent on some neurophysiological state. For instance an organism which has a goal G and which has the belief that movement, m, is necessary to achieve G will not emit movement m unless the organism has structure S and is in neurophysiological state q. In this sense neurophysiological explanations are more basic. This is in fact the sense of 'more basic' specified by Malcolm.

Now Malcolm's sense of 'more basic' would not apply if (1') is an *a priori* truth for if (1') is an *a priori* truth, the truth of (1') could not be dependent on some neurophysiological state. However, perhaps some other meaning of 'more basic' can be given which would apply. I believe a different and relevant sense of 'more basic' can be constructed.

First of all it is important to note that nothing Malcolm says rules out the possibility that goals and beliefs have neurophysiological sufficient conditions. Thus a law of the following form might well hold:

(5) Whenever an organism with structure S is in neurophysiological state q, the organism has goal G and believes that movement m is necessary for achieving G provided there are no countervailing factors.

(5) Combined with (2) and (3) would enable us to deduce

(6) Organism O has goal G and believes that movement m is necessary for achieving G.

Thus neurophysiology could explain all the movement which purposive explanations could and more. First, neurophysiological theory could explain the causes of purposive behavior that are postulated in purposive explanations, i.e. purposes and beliefs. Purposive explanations presumably could not explain this. Secondly, neurophysiological theory could explain nonpurposive behavior. By hypothesis purposive explanations could not explain this sort of behavior.

But in one important sense a theory T_1 is more basic than T_2 if T_1 can explain everything which T_2 can explain and more, and T_1 can explain the causes postulated by T_2 in explaining what T_2 can explain whereas T_2 cannot explain these causes. In this sense of 'more basic' a mechanist might argue that neurophysiology is more basic than the commonsense principles or "theories" used in purposive explanations. It is important to realize this sense of 'more basic' is compatible with the allegedly *a priori* nature of the principles of purposive explanations.

Now whether neurophysiological theory is (or will become) more basic in this sense I do not know. But it is clear that Malcolm has said nothing to show that it is not more basic or will not become so.

REFERENCE

[1] Malcolm, N., "The Conceivability of Mechanism," *Philosophical Review*, vol. 77, 1968, pp. 45–72.

METHODOLOGICAL INDIVIDUALISM AND THE REDUCTION OF CULTURAL ANTHROPOLOGY TO PSYCHOLOGY

A fundamental problem in the philosophy of science is to specify clearly what it means to reduce one science to another. This specification is preliminary to answering the question of whether cultural anthropology is or can be reduced to psychology. A weak and a strong sense of reduction is defined in terms of two conditions: definability and derivability. It is argued that in the light of present evidence it is unlikely that cultural anthropology is reducible to psychology in any of the senses of « reducible » specified. However, future developments in these sciences might make such a reduction possible. Once the notion of reduction is clarified the positions of Methodological Individualism and Methodological Holism are characterized. Methodological Individualism holds that all holistic sciences (e. g. macro-economic, sociology, cultural anthropology) are or can be reduced to individualistic sciences (e. g., psychology, biology). Methodological Holism denies what Methodological Individualism affirms. It is argued that the issue between these two positions — at least with respect to future reduction — is undecided; it does seem to be true, however, that such a reduction is not possible now. The question of the heuristic value of attempting such a reduction is discussed.

INTRODUCTION. — One of the fundamental theoretical questions in the social and behavioral sciences is whether one behavioral or social science is reducible to another. Sometimes this question takes the form, « Can social psychology be reduced to individual psychology? »; at other times it takes the form, « Can cultural anthropology be reduced to psychology? »; at still other times it takes the form, « Can macro-economics be reduced to micro-economics? » What is sometimes not realized in the heat of these controversies, however, is that these questions can not possibly be answered until one is clear on what it means to reduce social psychology to individual psychology, what it means to reduce cultural anthropology to psychology, what it means to reduce macro-economics to micro-economics.

These prior questions push to the fore a still more basic questions; What does it mean to reduce any science to any other? This question is a fundamental one in the philosophy of science. Philosophers of science have wanted to know not just what it means to reduce biology to physics or to reduce psychology to biology or to reduce cultural anthropology to psychology but what it means to reduce any science to any other science[1]. Stated more formally one can express the problem in this way: Let S_1 be the primary science — the reducing science. Let S_2 be the secondary science — the science to be reduced. We want to know what it means to say:

S_2 is reducible to S_1

[1] See for example, NAGEL (1961: 336-397).

Thus although the focus of much of this paper will be on the reduction of cultural anthropology to psychology this problem will be used to illustrate a quite general problem: the reduction of any science to any other. Moreover, as will be shown in the sequel, the analysis of a methodological position called methodological individualism can be construed as a special case of this general problem.

CONDITIONS OF REDUCTION. — Now in asking whether S_2 is re-reducible to S_1 one seems to be asking if two conditions hold: (The Describability Condition). All the entities and processes and so on which are the subject matter of S_2 can be completely described by the concepts of S_1; (The Explanability Condition) All phenomena studied by S_2 can be explained by means of the laws and theories of S_1.

Thus in the case of the reduction of biology to physics and chemistry, to ask whether the Describability Condition holds would be to ask whether all characteristics of living organisms can be fully described in physical-chemical terms; in the case of the reduction of cultural anthropology to psychology to ask whether the Describability Condition holds would be to ask whether all characteristics of cultures and societies[1] can be completely described using the concepts of psychology.

One plausible way of construing the Describability Condition is that the terms of the secondary science S_2 can be defined in terms of the primary science S_1. Let us call this particular version of the Describability Condition, the Definability Condition. In the case of the reduction of biology to physics to ask whether the Definability Condition holds is to ask whether terms like 'cell' and 'fertilization' can be defined with terms taken from the vocabulary of physics and chemistry. In relation to the reduction of cultural anthropology to psychology to ask whether the Definability Condition holds is to ask whether the terms of cultural anthropology, e.g. terms like 'clan' 'cargo cult' 'totem' 'myth' 'accession ceremony' can be defined with the help of terms taken from the vocabulary of psychology.

In relation to the reduction of biology to physics and chemistry to ask whether the Explanability Condition holds is to ask whether all the phenomena studied in biology can be explained by the laws and theories of physics and chemistry; with respect to the reduction of cultural anthropology to psychology to ask whether the Explanability Condition holds is to ask whether the phenomena studied by cultural anthropology can be explained by the laws and theories of psychology.

[1] For the present discussion we make no distinction between the subject matter of social and cultural anthropology; thus we assume cultural anthropology studies cultural and social phenomena.

One plausible interpretation of the Explanability Condition is that all well confirmed sentences describing the phenomena studied by S_2, i.e. all well confirmed sentences that contain descriptive terms of S_2 can be deduced from the laws and theories of the primary science S_1 given certain appropriate statements of initial conditions[1]. Let us call this interpretation of the Explanability Condition, the Derivability Condition[2]. In the case of the reduction of biology to physics and chemistry to ask whether the Derivability Condition holds would be to ask whether all well confirmed biological sentences, i.e. all well confirmed sentences that contain descriptive terms of biology could be deduced from the laws and theories of physics and chemistry plus appropriate initial conditions; with regard to the reduction of cultural anthropology to psychology to ask whether the Derivability Condition holds would be to ask whether all well confirmed cultural sentences, i.e. all well confirmed sentences that contain descriptive terms of cultural anthropology could be logically deduced from psychological laws and theoretical principles plus statements of initial conditions.

Thus the question of whether the Derivability Condition holds in relation to cultural anthropology and psychology comes down to the question of whether all well confirmed cultural sentences like « Papua had cargo cults » or « Nyoro accession ceremonies are lenghty and complex » can be deduced from psychological laws and theories given appropriate statements of initial conditions.

It should be stressed that the Definability Condition and the Derivability Condition are logically independent conditions: one condition does not imply the other. Thus it is logically possible that all terms of cultural anthropology could be defined by psychological terms and yet it not be the case that all sentences describing cultural phenomena could be deduced from psychological laws and theories[3].

Moreover, it is logically possible that all sentences describing cultural phenomena could be deduced from psychological laws and theories and yet it not be the case that all cultural terms could be defined in terms of psychology[4]. The logical independence of the two conditions suggest a strong and a weak sense of reduction.

In the strong sense:

S_2 is reducible to S_1 = the Definability Condition and the Derivability Condition hold.

---

[1] This view of explanation has been proposed by POPPER (1959: 59-77) and HEMPEL (1964: 229-290).

[2] Various alternative formulations of the Derivability Condition are possible.

[3] For example, if S_1 lacked laws then clearly the descriptive sentences of S_2 could not be derived from the laws and initial conditions of S_1. Whether psychology does have laws we need not decide here.

[4] An example of this possibility is given later in the paper when the Derivability Condition is discussed.

In the logically weaker sense:

S_2 is reducible to S_1 = the Derivability Condition holds.

KROEBER ON REDUCTION. — It would be useful at this point to relate our thesis to the classical discussion of KROEBER (1917: 163-213). Kroeber in this well known and widely discussed essay[1] argues that social phenomena are on another plane (KROEBER 1917: 209) from organic phenomena and that civilization « transcends » (KROEBER 1917: 212) both bodily and mental phenomena. Although Kroeber's language was imprecise and metaphysical it suggested to some commentators that Kroeber was denying that cultural anthropology could be reduced to psychology (SAPIR 1917, BIDNEY 1964). This seems to be to be one plausible interpretation of Kroeber's view. Unfortunately, discussion and criticism of Kroeber have failed to make clear what sense of reduction was at issue; these discussions have failed to clearly logically analyze the notion of reduction implicit in the paper[2].

It seems to me quite plausible to suppose that Kroeber was denying that cultural anthropology — at least in the historical perspective he viewed it — was reducible to psychology in both the strong and weaker sense of 'reducible' specified above. First of all, his statement that history « keeps its intent fixed upon the unaltered and irresolved facts of the social plane » (KROEBER 1917: 209) suggests Kroeber was denying that the Describability Condition holds; social and cultural facts could not be adequately described in psychological terms. In our terms Kroeber was denying that certain cultural or social terms could be defined in psychological terms. In short he was denying that the Definability Condition holds. Secondly, Kroeber's belief that cultural phenomena was « something new » (KROEBER 1917: 208) and could not have been inferred from non cultural phenomena as well as his statement that an historical anthropologist « does not explain » his phenomena (KROEBER 1917: 212) certainly suggests that he was denying that the Explanability Condition holds. In our terms he was denying that sentences describing cultural phenomena could be deduced from the laws and theories of psychology. In short, he was denying that the Derivability Condition holds.

It should be pointed out again that these two claims are logically independent; they must be separated and evaluated on their own merits. We shall return to Kroeber in a moment.

[1] See for example, SAPIR (1917: 441-447) and BIDNEY (1964: 34-53).

[2] SAPIR (1917: 444), for example, never makes clear what it means to say that cultural phenomena are « ideally resolvable » into « inorganic, organic, and psychic processes ». I take it that by « ideally resolvable » Sapir means « reducible ».

CLARIFICATION OF THE DEFINABILITY CONDITION. — More needs to be said however about these two conditions. Let us consider the Definability Condition first. What does it mean to define all the terms of one science in terms of another? In order to answer this question let us distinguish two different kinds of definitions: 1) analytic definitions, 2) extensional definitions.

An analytic definition has the following form:

————has the same meaning as........

For this kind of definition to be correct the blanks need to be filled in by synonyms. An example of an analytic definition would be the following:

« brother » has the same meaning as « male sibling ».

In the case of an analytic definition the Definability Condition amounts to this: Each terms in the secondary science S_2 is synonymous with some term (or combination of terms) in the primary science S_1. Let us call the Definability Condition interpreted in this way the Analytic Definability Condition.

Now it should be noted that to determine whether one term is synonymous with another is not an empirical question about the subject matter to which the terms refer. Thus to tell whether 'brother' has the same meaning as 'male sibling' is not a psychological, sociological or biological question about brothers and male siblings. What might be needed, of course, is empirical research into the linguistic practices of the uses of the language[1]. But this is an entirely different matter. Linguistic research about the ordinary meaning of the word 'brother' must not be confused with empirical research about brothers.

The import of this observation is the following: In order to tell whether the Analytic Definability Condition holds one does not ordinarily need empirical investigation of the subject matter of S_1 or S_2. Thus in order to tell whether the Analytic Definability Condition holds in relation to the reduction of cultural anthropology to psychology one does not do psychological or anthropological investigation of the typical sort. What one may need to do is empirical research into the linguistic practices of psychologists and anthropologists.

Now whether the Analytic Definability Condition does in fact hold in relation to cultural anthropology and psychology we do not know with any certainty. But it is unlikely that at the present time this condition does hold. It seems implausible, for example, to suppose that a term like 'clan' has the same meaning for any social scientists as any term or combination of terms of psychology.

---

[1] However, determining the meaning of an expression is no simple empirical task (QUINE 1960: 26-79).

However, although the Analytic Definability Condition may not hold now this may well change. Change in meaning of sociological and psychological terms, richer vocabularies in both disciplines may make it possible for this condition to be satisfied. It should also be noted that whether the Analytic Definability Condition does hold may be relative to a particular group's linguistic practices. The meaning of the same terms may indeed be different in different behavioral disciplines. Thus it could be that for psychologists but not sociologists all sociological terms would be synonymous with psychological terms. Thus, when one speaks of the Analytic Definability Condition holding one may have to specify the group of language users to which one is referring. We need not, however, speculate further here about these and other possibilities.

Another type of definition is extensional definition. It has the following form:

———— has the same extension as ....

To say that two terms have the same extension is not to say that the two terms have the same meaning; it is to say rather that the phenomenon referred to by the one term is a necessary and sufficient condition for the phenomenon designated by the other. For example the term 'man' has the same extension as 'featherless biped'. These terms do not have the same meaning but it is true that being a man is a necessary and sufficient condition for being a featherless biped and conversely.

Unlike an analytic definition the correctness of an extensional definition is established by empirical investigation of the subject matter to which the terms apply and is not established by the inversigation of the linguistic practices of the users of the language. Thus to tell whether the term 'man' does have the same extension as the term 'featherless biped' one would have to know whether being a man is a sufficient condition for being a featerless biped and conversely. And presumably empirical investigation of men and featherless bipeds would be needed.

In the case of extensional definitions the Definability Condition amounts to this: Each term in the secondary science S_2 has the same extension as some term (or combination of terms) in the primary science S_1. Let us call this interpretation of the Definability Condition, the Extensional Definability Condition. In relation to cultural anthropology and psychology this condition would be: Each cultural term has the same extension as some psychological term (or combination of psychological terms). It is important to note that the Extensional Definability Condition is a logically weaker condition that the Analytic Definability Condition[1]. Thus if the Analytic Definability Condition

---

[1] GOODMAN (1951) suggests that extensional isomorphism as an even logically weaker condition. Extensional isomorphism requires only that truth be preserved in translation of certain statements we are particularly interested in. See SCHEFFLER (1963: 156-160).

holds, so does the Extensional Definability Condition. But the converse is not the case. Thus if one would show that the Analytic Definability Condition did not hold in relation to cultural anthropology and psychology, one would have to show independently that the Extensional Definability Condition did not hold.

It seems clear that at the present time the Extensional Definability Condition has not been established: Each cultural term has not been shown to have the same extension as some term or combination of terms in psychology. Consider, for example, what hypothesis would have to be confirmed to make it at all plausible that, say, the term 'cargo cult' has the same extension as some psychological term 'P'. One would have to confirm the following statement: In all cases of cargo cults a particular psychological phenomenon P is present (which is referred to by the term 'P') and in all cases where psychological phenomenon P is present a cargo cult is present. In short, one would have to establish the law: A cargo cult is present if and only if psychological phenomenon P is present. But as far as I know social scientists at the present time do not know of any such psychological phenomenon P. Hence at the present time the term 'cargo cult' does not have the same extension as any psychological term and the Extensional Definability Condition does not hold.

This does not mean, however, that further empirical research may not reveal such a psychological phenomenon, a psychological phenomenon that is co-extensive with cargo cults. Thus a psychological phenomenon P referred to by the term 'P' may be found as social science develops. And, indeed, it might be the case that future research will establish that each cultural term has the same extension as some psychological term. But whether this day will ever come is any one's guess. It does seem safe to say that the satisfaction of the Extensional Derivability Condition is a long way off.

CLARIFICATION OF THE DERIVABILITY CONDITION. — We noted earlier that there is a weaker sense of reduction. In this sense only the Derivability Condition needs to hold. Thus in this weaker sense even if neither the Analytic or Extensional Definability Condition holds at the present or even if they will never hold, it still may be true that the sencondary science S_2 is reducible to primary science S_1. It is time to say a little bit more about the Derivability Condition.

However, once one starts to reflect on the Derivability Condition one sees trouble. For it appears that on logical grounds sentences describing cultural phenomena could *never* be derived from psychological laws alone in any non trivial way[1] since these sentences will presu-

---

[1] It is possible to derive any descriptive sentence from any psychological law in a trivial way. For example: From 'Lp' we can logically derive 'Either Lp or Ac'. But it is also possible to derive the formal contradiction of Ac in the same way. These and other trivial cases do not invalidate the point. For further discussion of this point see NAGEL (1961: 353n).

mably contain terms not found in psychological laws. Consider for example the following case: Let 'P_1' and 'P_2' be psychological terms referring to certain psychological phenomena P_1 and P_2 and 'C_1' be some cultural term, e.g. 'C_1' might be 'cargo cult' referring to some cultural phenomena C_1. Now consider some psychological law Lp containing terms 'P_1' and P_2', namely: In all cases where psychological phenomena P_1 is present, psychological phenomena P_2 is present, and consider some sentence of anthropology Ac containing the term 'C_1'. For example Ac might be « Papua had cargo cults ». Now clearly Ac could not be deduced from Lp given appropriate initial conditions since 'C_1' does not appear in Lp. And this would be true no matter how many purely psychological laws one would add. It looks as if the Derivability Condition could never be met.

One way to bring off the deduction is by some laws connecting psychological phenomena with cultural phenomena. Let us call these laws 'bridge laws' or 'cross discipline laws'. These laws could take many forms and, indeed one form they could take would be the sort of law mentioned in relation to extensional definitions. But this form is not the only one. Here is a schematic illustration of the derivation of Ac by means of a bridge law and Lp.

Lp	Whenever psychological phenomena P_1 is present, psychological phenomena P_2 is present.
Bridge law	Whenever psychological phenomena P_2 is present cultural phenomena C_1 is present.
Statement of Initial Condition	P_1 was present in Papua.
Ac	C_1 was present in Papua, i.e. Papua had C_1.

Notice that although Ac was derived from Lp plus a bridge law and initial conditions no definition of 'C_1' in terms of psychological terms was needed.

In the light of this discussion it is plausible to give the Derivability Condition a more liberal interpretation and say the Derivability Condition means: all sentences describing phenomena of S_2 are derivable from S_1 given certain appropriate bridge laws and initial conditions. Let us call this interpretation of the Derivability Condition, the Bridge Law Derivability Condition. With respect to cultural anthropology and psychology, therefore, to say that the Bridge Law Derivability Condition holds is to say that all sentences describing cultural phenomena are derivable from psychological laws when combined with appropriate bridge laws and initial conditions.

It seems highly unlikely in relation to cultural anthropology and psychology that at the present time this condition does hold; appropriate bridge laws have not been discovered and the derivation of all descriptive sentences of cultural anthropology from psychological laws and theories and initial conditions is not possible. This again does not mean that the Bridge Law Derivability Condition will not be satisfied as cultural anthropology and psychology develop. Whether this will ever happen is anyone's guess.

KROEBER'S VIEWS EVALUATED. — To return briefly to Kroeber one can say this: Kroeber as interpreted above does seem to have the evidence on his side for the present time; it would seem that cultural anthropology is not reducible to psychology in any of the senses I have specified[1]. Nevertheless, there is nothing final about this. As both psychology and cultural anthropology develop, as the vocabularies of both disciplines are enriched, as their theoretical sophistication increases, as bridge laws are developed, the thesis of Kroeber in 1917 may be shown to be wrong.

Above all what must be emphasized is that Kroeber's thesis as here interpreted is not something that can be refuted or established by *a priori* argument. After the notion of reducible has been clarified by logical analysis the question of Kroeber's correctness or incorrectness will have to wait on the development of anthropology and psychology. In particular, it cannot be argued that Kroeber as here interpreted made any fallacy (BIDNEY 1964: 51) in arguing for the irreducibility of cultural anthropology. The word 'fallacy' sugggests some sort of logical mistake. Now Kroeber may be shown ultimately to be mistaken. But it will not be on some logical point. If he is wrong at all, it will be shown on evidence that is not available at this time.

Moreover, those people who oppose Kroeber and who argue that cultural anthropology can be reduced to psychology have made no fallacy either (BIDNEY 1964: 51). As here interpreted they may have merely made a prediction about the future development of anthropology and psychology whose truth cannot now be determined.

It is true that Kroeber sometimes lapsed into an objectionable ontological vocabulary; he talked at times as if culture was some super entity. But we need not give his thesis this ontological interpretation (GOLDSTEIN 1959). The ontological question should be separated from the methodological one (GOLDSTEIN 1958) and we should interpret

---

[1] Nevertheless, there has been some noteworthy progress. WHITING and CHILD (1953: 16-39), for example, define the cultural term 'custom' in terms of behavior theory; this may be interpreted as a first step towards meeting the Definability Condition.

Kroeber methodologically[1]. Interpreted in this way his view is important and may even prove to be correct.

Moreover, even if Kroeber is wrong it does not follow that cultural anthropologists should attempt to reduce cultural anthropollogy to psychology. But this is a separate issue which we will take up at the end of the paper.

METHODOLOGICAL INDIVIDUALISM. — The problem posed by the reduction of cultural anthropology to psychology raises a more general question and a larger issue. Cultural anthropology is one of several social sciences that takes as its subject matter wholes — social, cultural or political. Let us call these sciences 'holistic sciences'. Psychology on the other hand, is one of several sciences which takes as its subject matter individuals. Let us call these sciences 'individualistic sciences'.

One may then pose the more general question: Are holistic sciences reducible to individualistic sciences? Notice that this question is independent of the question of the reduction of cultural anthropology to psychology. Cultural anthropology may be reducible to psychology without all holistic sciences being reducible to individualistic sciences. Conversely all holistic sciences may be reducible to individualistic sciences without cultural anthropology being reducible to psychology.

With the above analytic apparatus as our tools we can clarify this general problem and define two opposing methodologies.

Consider a class of terms found in the vocabulary of the social sciences. These terms for want of a better name might be called « social whole terms » since they refer to certain wholes that are the subject matter of some social sciences and to the properties of these wholes. Thus there are terms that refer to groups, organizations, institutions, cultures, economies and so on and to the properties of these wholes[2]. Such terms are found in cultural anthropology but they are also found in sociology, history, political science, parts of economics and social psychology.

Now let us consider the following proposition: All sciences or parts of sciences that use social whole terms are reducible to sciences or parts of sciences which do not contain social whole terms. Let us call this proposition: The Reducibility Thesis. The term 'reducible' here can be taken in either the weaker or stronger sense or in any of the various refinements specified earlier. It should also be noted that by « sciences that do not contain social whole terms » I do not mean

[1] Kroeber himself never seemed clear on the distinction between the ontological and methodological issues. Had he been this might have saved him his retraction of his earlier position (KROEBER 1952: 23). GOLDSTEIN (1959: 297n) suggests that the term 'methodological super organicism' would have been less misleading.

[2] For example, 'French Enlightenment', 'degree of social integration', 'class mobility', 'crowd' are social whole terms. This is not to suggest that the distinction between social terms and non social whole terms is completely clear. On this point see NAGEL (1963: 536-540).

just psychology. Such sciences would include psychology — or at least parts of psychology — but also much more, e.g. biology and physiology.

The position of Methodological Individualism can now be defined: Methodological Individualism is the position that maintains the Reducibility Thesis in any of the senses of 'reduce' specified above. On the other hand Methodological Holism is the position that denies the Reducibility Thesis in any of those senses of 'reduce'. It should be noted that depending on what sense of 'reduce' one chooses one can advocate a stronger or weaker Methodological Individualism or Holism. Indeed, one could be a Methodological Individualist *and* a Holist in different senses of 'reduce' at the same time with no inconsistency. Thus one might deny the Reducibility Thesis in the strong sense of reduce and affirm it in the weak sense.

Still the Reducibility Thesis and consequently the position of Methodological Individualism and Holism contains an ambiguity. Does the Reducibility Thesis refer to the present state of the sciences or to some future state? Let us eliminate this ambiguity by distinguishing two reducibility theses: (Reducibility Thesis 1). All those sciences (or parts of sciences) that use social whole terms are reducible to sciences or those parts of sciences which do not contain social whole terms *at the present* time; (Reducibility Thesis 2). All those sciences (or parts of sciences) that use social whole terms will be reducible to sciences or those parts of sciences which do not contain social whole terms at some time.

It is very unlikely that Reducibility Thesis 1 is true. For the present it seems Methodological Holists have the evidence on their side. This does not mean, however, that as social science develops things may not change. Reducibility Thesis 2 may be true; at the present we have no sure way of knowing. Thus any decision between Methodological Individualism and Methodological Holism in so far as the one affirms Reducibility Thesis 2 and the other denies Reducibility Thesis 2, will have to wait on further developments in the social sciences.

There is, however, another dimension to the Methodological Individualism and Methodological Holism controversy. One may wonder not about whether Reducibility Thesis 2 is true but whether it is fruitful to try to reduce holistic sciences to non-holistic sciences. Thus one may wonder about the fruitfulness of following a methodological rule M: Let us attempt to reduce all sciences or parts of sciences that contain holistic terms to sciences or parts of scineces that do not! This imperative is not true or false but it may be a fruitful or unfruitful one to follow. Let us call the thesis that M is a fruitful methodological rule: the Heuristic Thesis.

Now we can discuss another aspect of Methodological Individualism. Methodological Individualists seem to maintain the Heuristic Thesis while Methodological Holists deny the Heuristic Thesis. It must be stressed, however, that the Reducibility Thesis and the Heuristic Thesis are logically independent theses. Thus the Reducibility Thesis may be true but M may not be a fruitful methodological rule. On the other hand, M may be a fruitful rule and the Reducibility Thesis may not be true. Notice also that whether M is a fruitful rule or not may depend on the sense of 'reduce' one is talking about.

Whether the Heuristic Thesis is true, i.e. whether M is a fruitful methodological rule in any of the senses of « reduce » specified, I do not know and indeed it is a complicated question to answer. One would have to determine the advantages — direct and indirect — of following M. Some direct advantages might be the discovery of the relevance of laws and theories from one discipline in explaining the phenomena of another; some indirect advantages might be the closer relations established with scientists working in other fields and consequently the influx of new ideas and concepts. These possible advantages, even if they are at all likely, do not necessarily entail that M should be followed. The likely heuristic value of following M would have to be weighed against its likely disadvantages before a decision to actually follow M could be made. The disadvantages of following M might be a decrease in time and energy available for other research, a decrease in effective specialization, a decrease in group identity of the scientists at issue and the neglect of applied research.

It should also be noted that what may be heuristic at one time may not be at other times and that just because it would not be a rational decision to follow M at one time it would not follow that it would not be a rational decision to follow M at some other time. Thus the same ambiguity of temporal referent that affects the Reducibility Thesis also affects the Heuristic Thesis. For further precision, therefore, we should distinguish at least two interpretations of the Heuristic Thesis, Heuristic Thesis 1 and Heuristic Thesis 2, as we distinguished two interpretations of the Reducibility Thesis, Reducibility Thesis 1 and Reducibility Thesis 2.

Finally, we must not overlook the implications of following M for the larger social picture. For example, what effect would following M or not following M have on political ideology? Karl Popper (1952) has claimed to find a close connection between Methodological Holism and totalitarianism and Methodological Individualism and liberalism. Although Popper has never shown any logical connection between these positions in the sense defined here[1] there could be some sort of

---

[1] It is not completely clear from Popper's work whether he means by 'Methodological Individualism' or 'Methodological Holism' the same thing as I mean by these terms. If Agassi's interpretation of Popper (AGASSI 1960) is correct, there are some inportant differences between my analysis and Popper's view.

historical, sociological or psychological connection[1]. If so, it would be extremely important to know this before one advocated either methodological position. If not following M would tend to sow the seeds of totalitarianism and following M would reinforce liberalism, this surely would have to ve taken into account in our final decision to use or not use M.

ANTHROPOLOGY AND THE HEURISTIC THESIS. — Everything I have said concerning Methodological Individualism and Holism applies directly to the narrower issue of the reduction of cultural anthropology to psychology. Even if the reduction of cultural anthropology to psychology is possible or even likely — Kroeber not withstanding — it does not follow that anthropologists should devote their energies to the task of bringing this reduction about. It may be the better part of wisdom to pursue anthropology in a way that does not attempt to link up with psychology — at least at the present time. Thus for practical purposes at least it is conceivable that cultural anthropology should be an autonomous discipline despite the theoretical possibility and even likelihood of it being a branch of psycology; it may simply not be fruitful to attempt such a reduction at particular times even if such a reduction will ultimately be achieved. On the other hand it may be advisable for anthropology to give up their opposition to psychological reduction even if Kroeber is correct; the attempt to reduce although perhaps doomed to failure may have fruitful side effects and may achieve partial success. These results may make it well worth the effort. Whether cultural anthropologists should or should not take its rather traditional posture against psychological reduction is a decision anthropologists will have to make in the light of the methodological, practical and even political contingencies of the day.

Edmonton, University of Alberta, Center for Theoretical Psychology.

M. MARTIN

---

[1] Popper's main argument, as I understand it, is that holistic methodology is connected with holistic morality, i.e. the subservience of the individual to the state or group. Thus the battle against Methodological Holism is seen, by Popper, as a battle against holistic morality. However, there is surely no logical inconsistency with a Methodological Holism, at least as we have characterized it, and liberal democracy, advocation of individual rights, etc. Hence, Popper's thesis to be at all plausible must be a factual thesis — asserting some empirical connection — between these two phenomena. That there is such a connection seems dubious in the light of the present evidence.

REFERENCES

AGASSI J. (1960). - *Methodological Individualism*. British Journal of Sociology, 11: 244-270.
BIDNEY D. (1964). - *Theoretical Anthropology*. New York, Columbia University Press.
GOLDSTEIN L. (1958). - *The Two Theses of Methodological Individualism*. British Journal for the Philosophy of Science, 9: 11.
GOLDSTEIN L. (1959). - *Ontological Social Science*. American Anthropologist, 61: 290-298.
GOODMAN N. (1951). - *The Structure of Appearance*. Cambridge, Mass., Harvard University Press.
HEMPEL C. G. (1964). - *Aspects of Scientific Explanation*. New York, Free Press.
KROEBER A. L. (1917). - *The Superorganic*. American Anthropologist, 19: 163-212.
KROEBER A. L. (1952). - *The Nature of Culture*. Chicago, University of Chicago Press.
NAGEL E. (1961). - *The Structure of Science*. New York, Harcourt, Brace and World.
POPPER K. (1952). - *The Open Society and Its Enemies*. London, Routledge and Kegan Paul.
POPPER K. (1959). - *The Logic of Scientific Discovery*. New York, Basic Books.
QUINE W. V. O. (1960). - *Word and Object*. New York, Wiley and Sons.
SAPIR E. (1917). - *Do We Need A «Superorganic»?* American Anthropologist, 19: 441-447.
SCHEFFLER, I. (1963). - *The Anatomy of Inquiry*. New York, Knopf and Sons.
WHITING J. W. M. and CHILD I. L. (1953). - *Child Training and Personality*. New Haven, Yale University Press.

PART V: TECHNIQUES OF VALIDATION

The social scientist seems to use methods that are vastly different from those of the natural scientist. Thus, for example, one can hardly imagine a greater difference in methods than between those of a psychoanalyst or field anthropologist and those of an experimental physicist. Moreover, in the social sciences the evidence is sometimes so subtle and theory is so little developed that predictions are not made by deduction from a well articulated theory and a statement of initial conditions. Rather, they are made by experts who seem to have an intuitive feel for what will happen.

However, compelling as such differences in methodology and prediction may seem, they do not provide an adequate basis for the thesis that the methodology of the social sciences is fundamentally different from the methodology of the natural sciences. Not all social sciences involve clinical situations or field work. The differences between the methods of an experimental psychologist and an experimental physicist do not appear to be basic. Moreover, not all natural scientists work in the laboratory. Some biologists observe animals in their natural habitats and in this respect their work seems hardly different from that of the field anthropologist. There are even basic similarities in the methods of an experimental physicist and a clinical psychologist or field anthropologist; for example, they test their hypotheses by deducing consequences from them and testing these consequences against the evidence. In fact, differences in method only enter in once these consequences are tested against the evidence; that is, they are differences in techniques of validation.

There is also a similarity in the use made of experts by the social sciences and at least the applied natural sciences. In diagnostic prediction in clinical medicine, as in psychiatry, direct appeal to expert judgement is not uncommon. Direct appeal to expert judgement is even made when the subject matter is not a living organism. Thus there is no well articulated theory and statement of initial conditions that can yield reliable inferences about whether a violin is a Stradivari. But reliable inferences are made by members of the Hill family, experts in violin appraising.

Now one important job of the philosopher of the social sciences is to evaluate critically the techniques of validation used in the social sciences. In two papers in this section two such techniques are discussed; in "The Scientific Status of Psychoanalytic Clinical Evidence" the technique of validating clinical interpretations by means of free association is critically considered;[1] in "Understanding and Participant Observation in Cultural and Social Anthropology"[2] the great reliance on participant observation by anthropologists is evaluated.

In this latter paper the notion of scientific understanding is analysed and various senses of "understanding" are distinguished from scientific understanding. The analysis has relevance to the notion of Verstehen. As we saw in some of the essays in Part III, it has been argued that the use of Verstehen in the social sciences constitutes a methodological difference between the natural and social sciences. As we also saw, despite what some positivists might say, Verstehen has not usually been considered to be a way of validating hypotheses (or indeed a way of generating hypotheses). However, Michael Scriven has argued that Verstehen *is* a technique of validating hypotheses both in the social sciences and the natural sciences. Furthermore, despite the positivists, he has defended such a validating use of Verstehen by linking Verstehen to the use of experts in validating hypotheses. In the third paper in this section, "Justification by Verstehen," Scriven's interesting interpretation of Verstehen is critically considered. The major question is whether Scriven's interpretation of Verstehen in terms of experts is in conflict with the standard positivists' view of science as Scriven claims it is. Howard Cohen's critique of Scriven's interpretation of Verstehen is also discussed in the context of the use of experts in historical inquiry and violin appraising.

Footnotes

1. This paper is criticized by Sydney Margolin in "A Rejoinder to Dr. Martin," Inquiry, 7, 1964, 37-46 and Björn Christiansen in "Comments on the Issues Raised by Dr. Martin," Inquiry, 7, 1964, 47-79.

2. For comments on this paper see Judith B. Agassi, "Theory and Practice of Participant-Observation," and Sidney W. Mintz, "Participant-Observation and the Collection of Data," in Boston Studies in the Philosophy of Science, Vol. 4, 1966-68 (eds) R.S. Cohen and M.W. Wartofsky.

THE SCIENTIFIC STATUS OF PSYCHOANALYTIC CLINICAL EVIDENCE

by

Michael Martin

The main source of evidence for psychoanalytic theory comes from the clinical situation. Yet recent empirical studies in verbal conditioning and the social psychology of persuasion indicate that psychoanalysts and therapists of other schools are speciously validating their own theories by unwittingly influencing their patients' behavior. In the light of this evidence it is small wonder that psychoanalysts consistently 'validate' psychoanalytic theory in their clinical practice while therapists of other schools 'validate' their own theories in *their* clinical practice. Although Freud was not unaware of the problems of 'suggestion' and the conflicting evidence of rival schools of psychotherapy, he never met these problems successfully. Contemporary psychoanalysts have added little to Freud's original position. One recent attempt, by Fritz Schmidl, to formulate new criteria for the correctness of psychoanalytic clinical interpretations, does not completely escape the problem of suggestion and has new problems of its own.

It is well known that clinical data obtained from patients in the psychoanalytic session are considered by psychoanalysts to be the most important type of evidence for psychoanalytic theory. Thus Mortimer Ostow cites 'the rich source [of data] provided by twelve hours a day in the consulting room'[1] when the evidential ground of psychoanalysis is questioned, and David Rapaport notes that 'the major body of positive evidence for the theory lies in the field of accumulated clinical observations'.[2] It becomes important, therefore, to examine the clinical situation as a source of data for psychoanalysis.

Now Freud wrote repeatedly on the techniques of psychoanalytic therapy[3] and illustrated his techniques in case studies, and his followers have continued to elaborate and refine his initial proposals.[4] The neurotic patient reclining on a couch, free-associating with the analyst sitting behind maintaining a quiet attentiveness or an 'evenly-hovering attention', as Freud once called it,[5] constitutes a scene so well known it need not be elaborated upon here. Yet despite the importance that psychoanalysts attribute to the clinical evidence which is supposed to emerge from this well-known situation, *the logic of the validation* of clinical reconstruction is a subject too seldom critically considered.[6]

FREUD'S VIEWS ON CLINICAL VALIDATION

In a short paper in 1938 called 'Constructions in Analysis'[7] Freud gave his most systematic statement on the nature of the validation of psychoanalytic clinical interpretations. Freud argued that a simple verbal response of 'Yes' or 'No' by the patient to an interpretation presented to him is never conclusive evidence that the interpretation is correct. Freud did not deny that verbal acknowledgment by the patient is a strong source of confirmatory evidence for an interpretation; rather he denied that verbal acknowledgment *alone* constitutes such evidence. Actually, verbal acknowledgment by the patient of the correctness of the interpretation presented to him by the analyst (what Freud called direct confirmation) that tied in with the patient's subsequent free association and reports of dreams (indirect confirmation) was considered by Freud to be the strongest sort of confirmatory evidence.

It should be pointed out, however, that Freud did not require this verbal acknowledgment to be based on the recall of repressed memories of the events posited in the interpretation; he emphasized that it was sufficient that the patient become 'assured' of the correctness of the interpretation although the patient did not recall the past events.

THE TWO MAIN PROBLEMS IN THE VALIDATION OF CLINICAL INTERPRETATIONS

Freud's views on the validation of psychoanalytic clinical interpretations have a great deal of initial plausibility. To hear Freud tell the story, in order to explain to the patient the patient's behavior, he is doing nothing more than proposing hypotheses which become validated by certain subsequent evidence, i.e., acceptance by the patient (direct confirmation) combined with other behavior, e.g. certain kinds of free association (indirect confirmation). Freud was aware, however, that despite the apparent legitimacy and innocuousness of this clinical procedure important objections could be raised and he returned to these objections again and again in his writings.

First of all, there was the problem of 'suggestion'. It could be argued that Freud was subtly influencing his patients to act and talk in ways which validated his interpretations. In other words, Freud might actually be producing in his patients the very behavior which was supposed to count as validating evidence. If this were true, it would hardly be surprising that the psychoanalytic hypotheses became well-confirmed in the clinical situation, for the clinical procedure would be producing the very evidence that confirmed the hypotheses.

Secondly, Freud realized that the existence of rival schools of psychotherapy, resulting from schisms in the original ranks of psychoanalysis, was a source of embarrassment to psychoanalysis. How could he explain findings and theories which were different from his own and yet were derived from similar clinical situations? The members of the rival schools used methods of clinical interpretation and validation similar to his, yet came up with different results.

Freud tried to answer both of these objections. I will argue that in the light of recent empirical studies the problems of 'suggestion' and of rival theories are very closely related and that Freud did not answer either of these two objections to the scientific status of psychoanalytic clinical evidence successfully.

Suggestion

In general, Freud scornfully denied any hint that he forced or persuaded his patients to accept his interpretations. In his study of Little Hans, for example, a small boy with an animal phobia who was analyzed by the boy's father under Freud's direction, Freud attempted to answer the objection that the boy was influenced by his father — a father strongly influenced by Freud's views.[8] Freud's answer, however, consists in little more than vigorous reassurances that such influence was impossible.

His rejection of the possibility of suggestion was still evident in his last clinical writings. In 1938 Freud argued:

> The danger of our leading a patient astray by suggestion, by persuading him to accept things which we ourselves believe but which he ought not to, has certainly been enormously exaggerated. . . . I can assert without boasting that such an abuse of 'suggestion' has never occurred in my practice.[9]

It is ironic that Freud, of all people, should overlook the hypothesis that the influence of the analyst could be so subtle and insidious that the analyst as well as the patient would be unaware of it. In any case, he did seem to think of suggestion as operating only in such a way that it would be obvious to the analyst and, therefore, something that was easily detected and combated. But whether Freud's assumptions about suggestion are true cannot be determined *a priori* and recourse to carefully designed experimental studies is necessary. Moreover, in the light of recent empirical studies designed to test the influence of therapists in the clinical situation Freud's views seem naive and mistaken. We shall review this evidence in a moment. For the present we can say this evidence indicates that analysts very probably unwittingly influence their patients' verbal responses and hence speciously confirm their own theory.

Rival Schools

It is well known that Adler and Jung left the psychoanalytic movement in the early part of this century and set up their own schools of psychology and therapy. Freud was very sensitive about these splits within the ranks of psychoanalysis and returned to this subject again and again in his writings.[10] In the *New Introductory Lectures on Psychoanalysis* he stressed: 'That such splits have occurred is no argument for or against the truth of psycho-analysis'.[11] Freud, of course, is correct in this, but the important question remains: How is one to decide among the different schools? It does little good to say, as Freud does in his *History of the Psychoanalytic Movement*, 'Anyone who has followed the growth of scientific movements will know that quite similar disturbances and dissentions took place in all of them'.[12] To be sure, the history of science is full of controversy, but the question still remains of how the differences between parties are to be decided. In other fields means are available, at least in principle, by which opposing theories can be objectively tested, and by which false ones can be eliminated. In the history of the theory of gases, for instance, the controversy between the static and kinetic theories was finally decided after measuring techniques were improved and experiments were refined.[13] Today a controversy exists between scientific theories of cosmology in astral physics. But the opponents are clear on what sort of objective evidence would count against their theories and on what improvements in technology would be able to decide the issue.[14]

The situation is different in the case of psychoanalysis and its rivals. 'Verification' of clinical interpretations continues to be the main, perhaps the only, source of verification seriously accepted by therapists. But from the clinical point of view there is no way to decide among rival schools. Consider, for instance, the way Freud dismisses clinical findings that conflict with his own:

> One hears of analysts who boast that, though they have worked for dozens of years, they have never found a sign of the existence of a castration complex. We must bow our heads in recognition of this achievement, even though it is only a negative one, a piece of virtuosity in the art of overlooking and mistaking.[15]

Freud could thus dismiss Adler's theory as 'radically false' and Jung's views as 'unintelligible, muddled and confused',[16] while Jung and Adler could pay Freud similar compliments without there being any objective way available for deciding between them as long as the opposing parties relied upon clinical findings. To be sure, Freud noted that he would leave the task of refuting these rivals 'to other able workers in the field of psychoanalysis', but these 'able workers' have done little more than cite more and more clinical studies which in turn conflict with the clinical studies of their rivals.

Some Recent Empirical Studies

In the light of a recent and ever-growing body of experimental literature, it is becoming increasingly implausible to maintain that psychoanalysts do not affect their patients' behavior in the clinical situation and do not produce in their patients the very evidence that confirms the psychoanalytic interpretation. This literature, moreover, makes it understandable why rival schools of psychotherapy find confirmation *only* within their own therapeutic sessions: each school's theories are confirmed by its own practitioners in their own practice by producing in their patients the very behaviors that are supposed to be confirmatory.

The empirical evidence relevant to the problem of suggestion is so vast that it is impossible to review it completely here.[17] It will be necessary to select for discussion those experiments which bear the closest analogy to the therapeutic situation. These studies can be divided into two main groups:

(1) studies of verbal conditioning in the actual clinical situation and in situations analogous to the clinical situation; (2) studies of the psychology of persuasion in situations analogous to the clinical situation.

Verbal Conditioning

As we noted above, psychoanalysts take certain verbal responses, among other behaviors of the patient, as confirmatory evidence for their interpretations. These verbal responses may be free associations, reports of dreams, or acknowledgments of the correctness of the interpretation. Meerloo has recently remarked:

> The communication between patient and therapist ... may become itself an object of study — a fascinating world of uncharted dimensions of contact between man and his fellow man.[18]

Indeed, the communication involved in therapy and therapy-like situations *has* become an object of study.

But the results emerging from this study have completely escaped Meerloo's attention. Instead of the 'method of free association' being 'one of the best tools of self-revelation and deeper communication',[19] it looks now as if 'free' association may not be free at all, but may be determined by the therapist who, unknown to the patient or to himself, influences the patient's verbal responses so that they conform to the therapist's own theoretical bias.

In general, the experiments on verbal conditioning that have been done so far take this form: the subject behaves verbally (e.g., he talks, tells a story, answers questions, responds verbally to Rorschach cards) and the experimenter attempts to condition (e.g., by saying 'good', by smiling, by nodding) a certain class of the subject's verbal responses (e.g., the set of 'mother' responses in a story, M-responses on a Rorschach examination) without the subject being aware that conditioning is attempted. The results of the experiments indicate two things clearly: (1) verbal responses of all sorts can be conditioned; (2) the subjects are, in general, not aware that their responses are being conditioned.

Let us consider some of the experiments in detail. Some analysts draw an analogy between the psychoanalytic interview and an ordinary conversation, but deny that the content of a patient's verbal responses in the clinical situation is influenced by the listener.[20] But an experiment of Verplanck's indicates that the content of ordinary conversation (the statement of certain opinions) can be controlled by verbal conditioning methods (agreement or paraphrasing) of which the subject is unaware.[21] Hildum and Brown have shown that one can condition responses about attitudes over the phone (by saying 'good') without the subject being aware of the conditioning.[22]

Several studies indicate that the responses a subject makes to a test supposed to measure personality can be conditioned. Nuthmann showed that subjects' responses could be conditioned on a personality test simply by the examiners' uttering 'good' after those responses which were chosen to be conditioned.[23] Wiches demonstrated that examiners' smiles and nods were sufficient to condition M-responses on a Rorschach examination.[24] In both studies the subjects were unaware that their responses were being conditioned.

In psychoanalysis the recall of memories of certain kinds is supposed to constitute confirming evidence. But Quay has shown that by simply saying 'uh-huh' interviewers were able to condition verbal responses about early memories of the family.[25] Quay concludes his study by saying:

> This study has demonstrated that highly personal and emotionally charged memories can be manipulated by another person in an interview with very minimal verbal participation selectively placed after certain classes of these memories.[26]

It is well known that psychoanalysts put great emphasis on the relation of the child to his parents. In relation to men, the boy-mother relation is of crucial importance. Naturally, therefore, verbal responses of male patients about their mothers would be of great importance in validating psychoanalytic interpretations. But Krasner has shown that verbal responses about the mother figure can be conditioned in a therapy-like situation by the experimenter's nodding, smiling, or saying 'umm-hm'. Krasner's experiment makes quite plausible a suggestion made by Hildum and Brown several years before. They argued: 'The therapist who believes in the importance of the Oedipus complex could elicit Oedipal content by selective reinforcement'.[27]

Followers of non-directive therapy, a rival to psychoanalytic therapy, have maintained that changes in self-reference indicate a reorganization of the self. J. Maurice Rogers (not to be confused with Carl Rogers, the founder of non-directive therapy) has argued, however:

> Reinforcement theory, however, makes tenable an alternative explanation — that the reported changes in self-reference verbalizations are elicited via unintentional selective reinforcement by the Rogerian therapist.[28]

He goes on to report the results of his experiment, which demonstrated that in a situation analogous to the clinical situation verbal self-references could be conditioned by saying 'umm-hm' without the subject being aware of it.

The experiment of M. Dinoff et al. ties in closely with Rogers's study. They hypothesized:

> It is possible that the results which different therapists produce in therapy are determined by the individual therapist's theoretical bias and that his own emphasis will determine the nature of the data which will be obtained.[29]

To test this contention they set up the following therapy-like situation. They selected three experimental groups. Each member of each group was instructed to make up a story about the therapist, himself, and two other people. But in each group a different class of verbal responses was conditioned. The different classes of verbal responses corresponded roughly to three different theoretical approaches of psychotherapy: in the first group verbal responses about the self were conditioned (corresponding to Carl Rogers's emphasis on the reorganization of the self); in the second group verbal responses about the environment were conditioned (corresponding to Adler's emphasis on environment); and in the last group verbal responses about the therapist-client relationship were conditioned (corresponding to psychoanalysis's emphasis on the transference relationship). The investigators found that each group could be successfully conditioned in this way, and that, in general, the subjects were not aware of the fact that their verbal responses were being conditioned.

It might be argued that the experiments so far cited indicate that verbal conditioning can be performed on normal people without their being aware of it, but that we have no reason to think it can be performed on neurotics or psychotics. This would be a mistake, however. Adams et al. have demonstrated that the verbal behavior of psychotic patients can be conditioned by saying 'good' and 'fine' as well as by psychoanalytically phrased sentences;[30] Rickard et al. have shown that the periodic rational verbalizations of psychotic patients can be conditioned;[31] Leventhal has shown that neurotics and psychotics can be verbally conditioned.[32] *Indeed, a recent experiment gives us some reason to think that it is precisely the anxiety-ridden neurotic who goes to psychoanalysts who is the most easily conditioned*: Taffel has shown that there is a positive correlation between susceptibility to verbal conditioning and scores on the Taylor anxiety scale.[33]

It might be argued, further, that there is a large gap between experiments in a 'therapy-like' situation and the actual therapeutic session. To be sure, it might be said, it has been shown that the verbal behavior of subjects (analogous to patients) can be conditioned by examiners (analogous to therapists) and that the subjects are unaware of this process. It has also been shown that people with high anxiety, hence people who are likely to seek psychoanalytic help, can be more easily conditioned than people with low anxiety. But what has not been shown is that the *actual* verbal behavior of patients is in fact conditioned by *actual* psychoanalysts and that *both* patients and therapists are unaware of the conditioning.

Recent empirical studies of the content of actual recorded therapeutic sessions, however, go a long way toward closing this gap and silencing this argument. A. Bandura *et al.* have analyzed the content of *actual* recorded therapeutic sessions in terms of learning theory. They are able to account for changes in patients' verbal expressions of hostility in terms of 'avoidance' and 'approach' reactions of the therapists, i.e., in terms of punishments and rewards given unwittingly by the therapists.[34] Again, Murray has shown by a similar analysis of the content of *actual* recorded therapeutic sessions 'that the therapist employed subtle directive techniques which influence the verbal behavior of the patients'. [35] Murray notes:

> It was found that the therapist mildly approved various subcategories of independence and mildly disapproved independence anxiety, intellectual defenses, and various subcategories of sex. As would be expected from learning theory, the approved patient-content categories decreased throughout the course of psycho-therapy.[36]

In summary: The evidence from verbal conditioning studies indicates: (1) verbal conditioning of all sorts can be performed within a therapy-like experimental situation without the subject being aware of the conditioning; (2) analyses of recorded therapeutic sessions indicate that a similar procedure occurs in the actual therapeutic situation without the patient or the therapist being aware of the process. Naturally, more studies of verbal conditioning will have to be performed before we know to what extent this conditioning is possible and what factors affect it. But the fact remains that analysts are ignoring the experimental facts when they deny their own influence on the content of their patients' verbalizations; hence they are ignoring the possibility that they may unwittingly be speciously validating their own theories.

Persuasion Studies

The studies in verbal conditioning thus far considered have been drawn from the field of learning theory. They indicate that the therapeutic situation can be considered as a learning situation in which the patient, by means of unnoticed reinforcement from the therapist, learns to respond with a certain class of verbal responses. This class of verbal responses is then counted as evidence for the 'correctness' of the therapist's interpretation.

But there are data from a different field of psychology, namely the social psychology of communication and persuasion, that are relevant for showing that therapists are unwittingly influencing their patients. It has been suspected for some time by critics of psychoanalysis that psychoanalysts, because of their academic degrees, their plush offices, and the general psychoanalytic mystique, not only influence the patient to accept their interpretations, but actually change the person's concept of himself to conform to the analyst's interpretation. Until now, however, these suspicions were based primarily on evidence of the influence of prestige factors on attitude change outside the therapeutic situation.[37]

Recently, however, a most elaborate and ingenious experiment was carried out by Allen E. Bergin to test the influence of a therapeutic interpretation on a subject when it is given by a person possessing characteristics which convey trustworthiness and expertness to the subject.[38] Bergin's experiment stands as a model of imaginative and carefully designed experimental procedure, and its results make extremely plausible the suspicion mentioned above. For Bergin has shown that the characteristic of high credibility in a therapist can influence a patient to accept the therapist's interpretation and can even change the patient's concept of himself to correspond to the interpretation although in fact the interpretation is false.

Roughly, Bergin's experiment took this form.[39] One group of subjects (college students) was placed in a situation of high credibility and the other in a situation of low credibility. Members of the first group reported individually to the Psychiatry Department of the Stanford Medical Center. The experimenter assumed the role of Director of a Personality Assessment Project. To establish the experimenter's prestige the subject was sent to the experimenter by a receptionist and 'the experimental room was furnished with elaborate equipment, a couch, an impressive array of medical and psychological volumes, and a large portrait of Freud'.[40] The subject was told that the study was concerned with people's accuracy in evaluating their own personality.

The subject rated himself on a masculinity-femininity scale and afterward was 'tested' by an elaborate and impressive battery of tests. The battery of tests was designed to do one thing: to impress the subject with the rigor and scientific nature of the procedure (the results of the test were not used). In the second meeting with the experimenter, who still pretended to be the Director of a Personality Assessment Project, the subject was shown a diagram that was supposed to summarize the test material (actually the diagram was prearranged). The validity of the test procedure was emphasized, and the discrepancy between the subject's self-rating and the 'true' measure of masculinity-femininity was calculated from the diagram. The subject was then asked to rate himself again on the masculinity-femininity scale and this score was compared to the first self-rating.

The second group of subjects (college students) reported to a 'relatively decrepit room in the basement of the Education Building'.[41] Here each subject filled out a self-rating form on the masculinity-femininity scale. In the next session the subject was introduced to a high-school freshman who supposedly was another subject. Actually this 'other subject' was a confederate of the experimenter. The subject was told to rate the high-school freshman on the masculinity-femininity scale and told that the high-school freshman would rate him on the same scale. The confederate, however, only pretended to rate the subject; the rating was prearranged. Then the experimenter showed the subject the difference between the high-school freshman's rating and the subject's own rating, taking care to imply 'that high-school students may not be the best judges of the traits of others'. The subject was then asked to rate himself again. The differences between the first self-rating and this one were computed.

The results of the experiment were as one might have expected. When the 'true' estimates were made in a situation of high credibility, the subjects changed their self-ratings in the direction of the 'true' estimate.[42] The subjects were, in general, unaware that they had changed their ratings. On the other hand, when the 'true' estimates were given in a situation of low credibility, no significant changes occurred in the subjects' self-ratings.

Still, it may be argued that we do not know if the *kind* of person who actually goes to psychoanalysts is persuasible or suggestible. Perhaps persons in psychotherapy are not suggestible at all; if so, Bergin's experiment would not be telling. But Imber *et al.* have shown that there is a definite correlation between suggestibility and the tendency of patients to remain in psychotherapy.[43] So the result of Imber's study seems to close even this route of escape: *therapists have a longer time to influence the very patients who seem to be most suggestible.*

If the therapist's capacity to change a patient's attitude is a function of the therapist's prestige, and if the most suggestible patients stay in therapy the longest, it is hardly surprising to find patients talking the jargon of the school to which their therapist belongs. Thus Heine, in a study of the reports of patients in psychoanalytic, non-directive, and Adlerian therapy about the changes that took place within them during therapy,[44] found that patients explained the changes along the 'school' lines of their therapist.

In summary: The social psychology of persuasion suggests that prestige factors alone might influence the patient to change his attitude and hence validate the therapist's interpretation. Bergin's experiment indicates that this may be precisely what occurs in therapy. Moreover, it may account for the fact that different schools tend to verify their theories only within their own clinical situation.

SCHMIDL'S VIEWS ON VALIDATION

An examination of psychoanalytic literature on the logic of the validation of psychoanalytic clinical interpretation shows that in general there has been little change from Freud's original view; most psychoanalysts still seem to validate their interpretations by evidence obtained within the clinical situation.[45]

However, there is at least one important exception: Fritz Schmidl has produced one of the most systematic and novel approaches to the validation of clinical interpretation to be found in the recent literature.[46] Some aspects of Schmidl's views are exempt from the criticism given above since he does not think clinical interpretations can be validated completely within the therapeutic situation. For those aspects which he does think can be clinically validated he suggests a criterion different from Freud's. Let us examine his views in detail.

Schmidl's Views Considered

Fritz Schmidl argues that the correctness of an interpretation is constituted by (1) the correctness of 'the general principles' which 'determine the direction of the interpretation', and (2) the degree to which the specific 'gestalt' of the event to be interpreted 'fits' into the gestalt of the event which, according to the interpretation, is supposed to be causally related to it.

(1) Schmidl maintains that in psychoanalytic interpretations certain general principles are presupposed. Using the case of the 19-year-old girl with an obsessional neurosis discussed by Freud in *A General Introduction to Psychoanalysis*[47] as an example, he maintains that in Freud's interpretation of the girl's behavior two general principles are presupposed: (a) certain sexual symbols, i.e., clocks and watches, as well as flowerpots and vases, are interpreted as symbols representing the female genitals; (b) the Oedipus complex. Schmidl goes on to argue that the validation of any inference made from these general principles presupposes the *scientific* validity of the general principles themselves. He maintains:

> Since an inference [from a general principle] can be valid only if the general principle is valid on which it is based, we shall have to concern ourselves first with the problem as to what extent psycho-analytic theory has been or can be validated scientifically.[48]

In his remarks that follow and in his brief discussion of Sears[49] and Hilgard,[50] it becomes clear that Schmidl means by 'validated scientifically' something different from validation by clinical experience. Apparently Schmidl does not think that the general principles, e.g. the Oedipus complex, can be validated scientifically by clinical means, but rather that clinical interpretations must presuppose certain general principles validated by non-clinical objective standards.

(2) Schmidl argues, however, that Freud's interpretations are 'not exclusively' based upon these general principles. He maintains that Freud also connects 'the specific content of his patient's symptoms'[51] with specific material from the life of the patient. Schmidl argues that this connecting process is *different* from accounting for the behavior of a patient by means of general principles, because this aspect of the interpretation 'goes beyond' the general principles assumed in 'the framework' of the individual life of the patient, a life that has unique significance.

Schmidl, therefore, concludes that standard experimental methods for validating general principles are inapplicable for validating interpretations connecting the past and present of an individual life. Schmidl suggests instead a purely formal way of validating interpretations of this kind. He argues that the criterion of correctness for this aspect of an interpretation is whether the gestalt of the facts to be interpreted 'fits' the gestalt of the events that are causally related to it according to the interpretation.

Although it is not completely clear what Schmidl means by 'the fitting together of two gestalts', he gives an example to illustrate his point. This example, the famous case of the disappointed bride, is taken from Freud's *A General Introduction to Psychoanalysis*.[52] Schmidl analyzes the 'gestalt' of the patient's symptom in this way:

(a) Patient runs from one room into the other.
(b) She rings for her maid.
(c) She takes up a certain position in order to enable the maid to see a certain spot.
(d) This spot is a mark on a tablecloth.
(e) The process is repeated several times within a day.
(f) The elements (a) to (e) form part of one symptom. The 'gestalt' of the allegedly traumatic wedding night is broken down by Schmidl into a similar pattern.

(a)' During the wedding night the husband ran from his bedroom into that of the patient.
(b)' He expressed his anxiety about the maid missing the blood spot on the bed linen by saying, 'It is enough to disgrace one in the eyes of the maid who does the bed'.
(c)' He made a mark with red ink on
(d)' the bed linen.
(e)' He repeated his going from his to the patient's bedroom several times.
(f)' The fact that all this happened during one night, the wedding night, combines the elements (a)' to (e)' into a unit.

Schmidl seems to believe that the 'fitting together' of patterns of the two events shows that there is a significant relation between them. He notes that there are six factual elements which correlate with each other and he suggests that the degree of validation of the interpretation would correspond with the number of correlated elements, i.e., the more the elements of the gestalts matched, the more the relation between the two events would be validated. He notes: 'The idea suggests itself that there would be a positive correlation between the number of corresponding elements in the two gestalten constituting the interpretation and the degree of validity of the interpretation'.[53] Because of the perfect match of the two gestalts in the case of the disappointed bride, Schmidl cites with approval Freud's statement: 'There could no longer be any doubt about the connection between the current obsessive act and the scene of the wedding night'.[54]

In summary: Schmidl has argued that there are certain general principles involved in every interpretation. These general principles must be validated scientifically, where 'validated scientifically' involves objective experimental procedures, not clinical experience. Yet Schmidl argues that there is another aspect of an interpretation which does not have to do with general principles but rather with the unique individual; this aspect of the interpretation connects some earlier unique events in the person's life with some later unique events. Interpretations of these connections are to be validated according to the degree to which the gestalt of the event postulated as causally relevant in the interpretation and the facts to be interpreted 'fit together'. Although the criterion of 'fitting together' is never explicated fully, part of Schmidl's meaning is that the degree of the correlation of the number of elements in the gestalts indicates the degree of validity of the interpretations.

Critique of Schmidl's Views

(1) Schmidl makes the validation of the general principles used in psychoanalytic clinical interpretations dependent upon *non-clinical* objective procedures. We may infer, therefore, that any failure to confirm these general principles by non-clinical means indicates that clinical interpretations based upon them are unjustified. But Schmidl either does not realize or does not accept the implications of his position, for many of the most basic principles used in clinical interpretations have not been validated by objective methods. Indeed, Schmidl fails to realize that Sears's survey, which he cites with apparent approval, does not show that the Oedipus complex is validated. Indeed Sears argues that the Oedipus complex is one of the most suspect of all Freudian notions.[55] But the Oedipus complex is, we should recall, one of the general principles Schmidl finds presupposed in Freud's clinical interpretation of the 19-year-old girl with an obsessional neurosis. Hence, the very clinical interpretation Schmidl takes from Freud and uses as an example becomes invalid by his own criterion, i.e., the criterion of objective, non-clinical validation.

(2) Schmidl's criterion for the validation of the connections within the life history of a person can be considered from two points of view: (a) it can be asked if there is any need for a different kind of method of validating a clinical interpretation; (b) it can be asked whether Schmidl's own notion of validation, i.e., the fitting together of two 'gestalts', is adequate. Let us start with the first question.

(a) Schmidl's argument for the need of a different kind of method of validation turns in part on the standard arguments of defenders of the ideographic sciences, i.e., the appeal to the unique aspect of the individual person — a person who 'presents an indefinite number of experiences falling within an indefinite number of frames of reference'. But the differences between the ideographic sciences, which allegedly deal only with the unique and individual, and the nomothetic sciences, which allegedly deal only with the universal and general, have recently been so thoroughly criticized by philosophers of science[56] that it seems commonplace to make the following points:
(i) The nomothetic sciences do not merely deal with general laws; singular statements, statements of initial conditions, play an important role. Indeed, the 'general principles' of psychoanalysis that Schmidl cites *must* be used with some singular statements of initial conditions before they can be used in explanations of individual events.
(ii) The ideographic sciences do not deal just with individuals in all their concreteness or with an 'indefinite number of experiences' within an 'indefinite number of frames of reference'; they abstract and select from the properties of the individual they are studying. Moreover, the ideographic sciences tacitly assume a number of general laws that are never explicitly stated or acknowledged.

Now the curious thing about Schmidl's position is that he *admits* that psychoanalytic interpretations appeal to general principles. He argues, however, that there is another aspect of the interpretation, namely, the connection between past and present within an individual's life that cannot be accounted for by subsumption under these general principles. But, outside of the valid point that singular statements of initial conditions are needed, as well as some relevant general principles, to account for any event or sequence of events in a person's life, it is not clear what Schmidl's argument amounts to. In any case, the examples used by Schmidl to illustrate his point can all be analyzed in terms of certain general principles and statements of initial conditions.

Schmidl notes:

> Further inspection of the two interpretations [i.e., (1) clocks, watches, flowerpots and vases are symbolic of the female genitals; (2) the peculiar condition that the pillow must not touch the board is interpreted as a magic ceremony in order to keep man and woman, i.e. father and mother, apart], however, shows that they are not exclusively based upon the two general

principles [(1) sexual symbolism and (2) Oedipus complex]. In both interpretations Freud connects the specific content of his patient's symptom with specific material from her life experience. Discussing the patient's anxiety that the flowerpots and vases may break, Freud refers to an incident in her childhood when she had fallen while carrying a glass or porcelain vessel, and had cut her finger, which had bled badly. This incident, then, is connected with the patient's later concern about bleeding which, in turn, was part of her phantasies on defloration.[57]

The explanatory connections in this girl's life that Schmidl mentions can all be analyzed in terms of genetic laws of a probabilistic character and statements of initial conditions. Thus Freud seems tacitly to assume a law, whose exact content is unclear, but which states in effect:

(1) Girls who cut themselves with objects that are unconscious symbols for the female genitals will often later associate this bleeding with adolescent phantasy about defloration and consequently manifest anxiety about breaking symbolic objects of this sort.[58]

This probabilistic statement is combined with certain initial conditions:

(2) This girl cut herself in a fall while carrying a glass vessel, an unconscious symbol for the female genitals.

(1) and (2) together make probable the event in question which is described by the following statement:

(3) This girl had associated her bleeding with adolescent phantasy about defloration and consequently manifested anxiety about the breaking of the flowerpot, etc. in her room.

It should be noted that in the use of premise (2) one must tacitly assume some other probabilistic law and a set of initial conditions that are so obvious to psychoanalysts they hardly need mentioning, namely:

(2) (a) Receptacles are often unconscious symbols for female genitals.

(2) (b) This is a glass vessel.

(2) (a) and (2) (b) make probable:

(2) (c) This glass vessel is an unconscious symbol for the female genitals.

Naturally other probabilistic laws and initial conditions must be assumed in order to give a complete account of the clinical picture. It should be noted, however, that the probabilistic laws (2) (a) and (1) which are at least tacitly involved in this explanation could both be validated in the same way,[59] namely, by empirical investigation aimed at determining whether the probabilistic laws hold. It should be noted that Schmidl remarks on (2) (a), the 'general principle' of sexual symbolism of receptacles: 'If experiments, e.g., hypnotic experiments, show that a significant number of people use receptacles as symbols for the female genitals, we assume that this particular theory is validated'.[60] In an analogous manner (1), the genetic law, could be validated; i.e., if investigations showed that a sufficient number of girls who cut themselves with objects symbolic of female genitals associate their bleeding with phantasies about defloration and manifest anxiety about the falling and breaking of similar objects, 'We would assume that this particular theory is validated'.

To be sure, experiments of the latter kind would be more difficult to perform than Schmidl's suggested hypnotic experiment to test the symbolic significance of receptacles. For one reason, such experiments would involve longitudinal studies that would take years to execute; we would also be hesitant, for obvious ethical reasons, to perform them. Nevertheless, these practical and ethical considerations have nothing to do with the *logic* of the validation; in principle, both probabilistic laws (1) and (2)(a) could be validated in the same way.

I must conclude, therefore, that Schmidl has not shown that the genetic relation postulated to hold within an individual life necessitates a different pattern of analysis, hence different methods of validation.

(6) We have argued so far that Schmidl has not shown the necessity for a new way of validating clinical interpretations. But it can also be asked whether the 'fitting together' of two 'gestalts' is by itself either a necessary or a sufficient condition for indicating a significant causal relationship between the earlier and the later events in a person's life.

It should be clear that it is not a necessary one. Two events can be causally related without their gestalts having the same number of elements. Indeed, in the very example that Schmidl gives there could have been a different number of elements in each gestalt and there still could have been a causal relationship between the two events. I see no reason *a priori* why the disappointed bride might not have manifested only *one* symptom, e.g., (a) 'Patient runs from one room into the other', from among the several which are supposed to have occurred, with a significant relation between this symptom and the events (a)'–(f)' of the wedding night nevertheless holding. But using Schmidl's criterion of a correct interpretation this relation would have to be discounted because the gestalts of the two events do not fit together: one had six elements and the other only one.

But his criterion is not only not a necessary one for causal significance, it is not a sufficient one. It is clear that there *could* be many events with the same number of elements or the same form in a person's life that would have no significant relation to one another. But what is worse, in one respect the unique aspect of Freud's theory is completely clouded by Schmidl's account. Surely it was not just the *number* of correlated parts in each event that led Freud to think that the events in question were related; rather it was the knowledge that traumatic events often lead to neurotic behavior and that neurotic behavior manifests itself in a symbolic form related to its cause. Thus Schmidl's criterion of the fitting together of two gestalts gains plausibility only because of the tacit assumption of a probabilistic law whose exact content is unclear, but which would state in effect:

The events connected with a traumatic experience are often repeated in symbolic form in neurotic behavior.

To be sure, the behavior *might* take the symbolic form of element-to-element matching Schmidl uses as a paradigm. But it might take some other form. In any case, this probabilistic law is validated in the standard manner — not by the correlation of elements in each event. In the clinical situation it would have to be shown that there were regularities between manifest neurotic (symbolic) symptoms of a certain kind and *reports* by patients about traumatic incidents of which the neurotic behavior is symbolic. But we have shown that the evidential value of such reports is dubious because of the unwitting influence of analysts on patients' verbal reports. Because of this, independent evidence of such regularities would have to be found outside the clinical situation. Moreover, it would not be enough to show that symbolic behavior of such and such a kind occurred with a certain relative frequency p when traumatic events occurred. One would also have to show that the relative frequency of symbolic behavior in the absence of traumatic events, or the relative frequency of the non-occurrence of symbolic behavior in the presence of traumatic events, is significantly different from p.

I must conclude that Schmidl has not shown that the criterion of the fitting together of two gestalts or patterns of events in a person's life indicates any significant relation between them; his criterion is neither a necessary nor a sufficient condition for this relation. The only sense that can be made of his thesis of corresponding gestalts is to assume that a genetic law of a probabilistic character holds between the traumatic events and neurotic behavior which is symbolic of it. But this law would be verified by standard methods of verification, and not by an element-to-element matching of patterns of the two events.

In summary: Fritz Schmidl's account of the validation of psychoanalytic interpretations is untenable. In contending that psychoanalysis uses 'general principles' that must be scientifically validated he overlooks the fact that the general principles he mentions have not been scientifically validated. His thesis that another method of validation is needed for connections within a person's life is mistaken, for the standard methods of validation are adequate here. Moreover, his own criterion of an element-to-element matching of the two gestalts or pattern of events within the person's life is neither a necessary nor a sufficient condition for a significant causal relation.

Conclusion

Our arguments have thrown doubt on psychoanalytic clinical evidence and, therefore, on the 'validation' of psychoanalysis within the clinical situation. We have seen how Freud believed clinical constructions could be validated. Verbal acknowledgment of the correctness of the interpretation was not important, according to Freud, unless it was combined with other evidence, e.g., free association of a certain kind. But we have seen that there are two great problems in the acceptance of his account; namely the problem of suggestion and the problem of rival schools.

We have argued that Freud was aware of these problems but never met them satisfactorily. Moreover, recent empirical evidence from learning theory and social psychology seems to make highly probable the thesis that psychoanalysts are unwittingly producing in their patients the very evidence that validates their theory. There are equally good grounds for thinking that other schools of therapy are doing the same thing.

Except for Fritz Schmidl's work, recent accounts of the validation of psychoanalytic clinical interpretation add little to Freud's original view. But an examination of Schmidl's views indicates that they are untenable; in particular, his method could not be used to validate psychoanalytic interpretations.

We must conclude that if psychoanalysis is to be validated, it must be by some non-clinical means so that the influence of the therapist is eliminated. There have been numerous attempts to validate psychoanalytic theory by these non-clinical methods but their review and interpretation cannot be attempted here.

NOTES

1 Mortimer Ostow, 'The Structural Model: Ego, Id and Superego', *Conceptual and Methodological Problems in Psychoanalysis*, ed. L. Bellak, Annals of the New York Academy of Sciences, Vol. 76, Art. 4, p. 1134.
2 David Rapaport, 'The Structure of Psychoanalytic Theory: A Systematizing Attempt', *Psychology: A Study of a Science*, ed. S. Koch, McGraw-Hill, New York 1959, III, p. 140.
3 See Freud's papers on technique, in Sigmund Freud, *Collected Papers*, Basic Books, New York 1959, II, pp. 285–392.
4 See Karl Menninger, *Theory of Psychoanalytic Technique*, Basic Books, New York 1959; Trygve Braatoy, *Fundamentals of Psychoanalytic Technique*, Wiley, New York 1954; Otto Fenichel, 'Problems of Psychoanalytic Technique', *Psychoanalytic Quarterly*, New York 1941.
5 Sigmund Freud, 'Recommendations for Physicians on the Psychoanalytic Method of Treatment', *Collected Papers*, II, p. 324.
6 See Judd Marmor, 'Validation of Psychoanalytic Techniques', *Journal of the American Psychoanalytic Association*, III, 1955, pp. 496–505; Lawrence S. Kubie, 'Problems and Techniques of Psychoanalytic Validation and Progress', *Psychoanalysis as Science*, ed. E. Pumpian-Mindlin, Stanford University Press, Stanford 1952, pp. 74–90; Rudolph M. Loewenstein, 'The Problem of Interpretation', *Psychoanalytic Quarterly*, 20, 1951, pp. 1–14: Rudolph M. Loewenstein, 'Some Thoughts on Interpretation in the Theory and Practice of Psychoanalysis', *The Psychoanalytic Study of the Child*, Vol. XIII, pp. 127–50; Susan Isaacs, 'Criteria for Interpretation,' *International Journal of Psychoanalysis*, 20, 1939, pp. 143–60; J. Reid and J. Finesinger, 'Inference Testing in Psychotherapy', *American Journal of Psychiatry*, 107, 1950-1, pp. 894–900; Fritz Schmidl, 'The Problem of Scientific Validation in Psychoanalytic Interpretations', *International Journal of Psychoanalysis*, 1955, pp. 105–14; Ernest Kris, 'Nature and Validation of Psychoanalytic Propositions', *Readings in Philosophy of Science*, ed. P. Wiener, Charles Scribner's Sons, New York 1953, pp. 241–3.
7 Sigmund Freud, 'Constructions in Analysis', *Collected Papers*, V, pp. 358–71.
8 Sigmund Freud, 'Analysis of a Phobia in a Five-Year-Old Boy', *Collected Papers*, III, pp. 243–8.
9 Sigmund Freud, 'Constructions in Analysis', *Collected Papers*, V, pp. 363–4.
10 See S. Freud, *New Introductory Lectures on Psychoanalysis*, W. W. Norton and Co., New York 1933, pp. 191–7.
11 Ibid., p. 195.
12 Sigmund Freud, *History of the Psychoanalytic Movement*, *The Basic Writings of Sigmund Freud*, ed. A. A. Brill, Modern Library, New York 1938, p. 964.

[13] Gerald Holton and Duane H. D. Roller, *Foundations of Modern Physical Science*, Addison-Wesley Publishing Co., Reading 1958, pp. 365–458.
[14] H. Bondi et al., *Rival Theories of Cosmology*, Oxford University Press, London 1960, pp. 34–60.
[15] Sigmund Freud, 'Some Psychological Consequences of the Anatomical Distinction between the Sexes', *Collected Papers*, V, p. 192n.
[16] Sigmund Freud, *History of the Psychoanalytic Movement, The Basic Writings of Sigmund Freud*, p. 972.
[17] For reviews of the experimental literature on verbal conditioning see L. Krasner, 'Studies of the Conditioning of Verbal Behavior', *Psychol. Bull.*, 1958, 55, pp. 148–70; K. Salzinger, 'Experimental Manipulation of Verbal Behavior: A Review', *J. Gen. Psychol.*, 1959, 61, pp. 65–94.
[18] Joost A. M. Meerloo, 'Psychoanalysis as an Experiment in Communication', *Psychoanalytic Review*, 46, 1959, p. 75.
[19] Ibid.
[20] See Siegfried Bernfeld, 'The Facts of Observation in Psychoanalysis', *Journal of Psychology*, 1941, 12, pp. 23–25.
[21] William S. Verplanck, 'The Control of the Content of Conversation: Reinforcement of Statements of Opinion', *Journal of Abnormal and Social Psychology*, 50, 1955, pp. 668–76.
[22] Donald C. Hildum and Roger W. Brown, 'Verbal Reinforcement and Interviewer Bias', *Journal of Abnormal and Social Psychology*, 53, 1956, pp. 108–11.
[23] Anne M. Nuthmann, 'Conditioning of a Response on a Personality Test', *Journal of Abnormal and Social Psychology*, 54, 1957, pp. 19–23.
[24] Thomas A. Wiches, 'Examiner Influence in a Testing Situation', *Journal of Consulting Psychology*, 20, 1956, pp. 23–26; see also D. L. Miller and E. L. Walke, 'The Examiner's Influence on the Rorschach Protocol', *Journal of Consulting Psychology*, 17, 1953, pp. 424–8.
[25] Herbert Quay, 'The Effect of Verbal Reinforcement on the Recall of Early Memories', *Journal of Abnormal and Social Psychology*, 59, 1959, pp. 254–7.
[26] Ibid., p. 256.
[27] Hildum and Brown, op. cit., p. 108.
[28] J. Maurice Rogers, 'Operant Conditioning in a Quasi-Therapy Setting', *Journal of Abnormal and Social Psychology*, 60, 1960, p. 247.
[29] M. Dinoff et al., 'An Experimental Analogue of Three Psychotherapeutic Approaches', *Journal of Clinical Psychology*, 16, 1960, p. 70.
[30] Henry E. Adams et al., 'The Differential Effect of Psychoanalytically Derived Interpretations and Verbal Conditioning in Schizophrenics', *American Psychologist*, 16, 1961, p. 404. I am indebted to Adams et al. for a copy of their paper of which only an abstract was published in *American Psychologist*.
[31] Henry C. Rickard et al., 'Verbal Manipulation in a Psychotherapeutic Relationship', *Journal of Clinical Psychology*, 16, 1960, pp. 364–7.
[32] Allan M. Leventhal, 'The Effect of Diagnostic Category and Reinforcer on Learning without Awareness', *Journal of Abnormal and Social Psychology*, 59, 1959, pp. 162–6.
[33] Charles Taffel, 'Anxiety and the Conditioning of Verbal Behavior', *Journal of Abnormal and Social Psychology*, 51, 1955, pp. 496–501.
[34] Albert Bandura et al., 'Psychotherapists' Approach-Avoidance Reaction to Patients' Expressions of Hostility', *Journal of Consulting Psychology*, 24, 1960, pp. 1–8.

[35] Edward J. Murray, 'A Content Analysis Method for Studying Psychotherapy', *Psychological Monographs*, 1956, 70, No. 420, p. 25.
[36] Ibid., p. 23.
[37] See C. I. Hovland and W. Weiss, 'The Influence of Source Credibility on Communication Effectiveness', *Publ. Opin. Quart.*, 1951, 15, pp. 635–50; C. I. Hovland, I. L. Janis, and H. H. Kelly, *Communication and Persuasion*, Yale University Press, New Haven 1953; C. I. Hovland and I. L. Janis (eds.), *Personality and Persuasibility*, Yale University Press, New Haven 1959; P. H. Tannenbaum, 'Initial Attitude Toward Source and Concept as Factors in Attitude Change Through Communication', *Publ. Opin. Quart.*, 1956, 20, pp. 413–25; F. G. Zimbardo, 'Involvement and Communication Discrepancy as Determinants of Opinion Conformity', *Journal of Abnormal and Social Psychology*, 1960, 60, pp. 86–94.
[38] Allen E. Bergin, 'Personality "Interpretation" as Dissonant Persuasive Communication', *American Psychologist*, 16, 1961, p. 428. I am indebted to Professor Bergin for a copy of his paper, of which only an abstract was published in *American Psychologist*, and for other helpful suggestions.
[39] I am leaving out many of the details of this elaborate and well-designed experiment.
[40] Allen E. Bergin, 'Personality "Interpretations" as Dissonant Persuasive Communication', unpublished manuscript. (Abstract appears in *American Psychologist*, 16, 1961), p. 5.
[41] Ibid., p. 7.
[42] The amount of change increased as a monotonic function of the discrepancy between self-rating and 'true' estimate.
[43] Stanley D. Imber *et al.*, 'Suggestibility, Social Class, and the Acceptance of Psychotherapy', *Journal of Clinical Psychology*, 1956, 12, pp. 341–4.
[44] R. W. Heine, 'A Comparison of Patients' Reports on Psychotherapeutic Experience with Psychoanalytic, Non-Directive, and Adlerian Therapists', *American Journal of Psychotherapy*, 1953, 7, pp. 16–23.
[45] See note 6.
[46] Fritz Schmidl, 'The Problem of Scientific Validation in Psycho-analytic Interpretation', *International Journal of Psychoanalysis*, 36, 1955, pp. 105–13.
[47] Freud, *A General Introduction to Psychoanalysis*, Garden City Publishing Co., New York 1943, pp. 234–41.
[48] Schmidl, op. cit., pp. 108–9.
[49] R. R. Sears, *Survey of Objective Studies of Psychoanalytic Concepts*, Social Science Research Council, 1943.
[50] Ernest R. Hilgard, 'Experimental Approaches to Psychoanalysis', *Psychoanalysis as Science*, ed. E. Pumpian-Mindlin, Stanford University Press, Stanford 1952, pp. 3–42.
[51] Schmidl, op. cit., p. 108.
[52] Freud, *A General Introduction to Psychoanalysis*, pp. 231–2.
[53] Schmidl, op. cit., p. 111.
[54] Freud, *A General Introduction to Psychoanalysis*, p. 232.
[55] Sears, op. cit., pp. 41–45 and 136–7.
[56] See Karl Popper, *The Poverty of Historicism*, Beacon Press, Boston 1957; Ernest Nagel, *The Structure of Science*, Harcourt, Brace and World, New York 1961, pp. 547–92; Carl Hempel, 'The Function of General Laws in History', *Readings*

in Philosophical Analysis, ed. Feigl and Sellars, Appleton-Century-Croft, New York 1949, pp. 459–71; see also Carl Hempel and Paul Oppenheim, 'The Logic of Explanation', *Readings in the Philosophy of Science*, ed. Feigl and Brodbeck, Appleton-Century-Croft, New York 1953, pp. 319–52.

[57] Schmidl, op. cit., p. 108.

[58] It should be noted that psychoanalytic theory attempts to *explain* this probabilistic law by a number of theoretical constructs such as repression and unconscious defense. The theoretical constructs serve as connecting links between these temporally and spatially separate events.

[59] We assume here that a clear empirical content can be given to these statements, thus enabling them to be tested.

[60] Schmidl, op. cit., p. 110.

MICHAEL MARTIN

UNDERSTANDING AND PARTICIPANT OBSERVATION IN CULTURAL AND SOCIAL ANTHROPOLOGY

There was a time when cultural and social anthropologists did not do participant observation. Sir James Frazer, famous anthropologist of yesteryear, was once asked if he ever lived amongst savages. It is reported that he held up his hands "as though to ward off even the thought" and answered "God forbid!"[1]

Today things are quite different; field work and in particular participant observation seems, as one critic has put it, an initiation rite into the cult of professional anthropology.[2] How accurate this anthropological characterization of anthropology is I do not know. But it does seem to be true that great stress is laid on the method of participant observation in the profession today.

We will not consider here the anthropological significance of this phenomenon; after all this is a job for anthropologists or sociologists and not for philosophers. The philosophical questions connected with participant observation are rather different. First we want to know what 'participant observation' means. As we shall see the term is not clear and several things have been meant by it. Secondly, we want to know whether there is any methodological justification for participant observation in any of its various senses in cultural and social anthropology. After all there may be good methodological reasons why anthropologists have stressed participant observation and good reasons for its having the significance it does seem to have within the profession. In particular, we shall try to determine the relevance of participant observation in the various senses analyzed for understanding a community. This is necessary because the method of participant observation seems to be closely connected in anthropological thought with the goal of understanding a community. Indeed, so important is the notion of understanding for the evaluation of participant observation that it will be necessary to analyze it before we begin on participant observation.

The paper will thus be divided into three parts. In the first part we will consider the meaning of 'scientific understanding' in anthropology taking some time to separate out other concepts that may be confused with such understanding. In the second part of the paper we will consider the meaning of 'participant observation' in anthropology, clarifying and separating different senses to be found in anthropological literature. In the third part of the paper we will consider the methodological relevance of participant observation for a scientific understanding of a community.

I. UNDERSTANDING A COMMUNITY

A. *Scientific Understanding*

Traditionally one of the major tasks of cultural and social anthropology has been to understand particular communities. In this respect, it has been suggested, anthropology is like history.[3] Cultural and social anthropology and history, it is said, are ideographic, not nomothetic sciences; they do not aim at discovering laws or theories but in understanding particular phenomena.

Now whether such a description of cultural anthropology is accurate we need not decide here. Nor need we enter into two other closely related controversies: the question of whether anthropologists, although they may not aim to discover laws, nevertheless use laws in understanding particular communities; the question of whether anthropologists should aim to discover laws even if they do not do so.

Whatever the answers to these two questions and whatever the accuracy of the description of anthropology as an ideographic science, it does seem to be true that anthropologists have often aimed at understanding some particular community.

What does *understanding* a community mean? Although the term 'understanding' may be used in many senses in science and ordinary life, there is one sense that stands out. This might be called scientific or factual understanding. In this sense to understand something – a person, a subject, a community, and so on – is to know certain facts about the person, theory or community.[4] Thus in the case of persons expressions like, 'Jones understands Smith' are often reducible to expressions of the form 'Jones knows that P_1 and P_2 and ... P_n', where $P_1, P_2, ..., P_n$ refer to certain facts about Smith. What sort of facts these are will usually be clear from the context. Sometimes the facts concern Smith's motivation, his purposes or his character; at other times the facts will be facts of his social or cultural background and their relation to his present behavior. I interpret the term 'fact' quite broadly here. One fact about Smith that Jones might have to know in some context to understand Smith is that Smith's behavior is subsumable under certain laws. The present analysis remains neutral with respect to the question of whether knowledge of such facts would be necessary.[5] In any case, conceived in this way, understanding a person seems to be reducible to knowing certain facts about him. We call this type of knowledge propositional knowledge.[6] Propositional knowledge is simply knowledge that something is the case. In the case of Jones and Smith, Jones' understanding Smith consists in Jones' having certain propositional knowledge of Smith, i.e., knowledge that certain things are true about Smith.

Where the object of understanding is not a person a similar kind of analysis seems possible. To say that Jones understands psychoanalysis or Newton's Theory is usually to say that Jones has some particular kind of propositional knowledge. Again the context usually makes clear what this propositional knowledge will be. The suggestion is often that Jones' propositional knowledge consists in knowing that psychoanalysis or Newton's Theory has certain important structural properties or that the parts of these theories fit together in a certain way; at other times the suggestion is that the propositional knowledge consists in knowing certain facts about the history of psychoanalysis or physics.

The same sort of thing could be said about understanding a community. Understanding a community seems to consist in having certain propositional knowledge about this community. Again what this knowledge will be will depend on the context of the inquiry. Sometimes understanding a community may consist in knowing that certain aspects of the community are related to one another in certain ways. Thus to say that John Beattie understands Bunyoro[7] may mean only that Beattie knows that certain social institutions in Bunyoro are related to each other in certain ways, forming what has been called a functional system. In other contexts understanding a community may consist in knowing that the community has such and such a historical development.

It should be clear that the present analysis is opposed to the view that there is only one set of facts which, if known, gives understanding of a community. In anthropology, understanding a community will be relative to the perspective taken by the anthropologist, the theory utilized in the investigation, and the purposes of the investigation. A community can be understood functionally, historically, and in other ways[8], although given certain purposes some ways may be better than others. However all these different ways of understanding on the present analysis come down to having propositional knowledge about the community.

B. *Being Understanding*

Another notion of understanding which may not be clearly separated is anthropological thought from factual or scientific understanding is that of being understanding toward a community.[9] Now being understanding toward something or someone involves manifesting a certain attitude; one is understanding toward a person or group, for instance, if one is sympathetic, patient and tolerant towards the person or group.

It may be true that nowadays part of the ethical creed of the anthropological profession is humanitarianism and that part of this humanitarian attitude may be a sympathetic and tolerant attitude toward the community studied; that anthropologists are expected to be understanding toward the people they study. It must be stressed that however strong this commitment may be among field anthropologists and however justified it is on ethical grounds, there is no logical connection between this ethical posture and factual understanding of a community. As far as the logic of the two concepts is concerned, an anthropologist could fail to be understanding toward a community he studies and yet from a scientific standpoint understand the community very well; moreover, he might be understanding toward the community he studies yet have little scientific understanding of the community. To be sure, although there is no logical connection between these two concepts there might be some close practical connection. This might be true for a number of reasons: a failure to be understanding toward a community might be manifested in the anthropologist's behavior; this behavior might cause offense; as a result, the anthropologist might be denied access to vital information; this denial of vital information would in turn prevent scientific understanding of the community.

I say "might" because the degree of intolerance a community can tolerate from a visiting anthropologist without closing down necessary sources of information is not completely known. It may well vary from community to community and from anthropologist to anthropologist. We may suspect at least that in some communities a high degree of intolerance and lack of sympathy can be expressed by the anthropologist and yet a high degree of scientific understanding of that community still be achieved. Malinowski's recent diary[10], for example, indicates that Malinowski often felt and expressed great hatred toward the Trobriand Islanders; he was often not understanding toward them. Yet his study of these people[11] is usually considered to be a landmark in ethnographic understanding, i.e., he is considered to have scientific understanding of the community.

C. *Empathy and Understanding*

A discussion of understanding in anthropology is surely not complete without some mention of the notion of empathy. It is important to discuss the notion since empathy is often confused with the two notions of understanding I have already analyzed.

1. *The Adoption Sense*

I take it that on one common view, to say that someone empathizes with a person or group is to say that he 'puts himself' in the other's place, i.e., he adopts the attitudes, views, emotions, thought patterns, and so on of a person or group; he sees the world and emotionally reacts to the world in the same way as the person or group sees it and reacts to it. Thus an empathizing visiting anthropologist would see and think what the natives saw and thought, he would feel what the natives felt, and so on. Let us call this sense of 'empathy' the *adoption* sense of empathy. It might be said that only by this sort of empathy can the anthropologist understand the community at issue.

To evaluate this position one must sharply distinguish it from another position that may easily be confused with it. It has been maintained by some students of anthropological methodology that it is only by knowing that the natives have the beliefs, goals and attitudes they do have that one understands them. But it is one thing to say this and an entirely different thing to insist that it is only by seeing, feeling, and believing what the natives see, feel and believe that understanding can be achieved.

In short, there is a vast difference between *having* knowledge that people have such and such beliefs, goals and attitudes and *adopting* such beliefs, goals and attitudes. To make this point clear consider the following two expressions:

(1) Beattie knows that the Nyoro have a suspicious attitude towards Europeans.
(2) Beattie adopted the same suspicious attitude toward Europeans that the Nyoro have.

Notice that only in the second expression is there any question of empathy in the adoption sense. Notice also that these two expressions are logically independent. Beattie might know that Nyoro have a certain attitude without adopting that attitude. Beattie might, for instance, be psychologically incapable of being suspicious of Europeans although he knew perfectly well that the Nyoro are suspicious. Moreover, Beattie might adopt this attitude without knowing that the Nyoro have this attitude. For instance he might lack sufficient evidence that the Nyoro are suspicious. This would preclude his knowing that they do have such an attitude on most analyses of propositional knowledge. But it would not prevent him from adopting this attitude.

This example illustrates that propositional knowledge of people's beliefs, goals and attitudes is possible without empathy with the people in the adoption sense. And it is clear that this is true in general: scientific understanding as we have analyzed it in terms of propositional knowledge is possible without empathy in the adoption sense.

Indeed, empathy in this sense is at times incompatible with scientific understanding. For to empathize with a community in this sense may involve adopting their beliefs about their own culture and themselves. However, these beliefs may well be false and distorted and thus preclude scientific understanding. For example, suppose an anthropologist empathized with the natives of some community. This empathizing, let us suppose, involves adopting one of their false beliefs. For example suppose John Beattie in empathizing with the Nyoro believed that not p where not p is some false proposition about Bunyoro. On one standard analysis of propositional knowledge Beattie could not know that p if he believed that not p. If his knowing that p was essential to his understanding Bunyoro, his empathizing would have precluded his understanding Bunyoro.

Furthermore, empathizing with a community may at times be incompatible with being understanding toward the community. Recall that to be understanding toward a community is to be sympathetic and tolerant toward the community. But it is possible that an anthropologist could not in certain communities at one and the same time be both sympathetic and empathetic in the adoption sense. For to empathize with the natives in the present sense is at least to adopt the attitudes of the natives. But one attitude found in certain communities may be an attitude of intolerance and lack of sympathy toward everyone. Surely one could not at the same time be both sympathetic toward the natives and unsympathetic toward everyone.

I conclude that empathy in the adoption sense is usually irrelevant to the scientific understanding of a community and that under certain conditions it is incompatible with it. I conclude also that empathy in the adoption sense is at times incompatible with being understanding toward a community.

2. *The Assimilation Sense*

There is another sense of 'empathy' that must be distinguished from the adoption sense. This sense is suggested by a statement by Nadel. He remarked: "Much in this process of 'empathy' can be reduced to simple empirical facts. Complete knowledge and ready use of the vernacular; long sojourn in the community; and above all, the cumulative effect of constant enquiries into everything that is observed – all these built up a familiarity with the native society which in more poetic language, one might call 'entering into the soul of the savage'. When you find yourself making jokes at which the people laugh (no mean achievement, this); when you have mastered their ways of linking concepts and adducing proof, or when you can predict with fair accuracy what X will do and feel in such and such a situation, you have accomplished an adequate 'assimilation'."[12]

I take it that in this passage Nadel is using 'empathy' in a sense other than the adoption sense. In this new sense to say that someone has empathy with a group is to say that the person can get around in the group easily, that he speaks their language, is on joking terms with them, and so on. In this sense of 'empathy' empathy seems to consist in the utilization of a complex skill. To use Ryle's notion, empathy in this sense is the utilization of a type of knowledge how, or, as it has recently been called, procedural knowledge.[13] Borrowing from Nadel, one might call this sense of empathy the *assimilation* sense.

These two senses of 'empathy' distinguished here are logically independent. One might move about smoothly in a group, be on joking terms with them, and so on without adopting the beliefs, goals, and attitudes of the members of the group although it might be necessary at times to act as if one had adopted some of these beliefs and goals and attitudes. One might also adopt a people's beliefs, goals, and attitudes and yet not move smoothly in the group. For instance the group might not believe that one had adopted their beliefs, goals, and attitudes. This belief might prevent assimilation.

As we shall see in a moment the assimilation sense of 'empathy' is closely connected with one sense of 'participant observation'. Because of this close connection, the relevance of the assimilation sense of 'empathy' to scientific understanding will be discussed later when we discuss the relevance of participant observation for scientific understanding.

There is no logical connection between the assimilation sense of 'empathy' and being understanding toward a community. One could have empathy with a community in the assimilation sense and yet not be understanding toward the community – although one might have to act *as if* one were understanding toward it in order to be assimilated. Indeed, the process of becoming assimilated in a community may in certain cases breed contempt rather than sympathy. (Malinowski's experience is perhaps an example of this.)

Conversely one can be understanding toward a community without being assimilated in the community. Indeed, being understanding toward a community is possible over great periods of time and spans of space. Thus some contemporary classicists are understanding toward classical Greek civilization although these men could hardly be said to be assimilated in ancient Greek society.

To be sure, under certain conditions assimilation in a community may be conducive to being understanding toward a community; and conversely, under other circumstances not being assimilated in a community may prevent understanding toward the community from developing. However, under what conditions this may happen is unclear and is a matter for empirical investigation.

II. THE MEANING OF PARTICIPANT OBSERVATION

Although the term 'participant observation' is widely used in social science literature, little attempt has been made to separate the different strands involved and to clarify issues. There have been, however, some attempts to specify different senses of the term. In a well known article Becker and Geer differentiate different senses of 'participant observation' and we will consider some of these here.[14]

A. *Participant Observation as Being a Member of a Group*

1. *The Native Sense*

In one of Becker and Geer's senses to say that someone is a participant observer of a community is to say that one is a member of the community. This definition is hardly helpful until we are clearer on what being a member of a community involves. For example, is John Beattie a member of the African community of Bunyoro if he lives in this community or are only the Nyoro members of Bunyoro. To clarify this situation let us differentiate between two senses of being a member of a community: the sense in which the Nyoro are members of Bunyoro, let us call this the 'native sense' of being a member of a community; the sense in which Beattie was a member, let us call it the 'living-in' sense of being a member of a community.

It should be noted that although most of the Nyoro are members of the Bunyoro community in the living-in sense, not all are; presumably some of the Nyoro are away and are not actually living in the community at some particular time. Thus in the living-in sense Beattie was a participant observer of Bunyoro in 1951 although some of the Nyoro were not participant observers in 1951 in this sense. Moreover, all the Nyoro are participant observers in the native sense of participant observer of Bunyoro by virtue of *their* cultural background, although Beattie could never be a participant observer in this sense by virtue of *his* cultural background. It seems apparent that anthropologists are not interested in the native sense of participant observation; it is the living-in sense that has relevance for them.

2. *The Living-In Sense*

But what does living in a community involve in anthropological field work? Does it involve living in a community as the natives live? The answer is that it does but only to a certain extent. The extent will depend on the anthropologist and the culture. For Malinowski living in a community involved isolating oneself from white men, taking residence in the village, eating native food, seeking out native entertainment and conversation. Beattie did all of this and more: he gave banana beer parties, and even did some native work. On the other hand, for many anthropologists living in a community does not include dressing in native garb, engaging in native sexual practices, giving up certain Western customs. Thus it is not strictly speaking true, as Frazer suggests, that Malinowski "lived as a native" in his study of Trobriand Islanders.[15]

Why anthropologists should adopt some of the practices of a people and not others is an interesting question and we will consider it in a moment.

3. *The Assimilation Sense*

However, one needs to make a finer distinction in 'the living-in' sense of participant observation in order to do justice to anthropological method. For most anthropologists are not merely interested in living in a community in the sense just specified. One might live in a community in this sense and yet be unable to operate in the community with ease and comfort and familiarity: one might not know one's way about with respect to the customs of the people. It was only after some time that Malinowski said that he learned how to behave and to a certain extent acquired 'the feeling' for the natives' good and bad manners.[16] To say that Malinowski was a participant observer in a community is to say that he lived in a community and knew his way about the community socially. In this sense to be a participant observer is to utilize a certain social know-how while living among the natives.

It should be noted that this sense of participant observation is identical to the assimilation sense of empathy specified earlier. Indeed, let us call this sense of being a member of a community the *assimilation* sense of being a member of a community. Notice that in this sense, the extent to which an anthropologist is a member of a community and thus the extent to which he is a participant observer in this community will be a matter of degree.

It should also be noted that the extent to which an anthropologist follows native customs and practices may be closely connected with the degree of social know-how he develops and utilizes in the culture. A following of native customs and practices to a certain degree seems essential for developing social know-how. On the other hand the following of particular native customs and practices may bring ridicule and hostility and actually prevent social know-how from developing. The extent to which the customs and practices must be followed in order to achieve the maximal social know-how will undoubtedly vary from culture to culture and anthropologist to anthropologist. In any case, the possibility of adverse effects of following some customs of the natives does provide some methodological grounds for not going completely native.

Notice, however, that although it might be necessary for an anthropologist to follow some of the customs of the natives in order to gain social know-how and to avoid adopting others in order to maintain this know-how, it would not be necessary that the anthropologist adopt any of the natives' *beliefs*, *goals*, or *attitudes*. To be sure, it might be necessary for the anthropologist to act *as if* he had adopted some of them. But this is a different matter. Thus having empathy with the natives in the adoption sense of 'empathy' specified earlier, is not a necessary condition for participant observation in the assimilation or living-in senses just specified.

Of course, some methodologists have defined 'participant observation' in such a way that it includes being empathetic in the adoption sense.[17] On the other hand, others have suggested that the expression 'participant' excludes empathy in the adoption sense.[18] It seems to me that this latter view comes closer to the truth. As we shall see in a moment some of the standard senses of 'participant observation' in social science literature would tend in some cases to exclude empathy in the adoption sense.

Taking our point of departure from Becker and Geer we have thus far characterized two senses of 'participant observation' that seem quite relevant for anthropology and yet do not involve empathy in the adoption sense. First the living-in sense: in this sense a participant observer is a person who lives in a culture and adopts some of the customs and practices of the people. Second, the assimilation sense: in this sense a participant observer is a person who lives in a community, develops some social know-how, and is assimilated to a certain extent in the community. We have emphasized that these two senses are closely related to one another. To gain social know-how in a culture involves living in the community and following certain customs and practices of the natives. However gaining social know-how may also involve not following other customs and practices.

So far we have simply tried to clarify and expand one of Becker and Geer's condensed characterizations of participant observation. However, even with this clarification and expansion there is a fundamental omission in Becker and Geer's account. It leaves out all mention of the fact that the person living-in the culture and having certain social know-how has as one of his purposes observing the culture. A person who lived in the culture and had certain social know-how of the culture would normally not be considered to be a participant observer unless he had as one of his purposes observing the culture, i.e., studying it. Missionaries and traders would not normally be considered participant observers of a culture even if they lived in the culture and gained a certain social know-how unless they were attempting to study the culture as well as save souls or sell merchandise.

Thus the living-in sense of participant observation must be amended as follows: A participant observer is a person who lives in a culture, adopting some of the customs and practices of the natives, and has as one of his purposes while living in the culture observing the culture. The definition of 'participant observation' in the assimilation sense would have to be modified along similar lines.

Once it is admitted that this qualification is needed, empathy in the adoption sense would in certain cases be ruled out. To empathize with a person or group in the adoption sense is to adopt all the goals, attitudes and beliefs of the person or group. Moreover, since the basic idea is to put oneself in the other person's place, it would presumably involve repressing or eliminating some of one's own goals, attitudes and beliefs; namely those goals, attitudes and beliefs that are different from those of the person or group being empathized with. But then if a participant observer is a person who by definition has as his purpose the observation of the members of the group and the members of the group do not have this as one of their goals, being a participant observer of a group and being a complete empathizer with the group in the adoption sense at one and the same time is ruled out. This, of course, does not rule out being a participant observer in these senses at certain times and empathizing with a group at different times. Nor does it rule out adopting some of a group's goals, attitudes, and beliefs, i.e., *partially* empathizing, and being a participant observer in these senses at the same time. But it does seem to rule out *complete* empathy and participant observation in these senses at the same time, in certain cases.

B. *Participant Observation as Posing as a Member of a Community*

Becker and Geer differentiate another sense of participant observation. In this sense to say that someone is a participant observer is to say that the person is posing as a member of a group or community. To achieve participant observation in this sense would be difficult, if not impossible, in many typical field situations. Consider the native sense of being a member of a community. The anthropologist as a participant observer would have to pose as a member of the community under investigation. Beattie in this sense of participant observation would have to pose as a Nyoro, a most unlikely prospect! As Herskovits has noted, the white anthropologist in a black man's culture has a "high degree of social visibility"[19]; it is rather difficult to think of Beattie or Malinowski attempting to pass themselves off as one of their black subjects by disguises, make up, and so on.

Consider the living-in sense of being a member of a community. It is difficult to see how an anthropologist could pose as someone living in a community to the community, when the community is small and isolated as is typical in anthropological studies. How for example could Beattie have posed as a person who was living in the small Bunyoro village he wished to study to the members of the village? It might have been possible for Beattie to pose as someone living in a small Bunyoro community to his friends at Oxford and even to members of another distant village but hardly to the members of the small village he did study.

I think it can safely be said that participant observation in this sense has such severe limitations in most anthropological field work that it can be ignored, and we will so ignore it. In any case, this sense also would have to be modified in terms of the purposes of the person posing as a member of the group: the person posing as a member of a group would have to have as one of his purposes the observation of the group to be a participant observer.

C. *Participant Observation as the Role of an Observer in a Community*

Becker and Geer distinguish another type of participant observer. In this sense to be a participant observer one joins a group as "one who is there to observe". Although this kind of participant observation is not completely clarified, what they seem to have in mind is roughly this: on certain occasions a social scientist joins a group and makes it known that he is there to study the group. He takes the role of an observer or student of the group. Let us call this sense of 'participant observation' the *observer-role* sense of participant observation. One gathers that it was this type of participant observation that Becker and Geer themselves used in their study.

But what does joining the group consist of in the observer-role sense? Does it consist in living in the group, being assimilated to a certain extent, gaining a certain social know-how? Does this sense include the living-in sense and assimilation sense of participant observation specified above? Sometimes it does. Beattie, for instance, came to his Bunyoro village as an observer. He announced to the assembled villagers at the beginning of his stay:

"I have come to your country to learn your language, and about your history, your traditions and your customs and the way you live. I have come from a big school in Europe where grown-ups are taught, including some who come to Africa..."[20]

This speech and his subsequent behavior placed Beattie in the role of observer of the village while in the village. Nevertheless this did not prevent him from living in the village, gaining a certain amount of social know-how and to a certain extent being assimilated.

Although sometimes – as in Beattie's case – being a participant observer in an observer-role sense includes being a participant observer in the living-in and assimilation senses, there is no necessity in this. These senses of 'participant observation' are logically distinct. One could join a group in the role of an observer and yet never gain any social know-how, never be assimilated to any extent into the group, and adopt very few of the customs of the group.

Anthropologists who are participant observers in the living-in and assimilation senses of participant observation do not always take the role of an observer. Some argue that the fact that they are studying the community they are living in should be hidden from the natives. Florence

UNDERSTANDING AND PARTICIPANT OBSERVATION

Kluckhohn[21], for example, stresses the necessity for the participant observer not to disclose that he is studying the group while living in the group. She argues that such a disclosure might distort the information received while living in the community and indeed prevent the anthropologist from obtaining information that he might otherwise have received. Kluckhohn, it should be noted, was in a fortunate position: for reasons we need not go into here she was able to live in a New Mexican village and study the people without any need for disclosing that she was studying them.

Whether Kluckhohn's approach would be possible or even desirable in all cases is uncertain. Could Beattie, for example, have been a participant observer in the assimilation sense in his Bunyoro village without having taken the role of an observer of the group? What pretext could he have used to start to live in the village? What would have happened if it had been discovered that he was lying? Moreover, is it really true that the observer-role he did take distorted his information as Kluckhohn seems to maintain? We do not know the answers to these questions. Much more information about human psychology and culture will have to be secured before they can be answered with any confidence.

One suspects, however, that Kluckhohn's view is much too simple. Whether or not observer-role participant observation will distort will depend on many factors including the type of information one is after and the culture under study. For instance, there might be certain types of information which could be gathered by observer-role participant observation with much more success than by other types of observation. Moreover, the very role of an observer may loosen tongues and provoke confessions in certain people under certain circumstances. A similar phenomenon has been noticed by some anthropologists: it has been noticed that in some cases anthropologists have access to certain information because they are non-natives. Thus far from their outsider role being a handicap, it may under certain conditions be a help.

III. THE JUSTIFICATION OF PARTICIPANT OBSERVATION

Now that we have discussed several different senses of 'participant observation' we will consider some possible methodological justifications for participant observation.

A. *Participant Observation as a Sufficient Condition for Scientific Understanding of a Community*

One possible methodological reason for the use of participant observation in anthropology could be that participant observation in a community is a sufficient condition for achieving scientific understanding of the community. It seems to me, however, that this thesis is mistaken no matter what sense of 'participant observation' one considers.

Consider the living-in sense of participant observation. Surely living in a community and following some of the customs and practices of the natives with the purpose of observing them does not guarantee scientific understanding of the community in the sense defined above. This is true for any number of reasons. For instance, while living in a community one may have to adopt the customs or practices of one particular social class and this may alienate one from another social class in the community, in turn preventing one from getting needed information. Under precisely what conditions such alienation and information blockage would occur is not completely clear at the present time. We do know that it sometimes happens. Beattie, for example, had the following choice in Bunyoro: if he lived with the King and his court, he would alienate the people; if he lived with the people, he would alienate the King and his court. Beattie chose the latter course of action and as a result much of the inner workings of the King and his court remained unknown to him. There seems to be no doubt that living with the people and adopting their customs actually prevented Beattie from gaining complete scientific understanding of a certain major social relation in Bunyoro.[22] It should be noted that this was indeed a loss for Beattie since because of his theoretical orientation he was committed to studying all the major social relations of the Bunyoro. The curious fact is that Beattie was also committed to doing participant observation in the living-in sense. The commitment to this method conflicted with full realization of his theoretical goal.

But even if there were no problem of alienation other problems remain. I have already mentioned that merely living in a community and adopting some of the customs of the natives will not necessarily bring about assimilation. Whether it will or not depends on many factors. And without this assimilation it may be impossible to get the sort of information one needs to understand the community.

Now consider the assimilation sense of 'participant observation'. At least one of the problems of the living-in sense remains. In becoming assimilated to one class of a community one may alienate another class; this in turn may block some important sources of information, in turn preventing scientific understanding.

There is another problem. Being assimilated in a community involves moving easily in the community, having a feeling for the manners and mores of the natives, and so on, but it does not in any way guarantee that scientific understanding of the community has been achieved. Scientific understanding of a community as we have specified it above consists in having certain propositional knowledge about the community. Being assimilated need not and often does not involve such propositional knowledge. One might be assimilated in a community and yet be ignorant of facts about the structure or history of the community which it would be necessary to know in order to understand the community given one's purposes and perspective.

Much the same sort of thing can be said for the observer-role sense of 'participant observation'. Announcing to the natives that one is there to observe them may be the kiss of death to one's research project. Even if one is allowed to stay after the disclosure, necessary information may be blocked by it. However, aside from these problems the mere fact of being in a certain role in a community, i.e. the role of an observer of that community, does not guarantee that any propositional knowledge has been obtained. And since scientific understanding involves obtaining such knowledge, being in the role of an observer does not necessarily mean that scientific understanding has been achieved.

B. *Participant Observation as a Necessary Condition for Scientific Understanding of a Community*

It may be granted that participant observation in a community in the senses specified is not a sufficient condition for scientific understanding of the community. However, it may be maintained that participant observation is a necessary condition for scientific understanding. This certainly seems to be Beattie's view. He argues that "only by at least some participation in the community life"[23] can the anthropologist understand the community and that the "observer must live in and with the community he is studying; it is not enough to stay in a comfortable hotl or rest-home and to visit them for a few hours daily or less often ".[24]

Before we can evaluate this contention it is necessary to clear up a certain ambiguity in the thesis. Is the claim that no person could scientifically understand a community unless the person himself was a participant observer in the community? Or is the claim rather that no person could scientifically understand a community unless some person or other was a participant observer in the community? Presumably it is the latter claim that is at issue since the former claim seems to have implications that are obviously false: no mere reader of anthropological literature could ever have scientific understanding of a community; an anthropologist who lived in a community could never communicate his scientific understanding of the community in his books and monographs. But surely this is mistaken. It may be true that anthropologists sometimes fail to give their readers any scientific understanding of a community. But they are hardly doomed to this failure; there seems to be no *a priori* reason to suppose they could not succeed.

The latter claim must be taken more seriously, however, but still we have a problem of clarification. What sense of 'participant observation' it at issue: the living-in sense, the assimilation sense, the observer-role sense? Let us interpret the thesis to be this: for all cultures someone's participant observation in one of the relevant senses is a necessary condition for understanding the culture. The thesis stated in this way has some difficulties.

It is worth pointing out initially that Beattie and most British social anthropologists investigate cultures that are still existing; and it is well known that British social anthropologists often have a definite ahistorical or even anti-historical orientation.[25] American cultural anthropologists, because of the types of cultures they have investigated, have been forced sometimes to use different methods than their British colleagues. Thus the alternative to participant observation is not always, as Beattie seems to suggest, traveling from a comfortable hotel or rest-home to "visit the natives a few hours daily or less". American anthropologists have sometimes wanted to investigate Indian civilizations that are virtually extinct. They have used old native informants and not participant observation[26] in their work; sometimes they have not even left their hotel. The informant has come to them.

Cornelius Osgood[27], for example, reports his investigation of the old culture of the Northern Athapascans primarily by the use of the remarkable Indian informant Billy Williams. Williams, a man of remarkable intelligence and photographic recall, was interviewed by Osgood 8 hours a day for weeks on end. Williams on his own initiative would travel to remote settlements to quiz old Indian women and men on details he did not know and reported the results to Osgood. Williams would make models of the old buildings and of manufactured objects for Osgood in his spare time and would spend hours relating the intricate and complex old ceremonies and dances to Osgood. It is hard to accept the view that Osgood, because he was not a participant observer in the old culture, did not come to have a scientific understanding of old Northern Athapascan culture through the informant Williams.

Indeed, I am far from convinced that even in Beattie's own work participant observation in any of the senses at issue was necessary. Beattie's procedure was as follows: After studying all the written documents on the Bunyoro culture, Beattie went to Bunyoro and became a participant observer in the living-in, assimilation and observer-role senses in a small Bunyoro village; he learned the language, adopted some customs, observed the social relations, took notes and after 6 months returned to Oxford. In Oxford he studied his notes, continued to study the language, consulted with his teachers and after 4 months returned to Bunyoro. One gathers that on this visit he used very little participant observation. Primarily he used other methods: he used informants, studied court records and official documents, took surveys, gave questionnaires, had natives write essays, and so on.

One naturally wonders whether his first 6 months' visit as a participant observer in a small Bunyoro village was really necessary. Would it really have been impossible to proceed without this initial contact? Is there any particular piece of information that Beattie would not have obtained without the first 6 months of participant observation?

These questions must not be confused with another type of question. Was Beattie's stay in a Bunyoro village an enriching and aesthetically satisfying experience? Could this experience have been achieved in any other way? Could it have been achieved by non-participant observer methods? It is no doubt true that participant observation is often an enriching, moving and aesthetically significant experience for anthropologists. And it may also be true that such an experience is difficult or even impossible to achieve in other ways. But this, it seems to me, shows nothing about the necessity of participant observation for achieving scientific understanding. The question we are concerned with here is only: is there any good reason to suppose that every fact Beattie learned about Bunyoro's social structure – this was what Beattie was primarily interested in – could not have been learned from good informants and other non-participant observer methods? We are not interested in whether Beattie will always cherish his 6 months in a small Bunyoro village or whether this moving experience could not have been achieved in other ways.

It must be emphasized that Beattie advances very little in the way of explicit argument to substantiate his view that his 6 months as a participant observer was necessary for a scientific understanding of the Bunyoro. As far as I can discern, his belief that it was necessary rests upon two major considerations:

(1) It is necessary to learn the native language of a culture to understand the culture. Unless he knew the language he would not have been able to check his informants and interpreters, compose questionnaires, gain insight into the natives' thinking. Six months alone as a participant observer where he was forced to use the language was an ideal way to achieve this linguistic knowledge.

(2) In his 6 months as a participant observer he got a certain feel for the culture. Without this initial exposure he would not have been able to ask his informants the right questions or compose an insightful questionnaire. Thus the first 6 months of participant observation could not have been eliminated.

These considerations, however, are hardly persuasive. Consider the first point.

Whether learning the native language is necessary for achieving understanding of a community we need not decide here, but it should be noted that not all anthropologists have believed that learning the language is essential in field work.[28] Let us grant, however, that learning the native language is essential. The most Beattie's argument shows is that the *best* way to learn the language would be through participant observation. It does not prove, however, that participant observation was a necessary condition for learning the native language and hence a necessary condition for achieving understanding. And it is surely mistaken to suppose that participant observation was a necessary condition for learning the native language in Beattie's case. Thus although Beattie did master the essentials of the native language while a participant observer presumably other methods were available to him, e.g., hiring a native tutor. Moreover, it is not completely obvious that participant observation is even the best way to learn a native language. So little is known about language learning that one might well take a skeptical attitude to this contention. For all we now at the present time a native tutor might well be a much better method.

In order to criticize Beattie's second point one need not belittle Beattie's idea of getting an initial feel of the culture. This initial and terminal exploratory period may indeed be necessary for all empirical research. The question is whether participant observation is necessary for gaining this feel. It should be recalled that anthropologists like Osgood who used a single informant like Billy Williams managed to get a feel for the old culture without participant observation. By asking the informant questions – perhaps stupid questions or perhaps by just letting the informant talk at random – one may get a feel for the culture. After a while more penetrating and intelligent questions can be asked.

It might be objected, however, that it was still necessary to have a participant observer in order to obtain any scientific understanding of, for example, the old North Athapascans' culture; that Billy Williams himself was the participant observer. But Williams was not presumably a participant observer in any of the senses at issue. Recall that to be a participant observer of a community in the senses under discussion one must have as one of one's purposes to observe or study the community at issue. Now although Billy Williams was a man of remarkable observing powers there is no good reason to suppose that he engaged in a purposeful study of the culture in which he lived while he lived there. It is true that Williams was a participant observer in the native-sense of participant observer. But as we have seen, this sense has little relevance to anthropological discussion of participant observation. Williams was an informant and the use of informants is *contrasted* with participant observation in the relevant senses in anthropological discussions.

Moreover, if we consider cultures that have long since perished, the dubiousness of the necessity of reports of participant observers even in the native-sense of participant observation, e.g. informants, becomes apparent. It does not seem to be true that one can have no scientific understanding of a culture without reports of natives. In reconstructions of prehistorical cultures archaeologists do not base their reconstructions on the reports of participant observers in any of the senses specified – even the native sense. Material artifacts such as coins, pottery, art work and so on of the old cultures may be the only source of evidence available. Thus Larco Hoyle[29] reconstructed the ancient Mochica culture of Peru primarily on the basis of scenes portrayed on grave pottery. Other investigators have reconstructed ancient cultures on similar evidence.[30]

It is important not to neglect the limitations of these kinds of reconstructions; on the other hand it is equally important not to belittle what they can achieve. And what they can achieve will depend on many factors. The type of material artifacts that are used, the kinds of cultural facts that are inferred, the strength of analogical reasoning that can be brought to bear, will all affect the understanding that these reconstructions can give.

It would be incorrect to say that these reconstructions always give us a great understanding of ancient cultures. But it is equally incorrect to say that they give us no understanding of these cultures. It seems correct to say that they do sometimes give us a moderate degree of understanding although it may be easily admitted that different sorts of evidence could increase our understanding. The evidence obtained from informants and participant observation might well be evidence of this sort.

Since we have just made this small concession to the method of participant observation it is time to make another. There is a much weaker version of the thesis that participant observation is a necessary condition for understanding a culture. Instead of claiming that for *all* cultures someone's participant observation in one of the relevant senses is a necessary condition for anyone understanding the culture, the claim might rather be that for *some* cultures someone's participant observation in one of the relevant senses is a necessary condition for anyone understanding the culture. This claim is not so obviously mistaken and indeed may even be true. It may be impossible at certain times in certain cultures to get reliable and trustworthy informants, direct non-participant observation may be impossible, no written history or literature may be available archaeological reconstructions may be out of the question, and so on. Under these conditions participant observation may well have to be used if any understanding is to be achieved.

UNDERSTANDING AND PARTICIPANT OBSERVATION

How often such conditions are realized is difficult to say. In any case, it remains to be shown that these conditions occur often enough to justify the great stress placed on participant observation by the anthropological profession.

C. Participant Observation as the Most Efficient Way of Obtaining Information of Certain Kinds

If we reject the view that participant observation is always a necessary condition for obtaining scientific understanding of a community, we may attempt to justify the widespread use of participant observation on other grounds. One might argue that participant observation is the most efficient way of obtaining certain kinds of information in a community and that these kinds of information are necessary for a scientific understanding. This tack is taken by Morris Zelditch.[31]

Zelditch argues that there are three types of information that social scientists in community studies are interested in obtaining: information about frequency distributions, e.g. the number of married women in the community; information about certain incidents in the community, e.g. a recent wedding in the community; information about rules or norms in the community, e.g. marriage rules. Moreover, there are three methods that social scientists use to obtain these three types of information: surveys, participant observation, informants.

Zelditch maintains that these three methods should be judged by two criteria: (a) informational adequacy, and (b) efficiency. Judged in these terms he finds the following: Survey method has the greatest informational adequacy and most efficiency with respect to frequency distributions; participant observation has the least. On the other hand, participant observation has the greatest information adequacy and most efficiency with respect to incidents; survey methods has the least. Use of informants has the most informational adequacy and most efficiency with respect to rules and norms; participant observation, although it has good informational adequacy, is inefficient in obtaining this kind of information.

Zelditch's contention, if correct, would indeed provide some justification for the widespread use of participant observation in anthropology. There are, however, certain questions one can raise about Zelditch's views.

First of all, it is unclear what Zelditch means by 'participant observation'. What sense of 'participant observation' is being used in his claim that participant observation is the best method to obtain information about certain incidents in a community? Certainly this will make a difference since as we have seen certain types of participant observation may have particular problems in certain communities. For example, the role-observer type of participant observation may be difficult to carry out in certain types of communities and may be performed only at a great price.

Moreover, what is the range of his claims? Is Zelditch suggesting that participant observation in some sense is *always* more efficient and more informationally adequate in obtaining information about incidents in the community? What sort of incidents are these? If the incident occurred 40 years ago, far from participant observation in some sense being the best method, it is not possible to use it at all. An old reliable informant like Billy Williams may be an anthropologist's only hope. But this may be true even with a contemporary incident. For instance if Beattie had suddenly discovered that an important and rare ceremony was to occur in a Bunyoro village close to the Bunyoro village he was a participant observer in, it would have been impossible for him to have obtained information about this incident by his participant observation. He was not a participant observer in the neighboring village and in several relevant senses of 'participant observer' it would have been impossible under normal circumstances to have become one in the needed time. If Beattie needed this information to obtain an understanding of Bunyoro culture some nonparticipant observer method would have been his only hope.

Of course Beattie might have hoped that this rare ceremony would occur in the village in which he was a participant observer given enough time. However, he only had a limited time to perform his research and in any case a long wait would be inefficient.

Moreover, there may be certain kinds of contemporary incidents occurring in a community in which an anthropologist is a participant observer which are not and cannot be observed by the anthropologist. For instance, there may be secret ceremonies to which the anthropologist has no access despite his having lived in the community for an extended period of time and despite his having developed a sense of social know-how. In this case also it would be necessary to use trusted informants if any are available. To be sure, the anthropologist may maintain that given more time and patience these ceremonies will be opened to him. But the time and energy needed to gain entrance into the inner circle may well make other methods more efficient.

Of course, it may be admitted that in certain cultures under certain conditions relative to certain types of information participant observation in some of the senses discussed may be more efficient than other methods. But this is an extremely weak claim; indeed, it would hardly by itself justify any widespread use of participant observation or justify the status participant observation seems to enjoy in the profession.

CONCLUSION

The main conclusions of this paper are as follows:

(1) Scientific understanding of a community consists in knowing certain facts about the community. What these facts are will depend on the context of inquiry.

(2) Scientific understanding of a community is logically independent of being understanding toward a community although there may be certain important practical connections between achieving scientific understanding of a community and being understanding toward that community.

(3) Being empathetic with a community in one important sense of the term (the adoption sense) is usually independent of both scientific understanding of the community and being understanding toward the community. Moreover, there are cases in which being empathetic is incompatible with understanding in both senses of understanding.

(4) Participant observation in the senses specified here is neither a sufficient condition nor a necessary condition for achieving scientific understanding of all communities.

(5) Moreover, participant observation is not in all cases the most efficient way of obtaining certain types of information.

(6) However, it may be true that in certain cases participant observation is a necessary condition for achieving scientific understanding of a community and in certain cases it may be the most efficient way of obtaining needed information. How far ranging these cases are is uncertain. If anthropologists put great stress on participant observation as has been often claimed and if the number of such cases is small, this emphasis can not be justified on the methodological grounds here considered.[32]

Several cautions or perhaps disclaimers should be added to these conclusions:

(1) It may be a myth that anthropologists do put great emphasis on participant observation as a method. If so, I am attacking a straw man, and I should get myself new 'native' informants since I have gathered my impressions about the status of participant observation from people in or close to the profession.

(2) Other methodological justifications might indeed be possible. Naturally, I have not exhausted all possible ones in my paper.

(3) Even if no methodological justification is possible it does not follow that participant observation should be deemphasized in the profession for some other sort of justification may be possible. Participant observation may give anthropologists great enjoyment, pleasure, adventure and a sense of esprit de corps, for example, and this perhaps is all the justification that a widespread use of participant observation may need in anthropology.

One final thought: I have evaluated the relevance of participant observation for achieving scientific understanding, but it may be a mistake to suppose that anthropologists are after this type of understanding alone when they investigate some particular society or culture. Kroeber has noted that there is an aesthetic dimension to anthropological thought and method.[33] There is a sense of 'understanding' distinct from scientific understanding that I have not yet mentioned. For example, when one speaks of understanding a poem or painting or a piece of music one may well have something different in mind than knowing certain facts about the work of art.[34] Thus aesthetic understanding may indeed be analogous to what the anthropologist is after in understanding a culture or society and participant observation may be much more relevant to achieving this sort of understanding than to achieving scientific understanding. But a consideration of this suggestion is another paper.

Boston University

REFERENCES

[1] Patrick Gallagher's review of Malinowski's *A Diary in the Strict Sense of the Term*, in *New Republic*, June 17, 1967, p. 14.

[2] I. C. Jarvie, *The Revolution In Anthropology*, The Humanities Press, New York, 1964, p. 29.

UNDERSTANDING AND PARTICIPANT OBSERVATION

[3] See, for example, E. E. Evans-Pritchard's 'Social Anthropology: Past and Present', *Man* 50 (1950), 118–124; Conrad M. Arensberg, 'Anthropology as History', in K. Polanyi et al., *Trade and Market in Early Empires*.

[4] It is important to note here we are discussing the notion of understanding something', i.e. expressions of the form x understands y. In these expressions 'understands' takes a noun or noun phrase as its grammatical object. We are not discussing here expressions where 'understands' takes some propositional clause as its grammatical object. For an analysis of these latter kinds of expressions see May Brodbeck, 'Meaning and Action', in *Readings in the Philosophy of Social Science* (ed. by May Brodbeck), Macmillan Co., New York, 1968.

[5] Cf. C. G. Hempel, *Aspects of Scientific Explanation*, The Free Press, New York 1965, p. 488. According to Hempel to understand a phenomena is to show that it fits' "into a nomic nexus". In our terms this would involve knowing that the phenomena fits into a nomic nexus. According to the present analysis Hempel's view would be a special case of scientific understanding.

[6] For a discussion of propositional knowledge see Israel Scheffler, *Conditions of Knowledge*, Scott, Foresman, Chicago, 1965.

[7] See John Beattie, *Understanding an African Community: Bunyoro*, Holt, Rinehart and Winston, New York, 1965.

[8] Cf. Leslie White, 'History, Evolutionism and Functionalism: Three Types of Interpretation of Culture', *SJA*, 1945, 221–248. One need not agree with White's evolutionism to agree that there are more than two ways to interpret cultural phenomena.

[9] These two notions of understanding were first explicitly separated and analysed by Jane Roland Martin in her doctoral thesis. See Jane Roland, *Understanding, Explaining and Teaching History*, unpublished Ph.D. dissertation, Radcliffe College, 1961.

[10] Bronislaw Malinowski, *A Diary in the Strict Sense of the Term*, Harcourt, Brace and World, New York, 1967.

[11] See for example Bronislaw Malinowski, *Coral Gardens and Their Magic*, Indiana University Press, Urban, 1967. See also Clifford Geertz's discussion of this work as well as of Malinowski's *Diary* in *The New York Review of Books*, Sept. 14, 1967.

[12] S. F. Nadel, *The Foundations of Social Anthropology*, Cohen & West, London, 1951, p. 18.

[13] Scheffler, *op. cit.*

[14] Howard S. Becker and Blanche Geer, 'Participant Observation' in R. N. Adams and J. J. Preiss, *Human Organization Research* pp. 267–289; for another attempt to distinguish different senses of participant observation see Buford H. Junker, *Field Work*, University of Chicago Press, Chicago, 1960.

[15] Sir James Frazer, 'Preface' to *Argonauts of the Western Pacific*, pp. vii–viii.

[16] Malinowski, *Argonauts of the Western Pacific*, p. 8.

[17] John Madge, *The Tools of Social Science*, Doubleday, New York, 1965, p. 137.

[18] Eric Fromm, 'Psychoanalysis and Zen Buddhism', in Suzuki, Fromm, and De Martino, *Zen Buddhism and Psychoanalysis*, Grove Press, New York, 1963, p. 112.

[19] M. Herskovits, *Life in a Haitian Valley*, New York 1937, p. 323.

[20] Beattie, *op. cit.*, p. 14.

[21] Florence Kluckhohn, 'The Participant Observer Technique in Small Communities', *AJS*, 1940, 331–343.

[22] Beattie, *op. cit.*, p. 47.

[23] John Beattie, *Other Cultures*, The Free Press, New York, 1964, p. 87.

[24] *Ibid.*, p. 82.

[25] George P. Murdock, 'British Social Anthropology' *AA* **53** (1951) 465–473.
[26] See Margaret Mead and Rhoda Metraux (ed.), *The Study of Culture at a Distance*, University of Chicago Press, Chicago, 1953, pp. 41–49.
[27] Cornelius Osgood, 'Informants', in *Yale University Publication in Anthropology*, 1940, pp. 50–55.
[28] See Margaret Mead, 'Native Language as Field Work Tools', *AA*, 1939, 189–205.
[29] R. Larco Hoyle, *Los Mochicas*, Museo R. Larco Herrera, Trujillo (Peru), 1945.
[30] Irving Rouse, 'The Strategy of Culture History', in *Anthropology Today* (ed. by A. L. Kroeber), The University of Chicago Press, Chicago, 1953, pp. 61–62.
[31] Morris Zelditch, 'Some Methodological Problems of Field Studies', *AJS*, 1962, 566–576.
[32] For a criticism of the thesis that all anthropologists should do field work, see I. C. Jarvie, 'On Theories of Fieldwork and the Scientific Character of Social Anthropology', *Philosophy of Science* **34** (1967) 223–242.
[33] A. L. Kroeber, *An Anthropologist Looks at History*, University of California Press, Berkeley, 1966, p. 124.
[34] See Carl R. Hausman, 'Intradiction: An Interpretation of Aesthetic Understanding', *Journal of Aesthetics*, 1963–64, 249–261.

JUSTIFICATION BY VERSTEHEN

Michael Scriven[1] has recently argued that the traditional positivistic view of Verstehen is incorrect. According to the traditional view Verstehen cannot be used to verify or test hypotheses. Rather Verstehen is at best a heuristic device used in the discovery of hypotheses. Now according to Scriven Verstehen can be used to test hypotheses although in certain cases non-Verstehen methods would also have to be used. In short, Scriven argues that Verstehen "is a fine provider of knowledge" in the social sciences and history and even in the natural sciences.

Howard Cohen[2] has argued that Scriven is correct in supposing that the method of Verstehen is a provider of knowledge. But he maintains that with respect to historical knowledge the method of Verstehen is not appropriate; that the method of Verstehen should not be used to test hypotheses in history. For history--unlike violin appraising where according to Cohen Verstehen is used--intersubjective testing is necessary. In this paper we will consider Scriven's and Cohen's arguments.

Scriven on Verstehen

Scriven's general position on Verstehen and our basic criticism of it can be outlined as follows: Scriven argues that Verstehen is a useful tool in science for verifying hypotheses. He illustrates this use by showing how experts' empathetic judgments can and should be relied upon. Furthermore, he argues that positivists have wrongly rejected Verstehen as a means of testing hypotheses. After distinguishing two senses of Verstehen not clearly distinguished by Scriven, we argue that Scriven has not shown that Verstehen per se can verify hypotheses but only that Verstehen combined with independent knowledge can verify hypotheses. We argue further that positivists would not be opposed to this use of Verstehen. We further consider the possibility that Scriven differs from the positivists in whether this independent knowledge must be intersubjectively testable. We argue that although Scriven's position differs from the positivists' it is the positivists and not Scriven that are correct.

Two Types of Verstehen

It is not completely clear what Scriven means by Verstehen. To be sure Scriven speaks of Verstehen as "empathetic insight." But what exactly empathetic insight involves is not completely clear.

At times Scriven speaks of empathy in terms of "estimating our reactions and their transferability." One thinks "about the likely effect" of some event on himself and "its likely effects" on others.[3] In this sense "X has empathetic insight that p" could be defined as follows: (1) X believes that p and (2) X infers that p on the basis of X's estimate of X's reactions and X's estimate of the transferability of X's reaction to other people. Presumably in this case p would be some statement about some other person's or persons' reactions, behavioral or otherwise. Let us call this type of Verstehen transfer Verstehen.

However, given this sense of Verstehen it is difficult to understand Scriven's claim that empathetic insight is a reliable tool for the natural sciences as well

355

as the social sciences and history. Since it seems to be limited to establishing hypotheses about peoples' reactions it seems to have relevance only to the social sciences and history.

Scriven also speaks of "instant perception"[4] in connection with Verstehen. This suggests that when he is talking about Verstehen in the natural sciences he simply means intuitive insight. Thus to say that X has empathetic insight that p in the present sense means (1) X believes that p, (2) X's belief that p is not based on conscious or explicit inference and (3) X's belief that p came to X instantly. Let us call this sort of Verstehen <u>intuitive insight Verstehen</u>.

It is important to notice that there is some connection between transfer Verstehen and intuitive insight Verstehen. Under certain conditions transfer Verstehen is a special case of intuitive insight Verstehen. For in our characterization of intuitive insight Verstehen we left open the possibility that implicit inference was involved; we only excluded the possibility of explicit inference. On our characterization of transfer Verstehen we left open the possibility that the inference involved was implicit. Thus an instance of transfer Verstehen would be a special case of intuitive judgment Verstehen when the inferences involved were implicit and instantaneous.

In what follows we will examine Verstehen as a means of justification both in the intuitive insight sense and the transfer sense. Mainly however we will be concerned with transfer Verstehen as a case of intuitive insight Verstehen.

Verstehen as a Tool

Now in what way does Scriven claim that Verstehen is a useful tool in the natural and social sciences? Let us consider intuitive insight Verstehen. Given that someone X has empathetic insight that p in the intuitive insight sense defined above, Scriven wants to claim that under certain conditions such insight is reliable: we have a right to believe X's judgment and X does too. Now, of course, Scriven does not wish to argue that such empathetic insight is always free from error. People sometimes have an empathetic insight that p and p is false. However beliefs that are based on non-empathetic methods, e.g., traditional methods of verification, can also turn out to be false. Furthermore Scriven does not wish to claim that empathetic insight has more reliability than claims based on other grounds, e.g., traditional methods of verification. Although Scriven does not say so explicitly he seems to want to claim that empathetic insight is as reliable under certain conditions as belief based on the more standard methods. The crucial question is under what conditions is it as reliable?

One sort of condition Scriven apparently has in mind is the following: Let us suppose that some person is usually correct when he has an empathetic insight. We know he has been correct on independent grounds. Now in the present case he has an empathetic insight that p. Consequently on inductive grounds we can reasonably suppose he is correct in the present case. In this sort of case a man's empathetic insight (in the sense of intuitive insight) is used as an indicator or symptom of the truth of his belief in the same way that a barometer is used as a symptom or indicator of rain.[5] Now a person with much more reliable empathetic insight than the average person in a particular realm is considered an expert in this realm: he is an expert in so far as his empathetic insight in the intuitive insight sense can be better trusted than other people's.

It is clear that Scriven takes his position to be in sharp contrast with the traditional positivistic view of Verstehen. He says "The positivists argued that empathy was not a reliable tool at all, and that the methods of obtaining knowledge, especially knowledge in history, were just the same as those used in the physical sciences."[6] Scriven, as we have seen, goes on to argue that Verstehen does provide knowledge in history as well as in the natural sciences.

What is not clear, however, is in what way Scriven's construal of Verstehen is in conflict with the positivist's view. To be sure positivists did not think about the possibility of linking the intuitive judgments of experts with Verstehen. However the use of the intuitive judgments of experts in prediction in the inexact sciences was explored in some detail by Helmer and Rescher in a well-known monograph.[7] There is no reason to suppose that such use of experts was rejected by well known critics of Verstehen—some of whom were acquainted with this monograph.

Furthermore, it is extremely dubious that positivists, had they thought of such an identification, would have had any objections to it. For it is clear from the above that empathetic insight by itself provides no justification for knowledge claims. If one knows that X has empathetic insight that p this by itself gives no reason to suppose that p unless we also know that X's empathetic insights have been reliable in similar circumstances. However, as far as I know, the positivist critics of Verstehen would not have denied that someone's empathetic insight plus knowledge about the reliability of this person's empathetic insight established by non-Verstehen methods could provide knowledge. They argued that empathetic insight taken by itself provides no knowledge. Thus, as far as I can tell, critics of Verstehen like Abel, Nagel, and Rudner would not have denied the inductive strength of the following sort of argument:

(1) Jones is usually correct in his empathetic insight.
(2) Jones has an empathetic insight that p.

----

(3) ∴ p.

Premises (1) and (2), positivists would surely admit, make (3) probable. (They would have required, of course, that (1) and (2) be established by standard intersubjectively testable non-Verstehen methods.)

What positivists would deny, however, is the inductive strength of the following argument:

(1') Jones has empathetic insight that p.

(2') ∴ p.

Thus Abel says, "from the affirmation of a possible connection we cannot conclude that it is also probable. From the point of view of Verstehen alone, any connection that is possible is equally certain."[8] Nagel argues, "competent evidence for assumptions about the attitudes and actions of other men is often difficult to obtain; but it is certainly not obtained merely by introspecting one's own sentiments or by examining one's own beliefs as to how such sentiments are likely to be manifested in overt action."[9] Rudner goes so far as to consider the possibility of Verstehen as a means of verification and argues that such a method presupposes that the empathetic act is veridical and this must be established by nonempathetic means. He says "We need not argue against empathy or discard it as a validational step, but clearly, in order to accept some specific empathetic act as validational, we must presuppose an investigation establishing the hypothesis that this act is veridical....we must have established independently that the empathy is sufficiently like the state of which it is an empathy."[10] To be sure Rudner fails to notice that the independent validation he requires could be achieved by showing by non-empathetic methods that a person's empathetic acts are often veridical and arguing that probably this act is as well. But it is extremely dubious that he would have rejected such a suggestion if he had considered it. His major point, as well as Abel's and Nagel's, seems to be that empathetic insight by itself cannot verify any hypothesis.

I think we can safely say that although it may be true that positivists did not contemplate Scriven's particular use of intuitive insight Verstehen in science, such a use could be assimilated to the positivist program. Positivist critics of Verstehen simply were not talking about this use of Verstehen as characterized above when they objected to Verstehen.

What is not completely clear on Scriven's view of Verstehen is whether he believes that the statistical sort of justification of Verstehen considered above is essential for its defense. Let us consider an example used by Scriven to illustrate the use of empathetic insight combined with non-empathetic methods.[11] A reconstruction of Scriven's argument is as follows:

(1) Intensive bombing of a city (C_1) is a possible cause of defeatism in the populace of the city (E_2).
(2) Intensive bombing of city X occurred.
(3) Defeatism occurred in the populace of city $X(E_2)$.
(4) All other possible causes ($C_2, C_3 ..., C_n$) were not present in this case of defeatism in city X.
(5) This case of defeatism has a cause.
(6) ∴ Intensive bombing (C_1) is the cause of defeatism in city X (E_2).

Now Scriven argues that premises (2)-(5) are established by non-Verstehen methods. But without premise (1) these premises do not allow us to infer (6). However, (1) is established by empathetic insight--empathetic insight presumably of the transfer type and perhaps of the intuitive insight type. Thus Scriven argues that empathy (premise 1) and non-empathetic methods (premises (2) and (3)) combined allow us to infer the cause of some social phenomenon.

The crucial question, however, is whether empathy by itself gives any justification for supposing that (1) is true. One possible suggestion is similar to one we have already considered. Suppose some expert has an empathetic insight that (1). Consequently because of the high reliability of his past judgments (established by non-Verstehen methods) we have good inductive evidence that he is correct in this case as well. If this is what Scriven has in mind, empathy itself has not established premise (1). Independent knowledge about the reliability of the empathizer would also be necessary. Under this interpretation there is no clear conflict with the positivist's critique of empathy although, as we have suggested above, positivists never seemed to have considered cases like this.

However, another slightly different interpretation of Scriven is possible. Let us suppose that the person with empathetic insight in the transfer sense makes his inference explicit. He argues:

> (1a) Intensive bombing could cause me to become a defeatist.
> (1b) I am very similar to people in City X with respect to my reaction to bombing.
> _____
> (1) ∴ Intensive bombing is a possible cause of defeatism in the populace of City X.

Now positivist critics of Verstehen would, I believe, raise no objection to this argument as a strong inductive argument. Their question would be how (1a) and (1b) are to be established. Certainly (1b) can not be established by empathetic insight by itself (in the intuitive insight sense). It might be suggested that (1a) can be established by what Anscombe has called "knowledge without observation." Anscombe's example[12] of knowing without observation that the bark of a crocodile caused one to be startled, it might be said, is not unlike knowledge that (1a). Furthermore, Anscombe's knowledge without observation might well be considered as a special case of intuitive insight: it is direct--not based on any explicit inference and instantaneous. However, I am dubious that (1a) could be established by knowledge without observation.

First of all, if Anscombe's knowledge without observation establishes anything, it presumably would establish:

> (1a') Intensive bombing caused me to become a deafeatist.

But (1a') is not at issue in the above argument. In (1a) one must have knowledge of what could cause one to become a defeatist. Anscombe's knowledge without observation is not direct knowledge of psychological possibilities. To be sure (1a') entails (1a). That is given intensive bombing as the actual cause of my defeatism one can deductively infer that intensive bombing could cause my defeatism. However, without (1a') how is (1a) to be established? As far as I can determine Anscombe did not suppose one could establish (1a) independently of (1a').

Secondly, in the bombed city example, the empathizer may have never been in a city when it was bombed. Consequently he could not establish by knowing without observation that bombing causes any of his psychological states. Thus he would not be able to rely on knowledge without observation in establishing (1a') and then inferring (1a) from (1a').

Thirdly, even if (1a') is established it is dubious that (1a') could be established by intuition alone. Our reliance on someone's judgment about the causes of his own psychological states and reactions is usually a function of his past reliability in making such judgments--the truth of which is ascertained on independent grounds. People can be mistaken in their judgments about causes of their own psychological states and reactions and the more mistakes they have made in the past the more inclined one is to discount their judgment now.

On the other hand if it is suggested that (1a) and (1b) could be established by intuitive insights of people whose intuitive insights have been reliable in the past and this reliability has been established on independent grounds--it is unclear that positivists would have any objection. As we have emphasized above, although the positivists critics did not think of this use of Verstehen it is dubious they would have rejected it; this use of Verstehen seems quite compatible with positivism.

Verstehen and Intersubjective Testing

So far we have argued that Scriven has not shown that empathy itself provides any way of testing hypotheses either in the natural sciences or the social sciences. What seems to be true is that empathy plus independent knowledge about the past reliability of the empathizer provides a way of justifying belief in a hypothesis. But, as we have seen, positivist critics of empathy need not deny this so long as the independent knowledge is verified by standard inter-subjective methods.

What then can be the disagreement between Scriven and the positivists? Does Scriven believe that sometimes empathy by itself provides a test of hypotheses? Or does he think rather that although independent knowledge of reliability of the empathizer's judgment is necessary that independent knowledge does not have to be verified in the standard intersubjective way? His position unfortunately is unclear.

Some of the things Scriven says suggest that he thinks that empathy by itself can provide a way of testing hypotheses. Thus he says: "If empathy can in principle provide knowledge, does it in practice? ...To suppose that one cannot rightly be certain from empathy that an air raid is causing one's children the anxiety they are manifesting strikes me as unreasonable."[13] There is no mention here of the past reliability of one's empathetic insights in similar cases. But some sort of assumption of past successes certainly seems to be required. To see the necessity consider the following argument where this requirement is contradicted:

(1'') Jones is usually mistaken in his empathetic insights concerning the cause of children's anxiety.
(2'') Jones has an empathetic insight that his children's anxiety is caused by the bombing.

(3'') His children's anxiety is caused by the bombing.

Given (1''), (2'') tends to disconfirm (3'') rather than support it. So unless Scriven is assuming that empathetic insight has been successful in a certain type of case it is not unreasonable to suppose that one cannot be certain on the basis of empathy in this case. On the other hand if he is supposing this past success, how does his view conflict with positivist critiques of Verstehen?

Perhaps the answer is that Scriven, although assuming the past success of Verstehen, does not believe that the evidence for past success needs to be based on standard positivistic intersubjective methods of verification. It is unclear if this is Scriven's view. Scriven does emphasize in one place that empathetic insight is indeed inter-subjectively testable.[14] If he means by intersubjectively testable what positivists mean by intersubjectively testable is unclear.

Sometimes he seems to mean something different. At one point he seems to identify intersubjective testability with the possibility of "inter-judge agreement,"[15] i.e., the agreement between judges. Certainly this is not what the positivists were concerned with and for good reason. For it is obvious that agreement among judges by itself gives no support to what they are agreeing to. One must also have independent reason to think the judges are reliable. Scriven may be aware of this point. He points out that on technical issues we are only interested in agreement among experts since "other humans are unreliable instruments on such issues."[16] Here the suggestion seems to be that inter-judge agreement is only useful when the judges are reliable instruments. The positivist would certainly concur.

The question the positivist would raise is how is this reliability to be established. Scriven seems to agree that this is an important question and argues that we have independent criteria for identifying experts.[17] Positivists would insist that these criteria should be their past success as verified by intersubjective methods, that is methods that could be used by nonexperts and that give results open to public scrutiny. Moreover, they would insist even when experts need not be involved that intersubjective testing seems necessary. Although it may not take an expert to have a justified empathetic insight that his child's anxiety is caused by bombing, the justification, as we have seen, still requires past success of the empathizer in relevantly similar cases. And knowledge of this past success in turn seems to demand intersubjective verification. Now whether according to Scriven knowledge of such past success is intersubjectively verifiable in the sense required by the positivists is unclear. Scriven says:

> But intersubjective testability, taken in the usual sense, is not even a necessary condition for scientific knowledge. A single witness of a unique astronomical event may be reliable enough to justify us in believing his knowledge claim although it is not testable. We'll hesitate to drop a good theory that turns out to be incompatible with his observation, but that just shows it was (indirectly) testable; in the absence of such a conflict, we'll believe him.[18]

What is the relevance of these remarks to the intersubjective testability of Verstehen? Perhaps the suggestion is that knowledge claims by experts using empathetic insight are justifiable but not inter-subjectively testable in "the usual sense " (the sense required by the positivists?).

But what is this sense? Scriven's talk about unique events and single witnesses seems to suggest that positivists were committed to the view that a statement about an event was not intersubjectively testable unless the event was repeatable or was directly observed by more than one witness. But this is not so. Positivism allowed indirect intersubjective verification. As Scriven points out the testimony of the witness was indirectly intersubjectively testable when it conflicted with or confirmed some theory.[19] Moreover the witness' testimony was intersubjectively testable in other ways as well. For if the witness was reliable in cases where direct intersubjective test was possible, this gives inductive support to his reliability in general and in the case at issue.

In a similar way the expertise of empathizers (in the intuitive insight sense) is indirectly intersubjectively testable. Suppose, for example, we are considering the reliability of the empathetic insights (in the intuitive insight sense) of Cohen's violin appraisers. These experts are, among other things, called upon to judge the make of certain violins, e.g., whether the violin was made by Antonio Stradivari. Now non-experts apparently cannot intersubjectively test the judgment of these experts. Yet those experts' judgments are accepted. This is presumably because in those cases where their intuitive insights about violins can be directly verified they are usually correct and by straightforward inductive argument, it is assumed, they are probably correct in those cases where their judgments cannot be directly verified. The basic argument used to establish their conclusions has the following form:

Suppose our evidence is that

(1) In most cases where expert X's intuitive judgment could be directly intersubjectively tested it was correct.

By inductive generalization one concludes from (1)

(2) In most cases expert X's intuitive judgment was correct.

By another inductive generalization one infers from (2)

(3) In most cases expert X's intuitive judgment is correct.

And (3) combined with

(4) X intuitively judges that p.

allows one by direct inference to infer

(5) p.

Now it seems that such an argument may well be an inductively acceptable argument: further, there is nothing obvious in the positivist program that would be opposed to such an argument. An expert's intuitive judgment could be subject to intersubjective tests of an indirect kind. For if an alleged expert's intuitive judgments often turned out to be incorrect where one could directly intersubjectively test them this would tend to count against his judgments in cases where direct intersubjective testing were not possible.

Cohen on Verstehen in History

Howard Cohen's position on Verstehen may be summarized in this way: Scriven is correct to suppose that Verstehen is a way of verifying hypotheses. However the method of Verstehen is inappropriate in history although it is appropriate in violin appraising. This is because intersubjective testability is more important in history than in violin appraising and judgments based on Verstehen are not intersubjectively testable.

Like Scriven what exactly Cohen means by Verstehen is not too clear. Certainly Cohen does not mean what Scriven means by "Verstehen" in the transfer sense. For given this sense of Verstehen Cohen's example of the use of Verstehen in violin appraising is unintelligible. Expert violin appraisers do not presumably estimate their reaction to something and the transferability of their reaction to other people in making their judgments; their conclusions are not about the reactions of other people but about certain properties of old violins.

All of this suggests that Cohen is using Verstehen in the intuitive insight sense of Verstehen. This suggestion is reinforced when Cohen in introducing his discussion of Verstehen in relation to violin appraising quotes the following remark of Scriven:[20] "One may see (or understand) immediately why someone or some group did some thing, and not require further testing to be justifiably confident that this really is the reason."

This quotation from Scriven with its emphasis on immediate seeing again indicates that Cohen is talking about Verstehen in the intuitive insight sense in history. Cohen argues that the use of Verstehen in this sense is inappropriate in history as opposed to violin appraising. The difference, as Cohen sees it, is as follows: In violin appraising it is of the utmost importance to settle doubtful cases. The use of Verstehen--that is the intuitive insight of an expert violin appraiser--is the only available and plausible way of doing this in many cases. Furthermore, in appraising violins extremely precise distinctions must be drawn which cannot be drawn on the basis of the available explicitly formulatable evidence. The intuitive insight of experts is the only way this can be done. Thus the need for definite and very finely drawn conclusions makes the use of Verstehen appropriate in violin appraising.

In history, however, Cohen argues other needs are primary. In particular, objectivity, i.e, intersubjective verification, is of primary importance.

> When a historian's explanation is challenged--when it becomes doubtful or disputed--it must survive the judgment of his peers. Other historians--if they are interested-- must be in a position to examine the evidence and decide whether the conclusion follows or not...The class of historians is not a closed circle of experts. Nor, for that matter, is any small segment of the class--at least not in the sense that their judgments are authoritative in virtue of the proven reliability of the investigator.[21]

Furthermore, in history the historian is not required to draw finer conclusions than is justified by the historical evidence. However Cohen argues that the drawing of fine distinctions in violin certification "is the major need of the community."[22] Consequently Cohen maintains that Verstehen in history is not a provider of knowledge.

There is at least one misleading aspect of Cohen's argument. It is not true that the use of experts in history precludes intersubjective testing. As we have seen the intuitive judgment of experts can be indirectly intersubjectively tested. Cohen's thesis must be modified to read that in history, unlike violin appraising, intersubjective verifiability of a certain kind is appropriate. Consequently, the use of the intuitive insight of experts in history, although intersubjectively verifiable in one sense, is not intersubjectively verifiable in another sense. The sense in which the intuitive insight of experts is not intersubjectively verifiable makes the use of experts in history inappropriate.

The important question is why? Once we see that the intuitive judgment of experts in history can be indirectly intersubjectively verified in one sense the persuasiveness of Cohen's argument seems to be diminished. Further, his thesis is dubious on independent grounds.

Cohen argues that historians, unlike violin appraisers, are not required to make very fine distinctions—distinctions that are indeterminate in relation to the historical evidence. Now whether this view is correct or not depends on what one takes the function of history to be. If we are talking about the traditional view of history as a detached ethically neutral inquiry Cohen may be correct. But if other goals are given prominence, his restriction on the use of experts becomes more dubious.

Radical historians, for example, argue that historians should not be afforded the luxury of detachment and aloofness commonly associated with historical inquiry. Thus Howard Zinn argues that historians have an important social function to serve. Historians, according to Zinn, can "intensify, expand, sharpen our preception of how bad things are for victims of the world"; they can expose "the pretensions of government to either neutrality or beneficence"; they can expose the ideology that pervades our culture"; they can "recapture those few moments in the past which show a better way of life than that which has dominated the earth thus far."[23] Although Zinn does not, as far as I know, consider the possibility of using experts in historical inquiry and does not use such experts in his own historical work, there is good reason why he should not be opposed to the use of them since he believes that the use of historians should have an important social function. This social function may make it necessary to draw conclusions finer than those permitted by the historical data. In such cases the intuitive historian need not forsake objectivity in the sense of intersubjective testability. If it becomes necessary to fulfill history's social function by going beyond the historical evidence and relying on the intuitive insight of experts, such insight would be indirectly intersubjectively testable.

However, one need not embrace Zinn's program of radical history to see that in some cases social goals should be given special weight. The Warren Commission Report on the assassination of President Kennedy might well be considered an example of historical writing motivated by special social concerns. Critics as well as defenders of the Warren Report admit that many crucial points about the assassination cannot be discerned by recourse to the available historical evidence. It seems plausible to suppose in a report of such crucial national interest that the use of the intuitive judgment of experts would have been quite appropriate.

One does not even have to consider special cases like the Warren Commission to question Cohen's thesis. Cohen argues that historians—unlike violin appraisers—are not required to draw finer conclusions than are warranted by the explicitly statable evidence. However, he admits that historians may draw such conclusions. "The historian may if he wishes explain details for which there is no formulatable evidence. When he does so the explanation rests on his authority as a diagnostician if they are acknowledged to be known at all." Cohen goes on to argue: "One cannot reasonably say, however, that achieving that sort of precision is such an important part of historical knowledge that intersubjective verifiability should be sacrificed to it.[24]

What is puzzling about this quotation is that Cohen seems to admit that historians are permitted (but not required) to rely on experts' intuitive insights in order to make fine distinctions but he also claims that intersubjective verifiability (in his sense) should not be sacrificed in order to make such distinctions. But if historians are permitted to use such insights, then intersubjective verifiability (in his sense) can be (although it need not be) sacrificed in order to make such fine distinctions. What Cohen must say, I should think, in order to have a coherent thesis is that historians—unlike violin appraisors—are not even permitted to draw conclusions "for which there is not formulatable evidence."

But this thesis surely is too strong and I believe that Cohen's apparent inconsistency suggests that he does not want to embrace it. Historians, given a traditional view of historical inquiry, should be permitted to draw conclusions that are not warranted by formulatable evidence provided that such conclusions are based on the intuitive insight of historical experts. Although Cohen is correct to insist that historians should not be required to draw such conclusions, as we have stressed permitting such conclusions would not be sacrificing intersubjective verifiability in one important sense although it would be sacrificing intersubjective verifiability in the sense Cohen has in mind. The crucial question is whether such sacrifice is worth it.

There is another approach to the study of history besides the approach of the radical historians or the approach of historians with some special social task, e.g., the writing of the Warren Commission Report which suggests that the sacrifice of Cohen's type of intersubjective testability may be worth the price. Many historians have argued that although history may not be a social science, history would benefit from the use of social scientific techniques. The use of computers, mathematical models, statistical analysis, social scientific theories in history by historians testifies to the growing importance of social science in history.

Looked at from this vantage point the use of the intuitive judgment of experts in history is just one more use of social science techniques in history—something that many scientifically minded historians should welcome. For example, Helmer and Rescher[25] have suggested the use of experts in the inexact sciences (part of the social sciences are inexact on their view). These experts could be used in prediction, decision making, simulation techniques, gaming techniques and pseudo-experimentation. Some of their suggestions are already being used in social science and there seems to be no good reason why certain uses of experts could not be used in a scientifically oriented historical inquiry.

Now one might argue that the use of experts in history would restrict the freedom of the non-expert historian to challenge the expert historian's findings and this would create a historical elite. Thus Cohen argues:"When a historian is challenged—when it becomes doubtful or disputed—it must survive the judgement of his peers." He maintains "the class of historians is not a closed circle of experts. Nor for that matter is any small segment of that class....Any young or previously unacknowledged historian may dispute an old diagnostician."[26]

Would the use of experts undercut this attractive picture sketched by Cohen? It would not, I believe, in any objectionable way. First of all, non-expert historians would still be needed to check the judgement of experts where this could be checked. Thus the judgement of the non-expert would in an important sense be basic. Secondly, historians could challenge the judgement of accepted experts in at least two ways. They might argue that new evidence has come to light in terms of which the intuitive judgement of an expert could be directly tested. Moreover, they could challenge the authority of the expert indirectly by showing in those cases where his judgement could be checked that he was wrong much more often than previously thought. Consequently his judgement in cases where his insight could not be directly checked would become dubious. Thirdly, expert judgement might be needed only occasionally. (In this respect perhaps Cohen is correct. Violin appraising and historical inquiry are perhaps different. The number of cases in which an expert insight is needed may be much smaller in history than in violin appraising even if a radical approach a la Zinn is taken.)

All of the above suggests that the alleged elitism among historians if experts are used is something that would be tolerable. Whether there are experts in history in the sense that there are experts in violin appraising is another question. But if there are, then, it seems to me, historians should welcome their use rather than fear for the objectivity of history.

Conclusion

I have argued that Scriven's argument for the use of Verstehen as a provider of knowledge is misleading. Verstehen, as Scriven seems to understand it, does not by itself verify hypotheses in either science or history. (In this respect the positivists were correct.) Whether Scriven thinks it does is unclear. It is true that Verstehen combined with independently established knowledge, namely the reliability of someone's past empathetic insights, does enable hypotheses to be verified. Although positivists did not envisage this use of Verstehen it is doubtful they would be opposed to it as Scriven seems to suggest. Such a use of Verstehen is not incompatible with the general program of positivism or with the explicit statements of the critics of Verstehen. Whether Scriven thinks the independently established knowledge of the past reliability of the empathizer is intersubjectively testable in the sense desired by positivists is unclear. But in any case such knowledge does seem to be intersubjectively testable in an indirect way that is in keeping with positivism.

Cohen is therefore incorrect to suppose that if the intuitive judgements of experts are relied on in history the intersubjective testability of their judgements would be precluded. He is correct that a certain type of intersubjective testability would be precluded by their use. However, we have argued that the use of intuitive insights of experts may be necessary for certain special historical writing dominated by practical motives and in any case it seems in keeping with the desirability of using social science techniques in history. We have further suggested that the use of such experts correctly understood would not preclude criticism of these experts' judgments or establish an historical elite.

Footnotes

1. Michael Scriven, "Logical Positivism and the Behavioral Sciences," in The Legacy of Logical Positivism, eds. Peter Achinstein and Stephen F. Barker (Baltimore: Johns Hopkins Univ. Press, 1969), pp. 195-210; and Michael Scriven, "Verstehen Again," Theory and Decision, I, 1971, pp. 382-386.

2. Howard Cohen, "Das Verstehen and Historical Knowledge," American Philosophical Quarterly, 1973, pp. 299-396.

3. Scriven, "Logical Positism...", p. 204.

4. Ibid.

5. Scriven, "Verstehen Again," p. 383.

6. Scriven, "Logical Positivism," p. 201.

7. O. Helmer and N. Rescher, "On the Epistemology of the Inexact Sciences," Management Science, 6, 1969.

8. T. Abel, "The Operation Called 'Verstehen'", in The Structure of Scientific Thought, ed. E.H. Madden (Boston: Houghton-Mifflin, 1960), p. 164.

9. Ernest Nagel, The Structure of Science (New York: Harcourt, Brace and World, 1961), pp. 482-483.

10. Richard Rudner, Philosophy of Social Science, (Englewood Cliffs, N.J.: Prentice-Hall, 1966), p. 73.

11. Scriven, "Logical Positivism," pp. 202-205.

12. G.E.M. Anscombe, Intention, (Oxford: Blackwell, 1957), p. 15.

13. Scriven, "Verstehen Again," p. 383.

14. Ibid., This comment of Scriven's is in response to a criticism of Van Evra. See James W. Van Evra, "On Scriven on 'Verstehen'", in Theory and Decision, 1, 1971, pp. 377-381.

15. Ibid.

16. Ibid.

17. Ibid.

18. Ibid., p. 384.

19. See Carl G. Hempel, The Philosophy of Natural Science, (Englewood Cliffs, N.J.: Prentice-Hall, 1966), pp. 38-40, for a discussion of the indirect support given by a theory.

20. Cohen, op. cit., p. 300.

21. Ibid., pp. 304-305.

22. Ibid., p. 305.

23. Howard Zinn, The Politics of History (Boston: Beacon Press, 1970), pp. 33-55.

24. Cohen, op. cit., pp. 305-306.

25. Helmer and Rescher, op. cit.

26. Cohen, op. cit., pp. 304-305.

PART VI: CRITIQUE OF ALTERNATIVE PHILOSOPHIES

Despite the various positions argued for and the alternative views criticized in the previous essays, no systematic critique has been given of any alternative philosophical positions. In the three essays that follow three different approaches to the social sciences are systematically evaluated. Two of these positions represent attempts to apply a general philosophical position to the social sciences. In "Winch on Philosophy, Social Science and Explanation," a Wittgensteinian approach to the social sciences is critically evaluated; in "Popperian Anthropology" a Popperian approach to cultural and social anthropology is criticized; in "The Philosopher of Social Science as Participant Observer" Diesing's views on the methodology of the philosophy of social sciences are critically evaluated. In the first two essays the view that certain a priori restrictions should be placed on the methodology of the social sciences is rejected. In the third essay, the a priori restrictions that Diesing places on the methodology of the philosophy of the social sciences (in contrast to the methodology of the social sciences) are rejected. I end my paper on Diesing by outlining some ideas about the methodology of the philosophy of the social sciences —a methodology that I believe is manifested to a large extent in the essays reprinted in this volume.

Winch on Philosophy, Social Science and Explanation

Peter Winch in his book *The Idea of A Social Science*[1] presents a view of the nature of philosophy and the social sciences that has far reaching implications. It is the purpose of this paper to subject Winch's views to critical scrutiny.[2] I will argue first that Winch's view of the task of philosophy is severely limited and that what he takes to be the method of philosophy is wrong; secondly, I will maintain that Winch's view of the task of the social sciences has little relevance to what is going on in the social sciences today; finally, I will argue that Winch's views on the nature of explanation and prediction in the social sciences are mistaken.

THE NATURE OF PHILOSOPHY

Winch is opposed to the "underlaborer" concept of philosophy. According to this view philosophy has a very minor role to play; the lead role is played by empirical science. It is empirical science that discovers the nature of the universe, man and society; it is empirical science and empirical science alone that can tell us truths about reality. Philosophy's task is merely to straighten out certain confusions caused by the misuse of language; these confusions may stand in the way of the really important task—the advancement of science (pp. 3-7).

According to Winch this view of the task of philosophy errs mainly because of a mistaken assumption about the nature of language. It assumes that there is a way of separating our linguistic apparatus from reality. This assumption is false, according to Winch, since the way we conceive reality is determined by our linguistic apparatus; we cannot conceive reality apart from our language (pp. 10-15).

Once this false assumption is exposed, Winch believes, the underlaborer concept of philosophy is doomed; there is no reason why philosophy cannot give us knowledge of reality. Philosophy's job is still to examine language, but not just the language which causes linguistic confusions. Philosophy's job is to examine the social institutions of linguistic usage in order to discover the diverse linguistic rules that govern the manifold linguistic activities of man. Thus the study of what Wittgenstein called "forms of life" is the subject matter of philosophy: philosophy of religion would study the rules of religious discourse in that form of

370

life known as religion; philosophy of science would study the rules of scientific discourse in that form of life known as science; epistemology would study linguistic rules of forms of life as such (pp. 15-39). Philosophy conceived in this way is not an underlaborer with but a minor role to play. For since philosophy examines our linguistic apparatus and since this apparatus governs the way in which we must conceive reality, philosophy gives us knowledge of the way in which we must conceive reality, given our language (pp. 14-21).

Moreover, philosophy is an *a priori* discipline. Winch argues again and again against the empirical prejudices of the underlaborer concept of philosophy in which genuine knowledge of the world is only empirical knowledge. What must be realized, according to Winch, is that philosophy can give us knowledge of the world *a priori* (pp. 15-18). How much *a priori* knowledge of the world philosophy can give us Winch leaves unclear, but one thing is clear: philosophy can give us much more *a priori* knowledge than has been supposed. In particular we can know a great deal more about social reality by examining our language than has ever been supposed by empirically minded social scientists (p. 17).

In sum, Winch's main theses on the nature of philosophy are:

(1) The task of philosophy is to examine the linguistic rules of various forms of life
(2) This task is accomplished *a priori*
(3) Philosophy can in this way give us knowledge of reality
(4) This *a priori* knowledge of social reality is greater than has usually been supposed.

Let us consider these points in turn.

(1) Now it seems to me that Winch's view on the greater role that philosophy should play is correct; the underlaborer conception of philosophy is surely limited and Winch does us a great service by pointing this out so lucidly. On the other hand, one may wonder whether Winch's own view of philosophy is too narrow. Certainly an important task of philosophy is to understand the rules of language in religion, science, art and so on. But surely this is not the only one. Now-a-days one must be suspicious of anyone who ignores Wittgenstein and the thrust of Oxford linguistic philosophy. However, one must equally be

suspicious of anyone who seems to maintain, as Winch does, that the only task of philosophy is to understand the function of language in certain forms of life. There are at least *some* other jobs that philosophers have done which one could hardly deny are important.[3]

The linguistic rules which are implicit in certain forms of life can be made explicit and systematized by philosophers. There is but a short step indeed from this task to a philosopher's revising and modifying these linguistic rules.[4] Just because the ideal languages of the *Tractatus* and logical positivism were so removed from actual linguistic practice that they were irrelevant to it, it does not follow that no improvement in linguistic practice is possible or desirable. After all, as Wittgenstein made clear, ordinary language is intimately related to different forms of life. But forms of life may be built upon false beliefs, outmoded practices, and decadent social institutions. Ordinary language enshrines not only the wisdom of the ages[5] but also the prejudices of the ages and the conventional beliefs of the masses. The idealized excesses of the early Wittgenstein and of philosophers like Carnap should not drive us to the other extreme in which philosophy leaves everything as it is. Surely some judicial balance and tension between language as it is and language as it might be is the sane approach. But this means that the philosopher can and should take a more creative role than Winch would seem to allow. Instead of merely describing the rules of different areas of discourse the philosopher can make explicit, systematize, formalize, and revise this discourse; he can also criticize the beliefs, practices and institutions to which this discourse is so intimately related and can suggest revisions in the institutions. That Winch would *actually* object to this role of philosophy is difficult to say. But that he *seems* to object to it is quite obvious (p. 130).

(2) Even if we take philosophy to be the narrow discipline Winch seems to be advocating it would still be wrong to suppose philosophy's method is *a priori*. One surely cannot determine what the linguistic rules of a certain social activity are without some empirical investigation of these social activities. A statement of the rules governing religious discourse, for example, is surely an empirical hypothesis subject to empirical check and refutation.[6] This does not mean, of course, that the hypothesis must be established or refuted by mass polls and interviews (although these may be relevant if sufficiently subtle).[7] It does

mean that a philosopher cannot establish his view on the rules of ordinary language by sitting in his armchair and introspecting. Evidence from literature, lexicography, sociology, history and linguistics may all be relevant in substantiating his views.

Once philosophy is taken to have the broader task outlined above the relevance of empirical investigation is even more obvious. Surely, the justification for recommendations for revisions in linguistic rules will depend partly on the probable consequences of these revisions. Again, to criticize rationally a form of life will involve, in part, factual considerations of its origin and its consequences.

(3) The thesis that our language influences the way in which we conceive the world is surely not new and today seems to be widely accepted.[8] This view, however, gives no support to any of Winch's other theses. In particular, his view of the nature of philosophy finds no support in it. As I have already argued, philosophy might well change our language; if this thesis is true, then by so doing philosophy might improve our vision of the world. Moreover, it does not follow from the fact that language influences our view of the world that philosophy's task is performed *a priori*. The only way to learn about our linguistic apparatus is by the empirical methods of science. Now, to say that Winch's thesis is widely accepted today is not to say that all questions of the influence of language on our conception of reality are settled. Indeed, all sorts of questions remain. In what respect, under what circumstances, to what degree does language influence our conception of reality? How does language influence our view of reality? Why does it? Do all languages influence our conceptions of the world in the same way?

In short, what Winch says may well be true; but it hardly goes very far. Indeed, now-a-days it seems almost commonplace.

(4) To be sure, once we have investigated, by empirical methods, the answers to questions raised in (3) above we may begin to have some reliable knowledge of the extent to which and respect in which reality is structured by language. And it might be true, as Winch suggests, that our language structures much more of our world—in particular our own social world—than is usually supposed. But this again cannot be determined by sitting in one's armchair and considering one's own usage. In short, the extent to which our language does determine our conception of the world is a question for which evidence from various fields might be relevant. That Winch fails to see the need for

empirical check and the possibility of evidential refutation of this aspect of his thesis should not be surprising in the light of what has been said previously. But for all we know, our language may structure our conception of the world *much less* than is usually supposed.

THE NATURE OF SOCIAL SCIENCE

According to Winch social science's task is very close indeed to philosophy's. In fact, at times it is hard to see how on Winch's view philosophy and social science differ at all. Perhaps the only difference is this: philosophy's job is to discover the linguistic rules of different forms of life; social science's job is to discover all rules governing a form of life. But in order to determine what the linguistic rules of a form of life are, philosophy must investigate all rules of a form of life since all aspects of social behavior are intimately connected. The difference between philosophy and social science is perhaps at best only a matter of emphasis (pp. 40-45).

Whatever Winch's exact view on the relation between philosophy and social science, he does maintain that social science—in particular sociology—has as its task the "elucidation" of the notion of meaningful or ruled-governed behavior. By "meaningful behavior" Winch does not just mean behavior that is governed by certain standards of appropriateness, e.g., rules governing voting behavior; he means also behavior that is justified by reasons e.g., the reasons why someone voted one way rather than another. Let us call standards of appropriateness as well as reasons given by an individual actor "rules of social life." I take it that by the elucidation of the notion of meaningful behavior Winch means simply the discovery and specification of the rules of social life (pp. 45-65).

It is difficult to determine, however, just how important he believes the elucidation of the concept of meaningful behavior to be in relation to the overall task of social science. Indeed, one may distinguish several different things that Winch might mean:

(1) The only task of social science is to elucidate the concept of meaningful behavior
(2) The main task of social science is to elucidate the concept of meaningful behavior
(3) An important task of the social sciences is to elucidate the concept of meaningful behavior

(4) A task of the social sciences is to elucidate the concept of meaningful behavior.

It seems quite clear that Winch does not maintain (4), the weakest proposal. And it seems only a little less clear that he does not want to maintain (3), a thesis that is only a little stronger. Actually, he appears to hold either (1) or (2). But whatever his view, no other job for social science except the discovery and specification of the rules of social life is ever mentioned. So even if Winch is only asserting (3) or (4) he says nothing about the other tasks social scientists might have.

Surely this is a serious omission for their are many other jobs for social scientists; investigations that social scientists have and are continuing to carry on. Consider, as an example, the work of Robert Merton. I take it that Merton's work is typical of much of what goes on in contemporary sociology and that any account of social science that does not allow for, or at least does not show any awareness of, the sort of problems Merton deals with is out of touch with what is going on in the field. To be sure, Merton is interested in the rules of social life, but he does not limit his investigation to discovering and specifying what these rules are. Indeed, discovering and specifying the rules of social life is only the beginning for Merton. Consider some of the kinds of questions Merton raises and tries to deal with in his study on bureaucracy:[9]

(a) What is the function of a particular social rule R_1 in a bureaucratic institution?
(b) Why does rule R_1 have this function?
(c) What is the disfunction of some other social rule R_2 in a bureaucratic institution?
(d) Why does R_2 have this disfunction?
(e) What effect does conforming to social rules have on the personality of people in a bureaucratic institution?
(f) Why does it have this effect?
(g) Does a bureaucratic institution with social rules R_1 and R_2 attract a certain personality type?
(h) If so, why does it do this?

There are, of course, other questions that have been asked by social scientists but which Merton does not deal with explicitly in this study on bureaucracy. For example:

(i) What is the origin of this bureaucratic institution?
(j) How did social rules R_1 and R_2 develop in this institution?

It should be clear from this list of questions that the strongest thesis, (1) above, is out of contact with what is going on in the social sciences.[10] One might still wonder if either (2) or (3) or (4) is a more reasonable position.

Certainly (2) seems too strong. It suggests that once one has discovered and specified the rules of social life little work of any importance remains for social science. But, on the contrary, almost all important questions that social scientists actually are interested in and are working on remain. Now it might be objected that although (2) is too strong, (3) and (4) are too weak. (4) makes it seem as if the discovery and specification of social rules is one among many other tasks of social science; (3) makes it seem as if the discovery and specification of social rules is one among many other important tasks. It may be argued that both are misleading suggestions; that discovering and specifying what social rules are present is not merely a task among others—even a task among other important tasks—but rather a necessary step for social science to take before it can begin its other tasks. Perhaps, it may be argued, what Winch should have said was:

> (5) Elucidating the concept of meaningful behavior is a necessary condition for doing any other social scientific investigation.

But even (5) is liable to serious misunderstanding. It is surely mistaken to maintain that social scientists must discover and specify all or even a large part of the rules of social life *before* any other investigation can begin. It would be equally mistaken to believe that social scientists must have detailed and precise knowledge of any social rules *before* they can start their other work. Increase in knowledge of the rules of social life as well as their detailed specification can go hand in hand with other investigations such as the study of their origins, their acquisition, their effect on personality. Perhaps all that can be said is this:

> (6) The existence of meaningful behavior is a necessary condition for doing social science.

But (6) is hardly news. Indeed, as Brown has argued, "To say, that social scientists depend heavily upon the notion of rule-conforming behavior is to utter a platitude."[11] Without rules of social life there is no society and hence no social scientific investigation is possible.

Social Scientific Explanation and Prediction

Winch's views on the nature of philosophy and social science lead him to make certain inferences about the nature of explanation and prediction in the social sciences. Winch seems to maintain—explicitly or implicitly—all of the following theses (pp. 46-94):

- (a) Social scientific explanations must be in terms of rules of social life.
- (b) Social scientific explanations are always of rule-governed behavior.
- (c) Social scientific explanation of rule-governed behavior must be in terms of rules of social life.
- (d) Social scientific explanation must be in terms of what the actor can understand.
- (e) It is in principle impossible to completely predict rule-governed behavior. (See especially pp. 91-94.)

These theses, although closely connected, raise different issues and we will consider them separately.

(1) We have already seen reason to doubt thesis (a). Social scientists explain the origin of rules in a social institution,[12] the learning of social rules, the attitude people have towards rules, the effect of conforming to these rules on personality, and so on. And in general such explanations are not in terms of rules of social life.[13] It is perhaps only because Winch takes such a narrow view of the task of the social sciences that he seems unaware of these obvious points.

(2) It should be clear from the above considerations that (b) is mistaken. Sometimes social scientific explanations are about rule-governed behavior, but sometimes they are about the rules themselves e.g., their origin, how they are learned. Moreover, sometimes social scientists explain behavior that is not rule-governed in Winch's sense. Winch gives an example of a berserk lunatic (p. 53). Such a person's behavior is not meaningful i.e., it is not governed by rules of social life. Yet there seems to be no reason why social science cannot give an explanation of this behavior. This, of course, is not to say that the lunatic's behavior can be completely explained in social scientific terms: psychology and physiology may also be relevant. But a partial explanation may come from social science e.g., in terms of the social class or social origin of the lunatic.

(3) Thesis (c) is weaker than thesis (a). One may grant

that social scientists sometimes do explain the origin of social rules, the learning of social rules, and so on and that these explanations are not always in terms of social rules, and yet still insist that rule-governed behavior must be explained in terms of these rules.

This weaker thesis is wrong, however. Indeed, Winch gives what seems to be a counter example to his own view. He considers a man N who votes labor and and yet has no reason for doing so (p. 49). This man's behavior, according to Winch, is meaningful: it is governed by certain standards of appropriateness i.e., the rules of voting behavior. However, although we understand *what* he has done when we see his behavior in the context of these voting rules we do not understand *why* he has voted labor in terms of these rules. Moreover, since he has no reason for voting labor rather than, say, liberal or conservative we do not know *why* he voted labor in terms of his reasons. Hence, rules of social life (standards of appropriateness or reasons) do not explain why he voted the way he did.

But even if N did vote labor and could give reasons for his choice it is still dubious that his reasons would furnish a *complete* explanation for his behavior. Citing his reasons may, of course, completely *justify* his choice; there might be no more one could say in constructing a rationale for N's voting labor.[14] But giving a complete rationale for someone's choice is not necessarily to answer the question why he did what he did in the sense of what causal factors brought about his action. If one is asking for the total cause of N voting labor, N's reason may be only one aspect of the whole causal nexus. That this is true is shown by the fact that N may sometimes not vote labor although his reasons have not changed. His reasons are not a sufficient nomological condition for his action.

Winch would, of course, object to the above suggestion. He does not believe that rule-governed behavior can be causally explained. If it could be, then such behavior would be completely predictable, and he argues that rule-governed behavior is in general impossible to predict. We shall take up this argument when we consider thesis (e). First let us consider two other arguments Winch gives against construing reasons as part of the total cause of someone's action.[15]

First, he maintains that reasons justify someone's action whereas causes do not. However, reasons can both justify an action *and* be a causal factor of the action. There is nothing incompatible in this.

Secondly, Winch argues that part of learning the concept of cause is learning techniques of prediction. But although one can sometimes predict what someone will do by means of knowing his reasons, learning techniques of prediction is not involved in learning the concept of reason. Hence, reasons cannot be causes (pp. 82-83). However, not enough is known about the details of language learning to know whether Winch's view is correct;[16] in relation to our present knowledge Winch's view is pure speculation. But even granted that we do learn language in the way Winch says, nothing of philosophical importance follows. It still might be true that the reasons can be usefully assimilated to causes.

Consider an analogous case: The notion of number may not be learned as a notion that is set theoretically defined but it may be useful to assimilate number to set in a systematic account of mathematics. The same thing may be true of cause and reason: it may be useful to assimilate reasons to causes in a systematic account of social science.

(4) Now it should be evident that thesis (d) is parasitic on theses (a) and (b) and hence can be disposed of rather quickly.

Explanations of the origin of rules in institutions, for example, may not be in terms the members of the institution understand for the members of the institution may be ignorant of history or theoretical sociology. For obvious reasons the explanation of the behavior of a lunatic may not be in terms the lunatic can understand.

But even an explanation of a piece of meaningful behavior need not always be in terms that the actor can understand. Thus an explanation of N's choice to vote labor when N has no reason might be in terms of a sociological theory which uses abstract theoretical notions beyond N's ken e.g., group cohesiveness. Moreover, even if N has reasons for voting labor the complete explanation—the total cause—may transcend N's understanding. The total cause may be specified in terms of an abstract sociological theory which N cannot grasp.

(5) One might be inclined to say that only future empirical research will decide whether rule-governed behavior will ever be completely predictable. This is not Winch's position. Winch gives an *a priori* argument. He maintains that the notion of free

choice is an essential aspect of rule-governed behavior. To use one of Winch's examples: N voting labor is a free choice. But if we could unerringly predict N's behavior by means of causal laws we would not call N's behavior free. Hence, rule-governed behavior is not completely predictable by means of causal laws.

Two points should be noted here. First, Winch's thesis rests upon an assumption about the actual use of language that is not obvious: if behavior could be unerringly predicted we would not say that such behavior was free. Philosophers have in recent literature usually given two conflicting analyses of free will:

(1) X has free will to do x. ≡. If X were to choose to do x, X would succeed.

(2) X has free will to do x. ≡. If X were to choose to do x X would succeed, and X could choose to do x.

It should be noted that (2) is a stronger thesis than (1). Now (1) is perfectly compatible with the prediction of all human behavior by causal laws. Thus according to (1) N would be free to vote conservative despite the fact that we could predict by causal law that N will vote labor. As long as N were to choose to vote conservative, N *would* be successful. On the other hand, (2) is incompatible with the prediction of all human behavior by causal laws. According to (2) N would not be free to vote conservative if one could predict by causal law that he will vote labor since it would be nomologically impossible for N to choose to vote conservative.

Now whether (1) or (2) captures the ordinary meaning of "free choice" is difficult to say. Certainly Winch cites no evidence to show that (2) is more in accord with the way people speak. But even if (2) is a correct account of ordinary usage it would not follow that social scientists could not predict what has been *called* free choice behavior: one might well argue that such ordinary usage is mistaken; that really there are no free choices in the sense of (2). Here might be one of those cases where philosophers might well recommend a change in usage e.g., a change to (1).

Secondly, it should be noted that if social scientists are able to predict what is (perhaps incorrectly) called rule-governed behavior it is likely that they will have to take into account many more factors than Winch would allow. Winch seems to suppose that the only information available to an observer O, of N's social behavior, in order for O to predict N's social behavior, is information about the rules of social life governing this behavior (p. 91). But this is surely mistaken. Social scientists may have information about N's physiological, psychological, social background, and environmental facts to help them make accurate predictions.

Related to this point is Winch's argument that in the natural sciences if a prediction fails this shows that we have made a miscalculation or that our own theory is mistaken, while in the social sciences inaccurate predictions are perfectly compatible with no miscalculations and with completely adequate theories. But again this seems mistaken. If our prediction fails in social sciences, this seems to me to show exactly the same thing as in the natural sciences: we have made a miscalculation or our theory is inadequate. That Winch thinks otherwise is undoubtedly partly due to the very limited range of variables he thinks are open for a social scientist to investigate as ways of predicting human behavior.

In conclusion, I have tried to show that Winch's idea of a social science and his view of the relationship between social science and philosophy are ill-conceived. Only time will tell if Winch's view on the nature of social science will become fashionable in social scientific circles as his Wittgensteinian views on the nature of philosophy has apparently become in philosophical circles. But in any case, as it has been often noted, what is fashionable and what is reasonable do not always coincide.

MICHAEL MARTIN
Boston University

---

[1] Peter Winch, *The Idea of A Social Science* (New York: Humanities Press, 1958). Page references appearing in the body of the paper will refer to Winch's book.

[2] Winch's book has been ably reviewed by L. Goldstein and I. C. Jarvie. These reviews are quite short, however, and only touch on a few of the points that need to be raised. Moreover, when critical points are raised they tend to be very condensed. See L. Goldstein review of *The Idea of A Social Science* by Peter Winch, *Philosophical Review*, 1960, pp. 411-414; I. C. Jarvie review of *The Idea of A Social Science* by Peter Winch, *British Journal for the Philosophy of Science*, 1961, pp. 73-77.

[3] Cf., Jarvie, *op. cit.*, p. 76.

[4] See I. Scheffler, *Anatomy of Inquiry* (New York: Alfred A. Knopf, 1963), pp. 3-19.

[5] Cf., John L. Austin, "A Plea for Excuses," *Collected Papers* (Oxford: Clarendon Press, 1961), p. 130.

[6] See Benson Mates, "On the Verification of Statements About Ordinary Language," *Ordinary Language*, ed. V. C. Chappell (Englewood Cliffs, N. J.:

Prentice-Hall, 1964); John Passmore, "Professor Ryle's Use of 'Use' and 'Usage,'" *Philosophical Review*, 1954, pp. 58-64.

7 The trouble with Ness' work is not that he attempts to establish statements about ordinary language empirically, but that his methods appear to be too crude. See for example, A. Ness, "'Truth'" As Conceived By Those Who Are Not Professional Philosophers," *Skrifter Utgitt Av Det Norske Videnskaps-Akadem: Oslo, 11. Hist.-Filos. Klasse*, Vol. IV, Oslo, 1938.

8 See for example, Ernst Cassirer, *Language and Myth* (New York: Harper, 1946); Dorothy D. Lee, "Conceptual Implications of an Indian Language," *Philosophy of Science*, 1938, pp. 89-102; Edward Sapir, *Language* (New York, 1921); B. L. Whorf, *Language, Thought and Reality: Selected Writings of Benjamin Lee Whorf*, ed. J. B. Carroll (New York: Wiley, 1956).

9 Robert K. Merton, *Social Theory and Social Structure* (Glencoe, Ill.: The Free Press, 1957), chaps. 6 & 7.

10 Cf., Goldstein, *op. cit.*

11 Robert Brown, *Explanation in Social Science* (Chicago: Aldine Publishing Co., 1963), p. 98.

12 Cf., Goldstein, *op. cit.*

13 Cf., Brown, *op. cit.*, chaps. 7, 8.

14 Cf., Morton White, *Foundations of Historical Knowledge* (New York: Harper and Row, 1965), chap. 5.

15 For a refutation of some other arguments against construing reasons as causes see White, *op. cit.*; Donald Davidson, "Action, Reasons, and Causes," *Journal of Philosophy*, 1963, pp. 685-700.

16 Cf., Paul Ziff, *Semantic Analysis* (New York: Cornell University Press, 1960), pp. 35-36n.

POPPERIAN ANTHROPOLOGY

by

Michael Martin, Boston University

I.C. Jarvie's stimulating and important theoretical work in anthropology 1) has several facets: a critical history of recent anthropological thought, a critical review of anthropological literature on cargo cults, and the application of Karl Popper's views on the philosophy of science to anthropology. I will not be concerned with either Jarvie's interpretation of the history of anthropology or his critical evaluation of studies of cargo cults. I wish rather to consider critically Jarvie's application of Popper's philosophy of science to anthropology. My criticism will be divided into two parts. First, an evaluation of his criticism of inductivism in anthropology.
Secondly, a criticism of his method of situational logic.

---

1) We will be concerned primarily with the following works by Jarvie:
"Nadel on the Aims and Methods of Social Anthropology" The British Journal for the Philosophy of Science, 1961, pp. 1-24; The Revolution in Anthropology (New York: The Humanities Press, 1964).

Jarvie's Critique of Inductivism

Throughout Jarvie's work he is critical of a view he labels "inductivism". 2)
However, it is not completely clear from Jarvie's writing exactly what "inductivism" is. He seems to label almost anything he does not like in anthropology as "inductivism"--everything from a sober attitude (a psychological disposition) to the use of inductive generalizations (a type of non-demonstrative inference). We shall return to Jarvie's more psychological criticisms later. For now we shall consider his critical comments directed against certain non-demonstrative inferences.

Jarvie is opposed to the use of two basic types of non-demonstrative inference in anthropology. First of all, and perhaps primarily, he is opposed to any inference from all observed members of a class to the whole class   3).

---

2) Alternatively, Jarvie speaks of the "Baconian view of Science" and "Building up a Science". See for example, The Revolution in Anthropology, pp. 5-6, 18-22, 33, 42, 48-49, 108-109; "Nadel on The Aims and Methods of Social Anthropology", pp. 3, 19-22.

3) See The Revolution in Anthropology, p. 42; "Nadel on the Aims and Methods of Social Anthropology", p. 19.

Let us call such inferences 'inductive generalizations'. Thus when an anthropologist infers from the fact that all observed primitive societies he has studied have some form of incest taboo to the conclusion that probably all primitive societies have some form of incest taboo, he has made an inductive generalization and Jarvie would object. It is important to realize that his objection is of a radical kind. He is not objecting on the grounds e.g., that the anthropologist's sample is small or that there is reason to think that the sample may be biased 4) in that it was obtained from one geographic region. Nor is he objecting on the ground that given the generally unreliable nature of most ethnographic data, the probability is not high. His objection is to any inference from the examined members of a class to the whole class--no matter what the range, variety or amount of examined members.

Secondly, Jarvie objects to another type of non-demonstrative inference. Consider an anthropologist with some cross-cultural hypothesis. Let us suppose that empirical consequences corresponding quite accurately to the ethnographic data are deduced from the hypothesis.

---

4) For a discussion of such factors in inductive generalizations, see John P. Day, <u>Inductive Probability</u> (New York: Humanities Press, 1961).

The anthropologist would infer that probably the hypothesis is true (the probability would presumably be a function of the amount and variety of the verified consequences). 5) Let us call such inferences hypothetical inferences. Again Jarvie would object. 6) All hypothetical inferences--no matter how many or varied the verified consequences deduced from them--are in principle invalid.

Many anthropologists might wonder at such criticisms. It is one thing, they might think, to be selectively critical of inductive generalizations and hypothetical inferences but it is another thing to condemn all such inferences. To understand Jarvie's position let us ask: Why does Jarvie hold such a view? What alternative view of anthropological method does he propose? As Jarvie makes clear, his views are based on the philosophy of science of Karl Popper. 7) Thus, to understand Jarvie's rejection of these types of non-demonstrative inference it is necessary to consider Popper's views.

---

5) See Ernest Nagel, "Probability and Degree of Confirmation or Weight of Evidence", Probability, Confirmation and Simplicity (eds) M. Foster and M.Martin (New York: Odyssey Press, 1966) pp. 184-194; Day, op. cit.

6) The Revolution in Anthropology, p. 211.

7) Karl Popper The Logic of Scientific Discovery (New York: Basic Books, 1959); Karl Popper Conjectures and Refutations (New York: Basic Books, 1962).

Popper's critique of non-demonstrative inference is derived primarily from the objection against induction raised by David Hume. 8) Hume argued that no inference that goes beyond the evidence (and inductive generalizations and hypothetical inferences do go beyond the evidence) is valid. To be sure, such inferences are made by everyone. But, according to Hume, they are irrational; they are without logical foundation. Hume argued that one can not make a deductive inference to any conclusion that goes beyond the evidence and one can not make a probabilistic inference to any conclusion that goes beyond the evidence <u>unless</u> one assumes (without justification) that the world beyond the evidence is similar to the world revealed by the evidence.

In brief this was Hume's argument and philosophers ever since have been trying to show Hume to be mistaken and inductive generalization and hypothetical inferences to be warranted. Popper, however, accepts Hume's argument; indeed, he maintains that no one has ever answered Hume's arguments. 9)

---

8) David Hume, "An Abstract of a Treatise on Human Nature", <u>Probability, Confirmation and Simplicity</u> (eds.) M. Foster and M. Martin, pp. 341-343.

9) Popper <u>The Logic of Scientific Discovery</u>, p.29.

Many philosophers of science have thought that if Hume were correct, it would be the end of science. Popper argues, however, that this is not so. The invalidity of inductive generalization and hypothetical inference is perfectly compatible with scientific inquiry. Popper maintains "Has our attitude, then, to be one of resignation?...are it's (science's) intellectual problems unsoluble? I do not think so". 10) Popper proposes a radically new way of looking at science as a rational enterprise--a way that is free from Hume's problem. According to Popper, science proceeds neither by inductive generalization nor by hypothetical inference i.e., the proposal of hypotheses and their verification. Science proceeds rather by the proposal of hypotheses and their falsification--by "conjecture and refutation". Hypotheses are proposed and then vigorous attempts are made to refute them. False hypotheses are thus eliminated and truth is ultimately approximated by the elimination of error.

How does this meet Hume's problem? Since the refutation of a hypothesis is a deductive procedure, no inference is made that goes beyond the evidence. In eliminating a hypothesis we deduce a consequence from the hypothesis that turns out false. We can then be <u>deductively assured</u> that the hypothesis is in error. But Hume had no objection to deduction. Thus science proceeds simply by the elimination of error which is accomplished purely by deduction e.g., by the deduction of the consequences of conjectured hypotheses that prove to be false.

---

10) Popper, <u>loc. cit.</u>, p. 281.

The implications for anthropology, according to
Jarvie, should be clear. Since Hume has shown that
inductive generalizations and hypothetical inferences are invalid, their continued use in anthropology is irrational. The method of conjecture (proposing a hypothesis) and refutation is to be substituted since this method is free from Hume's problem.

According to Jarvie there is another argument for Popper's methodology of conjecture and refutation in anthropology. The use of Popper's methodology would give a rationale for bold and imaginative theorizing. Critics of anthropology have often pointed out the theoretical poverty of anthropology. 11) Jarvie seems to maintain that this theoretical poverty is due to the use of inductive generalizations and hypothetical inferences in anthropology. The use of such inferences gives a rationale for "fact worship" and endless field work which seem to have resulted in so little theoretical progress in anthropology.

But could it not be argued that Popper's methodology would give impetus to wild and undisciplined anthropological speculation, and a lack of attention to the ethnographic data? Such an argument, according to Jarvie, misses one of the pivotal points of Popper's view.

---

11) See for example, Clyde Kluckhohn, "The Place of Theory in Anthropological Studies", Philosophy of Science, 1939, pp. 328-334; C.W.M. Hart, "Cultural Anthropology and Sociology", Modern Sociological Theory, (eds.), H. Becker and A. Boskoff (New York: Holt, Rinehart, and Winston, 1957), pp. 528-549.

For not only does Popper emphasize bold conjecture, he stresses rigorous testing-- refutation--as well. Thus one cannot argue, according to Jarvie, that the use of Popper's theory would be a rationale for softheaded anthropology. On the contrary it would justify hardheaded testing of imaginative theory.

There are a number of questions that could be raised about this view. We shall concentrate on only a few: (1) Popper's acceptance of Hume's problem, (2) Popper's method as the answer to Hume, (3) Popper's method as an answer to Hume, (4) refutation as an approach to truth, (5) the theoretical poverty of inductivism.

Popper's Acceptance of Hume's Problem

It is clear that Popper and Jarvie believe that Hume has proposed a genuine problem: non-demonstrative inference needs a justification before it can be accepted and no justification is possible. Some contemporary philosophers have questioned this assumption. It has been argued persuasively that Hume's problem is illusory; that his problem is based on a misuse of language. Hume's problem is not to be solved but dissolved. No real problem was actually posed by Hume. 12)

Thus it has been argued that the use of certain types of non-demonstrative inference (e.g., inductive generalizations and hypothetical inference) is simply part of what is meant by "being rational". There is no more sense in asking for the justification of such inferences in general than there is in asking for the justification of deductive inference in general. To be sure, one can ask for the justification of a particular inductive generalization and hypothetical inference or deductive inference.

---

12) See for example, Peter Strawson, "The 'Justification' of Induction", Probability, Confirmation and Simplicity, (eds.), M. Foster and M. Martin; Paul Edwards, "Russell's Doubts About Induction", Mind, 1949.

In this case a significant answer is available in terms of commonly accepted canons of induction and deduction. Whether such an approach to Hume's problem is acceptable or not is not at issue here. It is important, however, to notice that unless such an approach is shown to be untenable much of Jarvie's attack against inductivism is unwarranted. I am not aware that Popper or any of his followers has answered this objection and recent attempts to answer such an approach by non-Popperians are by no means conclusive. 13)

Popper's Method As The Answer to Hume

But even if Hume did raise a genuine problem is Popper's approach the only rational way to do science? Is there no solution to the alleged invalidity of induction except the method of conjecture and refutation? Some philosophers have proposed an alternative that has been discussed in recent literature. These philosophers have agreed that inductive generalization and hypothetical inference cannot be validated. These inferences cannot be shown either to lead to truth or to probably lead to truth. In this respect Hume was correct. But they have argued that these procedures are nevertheless vindicated 14).

---

13) See for example, Wesley Salmon "Should We Attempt To Justify Induction? Philosophical Studies, 1957.

14) For an analysis of this approach see Jerrold J. Katz, The Problem of Induction and its Solution (Chicago: University of Chicago Press, 1962).

It is still rational to use non-demonstrative inference--Hume notwithstanding--despite the fact that such inference is not valid. For the use of such inference will in the long run arrive at truth if truth can be arrived at at all. 15) Hume only showed that if one uses non-demonstrative inference one need not--even probably--arrive at truth.

Whether such an approach is free from problems is not at issue here. The question is only whether the acceptance of Hume's argument as valid leaves Popper's approach as the only arguable alternative. The answer seems to be no. Although Jarvie does not explicitly say that Hume's problem is avoided only by Popper's methodology the present alternative is not critically considered. Thus Jarvie has not shown that the method of conjecture and refutation is the only plausible method in anthropology.

Popper's Method As An Answer to Hume

I have argued that it has not been shown that Popper's methodology is the only plausible way of handling Hume's attack. The question remains whether Popper's methodology is indeed a plausible way. For as I have already mentioned Popper's methodology may be interpreted as an attempt to produce a rational way of looking at and doing science within the skeptical framework of Hume. The only question is whether Popper succeeds.

---

15) To paraphrase Jarvie: Inductive method will deliver the cargo of science in the long run if there is any cargo to deliver. The Revolution in Anthropology, Chapter I.

I will argue that if by 'science' is meant what is usually meant Popper does not succeed. An essential part of what people usually call science becomes purely irrational on Popper's view. To be sure, Popper may show that science in another sense is possible but this sense is so removed from our usual notion of science as to have little interest. Let us consider what is excluded on Popper's account.

Critics of Popper seem to insist on interpreting Popper's methodology as a way of determining what hypotheses to accept as true. 16) So interpreted hypotheses that have been "corroborated" or "have proved their mettle" (in Popper's language) ie., have withstood attempts to refute them, are to be tentatively accepted as true. It is important to realize this is <u>not</u> Popper's view. Popper's methodology gives us no guide at all about what hypotheses we are to accept as true. The phrase "a hypothesis has been corroborated" and a "hypothesis has proved its mettle" are technical jargon in Popperian literature and must be divorced from their usual connotations. 17)

---

16) See for example, Gerd Buchdahl and H.G. Alexander, "Convention, Falsification and Induction", <u>Aristotelian Society</u>, Supp. Vol. XXXIV; Isaac Levi, "Decision Theory and Confirmation", <u>Journal of Philosophy</u>, 1961, pp. 621-622.

17) Cf., J. Agassi, "The Role of Corroboration in Popper's Methodology", <u>Australasian Journal of Philosophy</u>, 1961.

Thus, to say that a hypothesis has "proved its mettle" or "is highly corroborated", on Popper's view is not to say that one should accept—even tentatively—H as true; moreover, it is not to say that one's belief in H is rational; it is not to say that any action based on one's belief in H is rational; it is not to say that H will continue or is likely to continue to withstand refutation. It must be stressed that Popperian method <u>only</u> tells one what hypotheses to accept as false; namely those hypotheses that have not withstood tests. However, this acceptance can be no rational guide to our actions if Hume is right. Just because a false consequence is deduced from some hypothesis H in the past indicates nothing about the results of future deduction.

What is true of a single hypothesis is true of the body or system of hypotheses that constitute some contemporary science e.g., anthropology. To speak of a body of anthropological theory e.g., contemporary physical anthropology, as being highly corroborated is not to say that any justified prediction can be based on such corroboration. As far as prediction is concerned, a prediction of a native witch doctor and a distinguished anthropologist are equally unjustified. Neither prediction is justified by the evidence. The difference, as far as science is concerned, between the witch doctor and the anthropologist, according to Jarvie, is that the witch doctor's theories are not usually capable of empirical refutation and the anthropologist's are. The rationality of science comes in <u>only</u> in providing theories that are open to refutation and in the vigoous/ attempts to refute them.

It seems clear, however, that science in the usual sense means at least a body of theories and principles that can be a rational guide to prediction, action and control of our environment. Yet such a science, according to Popper, is impossible. Belief about the future and actions that are based on these beliefs, according to Popper, are based on a "metaphysical faith" on the uniformity of nature 18). They are completely irrational. Thus if science has been shown to be a rational enterprise despite Hume's objections, it is clearly not the science that people usually think of. Indeed, this Popperian 'science' is a science that many might believe to be without point or use.

Refutation as an Approach to Truth

It might be objected that our concern in the last section was too practical. It may be true that Popperian science cannot be a guide to life. Still science conceived of in the Popperian way can arrive at truth by the elimination of error. Perhaps this is all one should demand.

The question is whether Popperian science can achieve even this purely theoretical aim. After all why is the refutation of hypotheses a way to truth? The basic idea must be that the more hypothesis we eliminate by empirical refutation the fewer remain and the closer we approach true hypotheses. But if there are an infinite number of hypotheses, as Jarvie and other Popperians seem to admit, refutation will not bring us any nearer to truth. 19)

---

18) Popper, The Logic of Scientific Discovery, pp. 252-254.

19) See The Revolution in Anthropology, pp. 16-17; also see J. Agassi, "The Confusion Between Science and Technology in the Standard Philosophies of Science", Technology and Culture, 1966, pp. 359-360.

Surely the notion of coming closer to truth or approximating to truth by means of refutation in Popperian literature 20) is at least unclear and perhaps incoherent if an infinite number of hypotheses is admitted.

On the other hand what would be the justification of the postulate of a finite number of hypotheses? Surely not an inductive justification. And presumably this postulate could not be arrived at by the method of conjecture and refutation. One might maintain that the postulate of a finite number of hypotheses is a necessary (though unjustified) assumption of science. But if we allow one unjustified assumption why not another--one to justify induction?

It would seem then that Popperian 'science' is even more removed from science as it is usually conceived of than one might have first supposed. Not only can it not be a rational guide to action but unless a quite arbitrary assumption is made about the number of possible hypotheses it can not even be a way of approximating truth.

It might be suggested that Popperians should not say that their method is a means of approximating truth: what should be said is that their method is a means of eliminating error. This would surely be more consistent with the rest of their views, but one might wonder what is so good about the elimination of error. There is surely nothing intrinsically good about this; the elimination of error presumably is good only insofar as it is a means to truth, or a guide to future predictions, and so on. But this is precisely what it can not be if Hume is correct, unless quite arbitrary assumptions are made.

---

20) See The Revolution in Anthropology, pp. 16-17; Agassi, "The Role of Corroboration in Popper's Methodology", op. cit.

Theoretical Poverty and Inductivism.

Anthropologists may well wonder why they should be interested in such a methodology. Perhaps the Popperian method despite other drawbacks would give a unique rationale for theoretical speculation. For according to Jarvie anthropology's lack of theory is due to its disregard of the method of conjecture and refutation and its reliance on inductivism.

Is it true, however, that the use of inductive generalization and hypothetical inference gives a rationale for anthropology's theoretical poverty?

Now certainly the use of hypothetical inference does not give a rationale for theoretical poverty. Indeed Jarvie seems to admit as much. Thus he admits in one place 21) that some anthropologists have emphasized the use of hypotheses (via what we have called hypothetical inference). He commends these anthropologists because of this. He objects, however to their contention that these hypotheses are to be verified. Jarvie insists that the method of science is the production of hypotheses and their refutation-- not their verification. So insofar as inductivism allows for the construction of speculative hypotheses via hypothetical inference Popperian methodology and inductivism are equivalent with respect to allowing speculative hypotheses.

Let us consider, however, a narrow form of inductivism: in this form only inductive generalizations are permissible. Would this form of inductivism give a rationale for theoretical poverty in anthropology?

---

21) Revolution in Anthropology, p. 211

To decide this issue let us consider two different
uses of inductive generalizations:
(1) the discovery use, (2) the justification use 22).

In the discovery use inductive generalizations are
used to discover generalizations. In the justification use inductive generalizations are used not
to discover generalizations but to try to justify
their acceptance. These two uses are logically independent. 23)
On the one hand, one might discover a generalization by an inductive generalization but try to
justify its acceptance by some other method. On the
other hand, one might discover a generalization by
some method other than inductive generalization and
try to justify its acceptance by inductive inference.
For example, an anthropologist after examining
a certain phenomenon B in cultures of type A might
infer that all cultures of type A have phenomenon B.
Thus he would come to his hypothesis i.e., he
would discover it, by inductive generalization.
But he might try to justify his acceptance of this

---

22) Indeed, it seems to me that these two senses
are never clearly distinguished by Jarvie.
23) In one place Jarvie argues that Nadel's use of
induction and hypothetical inferences are inconsistent. "Nadel on the Aims and Methods of Social
Anthropology", p. 19. But in the first place the
discovery and justification use are perfectly compatible and in the second place there is no reason
to suppose that both types of inference could not
be used to try to justify the same conclusion.
Jarvie appears to believe they are inconsistent
because he thinks that inductive generalizations
are based upon pure observation where hypothetical
inference is not. This view will be criticized
later.

hypothesis by other methods e.g., by hypothetical inference, that is, by the deduction and subsequent verification of the consequences of the hypothesis. On the other hand an anthropologist may dream (or have a spontaneous thought) that all cultures of type A have phenomenon B. He might then try to justify his acceptance of this hypothesis by an inductive generalization.
In the light of the above discussion let us distinguish two different types of narrow inductivism: narrow inductivism #1 and narrow inductivism #2. The basic rule of #1 is: The only method of discovering generalization is inductive generalization. The basic rule of inductivism #2 is: The only method of justifying generalization is inductive generalization.
Would narrow inductivism #1 give a rationale for the theoretical poverty of anthropology? There is some reason to think that it would. Narrow inductivism #1 would allow the discovery of theories only by inductive generalizations. Such a requirement is unduly restrictive and may well have harmful consequences. Surely anthropological theories may be generated in *any* way; it is stultifying to put *any* restriction at all on the way anthropological theories are discovered. What is uncertain is whether anthropologists have actually held that such a restriction should be imposed. Those who have held such a view are certainly to be criticized. If this is all Jarvie is saying, there would be no objection.
However, there is some suggestion in Jarvie's writing of a stronger position.24)

---

24) "Nadel on the Aims and Methods of Social Anthropology", p.19 The Revolution in Anthropology, p. 210.

Jarvie seems at times to suggest that anthropological generalizations can never be discovered by inductive generalizations. This position must be sharply distinguished from the plausible position that anthropological theories need not be discovered by inductive generalizations ie., that they can be discovered by inductive generalizations as well as in other ways.
But why does Jarvie seem to believe that inductive generalization cannot be a method of discovery of anthropological generalizations? His argument is something like this: (1) All observation is based on certain explicit or implicit expectations. (Thus pure interpretation--free observation--is impossible.) (2) Inductive generalization as a means of discovering inductive generalizations presupposes that observation is pure and uninterpreted. Hence, (3) inductive generalizations as means of discovering generalizations is impossible. The argument seems to be a valid one. the only trouble is that the second premise is false. Inductive generalization as a means of discovery is logically compatible with the admission that there is no pure observation. One might observe phenomenon B in cultures of type A on the basis of some selective process P and yet still come to the conclusion that all cultures of type A have phenomenon B by inductive generalization.
Jarvie is perhaps misled into thinking otherwise by the following consideration.25)
The selective process P, it might be said, must be based on the expectation that all cultures of type A will have phenomenon B.

---

25) Cf. The Revolution in Anthropology, p. 109.

But then the conclusion of the inductive generalization, namely that all cultures of type A have phenomenon B, is already discovered. No _new_ hypothesis is therefore generated since the hypothesis that all cultures of type A have phenomenon B, is already implicit in the observer's selection of the data for the inductive generalization. If this is Jarvie's argument, it is dubious. I see no _a priori_ reason to suppose that the basis of the selective process involved in making a series of observations involves the conclusion of inductive generalizations based on these observations.

Would narrow inductivism # 2 give a rationale for theoretical poverty in anthropology? The answer seems to be no. Since narrow inductivism #2 is a method of trying to _justify_ the acceptance of anthropological generalizations and theories, the most freewheeling speculation is permissible. The only requirement is that the production of such speculation is to be accepted only if it can be inferred as a conclusion of an inductive generalization from the evidence. Even independently of Hume's problem, this may mean, of course, that many anthropological theories that are proposed cannot be accepted. In particular, hypotheses about unobservable processes and entities cannot be inferred from observational data via inductive generalization even if inductive generalization is a valid mode of inference. Whether hypotheses about unobservable processes and entities are necessary in anthropology is a debatable question. In any case, this does not mean that hypotheses whose acceptance cannot be justified cannot be _used_ in various ways in anthropology. These hypotheses, although not accepted as true, may be used as predictive devices, as heuristic tools, as guides for further inquiry and so on.

It may, of course, be the case that some anthropologists have mistakenly thought that the use of inductive generalization as the sole means of justifying one's acceptance of anthropological generalizations and theory excluded various uses of speculative theory. But their error can hardly be blamed on a narrow inductivism as we have conceived it. In particular, certain psychological traits that Jarvie finds objectionable e.g., a sober attitude, a lack of imagination, find no justification in narrow inductivism $\#2$ (let alone in an inductivism that would allow for hypothetical inference).

Situational logic

Jarvie argues that the correct explanatory approach to anthropological phenomena is in terms of "situational logic." 26) By this he means roughly that natives' underlying aims and beliefs and some other factors should serve as the explanation of both their actions and the consequences of their actions. Thus Jarvie maintains that although people's actions may superficially seem irrational, e.g., the actions of members of cargo cults, deeper analysis would reveal that given their aims and beliefs about the world their actions are perfectly reasonable.

---

26) See <u>The Revolution in Anthropology</u>, p. 34 - 42, 113-130, 163-169, 223-4; "Nadel on the Aims and Methods of Social Anthropology", pp. 11-24; See also I.C.Jarvie, Review of Robert Brown, <u>Explanation in Social Science</u>, The British Journal for the Philosophy of Science, 1964, pp. 143-150. It is curious that although Jarvie makes situational logic central to his approach to anthropology, Popper, his master, makes only passing reference to situational logic in his major work on the philosophy of the social sciences. See Karl Popper, <u>The Poverty of Historicism</u> (Boston: The Beacon Press, 1957), pp. 149-152.

These people's aims and beliefs and their rationality in the light of these values and beliefs explain what they do. Consequently Jarvie urges anthropologists to return to Frazer's notion that primitive myth and magic is rational in the light of the natives' beliefs and goals. Situational logic explains myth and magic. The accounts of myth and magic in terms of the function that myth and magic might serve do not explain myth and magic.

Explanation in terms of the logic of the situation may work in two ways: First, knowing what people value and believe we may explain the <u>intended</u> results of their action. For example, obtaining food would normally be an intended result of hunting and would be explained by situational logic. On the other hand a low standard of living that results from crude agricultural practice in a primitive society may be an <u>unintended</u> consequence of certain actions of the people. This would also be explained by situational logic.

There are a number of questions that must be raised about situational logic as presented by Jarvie: (1) The relation between situational logic and the method of conjecture and refutation, (2) the unique adequacy of situational logic explanations, (3) the meaning of rationality, (4) the causal sufficiency of situational logic explanations, (5) the causal importance of beliefs, aims and rationality in causal explanations.

The Relation Between Situational Logic and the Method of Conjecture and Refutation

A hasty reader might be led to suppose from Jarvie's writings that situational logic explanations in anthropology are somehow implied by the method of

conjecture and refutation. Thus one might suppose that once we have seen the errors of inductivism and the virtue of the method of conjecture and refutation the acceptance of situational logic as the fundamental method of anthropology follows as a matter of course. That this is not so can be easily seen. The method of conjecture and refutation does not prescribe <u>any</u> particular content for the conjecture. An hypothesis in terms of peoples' beliefs, aims and rationality would be one possible hypothesis among many. One might well accept the method of conjecture and refutation as the method of science and with no inconsistency be opposed to situational logic as the method of explanation in anthropology. 27) Conversely one may accept situational logic and yet not accept the method of conjecture and refutation. Indeed, situational logic is perfectly compatible with, e.g., the use of hypothetical inference. Hypotheses about peoples' expectations, aims and rationality might be construed as verified by verbal and non-verbal behavior. Thus there is no inconsistency in using situational logic and one form of inductivism. 28).
So unless independent arguments are produced the advantages of situational logic in anthropology are by no means established by establishing the method of conjecture and refutation as the fundamental method of anthropology.

---

27) For example, it could be shown that situational logic explanations are difficult to refute.
28) See for example the use of such explanations by Hempel. C.G. Hempel <u>Aspects of Scientific Explanation</u> (New York: The Free Press, 1965), pp. 463-489.

Indeed, it would seem that unless independent arguments were given the method of situational logic would be inconsistent with the method of conjecture and refutation

To see this we must recall that Jarvie emphasizes that the method of conjecture and refutation would justify bold and speculative theories in anthropology. Presumably an essential part of bold and speculative anthropological theorizing would be the introduction of new and unfamiliar notions, the postulation of unheard of processes and entities. However, the method of situational logic as the fundamental method in anthropology far from justifying such freewheeling speculation would put some restrictions on it. Jarvie himself says that in social science explanations are to be in terms of the familiar i.e., in terms of goals and beliefs and the rationality of acting in terms of these values and beliefs. But surely restricting anthropological explanation to explanation in terms of the familiar notions of aim and beliefs and rational action would prevent the formulation of explanatory hypotheses conceived in unfamiliar notions. Many explanations in the social sciences are formulated in these unfamiliar terms.

The Unique Adequacy of Situational Logic Explanation

To avoid this inconsistency Jarvie must somehow show that other types of explanations, i.e., non-situational logic explanations, are not worth considering; he must show that one ought not to conjecture in terms of these other hypotheses. But how <u>could</u> this be shown?

Presumably it could not be shown by refuting existing alternative explanatory theories on factual grounds. Thus even if it is shown that existing functional theories (Malinowski's and Radcliff-Brown's) have false premises this would not show that other new types of functional theories will have false premises let alone that new non-functionalistic non-situational logic explanations will have such premises.[29] Jarvie's argument would have to proceed on methodological grounds; he would have to show that all possible non-situation logic explanations were methodologically inadequate. Has Jarvie done this?

Jarvie, as well as other Popperians, advocate methodological individualism as against methodological holism, i.e., the view that explanation of social phenomena should be in terms of individuals rather than in terms of social wholes. The issue is an extremely complicated one. But at least this can be said here. It is quite possible that the issue between these two positions is not a methodological one at all, that it can be resolved into a purely factual question about the existence of certain laws.[30] In any case, even if methodological individualism is established it does not follow that situational logic is thereby shown to be uniquely adequate. Situational logic explanation is merely one kind of methodological individualistic explanation; physiological explanation, for instance, is another type.

---

[29] The Revolution in Anthropology, pp.176-198; See also I.C. Jarvie "The Nature and Value of Functionalism in Anthropology" Functionalism in The Social Sciences, (ed.) Don Martindale (Philadelphia: The American Academy of Political and Social Science, 1965),pp.19-35. See also Brown's critique of Jarvie's critique of functionalism. Robert Brown, Review of I.C. Jarvie, "The Revolution in Anthropology", The British Journal for the Philosophy of Science, 1964, pp. 143-150.

[30] For this view see Arthur Danto Analytic Philosophy of History (Cambridge: Cambridge University Press, 1965), Chapter 12; Michael Martin "Methodological Individualism and the Reduction of Cultural Anthropology to Psychology" Scientia, 1969.

Moreover, even if physiological explanations are somehow ruled out, psychological explanations would remain. But even if one ruled out all psychological explanations except those that dealt with common sense categories like beliefs, aims-- rather than categories like psychic energy-- this would still not establish the unique adequacy of situational logic explanations. Situation logic explanations are in terms of beliefs, aims <u>and</u> the rationality of the actor.

It is curious that although all these possibilities must be eliminated as live opinions to establish Jarvie's thesis, Jarvie does little to eliminate them. He excluded explanations in terms of the irrationality of the actor as beyond the purview of social science; he maintains that to "appeal to irrationality [is to] give up the possibility of any explanation at all." 31) No argument is given for the contention that the irrationality of the actor could not explain-- at least partially-- what he did. Surely, the only thing that is necessary to explain a person's action (if Popper's view of explanation is correct) 32) is to deduce a description of the action from general laws and initial conditions. There is no <u>a priori</u> reason why the predicate "is irrational" could not appear in the antecedent of a general law and in the statement of initial conditions. Naturally other factors beside the irrationality of the actor would have to be taken into account to provide a complete explanation. But the same thing is true in situational logic explanations; more factors than the rationality of the actor must be taken into account.

It is possible that Jarvie supposes that an irrational action cannot be subsumed under some general law. But this is surely not the case. One might speculate that Jarvie has confused here two different senses of "irrational". In one sense "irrational" means "not lawful,

---

31) The Revolution in Anthropology, p. 92

32) See Popper, The Logic of Scientific Discovery, pp. 59-64.

spontaneous or random"; in another sense "irrational" means "not guided by reason or rational principles." Irrational action in the second sense-- presumably the sense Jarvie is talking about-- does not entail irrational action in the first sense.

Although Jarvie explicitly rejects physiological explanations his arguments are far from persuasive. He argues that Nadel is wrong to suppose that there are levels of explanation and that social phenomena, e.g.,joking relations, can be explained at the level of neurophysiology. His argument seems to be that since neurophysiological processes are influenced by environmental factors (including social environment), and conversely, social phenomena therefore could not be explained in terms of neurophysiology 33). Situational logic alone seems able to take into account the mutual influence between environment and people on his view.

Whatever the validity of Nadel's position, Jarvie seems surely to be guilty of a non-sequitor. One need not suggest that only neurological factors alone are sufficient to explain the joking relation. But one might argue that neuro-physiological and environmental variables together might be sufficient to explain social phenomena, e.g., joking relations. One might suggest that beliefs, goals etc. are not needed. Thus the refutation of completely physiological explanations of social phenomena does not leave situational logic as the only alternative.

Jarvie does not consider explicitly behavior theory, despite the fact that this theory has been used in anthropological studies 34). When he does consider psychological theories which are not in terms of beliefs, aims and so on, his argument is the same as the one he used

---

33) Nadel on the Aims and Methods of Social Anthropology", pp. 16-17.
34) John W.M.Whiting and Irvin L. Child Child Training and Personality (New York:Yale University Press,1953).

against neuro-physiology: since psychological variables are influenced by social variables, and conversely, purely psychological explanations are inadequate.

But advocates of psychological theories in anthropology need not argue that psychological factors (for instance action potentials, mental energy) alone provide a sufficient condition of social phenomena any more than Jarvie needs to maintain that beliefs, aims etc. are not necessary and that some particular psychological variables <u>and</u> some environmental variables do provide a sufficient condition of social phenomena.

Jarvie hints at times that other types of explanations--non-situational logic explanations--are or at least tend to be untestable (unfalsifiable) 35).

No argument is given for this remarkable contention. Surely this thesis cannot be decided on <u>a priori</u> grounds. Even if all existing alternative theories are shown to be untestable (something Jarvie does not begin to show) this would not show that all alternative theories will be untestable.

In summary, we must conclude that Jarvie has done nothing to establish the unique adequacy of situational logic explanations.

The Meaning of Rationality

Although Jarvie uses the notion of rational action throughout his work it is surprising how little he does to clarify what he means.

At times he seems to identify goal directed activity

---

35) See for example, <u>The Revolution in Anthropology</u>, p. 73.

and rational action 36). But surely this must not be
his view since not all goal directed activity is rational. A native might want to produce rain and believe that
doing a rain dance is the only way to do this and yet
not do this dance, but do, e.g., a war dance. Although
his action is goal directed, i.e., he aims to produce
rain by the dance, it would not be rational in the
light of his beliefs (unless we found out, e.g., that
he thought he was doing the rain dance). Goal directedness may be a necessary condition of rational action,
but it is surely not a sufficient condition. It does
not uniquely separate rational from non-rational action.

Closer reading of Jarvie suggests, however, that this
is probably not his view. What he may intend is that
rational action is goal directed action in which the
goal is in keeping with the beliefs of the natives, in
keeping with the natives' "horizon of expectations"
37). The native's actions would be rational if he did
the rain dance and believed that the dance was necessary
to achieve rain and he wanted rain.

However, given more complex cases the rational thing
to do given certain beliefs and goals is more difficult
to determine. And Jarvie's simple model of rational
action is less appropriate. Consider a native with
various goals $G_1, G_2, \ldots, G_n$ and beliefs $B_1, B_2, \ldots, B_n$ about the likelihood of reaching these goals. One
may suppose that these goals have different utilities
for the native. What is rational action for this native
in this situation?

---

36) *The Revolution in Anthropology,* p. 132, 137.

37) Ibid., p. 134.

The mathematical theory of decision may be useful in cases of this sort (so called decision under risk). The usual procedure is to define rational action as that which maximizes expected utility. Expected utility is computed by multiplying, say, the believed likelihood of obtaining each goal G with the utility of achieving the goal. It should be noted that two or more courses of action may have equal expected utility; hence these courses of action are equally rational. Clearly in this case there is no one course of rational action relative to the person's expectations and goals.

This problem is even more pronounced when we come to other situations (so called decisions under uncertainty). Suppose that on one's beliefs $B_1, B_2, \ldots, B_n$ a set of mutually exclusive courses of action $A_1, A_2, \ldots, A_n$ are possible with mutually exclusive outcomes $C_1, C_2, \ldots, C_n$ for each course of action; suppose further that each outcome has an associated utility. For example, suppose a native in a primitive society believes he has the following two courses of action open to him: he can either pray to the Sun God or he can pray to the Moon God (he believes he cannot do both). Suppose he believes that if he prays to the Moon God there will be either rain (1) for a week or (2) for five minutes; if he prays to the Sun God, there will either be rain (3) for a day or (4) for an hour. Now suppose the native values each outcome in the following way: (1) 1000: (3) 100: (4) 10: (2) 1. i.e., suppose these are subjective utilities of the native for each outcome.

What is the rational thing to do in terms of which his action could be viewed. The <u>maximin rule</u> would direct him to act on the assumption that the worst possible outcome will result from his action. In this case he would be directed to pray to the Sun God.

On the other hand, the <u>maximax rule</u> would direct him to pray to the Moon God since one of the possible outcomes of this action is at least as good as the best possible outcome of the alternative. Moreover, various alternative rules have been proposed 38).

To say that Jarvie is not alive to these complexities is perhaps to understate the case: He speaks glibly of <u>the</u> rationality principle 39) as if there was one criterion of rationality. But as we have seen, this is not the case. Moreover, even if a criterion of rationality is chosen, it does not always uniquely determine one course of action as rational.

The Causal Sufficiency of Situational Logic Explanations

So far although we have criticized Jarvie for maintaining the unique adequacy of situational logic explanations and for his too simple views on the nature of rationality, we have supposed that sometimes at least situational logic (when a suitable criterion of rationality is specified) can explain human action. Now we must consider this assumption more critically. We shall now ask: Is it ever the case that situational logic gives a complete explanation of human action or of the result of human action?

---

38) For a discussion of this and related points, see Hempel, <u>op. cit.</u>

39) <u>The Revolution in Anthropology</u>, p. 218

We will assume that a complete explanation of human action or of the results of human action will specify causally sufficient conditions of the action. Such a view of explanation seems in keeping with a general Popperian view of explanation.

The answer to this question will depend on how much is included in a situational logic explanation. Some isolated passages in Jarvie suggest that an explanation in terms of situational logic takes into account <u>only</u> a person's beliefs and aims and rationality. If these were Jarvie's views, they would be easily criticized. For it is clear that the aims and beliefs and rationality of an actor taken alone are never a sufficient causal condition of his doing anything.

No matter what aims or beliefs a person holds and no matter how rational he may be, it is still physically possible that no action will result because, e.g., of certain environmental or physiological factors. Thus in relation to a native's beliefs and values the rational thing to do might be to perform a rain dance and yet the native might not perform the dance even though he was rational: he might be paralized or environmental circumstances might prevent his dancing. There is then always a nomological gap between beliefs, desires and rationality taken alone and <u>actual</u> rational action. Thus accurate prediction and explanation of rational human action must always take into account other factors besides beliefs, values and rationality. The general schema would be this:

If X has belief b and desire d and X is rational and certain other factors $f_1, f_2, \ldots, f_n$ are present and x is the rational thing to do given b and d, X will do x.

Other passages in Jarvie indicate quite clearly, however, that he includes more than beliefs, values and rationality in situational logic explanations.

What is not clear is exactly what else he intends
to include. In some passages he speaks vaguely of
the necessity of taking into account "other factors"
40). Until these other factors are specified, however, it is uncertain that situational logic could
give a sufficient causal explanation of any piece
of human behavior.
In other passages he is more specific. He says about
his explanation of cargo cults:

> This explanation, which takes into account the
> aims of the prophet and the circumstances as
> he sees them; the aims of the followers and
> the circumstances as they see them; and the
> circumstances as they are, consisting of
> people, prophets, followers, white men,
> institutions, cosmological and moral ideas
> (which are institutional), is what I would
> call situational logic 41).

However, if this is all that situational logic explanations take into account, they will not provide
a sufficient causal explanation of even cargo cult
activity. Presumably meteorological factors at least
would also have to be taken into account for a
sufficient causal explanation. Cargo cults would
not presumably occur in sub-zero temperatures or
violent hurricanes. Moreover, Jarvie's statement
that "the circumstances as they are consisting of
people, prophets....." still leaves open which specific factors of the people, prophets and so on are
to be taken into account.

---

40) The Revolution in Anthropology, p. 128
41) Ibid. p. 93.

Presumably only certain factors would be causally relevant. Until such factors are specified, even if other circumstances, e.g., meteorological conditions, are taken into account it will be impossible to evaluate the causal sufficiency of Jarvie's situational logic explanation.

It may be argued, however, that Jarvie's situational logic need not be interpreted as specifying any <u>particular</u> factors independent of beliefs, aims and rationality. On this interpretation Jarvie's vagueness when he speaks of the necessity of taking "other factors" into account reveals his views on situational logic more clearly than his more specific statements. By a situational logic explanation Jarvie may mean any causal explanation that takes <u>at least</u> some other factors into account besides the aims, beliefs and rationality of the actor.

On this interpretation our problem of whether situational logic can ever give a sufficient causal explanation of any human behavior reduces to whether it is ever possible to specify the beliefs, aims and rationality of an actor <u>plus</u> some factor or other that would constitute a sufficient causal condition of his behavior. The answer is undoubtedly yes.
But this is hardly an interesting result. The only people who would oppose such a view would be those people who believe that beliefs, aims and rationality have no causal importance at all, i.e., that they could not even be part of a sufficient causal condition of a piece of human behavior.

The Causal Importance of Belief, Aims and Rationality

We have argued so far that the beliefs, aims and rationality of the members of a society taken alone cannot provide a causally sufficient explanation of their behavior. Jarvie admits this.

But what else he wants to include is uncertain. We have suggested that Jarvie's thesis may be only that some unspecified factors must be included. If so, it is certainly true that sometimes situational logic so interpreted can provide a causally sufficient explanation of human behavior. But this is surely of little interest and may well be unfair to Jarvie's intention. For Jarvie above all wants to emphasize the importance of beliefs, aims and rationality in causal explanation whatever <u>other</u> factors may be causally relevant.

Thus one may perhaps interpret Jarvie as claiming that belief, aims and rationality are the most <u>important</u> causal factors 42) in the total cause of a piece of behavior, e.g., cargo cult activity, whatever else the total cause may include. The truth of Jarvie's thesis so interpreted will depend on what is meant by "the most important causal factor or factors." On some analyses Jarvie's thesis may not be true.

One analysis is this: 43) Suppose factors A and B when taken together are causally sufficient for C although neither A nor B taken alone is causally sufficient. Thus all A's and B's are C but it is not the case that All A's are B and it is not the case that All B's are C.

---

42)
I can not find any specific passages in Jarvie to justify this interpretation; however this interpretation does make sense out of his apparent emphasis on these factors in explanations in the social science.

43)
Cf. Morton White, <u>Foundations of Historical Knowledge</u> (New York: Harper and Row, 1965), chapter 4.

Now if Most A's are C and it is not the case that Most
B's are C, then let us say that A is a more important
causal factor for C than B. However, if Most B's are
C and it is not the case that Most A's are C, let us
say that B is a more important causal factor for C tha[n]
A. Finally, if Most A's are C and Most B's are C let u[s]
say that A and B are equally causally important for C.

The application of this to situational logic should b[e]
obvious. Let A be the complex factor of beliefs, aims [and]
rationality and let B be all other causally relevant
factors, e.g., physiological factors and environmenta[l]
factors. Now it is an empirical question whether the
factors Jarvie emphasizes in situational logic explana[-]
tion are the more important causal factors in any give[n]
situation; it is not something that can be decided by
<u>a priori</u> reasoning.

Let us illustrate this more fully. Suppose we are
interested in knowing the most important causal factor
in a native's hunting for game. Let us suppose we know
that the native is rational and in relation to his
desires and belief the rational thing to do would be t[o]
hunt game. However, the native will not hunt if for
example he becomes very ill or if certain environmenta[l]
factors prevent him. Now it is an empirical question
whether (1) "Most natives for which hunting game is th[e]
rational thing to do and who are rational hunt game" i[s]
true and whether (2) "Most natives who are not ill and
no environmental factors prevent them from hunting gam[e]
hunt game" is false or vice versa or whether (1) and
(2) are both true.

    Thus in general the sentences resulting from inte[r-]
preting the schemata:

(1)'   Most people for whom doing x is the rationa[l]
      thing to do given their aims y and beliefs v
      and who are rational do x

(2)' Most people who are in physiological condition c and environmental condition e do x

will be true or false depending on the particular values of x, y, w, c and e which are substituted even if the sentence is true which results from substitution in the following schema:

(3) All people for whom doing x is the rational thing to do given their values y and beliefs w and who are rational and who are in physiological condition x and environmental condition e, do x.

Thus on this analysis of causal importance the causal importance of beliefs, aims and rationality may vary from context to context. Jarvie's thesis interpreted as stressing the causal importance of belief, aims and rationality in all or most contexts will require the support of evidence not found in his work.

But even if this is not Jarvie's thesis, the above considerations throw light on an important aspect of social scientific explanation. If it were true that beliefs, aims and rationality were not in general important causal factors in the explanation of human behavior, social scientists might well choose to ignore them.

To be sure, it might be true that slight precise predictions could be had by taking into account beliefs, aims and rationality than if only pshysiological and environmental factors are taken into account. But such precision may not be needed and indeed may be had only at a high proce. For example it often is difficult to find out what a person's beliefs and aims are. This difficulty may be too high a price to pay for a slight increase in predictive accuracy.

On the other hand if beliefs, aims and rationality are causally important and environmental and other factors are not, Jarvie's apparent stress on the former may indeed be vindicated. Social scientists may be well advised to concentrate on beliefs, aims and rationality rather than on environmental and other factors despite the problems involved in discovering what an actor's beliefs and aims are. For if one takes beliefs, aims and rationality into account a large increase in predictive accuracy will result. Environmental factors, in this case, may well be relatively ignored.

However, if Jarvie is not stressing the causal importance of aims, beliefs and rationality above other factors and in fact is urging social scientists to concentrate equally on both sorts of factors, this view may prove ill-advised as social science progresses. Either sort of factor might warrant special concentration in the light of new evidence and theories. What <u>exactly</u> Jarvie thesis is is difficult to discern on this issue. But that he does not discuss these crucial issues is obvious

CONCLUSION

I have argued that Popperian anthropology has serious problems. Jarvie's rejection of non-demonstrative inference is based on arguments that seem in the light of contemporary philosophical discussion to be at worst meaningless and at best outmoded. In any case, Jarvie's attack will have to be reconsidered in the light of this recent discussion. Moreover, once certain distinctions are made there seems to be no reason to suppose that the use of non-demonstrative inference provides a rationale for anthropology's theoretical shortcomings. Furthermore the alternative to the use of non-demonstrative inference proposed by Jarvie--the method of conjecture and refutation--makes science in its usual sense quite irrational and pointless.

Jarvie's advocacy of situational logic seems inconsistent with his stress on free speculation in anthropology unless non-situational logic explanations are excluded from anthropology a priori. This Jarvie does not do. Moreover, his views on rationality--an essential notion in situational logic explanations--are too simple; a precise characterization of situational logic explanations is never given; his stress on aims and beliefs is never justified.

I do not intend to suggest that there is no value in Jarvie's theoretical work in anthropology. On the contrary, because of its great importance and potential influence I have felt the need to criticize it in some detail.

THE PHILOSOPHER OF SOCIAL SCIENCE
AS A PARTICIPANT OBSERVER

What method should a philosopher of science use? Paul Diesing has recently argued[1] for participant observation as a methodology of the philosophy of social science. In this paper I will evaluate Diesing's view.

The Method of Participant Observation

As a philosopher of social science Diesing sees his major task as describing the methods of the social sciences as they actually exist. Thus, in his philosophical work he uses the participant observer method[2] (at least as he understands it). Various methods of the social sciences are treated as subcultures within the general culture of science. Diesing uses articles on methodology as informants' reports; he attends social scientific conventions; he talks and listens to social scientists; he participates in social scientific work. As a participant observer, moreover, he constructs typologies. He has to date constructed a typology of participant observation, of experimental method, of formal method and of survey research method.

According to Diesing the philosopher of social science as a participant observer does not merely describe; he also evaluates scientific work. But like the participant observer in social science itself, he must not use external standards. Each scientific tradition has its own standards and the participant observer should use these standards rather than external ones.

Not only is the philosopher of the social sciences as a participant observer restricted to standards of evaluation internal to the method he is observing, but according to Diesing he is also restricted to the concepts or language of that methodological tradition as well. Philosophers of social science are criticized by Diesing for making conceptual distinctions which are not present in a given methodological tradition and for using language "inoperative" in that tradition. In general, Diesing finds little to praise in the work of most philosophers of social science. For according to Diesing they display arrogance, superiority, and gross ethnocentrism.

Evaluation of the Method

Now it is no doubt true that many philosophers have not taken the trouble to understand the scientific traditions they are philosophizing about and have imposed standards that are inappropriate; it is also no doubt true that many philosophers have shown a distasteful arrogance and superiority. Diesing's emphasis on trying to find out what social scientists are doing—instead of merely saying what they are doing, his stress on getting some direct acquaintance with scientific work, his emphasis on taking an inside look at social scientific methods are, I believe, important corrections of typical philosophical methodology.

However, it is one thing to admit this and another thing to say that no external criticism of a social scientific method is possible. Furthermore, to some readers at least it may seem that the restrictions Diesing places on philosophers of social science reflect an attitude if not of arrogance, at least of unwarranted conservatism. Let us examine several aspects of Diesing's view: first, his characterization of participant observation in the social sciences; second, his defence of psychoanalysis against certain external criticisms; third, his empirical definition of social science.

Characterization of Participant Observation

Since Diesing argues for the use of participant observation as a method of the philosophy of social science and this method is borrowed from the social sciences, it is extremely important to evaluate Diesing's characterization of participant observation in the social sciences. If Diesing's characterization is mistaken, this will adversely affect his view about philosophical method. For our purposes only one aspect of his characterization of participant observation method needs to be considered: the restrictions he claims to find built into the participant observer method.

At one point in his book Diesing seems to restrict the participant observer to concepts derived from the thinking of the people he is studying, or at least not foreign to these people's way of thinking.[3] However, later in the book he distinguishes between two types of concepts used in social science: observation concepts and theoretical concepts. He calls observation concepts concrete concepts since they are directly developed from the subject matter. On a theoretical level there are what Diesing calls anthropomorphic-sensitizing concepts. These concepts are not directly derivable from the subject matter but are developed by comparing cases and finding common elements.[4] Some of these concepts presumably would be foreign to the natives' way of thinking.

It would seem that participant observers at least on a theoretical level can use concepts that are foreign to the natives' thinking. But even on a theoretical level there are certain restrictions. This is brought out when Diesing contrasts anthropomorphic-sensitizing concepts with theoretical concepts appropriate to other methods. Theoretical concepts of the participant observer must point to similarities between the observer's experience and that of his subjects. Thus, for example, the concept of kinship relates the phenomena the participant observer is studying to his own experience, the concept of latent function "focuses attention on people's awareness and its limits and thus forces the participant observer to learn the point of view of his subject...The concept also reminds one of the various defense mechanisms that prevent awareness--repression, projection, etc. --and raises the question of which one might be operating."[5] Diesing contrasts latent function, an anthropomorphic-sensitizing concept appropriate to participant observation, with response latency, a theoretical concept appropriate to experimental psychology. Response latency is the amount of time between stimulus and response and as a result "the experimenter's possible empathy with the subject matter is closed off by the strict behavioristic nature of the concept."[6]

Besides this restriction on the kind of concepts a participant observer can use there is a restriction on the practical use of the method of participant observation. According to Diesing a participant observer can use knowledge of a society to bring about certain change in the society or to keep the society in a certain state so long as changing or maintaining the society is a goal of the society itself. The participant observer cannot help to bring about change or to resist change if changing or resisting change is an external goal, a goal that is not a goal of the society. Thus if an economically dependent society has a goal of economic independence, the participant observer can help the society change by, e.g., introducing certain industries or new farming methods. But if the society does not have economic independence as a goal, then the participant observer cannot help introduce new industries or farming methods. Diesing argues that anthropologist participant observers have often helped a native society resist the influence of Western culture on their societies. But resisting such influence was a goal of the society itself. According to Diesing anthropologists found native societies preoccupied with the problem of maintaining their integrity against Western society. Thus Diesing argues that the method of participant observation involves cultural relativism[7], i.e. accepting the goals of the culture that one is in.

However, Diesing also says that participant observers are opposed to any manipulation of human beings (which according to Diesing is involved in the practical use of experimental methods). The participant observer believes that such manipulation is immoral, that it shows lack of respect for freedom and dignity.[8]

As I understand Diesing he is claiming that not only do participant observers in fact limit themselves conceptually and practically in the ways outlined above but that these restrictions should or must be part of the participant observation method. I have serious doubts that all participant observers have so restricted themselves. But there would not be much point in citing cases where I believe that participant observers have not followed the restrictions that Diesing finds in participant observer method. Diesing could argue either that in the cases I cite the social scientists were not really participant observers or that they were participant observers doing things they should not have done. Diesing's thesis about participant observation primarily functions as a norm, a norm that he would claim is internal to the participant observer method itself. A more useful criticism will be to consider Diesing's characterization as a norm and not a description of social scientists' behavior. So construed I will argue that Diesing has given no good reason why participant observers should follow this norm, no good reason why these restrictions should be taken seriously. Consequently by analogy he has not shown that participant observation as a method of philosophizing should have these restrictions. Let us consider first his restriction on the practical use of the participant observer method.

There seems to be a contradiction in the restriction outlined by Diesing for there is a possible conflict between (1) the goal of maintaining the freedom and dignity of human beings and (2) the goal of furthering the goals of society. One of the goals of a society (group, family, culture, etc.,) could be destructive of the freedom and dignity of human beings. Clearly one could not maintain both (1) and (2) in such a case. To put it in a slightly different way, participant observers who work for the dignity and freedom of human beings cannot be cultural relativists and insofar as they are cultural relativists they must in certain cultures work for the destruction of freedom and dignity.

Imagine, if you will, a participant observer in the White House in recent years or in the Nazi Party during the 1930's. One primary goal of both of these sub-cultures was the manipulation of people—exactly what participant observers are supposed to be against. Yet this is precisely what they would have to work for given Diesing's cultural relativism. One hopes that in the case of a conflict Diesing and anthropologist participant observers would opt for freedom and dignity. And insofar as they would they would be using a standard not derived from the group they were working with.

After all why should a participant observer in his practical role just attempt to realize the goals of the natives? Might he not suggest new goals and criticize old goals? Such an activity would not constitute an imposition of goals on the natives (for this would interfere with their freedom and dignity). There is all the difference in the world between imposing goals and suggesting and arguing for new ones. The natives may or may not appreciate the participant observer's suggestions in the long run. But at least the participant observer would be acting honestly, being true to his own principles and not hiding his moral views and feelings from the natives[9]--a stance that Diesing (from other remarks he has made) should approve.[10]

Indeed, at one point Diesing says something that implies that anthropologists may go farther in practice than simply helping to achieve the goals of the natives. Diesing argues that a participant observer may produce an "intellectual challenge" to the people he is observing.[11] However, producing an intellectual challenge may well involve challenging some of the goals of the natives and arguing for different goals.

One must conclude that the restrictions Diesing finds in the practical use of the participant observer method conflict with other ethical goals stated by Diesing and in any case seem unjustified. Moreover, the means of going beyond these restrictions seem implicit in other things Diesing says. Consequently there is no reason to think that the use of participant observer method in philosophy has similar restrictions.

What about the restriction built into the conceptual apparatus available to participant observers characterized by Diesing? There seems to be good reasons why participant observers should not be so restricted. First, there is the problem of the influence of theory on observation. It has been persuasively argued that there are no such things as observational and theoretical concepts *per se* as Diesing assumes. What one sees and in what categories one sees it are largely determined by one's background, training and theoretical orientation.[12] A trained anthropologist may well see a particular cultural phenomenon in what (in Diesing's view) would be called theoretical concepts. He might, for example, see that Abuta in the role of medicine man is lessening the natives' anxiety. However, the concepts of anxiety and role are theoretical concepts--not observational concepts--according to Diesing. A trained observer might be able to see this just as clearly as an ordinary man might see that a black man in animal skins is dancing around a fire. Diesing's apparent restriction of observational concepts to concepts intelligible to the natives could absurdly restrict what expert observers could observe.

Secondly, anthropomorphic-sensitizing concepts make cross-cultural comparisons possible by relating the native's concepts to something in the observer's cultural experience. The concept of kinship relates concepts in the native culture to the observer's culture making the observer "feel at home." But this requirement seems unduly restrictive. Suppose one had a theoretical concept that related phenomena in different cultures but did not tie into any of the observer's cultural experiences. Why should it be excluded from anthropological theory? The concept of a folk community, for example, may be quite useful to an anthropologist who comes from New York City but it does not relate

425

the native concepts to his own, it does not make him feel at home.

Anthropomorphic-sensitizing concepts are also supposed to increase the anthropologist's ability to emphathize with his subjects. It is unclear why this empathy should be crucial. There does not seem to be any reason why the study of society, the building of typologies, the verification of hypotheses and models and all the rest of the goals of a participant observer could not proceed without the anthropologist having empathy with the natives. Indeed, there is reason to suppose that Malinowski despised the Trobriand Islanders and had very little empathy with them.[13] Yet his work is a land-mark in participant observer method.

Thus there seems to be no good reason why anthropologists must be restricted to observation and anthropomorphic-sensitizing concepts as Diesing construes them. Consequently there is no good reason to suppose that philosophers of social science (like Diesing) who use the participant observer method need to be restricted in the ways Diesing maintains. In particular, there is no good reason to suppose that a philosopher of the social sciences needs to be restricted to the language and concepts of social scientists, e.g. anthropologists.

To see this more clearly consider the following example. Elsewhere I have suggested[14] that three distinct ideas are often not clearly distinguished in anthropological literature. All of these have, I believe, been referred to as empathy although only the last is close to the typical dictionary definition: (1) understanding someone's behavior in terms of the person's beliefs and goals, (2) being understanding towards someone, i.e., taking a sympathetic attitude towards someone (3) putting oneself in someone else's place by feeling what they feel, thinking what they think (empathy in the strict sense). I have argued that these are logically distinct ideas although they have certain interesting relations to one another.

Diesing does not make these distinctions in his writing because the anthropologists whose concepts he uses do not make these distinctions. As a result it is unclear whether he is talking about (1), (2), or (3) when he talks about empathy. Diesing seems to be committed to the view that philosophers of the social sciences should not try to bring distinctions like these to the surface and explore their interconnections even though such an analysis might be clarifying to anthropologists themselves.

The reply to Diesing has already been stated by an unnamed philosopher quoted in his book. "You talk as if I, a philosopher, have to stick to the vague, ambiguous and philosophically naive things an anthropologist says."[15] To Diesing such a statement reflects philosophical arrogance. But it is more likely that such a statement reflects frustration and outrage over Diesing's arbitrary restrictions on philosophical method.

Defense of Psychoanalysis

To see Diesing's methodological conservatism in action in another context, let us examine his defense of psychoanalysis against three common criticisms. First, it has been argued, e.g., by Eysenck, that psychoanalytic therapy is not effective. Secondly, it has been maintained that psychoanalysts produce their results by operant conditioning. Thirdly, it has been argued that psychoanalytic theory is not a refutable theory.

With respect to the first criticism, Diesing argues that Eysenck's evaluations cannot be taken seriously because of his misuse of statistical method. But he also argues that even if Eysenck had used statistics correctly his criticism would be inappropriate, for Eysenck imposed goals on psychotherapy externally whereas the goals of psychotherapy must be set within the therapeutic situation by the patient and the therapist.

However, it seems to me that these objections miss the major thrust of Eysenck's critique. Whatever the trouble with Eysenck's statistical evaluation, the basic question posed by Eysenck remains unanswered: Is there any good reason to suppose that psychoanalysis is effective? It makes little difference, I think, whether the goals are imposed from the outside or created from within.

Diesing admits that even when the goals are created from within the therapeutic situation "some 'spontaneous remissions' may be similar to therapy . in their outcome, though they are accomplished without the aid of a professional therapist."[16] But the question remains: Is there any reason to think that the spontaneous remission rate is lower than the rate of cures claimed by psychoanalysts (however cure is defined)? Diesing's statement that clinical methods "are valuable when used properly"[17] is, as far as one can determine, based on the clinical impression of psychoanalysts and other clinicians. But the validity of these impressions is precisely what is in question. It would seem that in order to evaluate any such impression (and thus the value of clinical method itself) one is forced to use a different method, namely the method of statistical analysis and control group experiments. However, this would be to evaluate the clinical method externally.

With respect to the second criticism Diesing admits that verbal conditioning occurs in the therapeutic situation. He stresses that this is only a partial account of the therapeutic situation and in no way "invalidates the more rounded account that I have given above".[18] Such an answer is hardly adequate. For part of the "rounded account" given by Diesing and by psychoanalysts is that psychoanalytic theory is validated by the behavior of the patient in the therapeutic situation. The import of verbal conditioning studies is that the verbal behavior of the patient is subtly and unwittingly influenced by the therapist in a way that conforms to his own biases. This hypothesis is also supported by evidence from the psychology of persuasion as well as by the fact (admitted by some therapists) that psychodynamic theory X is only confirmed by therapists committed to X: psychoanalytic theory is confirmed by psychoanalysts, Jungian theory is confirmed by Jungian therapists and so on.[19]

These problems seem absolutely crucial to the validity of clinical method. Why Diesing thinks they can be answered by pointing out that more than verbal conditioning occurs in the therapeutic situation is difficult to understand. The critics may well admit that more occurs but hold that the more that occurs, e.g., the non-verbal behavior of the patient and the beliefs of the patient, may be subtly influenced by the therapist to conform to his theory. Secondly, psychoanalysts claim that the more that occurs is hidden psychodynamics. However, the inference that such dynamics exists is based in the behavior--verbal and otherwise-- that is brought into question by verbal conditioning studies and by other studies.

With respect to the refutability of psychoanalysis Diesing dismissed Sidney Hook's question (posed to psychoanalysts): "On what specific evidence would you decide that a child did not have an Oedipus complex?"[20] According to Diesing, Hook and many other philosophers have badly misunderstood the status of psychoanalytic theory. They have wrongly supposed that the Oedipal theory is stated in propositions, e.g., "Every boy has an Oedipal complex". However, the Oedipal theory is part of a developmental typology. This typology is tested by how it guides a therapist's observations to the essentials of the case, how it organizes his clinical experience. If the typology is not useful in these respects, this constitutes a partial disconfirmation of the type. Diesing argues that the typology has been tested by thousands of clinical cases and has been partially disconfirmed and has led to changes in typology, e.g., Fromm's theory and Erikson's theory.

It is important to see that Diesing's defense of psychoanalysis is based on an instrumental account of the nature of clinical theory: the Oedipal theory is not true or false, but useful or not useful in guiding clinical practice and observation. That this is a correct way to interpret scientific theorizing in this area is certainly not obvious. I think one could show by citations from Freud and many latter day psychoanalysts that they did believe that every boy had an Oedipal complex, not just that the Oedipal complex was conceptually useful in organizing and approaching their clinical experience. But I will not attempt to show this here.

For even if Diesing's interpretation is accepted, Hook's question can easily be reformulated without losing its import: "On what evidence would you decide that the Oedipus complex was not a useful way of organizing and approaching clinical experience?" Hook was impressed, as have been other observers of the psychoanalytic movement, e.g. Popper, with the dogmatic orthodoxy of many psychoanalysts, especially the so-called orthodox psychoanalysts. An inability to answer Hook's question (whether one interprets psychoanalysis as a set of propositions or as a clinical tool) strongly suggests that Hook's impression is correct. Now whether Diesing believes that there is no dogmatic orthodoxy in psychoanalysis is unclear. He certainly shows no awareness of the problem. In any case, one cannot help but be impressed by the fact that the therapists he cites as changing Oedipal theory are not typical orthodox analysts. Fromm is regarded as neo-Freudian and Erikson could hardly be considered as typical.

I, for one, have grave doubts whether typical orthodox analysts have admitted to the partial disconfirmation of the usefulness of the Oedipal typology and even whether they could characterize the evidence that would show the Oedipal typology was not useful. The question is an empirical one and I would certainly be willing to change my mind if evidence was produced. One thing is clear: Diesing has not produced that evidence.

Suppose that my suspicions are correct. This would not show, of course, that (given Diesing's instrumental intepretation) the Oedipal theory is irrefutable. What it would show is that as the theory functions among a group of psychoanalysts it is not refutable,[21] that it functions as a dogma not as a changing therapeutic tool. But given Diesing's methodological relativism a philosopher of social science would be unable to criticize psychoanalysis on this point. For to do so would be to impose some external standard on a scientific subculture. This result seems to me to constitute a <u>reductio ad absurdum</u> of the view from which it is derived.

One must conclude that Diesing's defense of psychoanalysis is based on an arbitrary restriction of social science from external criticism.

Empirical Definition of Science

Diesing's restrictions get him into further trouble later in his book. He proposes what he calls "an empirical definition" of science. Psychoanalysis is supposed to qualify as a science on his definition and astrology is not. The definition is as follows: "A method is scientific if it is used by members of the scientific community. The criterion of membership is the empirical one of regular, effective collaboration with the other members. Community boundaries are marked by non-interaction, misunderstanding, and polemics. In cases where interaction between groups is partly friendly and partially hostile, I have marked off sub-communities boundaries and have looked for subcultural differences to explain the partial hostilities."[22] According to Diesing, given his criterion the whole of social science forms a single community. Collaboration is defined as a two way process "excluding one-way borrowing".[23] The practitioner of dianetics borrows from psychology but the psychologist does not borrow from dianetics. Consequently, dianetics is not a science. As far as astrology is concerned, since there is no collaboration between astrology and modern astronomy or other sciences astrology is not a science.

There are several questions to be asked about this definition of science. First, does it make psychoanalysis a science as Diesing supposes? Secondly, does his definition exclude certain disciplines from being sciences that should not be excluded? Thirdly, does Diesing's definition assume some external standard of what a science should be? Let us consider these questions in turn.

Diesing seems to mean by collaboration between scientific subcultures the mutual borrowing of ideas. Given this reading it is unclear why psychoanalysis is a science. It is true that anthropologists and psychologists have borrowed from psychoanalysis. However, it is not so clear that psychoanalysts have borrowed from other fields. Indeed, the thesis that orthodox psychoanalysts form a closed society with respect to new ideas is not a new one.[24]

Given this interpretation of collaboration there is reason to think that certain parts of experimental psychology are not a science. There is little reason, for example, to suppose that Skinnerians collaborate, i.e., borrow ideas from non-Skinnerians. Consequently, on Diesing's definition Skinnerians are not scientists. Interestingly enough Diesing seems to admit that experimental psychologists form a closed group. He says "Whenever a field (such as experimental psychology recently or economics fifty years ago) achieves substantial unity of method and high internal cohesion, contact with other methods is weakened and theory stagnates. The field moves into a scholastic phase in which..."[25] But what he does not seem to see is that given his account of science this would mean that experimental psychology is close to becoming a non-science. This seems to me to be absurd. There may be serious limitations to Skinnerian experimental psychology but to be committed to the idea at least by implication that it is non-scientific simply because there is no collaboration between it and other fields is bizarre. Applying Diesing's criteria to the natural sciences one gets even stranger results, for although it is true that many natural sciences borrow from physics it is not obvious that physics borrows ideas from other natural sciences. If it does not, according to Diesing's criteria, physics is not a science.

Finally, Diesing's criterion of collaboration and interaction seems not to be simply a descriptive criterion. Disciplines that do not collaborate, e.g. experimental psychology, are said to "stagnate" and go into a "scholastic phase." Such language suggests the normative criterion that sciences should collaborate and interact. One wonders, of course, how a normative criterion is justified given Diesing's relativism. Psychoanalysts and Skinnerians may not accept such a criterion; it is not their criterion of science. There seems to be some danger here of Diesing inconsistently using _external_ standards in evaluating sciences.

In sum, Diesing's empirical definition of science based on his participant observer method fails--again suggesting the inadequacies of the method as he construes it. It leads to mis-classification of legitimate sciences and seems in the end to rely on external standards, something it cannot do.

Conclusion

Once Diesing's restrictions are removed one can begin to assess the strengths and weaknesses of participant observation as a method of the philosophy of the social sciences. For with these restrictions out of the way participant observation can be seen as simply a way that philosophers can study the social sciences in order to do what traditionally they have always done: criticize, evaluate, and philosophize about social science.

One of the major strengths of the method of participant observation is the advantage of seeing first hand the workings of science, of seeing how it in fact operates. As a result the philosopher as a participant observer will be in a good position to see the weaknesses and shortcomings of a particular scientific method or scientific tradition. Consequently he will be in a good position to make clarifying conceptual distinctions and penetrating criticisms, distinctions and criticisms that may go beyond the distinctions and standards implicit in the method or tradition itself.

Secondly, and closely related to the first point, as an insider and friend the philosopher as a participant observer will be in a good position to get social scientists to take him seriously. Although his distinctions and suggestions may at first be foreign to social scientists he will be in a position to argue his case and achieve acceptance. Consequently, the philosopher of science as a participant observer may actually be able to effect change with his philosophical analyses and criticism.

Thirdly, the philosopher of the social sciences as participant observer working at close range to social science will be in a good position to test and modify his philosophical theories about social science, especially those theories about the detailed workings of social science.

But the participant observer method (even disallowing Diesing's restrictions) has some disadvantages.

First, too close a contact with social science may tend to dull philosophers' critical ability. It is all too easy for a participant observer to "go native" and forsake his objectivity. As a result the philosopher of the social sciences may lose his philosophical perspective and insight and unconsciously fall into the habit of always viewing things as social scientists do. For Diesing such a habit is a requirement of participant observation; in fact it is one of the great dangers of participant observation that always must be guarded against.

Secondly, the participant observer method is tremendously time-consuming and demanding. Recall that it involves first hand observation of and participation in social science activity. Reading social science literature and even talking to social scientists is not enough. Philosophers of social science may well wonder whether the possible benefits of direct participation is worth the price. After all is direct observation and participation a necessary way or even the most efficient way to solve many of the problems that concern philosophers of the social sciences?[26]

Several reasons might be given that suggest that the answer to this question is no. First of all, consider Diesing's own work. Although his book is packed with information about the methods of the social sciences it is likely that most of this information could have been achieved by merely reading social science literature. Secondly, anthropologists sometimes investigate whole cultures by methods which do not use direct observation. Thus dying Indian cultures have been investigated purely by interviewing old reliable informants.[27] One might suppose that by analogy scientific cultures could be studied by interviewing members of these cultures. Thirdly, Diesing suggests that a method akin to participant observation is the historical reconstruction of a whole historical period.[28] However, in such cases the examination of artifacts and documents must be used and direct observation cannot be used. This suggests that the results of participant observation can be achieved without direct observation and participation. Again by analogy one might suppose that scientific methods and traditions could be studied without direct observation by reading methodological and scientific documents.

Now Diesing might object to the above suggestions on the following grounds: Treatises on social scientific methodology and verbal statements of social scientists are idealized accounts and do not give an accurate picture of social science practice. Consequently there is need for direct observation and participation.

Now whether Diesing's contention is true or not is at least questionable. For example, Diesing's account of formal method in social science was presumably arrived at (at least in part) by direct observation. But his account agrees in broad outline with my understanding of formal method in the social sciences. My understanding was achieved exclusively by reading social science literature. Were there the great difference Diesing supposes between the written word and actual practice there should be wide divergence in my basic understanding of formal method and Diesing's understanding. But there is not. The difference between Diesing's understanding of formal method and mine is not over basics. Rather Diesing's knowledge in contrast to mine is characterized by great detail and breadth. However, as far as I can determine, such detail and breadth of knowledge could have been achieved by simply reading extensively in social science literature.

Let us suppose the worst and suppose that social scientific behavior does not live up to the written or spoken pronouncements of social scientists. It is not clear that a divergence between actual methodological practice and written or verbal articulation of that practice should make much difference to philosophical evaluation. Philosophers of social science are often interested not in actual social scientific practice but rather in the norms which guide and justify practice. That practice should diverge from these norms is hardly surprising. Moreover, it is the norms of practice that are usually articulated in written treatises and verbal statements. Consequently philosophers of social science do not have to do direct observation to know what these norms are. Of course, philosophers of social science may be interested in knowing if actual scientific practice diverges from the norm. Participant observation may be the only way to get the needed information. On the other hand, participant observation may not be the only way. There is no *a priori* way of knowing and much depends on the situation.

All in all, philosophers of social science may be well advised in certain situations and given certain purposes to use participant observation and well advised in other situations and given other purposes not to use participant observation. In all cases philosophers must remember that participant observation has the potential for achieving insight but also blindness. Philosophers will have to weigh the results that could be achieved by participant observation against its possible dangers and inefficiencies and even against the possibility that the result could be achieved in less troublesome ways. That Diesing is perhaps not completely aware of these problems is to be regretted, but that he has called our attention to participant observation as a method of philosophers of the social sciences is to be applauded. For this we are in his debt.

Footnotes

1. Paul Diesing, Patterns of Discovery in the Social Sciences (New York: Aldine 1971).

2. Ibid., pp. 17-22; 291-303.

3. Ibid., p. 139.

4. Ibid., pp. 205-210.

5. Ibid., p. 206.

6. Ibid., p. 207.

7. Ibid., p. 273.

8. Ibid., pp. 260-261.

9. On this point see I.C. Jarvie, "The Problem of Ethical Integrity in Participant Observation," Current Anthropology, 10, 1969, pp. 505-522.

10. Diesing, op. cit., p. 155.

11. Ibid., p. 265.

12. Israel Scheffler, Science and Subjectivity (New York: Bobbs-Merrill, 1967); Peter Achinstein, Concepts of Science (Baltimore: The Johns Hopkins University Press, 1968), pp. 157-202; Michael Martin, Concepts of Science Education (Glenview, Ill.: Scott-Foresman, 1972), pp. 103-131.

13. Bronislaw Malinowski, *A Diary in the Strict Sense of the Term* (New York: Harcourt, Brace and World, 1967). See also Clifford Geertz's discussion in the *New York Review of Books*, Sept. 4, 1967.

14. Michael Martin, "Understanding Participant Observation in Cultural and Social Anthropology" *Boston Studies in the Philosophy of Science*, eds. R.S. Cohen and M.W. Wartofsky (New York: Humanities Press, 1967), Vol. IV, pp. 303-330.

15. Diesing, op. cit., p. 292.

16. Ibid., p. 268.

17. Ibid., p. 267.

18. Ibid., p. 270.

19. See Michael Martin, "The Scientific Status of Psychoanalysis Clinical Evidence" *Inquiry* 7, 1964.

20. Diesing, op. cit., pp. 232-233.

21. On this point see Michael Martin, "Mr. Farrell and the Refutability of Psychoanalysis," *Inquiry* 7, pp. 80-98; Frank Cioffi, "Freud and the Idea of Pseudo-Science," *Explanation in the Behavioral Sciences* eds. Robert Borger and Frank Cioffi, (Cambridge University Press, 1970), pp. 471-499.

22. Diesing, op. cit,. pp. 319-320.

23. Ibid., p. 320.

24. See Albert Ellis, "An Introduction to the Principles of Scientific Psychoanalysis," *Genetic Psychology Monographs*, 41, 1950.

25. Diesing, op. cit., pp. 22-23.

26. See Martin, "Understanding Participant Observation in Cultural and Social Anthropology," op. cit.

27. Ibid.

28. Diesing, op. cit., p. 7.